# Striving for Gro

# after Adjustment

*The Role of Capital Formation*

**WORLD BANK**

**REGIONAL AND**

**SECTORAL STUDIES**

# Striving for Growth

# after Adjustment

*The Role of Capital Formation*

EDITED BY

LUIS SERVEN

AND

ANDRES SOLIMANO

The World Bank
*Washington*, D.C.

© 1993 The International Bank for Reconstruction
and Development / The World Bank
1818 H Street, N.W., Washington, D.C. 20433

The World Bank Regional and Sectoral Studies series provides an outlet for work that is relatively limited in its subject matter or geographic coverage but that contributes to the intellectual foundations of development operations and policy formulation.

The findings, interpretations, and conclusions expressed in this publication are those of the authors and should not be attributed in any manner to the World Bank, to its affiliated organizations, or to the members of its Board of Executive Directors or the countries they represent.

The material in this publication is copyrighted. Requests for permission to reproduce portions of it should be sent to the Office of the Publisher at the address shown in the copyright notice above. The World Bank encourages dissemination of its work and will normally give permission promptly and, when the reproduction is for noncommercial purposes, without asking a fee. Permission to copy portions for classroom use is granted through the Copyright Clearance Center, 27 Congress Street, Salem, Massachusetts 01970, U.S.A.

The complete backlist of publications from the World Bank is shown in the annual *Index of Publications*, which contains an alphabetical title list and indexes of subjects, authors, and countries and regions. The latest edition is available free of charge from Distribution Unit, Office of the Publisher, The World Bank, 1818 H Street, N.W., Washington, D.C. 20433, U.S.A., or from Publications, The World Bank, 66, avenue d'Iéna, 75116 Paris, France.

Luis Servén and Andrés Solimano are economists in the Transition and Macro-Adjustment Division of the World Bank.

*Cover design by Sam Ferro*

*Library of Congress Cataloging-in-Publication Data*

Striving for growth after adjustment : the role of capital formation /
  edited by Luis Servén and Andrés Solimano.
    p.  cm. — (World Bank regional and sectoral studies)
    ISBN 0-8213-2484-5
    1. Saving and investment—Developing countries.  2. Economic
  stabilization—Developing countries.  3. Investments—Developing
  countries.  I. Servén, Luis.  II. Solimano, Andrés.  III. Series.
  HC59.72.S3S77    1994
  338.9'009172'4—dc20                                          93-23833
                                                                  CIP

# Contents

# Part B

**Adjustment and Investment Performance**

# Preface

This book presents the results of about three years of work finished in early 1992 in the area of private investment and macroeconomic adjustment. Its purpose is to explore the macroeconomic determinants of investment and the causes and cures for the gap between macroeconomic adjustment and stabilization and the resumption of economic growth in developing countries, a gap that even today—10 years after the debt crisis and the subsequent adjustment of the eighties—remains wide. This volume highlights the central role of capital formation (private and public) in the restoration of sustainable growth.

Most of the book's chapters were developed as part of a research project, "Private Investment and Macroeconomic Adjustment," financed by the Research Committee of the World Bank. They were presented in several seminars both within and outside the Bank. A conference was held at the World Bank in Washington, D.C. in March 1991, where the work in progress was presented. The panel discussion that closed the conference is contained in the final chapter of the book.

Three of the chapters contain previously published material, which is reproduced here with the kind permission of the copyright holders: chapter 2, by Luis Servén and Andrés Solimano, was originally published by *The World Bank Research Observer*. Chapter 3, by Robert Pindyck, was published by the *Journal of Economic Literature*. Chapter 6 by Luis Servén and Andrés Solimano, was published in *Adjustment Lending Revisited: Policies to Restore Growth*, edited by V. Corbo, S. Fischer and S. Webb.

In developing this work we benefited greatly from the encouragement and advice provided by many colleagues at the World Bank and elsewhere. Among them, our greatest debt is probably to Vittorio Corbo for his constant support from the early stages of this project. We are also grateful to Alan Gelb for his advice, to Anna Maranon and Sabah Moussa for their patient typing of our many revisions to the manuscript, and to Whitney Watriss for her careful editing. Special thanks go to Cecilia Guido-Spano and also Jenepher Moseley and Lauralee Wilson for their valuable assistance in the editorial process, and to Fernando Lefort and Raimundo Soto for assistance.

# List of Contributors

*Editors*

**Luis Servén.** Macroeconomics and Growth Division, Policy and Research Department, The World Bank.

**Andrés Solimano.** Macroeconomics and Growth Division, Policy and Research Department, The World Bank.


*Other Contributors*

**Ricardo J. Caballero.** Massachusetts Institute of Technology, and National Bureau of Economic Research

**Eliana Cardoso.** Fletcher School of Diplomacy, and National Bureau of Economic Research

**Rudiger Dornbusch.** Massachusetts Institute of Technology, and National Bureau of Economic Research

**Felipe Larrain.** Catholic University of Chile

**Robert S. Pindyck.** Sloan School of Management, Massachusetts Institute of Technology, and National Bureau of Economic Research

**Martin Rama**. The World Bank, University of Paris-VI, and CINVE, Uruguay

**Dani Rodrik.** Columbia University and National Bureau of Economic Research

**Rodrigo Vergara.** Central Bank of Chile

# Part A. Investment Theory and Adjustment Policies

# Introduction

*Luis Servén*
*and*
*Andrés Solimano*

Almost a decade ago, the debt crisis and the global shocks affecting developing countries set off a protracted period of macro instability and lack of external financing that led to a drastic decline in capital formation. This worrisome trend endangers the social sustainability of stabilization and reform programs in the developing world. In fact, the paradigm of adjustment *with* growth involves an apparent circularity: for adjustment policies to be followed by growth (that is, to be sustainable), a robust response by investment is required, particularly by the private sector, which is expected to play a key role in market-oriented reform. However, for that investment response to materialize, and for the private sector to engage in intrinsically irreversible investment decisions, it needs to perceive adjustment as sustainable. Lack of confidence in, or just mere skepticism about, the permanence of policy measures may be self-defeating and postpone the benefits of reform.

The study of different experiences with economic reform reveals that private investment follows a cycle during adjustment. In the initial phase of an adjustment program, private (and often public) investment falls, following which it reaches a "plateau" in which neither a substantial recovery (nor further decline) in private investment takes place. The implication is that private investors are adopting a "wait-and-see" attitude. Then, in economies where reform is consolidated and external factors improve, sustained private capital formation resumes, although this phase may not get underway for several years.

## The questions

Important policy questions regarding the effects of macroeconomic adjustment on the recent performance of investment motivated the research covered in this volume. The questions below derive from important aspects

3

of the recent adjustment experience of developing countries. Answers to these questions are critical to advancing the design of growth-enhancing adjustment programs. They are:

- A crucial component of most adjustment programs is a real depreciation of the exchange rate, aimed at restoring external balance and making room for growth to resume. What is the impact of a real currency depreciation on private investment? Through which channels are the level and composition of investment affected?
- What has been the impact of the observed cuts in public investment on private investment? Has private investment suffered from the decline in public capital formation that resulted from the fiscal adjustment, as suggested by the hypothesis of complementarity between private and public investment? Or has it benefitted from a crowding-in effect of reduced government expenditures?
- Why do private investors adopt a wait-and-see attitude during adjustment? Do countries that undertake radical changes in the structure of incentives and the rules of the game as part of their economic reforms face an intrinsic credibility problem? Is there a coordination failure by decentralized markets affecting private investment in the aftermath of adjustment? What other forms of systemic instability affect capital formation? Is a lack of credibility the main reason behind the slow recovery of investment after adjustment?
- What effect did the external debt burden and the cut in external financing to developing countries in the eighties have on investment? What are the relevant transmission mechanisms and orders of magnitude of the impact of debt on investment?
- What policies can be devised to speed up the response of private investment after economic adjustment?

## Main conclusions

The main conclusions of this volume are as follows.

(1) The *debt crisis, and subsequent adjustment* effort in Latin America and other developing countries led to a substantial reduction in capital formation in the 1980s. Private investment recovered somewhat after 1987, but as of the early 1990s public investment showed no signs of recovery. Regionally, the cuts in private and public investment occurred mainly in Latin America and Sub-Saharan Africa. The economies of Southeast Asia did not experience a serious and protracted decline in investment rates in the last decade.

(2) The *external debt* burden hampered investment through at least three main channels: first, debt service requires an external transfer that, under conditions of limited external financing, leads to reduced investible resources; second, the anticipated "tax" associated with future debt service (the debt overhang) reduces the anticipated return on investment; and, third, uncertainty about the policies needed in the future to meet an equally uncertain debt service also tends to depress investment.

Empirically, the adverse impact of the debt burden on investment is confirmed in investment equations estimated for samples of Latin American (see chapter 7) and East Asian countries (see chapter 8), and also on a larger panel of developing countries (see chapter 6). In all cases the relevant debt measure was found to exert a negative and significant effect on the rate of private investment.

(3) The analytical results (see chapters 2-4) underscore the importance of *irreversibility and uncertainty* in investment decisions. A practical implication of the irreversibility of most fixed investment decisions is that the response of capital accumulation to the new set of economic incentives brought about by an adjustment program is bound to be weak if the macro environment is unstable and the new policy regime perceived to be fragile. From the viewpoint of investment, the stability and predictability of the incentive structure are likely to be at least as important as the *level* of the incentives. While attractive incentives for capital formation are a precondition for the resumption of private investment and growth, they do not guarantee it will take place. Private investors may wait and see for several years (three or more) before deciding to invest at a sustained pace.

At the empirical level, investment equations with irreversibility constraints were estimated using data for selected developing countries. The results show that investment incentives may have to be very large to promote a significant recovery of capital accumulation (see chapter 3). The implication is that macro stability, predictable policy, and clear rules of the game are key ingredients for a strong response of private investment to changes in incentives. These elements probably played a major role in the mixed response of private investment to structural reforms (trade liberalization, financial reform, labor market reform, and privatization) in different Latin American countries: private investment reacted quite forcefully in Chile in the late 1970s and since the mid-1980s, did so more moderately in Mexico in the late 1980s, and failed to respond in Bolivia to the stabilization cum structural reform launched in the mid-1980s.

Empirically, these factors can go a long way in explaining the differences in investment and growth between Latin America and East Asia in the last two decades. Econometric analyses for both regions, as well as for a larger group of developing countries, reveal the adverse effect of measures of macro instability (that is, the variability of inflation and of the real exchange rate) on private investment.

(4) *The relationship between public and private investment* depends crucially on the composition of the former. Investment in infrastructure—and public expenditures for the maintenance of infrastructure and human capital formation—are likely to *crowd in* private investment; other types of public investment tend to have the opposite effect. As a consequence, excessive compression of expenditures on infrastructure in the course of fiscal adjustment (a common pattern in developing countries) may jeopardize the recovery of private investment.

Interestingly, the empirical studies included in this book suggest that there are strong complementarities between public and private investment for a panel of Latin American, African, and East Asian countries. The same result emerged from separate cross country studies of Latin America and East Asia. In all cases, the coefficient of the ratio of public investment to gross domestic product (GDP) in the estimated private investment equations is positive and significant. Nevertheless, separate empirical analyses for Latin America and Asia also suggest that public sector deficits, for a given level of public investment, crowd out private investment, as the financing of these deficits pushes real interest rates up and/or reduces the credit available to the private sector.

(5) The effect of changes in the *real exchange rate* on the *level of aggregate private investment* is complex. Time-series studies for individual countries tend to show a kind of J-dynamics in the response of private investment to a real devaluation. The volume of private investment may initially drop and then recover following a real currency depreciation. In fact, a real devaluation squeezes real balances (or real credit) and increases the real price of imported capital goods, all of which lead to a contraction in capital formation in the short run. Over time, however, a real depreciation of the exchange rate stimulates an increase in exports and investment that gives rise to an expansion in output. Empirical work combining cross-section data with time series for country groups in Latin America, East Asia, and some African countries tend to show that the *level* of the exchange rate has an ambiguous and statistically insignificant impact on the *level* of private investment. By contrast, the *variability* of the real exchange rate (as a measure of macroeconomic uncertainty) has a much stronger (and adverse) effect on capital formation than does its *level*.

(6) From a policy perspective the analysis identifies *areas where public policies can promote investment*. In general, sound public investment in physical infrastructure and human capital must be protected during adjustment, both to boost complementary private investment and to contribute to long—term growth. Macroeconomic stabilization and maintenance of stable rules during the design of adjustment programs should be a policy priority. Sustainable policies often promote private investment better than do certain liberalization moves that can be reversed because they lack solid macro foundations. The analysis in this project points to a wait-and-see attitude on the part of private investors that may reflect pervasive coordination failures. In that sense, policies that increase the perceived set of opportunities for the private sector are required to boost investment. A free trade agreement, debt relief, and other measures can help break investors' reluctance to commit real resources to capital formation, a shift that can make adjustment with growth more a reality than a hope.

### Summary of the chapters

Chapter 2, "Private Investment and Macroeconomic Adjustment: A Survey," by Luis Servén and Andrés Solimano, provides a general analytical and methodological background for the study of the determinants of private investment in developing countries. It describes the puzzles posed by the response (or lack thereof) of private investment in developing countries to the macroeconomic adjustment and reform measures in recent years. It also reviews, broadly, the theoretical and empirical literature, examining its ability to solve those puzzles. Particular attention is paid to two issues: first, the impact of macroeconomic adjustment policies, including currency depreciation and demand restraint, on private investment; and, second, the role of uncertainty, credibility, and coordination failures in shaping the response of private investment to changes in incentives and policy reform. The chapter singles out two areas in which additional research could yield valuable lessons for policy design: (a) the impact of changes in public investment and exchange rates on private investment; and (b) the policy options for reducing the duration of the wait-and-see attitude of private investors after adjustment and for speeding up the resumption of growth.

In chapter 3, "Irreversibility, Uncertainty, and Investment," Robert S. Pindyck surveys the relevant literature on the topic and explores the microeconomic implications of irreversibility for investment decisions. He explains why the conventional net present value criterion for investment could be seriously mistaken when investment is irreversible and shows that the magnitude of the error can be very large. The chapter describes the solution of the optimal investment problem under irreversibility, proves the equivalence of the option pricing and dynamic programming approaches, and investigates the consequences of different types of uncertainty (as relates, for example, to relative prices, interest rates, and demand conditions) for investment decisions. Pindyck concludes that, under reasonable assumptions, uncertainty can be a powerful deterrent to investment.

Chapter 4, "On the Dynamics of Aggregate Investment," by Ricardo J. Caballero, makes two important contributions. First, it explores the implications of uncertainty and irreversibility for *aggregate* investment. Second, it proposes an econometric methodology for evaluating uncertainty and irreversibility empirically. Caballero solves a very difficult aggregation problem and confirms rigorously that the main implication of irreversibility is "asymmetric inertia" in aggregate investment: in general, investment responds differently to positive and negative shocks. Moreover, the asymmetry is strongly dependent on initial conditions: specifically, after a deep recession irreversibility will make investment very insensitive to incentive measures. This dependence suggests that further progress with the empirical evaluation of the effects of uncertainty requires in-depth analysis of specific country cases. The author presents some illustrative applications of his proposed empirical methodology to a selected group of developing countries.

In chapter 5, "Empirical Investment Equations in Developing Countries," Martin Rama surveys selected *empirical* studies of investment in developing countries. He provides an integrative analytical framework that encompasses different investment models as particular cases: the monopolistic competition model; the neoclassical approach; the demand-constrained case; Tobin's Q model; the credit-constrained model; and the foreign exchange shortage case. Each of the empirical studies on investment in developing countries the chapter examines can be viewed as testing one (or more) of these models—although in many cases with potential specification and/or measurement errors. Common results from these studies are: (a) the importance of accelerator-type effects on investment; (b) the failure to identify empirically strong effects from the cost of capital and other factor prices; (c) conflicting results on the effect of public investment on private investment; (d) the importance in some cases of credit and foreign exchange availability measures; and (e) the generally adverse impact on investment of selected measures of instability.

Chapter 6, "Economic Adjustment and Investment Performance in Developing Countries: The Experience of the 1980s," by Luis Servén and Andrés Solimano, provides a general overview and empirical analysis of the performance of investment in developing countries in the 1980s. First, it examines the behavior of investment in a group of 75 developing countries, with a breakdown between private and public investment for a smaller sample. The chapter then turns to the impact of external shocks, stabilization policies, and structural reforms on investment by comparing the experiences of three selected groups of countries: (a) three Latin American countries that pursued successful stabilization and embarked on structural reforms in the 1980s or before (Chile, Mexico, and Bolivia); (b) two Latin American countries that suffered severe macroeconomic instability in the 1980s and did not pursue the extensive structural reforms of the first group (Argentina and Brazil); and (c) three East Asian economies that adjusted to the adverse shocks of the 1980s, while preserving a remarkable degree of macro stability and high growth (Korea, Singapore, and Thailand). A major lesson from the country experiences is that the response of private investment to structural reform is mixed (ranging from strong [Chile] to very weak [Bolivia]). In turn, the East Asian countries suffered only a mild and shortlived slowdown in the face of the adverse external shocks of the eighties. Argentina, and to a lesser extent Brazil, show that protracted economic instability is a powerful deterrent to investment.

The chapter carries out an econometric analysis of the determinants of private investment for a sample of Latin American, African, and Asian countries for the period 1976-88, followed by a decomposition analysis of the sources of the variation in private investment after 1982. The analysis reveals that the increase in the level of external debt was the chief determinant of the decline in private investment in the sample. In addition, the increase in macroeconomic instability and the decline in public investment rates play an important role in the decline in private investment rates in Latin America after 1982.

In chapter 7, "Macroeconomic Environment and Capital Formation in Latin America," Eliana Cardoso focuses on the interactions between private investment and macroeconomic policies in Latin America. She reviews the experiences of Chile and Mexico as examples of adjusting countries and Argentina and Brazil as cases of "accommodative" economic policies in the 1980s. She then turns to the negative relationship between the real exchange rate and investment observed in the 1980s, arguing that a third variable—the terms of trade—is the driving force, affecting both the real price of capital and the real exchange rate. Cardoso formally shows that a deterioration in the terms of trade reduces the real price of capital and thus investment, and also forces a real depreciation of the exchange rate.

Cardoso also performs an empirical analysis of private investment on data for the period 1970-85 for six Latin American countries (which account for 86 percent of total GDP in Latin America). Her results confirm the positive (and significant) effect of improvements in the terms of trade and the irrelevance of the real exchange rate once the former variable is included. The results also support the complementarity between public and private investment—although they also provide (limited) evidence of financial crowding-out of private investment by public expenditures—and the adverse effect of the foreign debt burden. Finally, Cardoso addresses measurement issues by comparing real and nominal shares of total investment in GDP from the World Bank and from the Summers-Heston data set for 13 Latin American countries. The Summers-Heston data often yield substantially higher investment to GDP ratios than do the World Bank and national accounts sources.

Chapter 8, "Investment and Macroeconomic Adjustment: The Case of East Asia," by Felipe Larrain and Rodrigo Vergara, examines the experience with investment and macroeconomic adjustment in Korea, Singapore, Thailand, and Malaysia in the 1970s and 1980s. The high investment-high growth record of these countries in the 1970s and 1980s is reviewed in the light of their financial and exchange rate policies, domestic saving, and income distribution patterns. Larrain and Vergara argue that no clear causality emerges from financial liberalization to growth; moreover, in several instances (subsidized) interest rates have been used to direct investment to specific sectors. On the other hand, the degree of public intervention in the economy varies across the group of countries, with Korea the most interventionist and Singapore the least. In general, state intervention is found to be pro-business, and evidence that regulation and direct public intervention crowded out private investment is not openly detected. An interesting fact concerns income distribution in these countries. It is found to be quite equitable—particularly when compared with Latin America. The authors argue that an equitable distribution of income supports macro stability in two ways: first, it reduces potential social conflict, with an ensuing favorable effect on the socioeconomic climate and thus on private investment; and, second, it leaves less ground for populist cycles that are eventually destabilizing.

The chapter also contains an econometric analysis of investment in Korea, Singapore, Thailand, and Malaysia for the period 1975-88. The empirical results show a positive and significant effect of GDP growth, of the public investment ratio—a result that again suggests complementarity in the sample—and of the real stock of credit to the private sector on the ratio of private investment to GDP; and a negative effect of the external debt to GDP ratio, of the real interest rate, and of macroeconomic instability (measured by the variability of the real exchange rate). In turn, the level of the real exchange rate exerts no significant influence on the level of investment.

The volume concludes with chapter 9, "Policies for the Recovery of Investment: Panel Presentations." It contains the presentations by Rudiger Dornbusch, Robert Pindyck, Dani Rodrik, Luis Servén, and Andrés Solimano at a panel discussion at the conference 'Private Investment and Macroeconomic Adjustment in Developing Countries' that was held at the World Bank in March 1991.

## 2

---

# Private Investment and Macroeconomic Adjustment: A Survey

*Luis Servén*
*and*
*Andrés Solimano*

The correction of external imbalances in many developing countries during the 1980s took the form of large cuts in investment rather than increases in domestic savings.[1] This decline in investment, which mirrored the decline in the transfer of external resources after 1982, was especially sharp in the highly-indebted countries and was accompanied by slower growth in these and other developing countries. In addition, both public and private rates of investment fell, although the decline in private investment was more drastic. If this trend continues, it will slow potential growth in these economies and will reduce long-run levels of per capita consumption and income, endangering the sustainability of the adjustment effort.

This reduction in investment seems to reflect several factors. First, the decline in the availability of foreign savings has not been matched by a corresponding increase in domestic savings. Second, the deterioration in fiscal conditions attributable to cuts in foreign lending, higher domestic interest rates, and the acceleration of inflation in several countries forced a fiscal adjustment that in many cases took the form of a contraction in public investment. Third, the macroeconomic instability associated with external shocks has hampered private investment. Fourth, the debt overhang has discouraged investors through its implied tax on future output and the ensuing credit constraints in the international capital markets.

In many countries, macroeconomic adjustment has not improved the response of private investment. Even in countries that made substantial progress in correcting imbalances and restoring profitability—often through drastic cuts in real wages—the effect on private investment has been weak and slow to appear.   Many of these issues are difficult to explain in the context of conventional investment theories.

This chapter reviews recent developments in investment theory and empirical studies on investment in developing countries to explain some features of investment behavior that were important in the 1980s:

• The relation between public and private investment that results from the traditional financial crowding-out effect and the complementarity between public and private capital.

• The importance of imperfections in financial markets and financial constraints in a world of imperfect and asymmetric information.

• The effects of changes in the real exchange rate on the volume, timing, and composition of investment. These effects are especially important in developing countries because of the typically high import content of investment.

• The irreversible nature of most investments, which makes private investors particularly sensitive to risk and dampens their response to changes in economic incentives.[2]

• The complex relationship between the foreign debt overhang and the volume of private investment.

• The dependence between the returns to individual investors and the level of aggregate investment, which opens a gap between the private and social returns on investment and creates a potential coordination failure. Such a failure can leave the economy trapped in a low-investment, low-growth equilibrium.

This chapter looks first at theories of investment. It then examines the effect of monetary, fiscal, and exchange rate policies on private investment, emphasizing economic or institutional features that are specific to developing countries (for instance, pervasive rationing in the financial markets, complementarities between public and private investment, considerable reliance on imported capital goods, and shifts in the distribution of income). Such features may determine how macroeconomic policies influence private investment. Finally, this chapter discusses recent literature on credibility, uncertainty, and irreversibility in investment decisions and looks at how such factors influence the investment response.

## Investment theory

Keynes (1936), who first called attention to the existence of an independent investment decision in the economy, observed that investment depends on the prospective marginal efficiency of capital relative to some interest rate that is reflective of the opportunity cost of the invested funds. He pointed out that private investment was intrinsically volatile since any rational assessment of the return on investment was bound to be uncertain. The "animal spirits" of private investors would be the main driving force in investment decisions.

After Keynes, the evolution of investment theory was linked to simple growth models. These models gave rise to the accelerator theory, popular in the 1950s and early 1960s and widely used even today in practical growth exercises. The accelerator theory makes investment a linear proportion of changes in output. Its extreme simplicity explains its popularity: given an incremental capital/output ratio (ICOR), it is easy to compute the investment requirements associated with a given target for output growth. In this view, expectations, profitability, and capital costs play no role.

The restrictive assumptions behind the accelerator theory led Jorgenson (1967) and Hall and Jorgenson (1971) to formulate the neoclassical approach. Here the desired (or optimal) capital stock depends on the level of output and the user cost of capital (which in turn depends on the price of capital goods, the real interest rate, and the depreciation rate). Lags in decisionmaking and delivery create a gap between current and desired capital stocks, giving rise to an investment equation, that is, an equation for the change in the capital stock.

The foundations of this approach have been criticized on the grounds that: the assumptions of perfect competition and exogenously given output are inconsistent; the assumption of static expectations about future prices, output, and interest rates is inappropriate, since investment is essentially forward-looking; and the lags in delivery are introduced ad hoc.

An alternative view, associated with Tobin (1969), is that what matters is the relation between the increase in the value of the firm as a result of the installation of an additional unit of capital and its replacement cost. When the increase in the firm's market value exceeds (or is less than) the replacement cost, firms will want to increase (or decrease) their capital stock. This ratio, known in the literature as marginal Q, may differ from unity because of delivery lags and adjustment or installation costs. However, it is not easy to measure marginal Q, and the ratio of the market value of the entire existing capital stock to its replacement cost (the average Q ratio) is used instead.

Abel (1980), Hayashi (1982), and Precious (1985) point to problems in using average Q. If firms enjoy economies of scale or market power, or if they cannot sell all they want, marginal and average Q will systematically differ. Moreover, the assumption of increasing marginal installation costs underlying the Q theory is dubious. The cost of additions to an individual firm's capital stock is likely to be proportional—or even less than proportional—to the volume of investment because of the lumpy nature of many investment projects. More important, disinvestment, if feasible, is more costly than positive investment: capital goods often are firm-specific and have a low resale value.

An extreme but useful view of this asymmetry is to consider investment completely irreversible. This notion, introduced by Arrow (1968), suggests that under conditions of certainty, irreversibility creates a wedge between the cost of capital and its marginal contribution to profits. However, it is under conditions of uncertainty that irreversibility can have important implications for investment decisions. Recent literature (Bernanke 1983; McDonald and Siegel 1986; Pindyck 1988; Bertola 1989; Bertola and Caballero 1990; and chapter 3, "Irreversibility, Uncertainty, and Investment," in this volume) emphasizes that risk factors can have a very negative effect on irreversible investment. The intuitive reason is that if the future is uncertain, any addition to productive capacity today risks the chance that the firm may find itself stuck tomorrow with excess capital that cannot be eliminated (costlessly). This point implies that uncertainty may be as relevant for investment decisions as such conventional variables as interest rates or taxes are.

In the Keynesian tradition, the disequilibrium approach (Malinvaud 1980, 1982; Sneesens 1987) views investment as a function of both profitability and demand for output. In Malinvaud (1982) investment decisions have two stages: first, the decision to expand the level of productive capacity; and, second, the decision about the capital intensity of the additional capacity. The former decision depends on the expected degree of capacity utilization in the economy, which provides an indicator of demand conditions; the latter decision depends on relative prices such as the cost of capital and labor. The distinction between the decisions is meaningful because factor proportions are assumed to be variable before the investment but fixed after it. The investment decision, in turn, takes place in a setting in which firms may be facing current and expected constraints on future sales, an important departure from the continuous market-clearing assumed by both neoclassical (Jorgenson's) and Tobin's Q models. Therefore, investment depends both on profitability and on the prevailing sales constraints, which determine the rate of capacity utilization (see Sneesens 1987).

Disequilibrium models have often been criticized on the grounds that their assumptions regarding expectations are too simple and that they do not explain why prices are rigid. Market disequilibrium and rational expectations are not, however, necessarily inconsistent hypotheses. Neary and Stiglitz (1983) have developed rational expectations models in which the markets for goods and labor do not clear, in a context of forward-looking agents that anticipate future sales constraints and wage and price rigidities (see also Precious 1985). This point is particularly relevant since investors are concerned whether investment decisions made today will be justified by events in the future. From the policy viewpoint, important problems of macroeconomic adjustment, such as a persistent decline in output, are associated with (transitory) disequilibrium in the goods and labor markets. In such conditions investment behavior may involve a combination of expectations and market disequilibrium.

The macroeconomic models of coordination failure, which emphasize the inability of individual agents to coordinate successfully their decisions in a decentralized economic system, provide another view. Although there are many potential sources for such failure (see Cooper and John 1988), the most common one is the existence of monopolistic competition with increasing returns to scale. In this context, the returns on investment depend on the overall level of economic activity, which in turn is positively affected by the volume of aggregate investment. Since each individual firm is likely to view its own contribution to aggregate investment as negligible, the social and private returns on investment diverge, with the former exceeding the latter. Under certain conditions the economy may get stuck in an "insufficient investment" equilibrium, in which individual firms invest too little—lowering aggregate investment—precisely because each firm expects aggregate investment to be low (Kiyotaki 1988; Schleifer and Vishny 1988). As is emphasized later, this mechanism may play an important role in adjustment programs.

There is a growing literature on the effects of financial constraints on investment. At the micro level firms may face binding financial constraints in the domestic capital markets because interest rates are controlled or because of endogenous credit rationing (Stiglitz and Weiss 1981). Asymmetric information, adverse selection, and incentive effects may make interest rate changes an inefficient device to sort out good borrowers from bad borrowers. Under those conditions creditors may prefer credit rationing and quantitative constraints. The recent literature on the financial determinants of investment (see Fazzari, Hubbard, and Petersen 1988a, 1988b; Calomiris and Hubbard 1989; Mayer 1989; Mackie-Mason 1989; and Hubbard 1990) emphasizes that internal finance (retained profits) and external finance (bonds, equity, or bank credit) are not perfect substitutes. The discrepancy in the cost of financing is the result of asymmetric information: lenders in capital markets cannot evaluate accurately the quality of investment opportunities. This situation raises the cost of new debt and equity above the opportunity cost of internal funds. In this view, investment is sensitive to such financial factors—a departure from the idea of the perfect capital market.

Fazzari, Hubbard, and Petersen (1988a) and Hubbard (1990) report empirical research along these lines for industrial countries. They test the role of the financial structure of the firm in the Q, neoclassical, and accelerator models of investment by firm size. They find that financial effects are important for investment but also that there are differences in the sensitivity of investment to liquidity, depending on firms' policies regarding retained earnings. An important macroeconomic dimension of these findings is that, provided fluctuations in cash flow and liquidity are correlated with movements in aggregate economic activity and the business cycle, macroeconomic instability may affect investment mainly by firms that rely heavily on internal finance.

Chenery and Bruno (1962) raise an important point: in developing economies where domestic and foreign capital goods are highly complementary, the lack of foreign exchange to import machinery and equipment can constrain growth, although in the medium run substitution between domestic and foreign capital goods, as well as export promotion, can ease the foreign exchange constraint (see Bacha 1984, 1990).

### Macroeconomic policies and private investment

Monetary, fiscal, and exchange rate policies aimed at correcting unsustainable macroeconomic imbalances are bound to affect private investment. The standard macroeconomic package oriented toward improving the balance of payments and reducing inflation includes restrictive fiscal and monetary policies supplemented by real devaluation. The relevant empirical litera-ture on the macroeconomic determinants of investment in developing countries is reviewed here. The transmission mechanisms through which such policies affect capital formation are highlighted.

*Monetary policy*

The restrictive monetary and credit policies included in stabilization pack-ages affect investment in two ways: they raise the real cost of bank credit; and, by raising interest rates, they increase the opportunity cost of retained earnings. Both mechanisms raise the user cost of capital and lead to a reduction in investment. Studies by de Melo and Tybout (1986), Greene and Villanueva (1991), and Solimano (1989) confirm this effect. Other econo-mists disagree, however. van Wijnbergen (1982), Blejer and Khan (1984), Lim (1987), and Dailami (1990), for example, find that in the repressed financial markets typical of many developing countries, credit policy affects investment directly because credit is allocated to firms with access to borrowing at preferential interest rates rather than through the indirect interest rate channel—although interest rates also affect firms that borrow in the unofficial money market (van Wijnbergen 1983a, 1983b). Thus the institutional structure of the financial markets in developing countries is important in determining the effect of monetary and credit policy on investment and how such policy is transmitted.

*Fiscal policy*

High fiscal deficits push interest rates up or reduce the availability of credit to the private sector, or both, crowding out private investment. Hence the reduction of the public deficit during macroeconomic adjustment should allow private investment to expand (as confirmed by van Wijnbergen 1982 in the case of Korea). However, the way a fiscal deficit is corrected also matters. The mix of tax increases and spending reductions will affect aggregate private investment. Efforts to reduce the public deficit often involve cutting back on public investment. Some of these expenditures (especially those for such components of infrastructure as roads, ports, and communication networks) may be complementary with private invest-ment, and the cutback will cause private investment to fall. This pattern underscores the need to protect public expenditure on infrastructure dur-ing adjustment to encourage the recovery of investment and growth.

Several empirical studies shed light on this issue. A study by Blejer and Khan (1984), based on cross-country data, finds that government invest-ment in infrastructure is complementary with private investment (and other types of government investment are not). Greene and Villanueva (1991) and chapter 6, "Economic Adjustment and Investment Performance in Developing Countries: The Experience of the 1980s," in this volume arrive at similar conclusions using multicountry panel data. Musalem (1989) reports that private and public investment was complementary in a time-series study of investment in Mexico. Balassa (1988), however, reports cross-section estimates showing that an increase in public investment leads to a decline in private investment. He further finds a negative correlation between the share of public investment in total investment and the size of ICORs, an indicator that public investment is less efficient than private investment. Khan and Reinhart (1990) reexamine the differences in productivity between private and public investment for a sample of 24 developing countries and find that the marginal productivity of public sector capital is negative (although not significantly so), whereas that of private investment is significantly positive.

*Changes in output*

Empirical studies of investment in developing countries show that changes in output are the most important determinant of private investment (see Blejer and Khan 1984; Faini and de Melo 1990; Greene and Villanueva 1991; and chapter 6, "Economic Adjustment and Investment Performance in Developing Countries: The Experience of the 1980s," in this volume). To a certain extent this finding is puzzling, since a substantial amount of fluctuation in output appears to be transitory and therefore should not affect investment. Further, it is costly to install capital, so that adjusting to transitory shocks is suboptimal. Thus the puzzle remains largely unexplained (see Shapiro 1986), although it might be the product of investors' myopic expectations or short planning horizon.

Whatever the cause, the implication is that the contraction in demand induced by adjustment measures is likely to have an adverse short-run effect on investment because of its negative effect on the growth of output. This effect is apparent in the context of the Q theory of investment. Solimano (1989) shows that in Chile aggregate investment profitability is procyclical—Tobin's Q increases in upturns and falls in downturns—so that the market value of capital, and hence investment, would be expected to fall in the short run in response to a exogenous slowdown in economic activity.

The downturn may also affect investment through its effect on expectations. A recession, for instance, could lead investors to postpone investing until the economy recovered. This response might in turn delay the recovery, and the economy might get stuck in a low investment equilibrium because of self-fulfilling pessimism. To avoid such an outcome, it is important that governments design demand adjustment policies that minimize the potentially adverse effects on investment and growth.

*Exchange rate policy*

To reduce the external imbalance, adjustment programs rely on a combination of policies that reduce expenditures and switch spending toward domestic goods. The switch generally includes a real devaluation, with significant consequences for investment.

**Profitability.** Devaluation has important effects on profitability through its impact on the relative price of capital goods. Because investment goods combine domestic components (that is, construction or infrastructure) and foreign components (machinery and equipment), a real depreciation raises the real cost of imported components and acts like an adverse supply shock on the "production" of investment goods. Buffie (1986) and Branson (1986) note that a real depreciation increases the real cost of new capital goods relative to domestic goods, a phenomenon that depresses investment in nontradable activities. In the tradable goods sector, however, the cost of new capital goods—relative to the price of output—falls, and investment rises. The result for aggregate investment is therefore uncertain.

The empirical studies reflect this theoretical ambiguity. In the short run real depreciation adversely affects investment (although its long-run effect may be positive). For example, Musalem (1989) finds that devaluation has had an adverse effect on investment in Mexico. Faini and de Melo (1990) arrive at similar results using data for 24 developing countries. Branson (1986) explicitly calculates the impact of a devaluation on Tobin's Q in the home goods sector, concluding that profits fall (along with the market value of capital) at the same time that the real cost of new capital goods rises. Solimano (1989), using an empirical simultaneous equation model for Chile, also concludes that a real depreciation reduces investment in the short run, although it recovers in the medium term. Moreover, this study finds that a real appreciation produces an unsustainable expansion in investment. In contrast, the empirical analysis of panel data on private investment for a number of developing countries (see chapter 6, "Economic Adjustment and Investment Performance in Developing Countries: The Experience of the 1980s," chapter 7, "Macroeconomic Environment and Capital Formation in Latin America," and chapter 8, "Investment and Macroeconomic Adjustment: The Case of East Asia," in this volume) shows that the real exchange rate has an insignificant effect, in the statistical sense, on aggregate investment; however, its variability does have a significantly adverse effect.

In general, a high dependence on imported capital and intermediate goods, along with a relatively low share of traded goods in total investment, results in a contraction in investment after a real devaluation. Lizondo and Montiel (1989) distinguish between investment in traded and nontraded goods in a model in which capital is sector-specific. They decompose the effect of devaluation on the cost of capital, the product wage in both sectors (also examined by van Wijnbergen 1985 and Risager 1988), and the cost of imported intermediate inputs. The results show that the net effect of a real depreciation is ambiguous: investment in tradable goods increases at the same time that investment in domestic goods declines.

Anticipated and unanticipated devaluation may affect the profitability of investment by raising the real interest rate. Devaluation will raise the price of imported intermediate inputs, and wages under indexation will rise. If monetary policy does not fully accommodate the increase in prices, real money balances will fall, pushing the real interest rate up for a given rate of (expected) inflation. In this way, an unanticipated devaluation depresses the market value of existing capital and exerts an adverse effect on investment In contrast, if devaluation was anticipated and if it eliminated expectations that the currency would be devalued, investment might expand, since the required return on capital would tend to fall, mirroring the reduction in the anticipated rate of depreciation. This result depends on the degree of financial openness and on the import content of investment.

**Financial Effects of Devaluation.** The debt crisis of the 1980s attracted attention to the effect of devaluation on the real value of foreign currency liabilities. In the case of firms with foreign debts, devaluation automatically raises the burden of debt and thereby reduces the net worth of firms producing home goods. If the domestic credit markets are imperfect (as is often the case in developing countries), these firms may face credit constraints or higher financing costs as creditors raise interest rates to compensate for the increased risk of default. These financial pressures will lead directly to reduced investment for indebted firms at risk of bankruptcy. The increase in the real value of the firms' foreign debt also affects investment indirectly. As the net worth of these firms falls, so does the quality of the portfolios of their domestic creditors. Banks and financial intermediaries may be forced to reduce their exposure by cutting their loans—or they may simply go bankrupt. The ensuing tightening of credit markets may reduce the supply of credit (or raise interest rates), even for firms that have no foreign currency liabilities. The implications for investment as financing becomes scarce and expensive are obvious.

The financial effects of an unanticipated devaluation may require that the government bail firms or financial intermediaries out to avoid an epidemic of bankruptcies that could jeopardize the adjustment effort. Financing the bailout, however, may lead to a domestic debt overhang, if the government or the central bank issues bonds to cover the foreign exchange losses of commercial banks or firms. The ensuing rise in public debt puts upward pressure on interest rates that crowds out private investment. It is important to note the implicit tradeoff between supporting investment today (by subsidizing indebted firms) and supporting it tomorrow, when previously issued public debt may crowd out investment.

Empirical studies of the financial effects of devaluation and its impact on investment are scarce; the exceptions are Easterly (1990) and Rosensweig and Taylor (1990). In Easterly's model, devaluation results in a drop in gross domestic product (GDP) and in private investment, but the decline in investment is greater than the reduction in GDP. The main cut in investment comes from corporations and is the result of a sharp increase in real foreign indebtedness. Easterly reports that the cash flow of corporations declines substantially as a result of capital losses on dollar debt, while the replacement cost of capital rises sharply. Rosensweig and Taylor (1990) also underscore the importance of foreign currency liabilities. In their model for Thailand, GDP increases following a real depreciation, under the assumption of a strong export response to relative price incentives (ignoring capital losses on foreign debt). Higher net worth results in more deposits to banks, the supply of credit rises, and interest rates fall. The result is an increase in investment. When the capital losses on foreign liabilities associated with a devaluation are taken into consideration, however, the expansionary net effect on exports may be offset, and domestic capital formation may fall.

**Devaluation, Output, and Investment.** Devaluation may also reduce investment by depressing aggregate demand. Moreover, if investment has a significant import content, the expansion of output is likely to be a necessary (but not sufficient) condition to sustain investment (Servén 1990). The literature on contractionary devaluation (Krugman and Taylor 1978; van Wijnbergen 1982; Edwards 1988; Solimano 1986; Lizondo and Montiel 1989) emphasizes the slow working of the substitution effects arising from devaluation. In the short run its adverse income effects are dominant. These effects operate through two channels on the demand side: one is the likely trade imbalance, which results in a real income transfer to the rest of the world (even at given terms of trade); the other is the negative effect on consumption as real income is redistributed from wages to profits. On the supply side three mechanisms of transmission may contribute to the contraction in output: the increased real price of imported inputs for domestic goods; the rise in the price of working capital (because of the increased interest rates); and real wage resistance. If the currency devaluation leads to a drop in GDP, the slump in economic activity will prompt a cut in investment (unless the slump is perceived to be transitory). Given strong substitution effects, however, such as a large rise in exports, GDP will expand, a trend that will raise real income and stimulate investment spending as the degree of capacity utilization increases. This outcome is more likely as time passes and substitution effects gradually come into play.

**The Timing of Investment.** An anticipated devaluation can have a substantial effect on the timing of investment through its effect on interest rates and the future price of imported capital goods (for a detailed exposition, see Servén 1990). Its effect on interest rates depends on the degree of financial openness, that is, the costs of portfolio adjustment. In the case of imperfect capital mobility, the domestic real interest rate is an increasing function of the foreign real interest rate plus the expected rate of depreciation of the real exchange rate (it may also depend on the relative or absolute stocks of financial assets). The perception that a real depreciation is imminent will be reflected in higher real interest rates—according to the degree of capital mobility. In this way expectations of a devaluation represent a transitory disincentive to invest: pending the depreciation, the real interest rate is high and investment is low. Once devaluation has taken place, the disincentive is eliminated, and investment rises.

The import content of capital goods operates in the opposite direction.

When a real depreciation is anticipated, the real price of imported capital goods is expected to rise. Before the depreciation, imports of capital goods are cheap and investment high (the mechanism is similar to an anticipated increase in tariffs on investment goods). Dornbusch (1985) notes that this amounts to a transitory investment incentive that disappears once the depreciation is implemented. The net effect on investment depends on the degree of international capital mobility relative to the import content of investment. When capital is highly mobile, the effect on the interest rate dominates, and expectations of a devaluation lead to an investment slump that will persist until the depreciation is actually undertaken. When capital is relatively immobile and investment requires a high proportion of imported capital goods, an anticipated depreciation may result in a transitory investment boom that subsides when the depreciation occurs.

## The incentive structure

A key ingredient of most adjustment packages is a change in economic incentives that switches spending to domestic goods and raises profitability in the tradable sector. This change in incentives is expected to lead to a burst of investment in tradables that boost production and economic growth and thus ensure the sustainability of the adjustment effort.

In practice, however, the investment response often is unexpectedly slow and weak. In the meantime the short-run deflationary consequences of cuts in expenditures may be magnified, causing a slump in growth. In the face of the high costs of adjustment in terms of employment and growth, the stabilization effort may fail.

Conventional investment theories do not explain this slow response except by the (unconvincing) arguments that firms face rapidly increasing costs of adjustment (an assertion that does not seem realistic), or that investors' expectations adapt very slowly to economic changes. A more satisfactory explanation takes into account the importance of uncertainty.

### *Irreversibility, uncertainty, and investment*

Uncertainty plays a key role in investment decisions because they are largely irreversible. These investments represent sunk costs, since capital, once installed, cannot be used in a different activity (without incurring a substantial cost). As chapter 3, "Irreversibility, Uncertainty, and Investment," describes in detail, the decision to invest in an uncertain environment involves exercising an option—the option to wait for new information. The loss of this option, which must be considered part of the opportunity cost of investment, is overlooked in conventional calculations of net present value. As recent studies show, this opportunity cost can be substantial and is also very sensitive to the prevailing degree of uncertainty about returns on the investment. Thus changes in uncertainty can have a strong effect on aggregate investment.

From a policy perspective, a stable incentive structure and macroeconomic policy environment may be as important for investment as the level of the tax incentives or the interest rate. In other words, if uncertainty is high, investment incentives may have to be prohibitively large to have any significant effect.

The effect of uncertainty is independent of investors' risk preferences or the extent to which risks may be diversifiable. Investors may be risk-neutral (as most of the literature on irreversibility assumes) and their risks diversifiable, but investment will still be hostage to the perceived degree of uncertainty.

From a macroeconomic perspective, different forms of uncertainty may be relevant for investment decisions. For example, in the face of uncertain demand (see Pindyck 1988 and Bertola 1989), firms will opt for lower capacity if the investment is irreversible than they would under conditions of reversibility. The ex-post capacity level may, however, actually be higher under irreversibility, because if demand is unexpectedly low, an irreversible investment cannot be undone. Pindyck and Bertola also show that increased volatility in demand will generally lead to reduced investment.

Dixit (1987), Krugman (1988), and Krugman and Baldwin (1987) find that when sunk costs of entry are combined with uncertain future real exchange rates, firms are discouraged from entering the market even though favorable current exchange rates would seem to make entry profitable. Similarly, Caballero and Corbo (1988) show that uncertainty over future real exchange rates can depress exports. Dornbusch (1988) examines the related issue of reversing capital flight following a real depreciation. He argues that if a country wants to attract capital to irreversible fixed investment, an overdepreciation of the exchange rate may be needed to compensate for the uncertainty faced by investors. The reason is that, unlike fixed investment, foreign exchange or assets held abroad do not involve an irreversible commitment and may be preferable to investors in the face of high uncertainty, even though they offer a lower rate of return. Likewise, it may be difficult to stem or reverse capital flight if the perception is that it may become more difficult to take capital out of the country than to bring it in.

Ingersoll and Ross (1988) and Tornell (1989) examine interest rate uncertainty in the context of irreversible investment where future returns are known with certainty. They conclude that the effect of changes in interest rate uncertainty on the optimal timing of investment may be sizable. Moreover, an expected decline in future interest rates may not lead to increased investment because the change lowers the cost of waiting, so that the effect on investment is ambiguous. In other words, the volatility of interest rates may have a more important effect on investment than the actual levels of interest rates do.

The relevance of these results for macroeconomic policy in developing countries cannot be overemphasized. Many developing countries suffer from high, unpredictable inflation and variability of relative prices. The findings on irreversible investment suggest that changes in prices that affect sectoral incentives may then be ineffective in stimulating investment. It may take some time before investors are convinced that the changes are permanent. The decision to implement an adjustment program may well increase uncertainty in the short run, as private agents get mixed signals about which incentives apply to previous policies, which to stabilization, and which to structural reforms. Along these lines, van Wijnbergen (1985) shows that a trade reform suspected of being only temporary can reduce investment in both the tradable and nontradable sectors as economic agents postpone decisions in order to receive additional information about the extent to which the reform measures can be viewed as permanent.

The foreign debt burden faced by highly—indebted countries and the associated income transfers to foreign creditors are another source of instability (Sachs 1988). In a context of uncertainty the real exchange rate and demand management policies consistent with the required income transfer are also uncertain. Even the amount of the income transfer is unknown, since it depends on uncontrollable factors such as future interest rates and terms of trade. The transfer may require changes in the real exchange rate or fiscal contraction, or both. Thus investors face the risk of large swings in relative prices, taxes, or aggregate demand, each of which leads to reduced investment.

This effect may be hard to identify because foreign debt may affect investment adversely through two additional channels (Borensztein 1990): the debt overhang, which acts as an anticipated foreign tax on current and future income (as part of the returns on investment accrue to foreign creditors in the form of debt service payments); and credit rationing, because a highly—indebted country is likely to face credit constraints in the international capital markets. Empirical studies (see Faini and de Melo 1990; Greene and Villanueva 1991; chapter 6, "Economic Adjustment and Investment Performance in Developing Countries: The Experience of the 1980s," in this volume) confirm that the debt burden has an adverse effect on investment.

## The role of credibility

From a policy perspective the credibility of policy reforms is an important source of uncertainty. Unless investors view the adjustment program as internally consistent and are convinced the government will carry it out despite the implied social costs, the possibility of reversal will become a key determinant of the investment response. Governments can reverse adjustment policies, but investors cannot undo decisions about fixed capital. In such conditions the value of waiting arises from the losses that investors would incur if the policies were reversed in the future.

Any given set of policies will affect investment depending on the level of public confidence. Stabilization may entail marked social and economic costs if the government's credibility is low, because the investment response will be too low to offset the deflationary bias of demand restraint. Thus a deep recession may develop before investors are persuaded that the government will maintain the adjustment measures. This skepticism is particularly relevant in economies with a history of frequent policy swings or failed stabilization attempts—two features shared by many developing countries.

The right economic incentives are a precondition for investment and growth but not a guarantee. Obviously, credibility would help speed the investment response and reduce the costs of adjustment, but how can governments improve their credibility? In this context the choice between gradual and abrupt stabilization is important. Gradual adjustment involves modest objectives that can be achieved and that are intended to strengthen the government's reputation. In contrast, an abrupt adjustment involves drastic measures—an overdepreciation of the exchange rate, for instance—to stimulate the prompt reallocation of resources (although it could also increase the social costs). The choice will largely depend on the social distribution of the costs of adjustment.

It is important to emphasize that a reversal of policy is an endogenous outcome, since the private sector ultimately determines whether the adjustment program can be sustained. For example, when a large real depreciation does not attract investment to the tradable sector because confidence is low, its only visible effects will be a decline in real income and a redistribution of income from labor to capital, especially in the tradable sector. Because the depreciation does not compensate for the lack of credibility, however, the increased profits will be reflected in increased capital flight. Social pressure and balance of payments problems may eventually force a reversal of policy, a move that confirms the initial skepticism of investors. The same policy in a situation of high confidence can, however, lead to an investment boom that validates the adjustment program.

This indeterminacy of the final outcome is the result of the difference between the social and private returns on investment: higher aggregate investment helps sustain the adjustment effort and therefore results in higher returns on investment—a mechanism individual investors will ignore. If left to its own resources, the economy might get stuck in the "low confidence—low investment—adjustment failure" cycle.

How can such a cycle be avoided? The answer is not simple. While transitory investment incentives appear to be the most appropriate tool to spur investment, in practice they run the risk of destabilizing public finances, which often are a key element in adjustment programs. In contrast, sufficient external support for the stabilization effort may raise investors' confidence in the sustainability of the adjustment and set the stage for the investment takeoff (Dornbusch 1991).

## Uncertainty and investment: Empirical applications

The empirical literature on the effects of uncertainty and irreversibility on investment in developing countries is sparse. Because structural models of irreversible investment are analytically cumbersome, empirical studies typically test for the effects of uncertainty by adding some measures of risk to otherwise conventional investment equations. For example, Solimano (1989) investigates the effects of economic instability in an empirical simultaneous equation model applied to Chile. He finds that the volatility of both the real exchange rate and output has a significant negative effect on private investment, and he argues that the large swings in both variables in the 1980s may have reduced private investment as compared with a scenario of lower variability in relative prices and output. Dailami (1987) reports similar results for Brazil. Dailami and Walton (1989) argue that macroeconomic instability may be a major cause of low investment in Zimbabwe. Multicountry studies of investment based on panel data (see chapter 6, "Economic Adjustment and Investment Performance in Developing Countries: The Experience of the 1980s," chapter 7, "Macroeconomic Environment and Capital Formation in Latin America," and chapter 8, "Investment and Macroeconomic Adjustment: The Case of East Asia," in this volume) also find that measures of macroeconomic instability, such as the variability of the real exchange rate or of the inflation rate, have an adverse effect on investment.

In contrast, empirical applications of structural models of irreversible investment in developing countries have so far been very limited. Chapter 4, "On the Dynamics of Aggregate Investment," in this volume applies a formal model based on the aggregation of individual firms' irreversible investments to data on some developing countries (Brazil, Korea, Mexico, and Turkey), with highly promising results.

### Issues for further research

This chapter reviewed the theoretical and empirical literature on macroeconomic adjustment and private capital formation. Further research should be a priority in the following areas:

• The specific mechanisms through which the level and composition of public investment affect private investment.

• The relationships between different types of investment, for instance, between investment in human capital and investment in physical capital, or between foreign and domestic investment.

• The effects of macroeconomic adjustment policies on the composition and quality of investment.

• The consequences of income distribution and redistributive policies for private investment.

• The relationship between the political regime and private capital accumulation.

### Notes

1. The authors thank the late Bela Balassa, William Branson, Ricardo Caballero, Vittorio Corbo, Rudiger Dornbusch, and Robert Pindyck for

helpful comments and discussion. Raimundo Soto and Walter Novaes provided research assistance. A version of this chapter appeared in *The World Bank Research Observer* (Servén and Solimano, 1992).
2.  See Chapter 3, "Irreversibility, Uncertainty, and Investment," in this volume, which presents a thorough analysis of the effects of uncertainty on irreversible investment decisions.

## References

Abel, A. 1980. "Empirical Investment Equations: An Integrative Approach." Carnegie-Rochester Conference Series on Public Policy on the State of Macroeconomics. University of Rochester, Rochester, N.Y.

Arrow, K. 1968. "Optimal Capital Policy with Irreversible Investment," in John Wolfe, ed., *Value, Capital, and Growth: Essays in Honor of Sir John Hicks.* Edinburgh: Edinburgh University Press.

Bacha, E. L. 1984. "Growth with Limited Supplies of Foreign Exchange: A Reappraisal of the Two Gaps Model," in M. Syrquin, L. Taylor, and L. Westphal, eds., *Economic Structure and Performance: Essays in Honor of Hollis B. Chenery.* New York: Academic Press.

———. 1990. "A Three-Gap Model of Foreign Transfers and the GDP Growth Rate in Developing Countries." *Journal of Development Economics* 32 (April):279-96.

Balassa, B. 1988. "Public Finance and Economic Development." World Bank, Policy, Research, and External Affairs (PRE) Working Paper 31. Office of the Vice President for Development Economics. Washington, D.C.

Bernanke, B. 1983. "Irreversibility, Uncertainty, and Cyclical Investment." *Quarterly Journal of Economics* 98(1) (February):85-106.

Bertola, G. 1989. "Irreversible Investment." Princeton University, Department of Economics, Princeton, N.J.

Bertola, G., and R. J. Caballero. 1990. "Irreversibility and Aggregate Investment." Columbia University, Department of Economics, New York.

Blejer, M., and M. Khan. 1984. "Government Policy and Private Investment in Developing Countries." *IMF Staff Papers* 31(2): 379-403.

Borensztein, E. 1990. "Debt Overhang, Credit Rationing, and Investment." *Journal of Development Economics* 32 (April): 315-35.

Branson, W. 1986. "Stabilization, Stagflation, and Investment Incentives: The Case of Kenya, 1979-1980," in S. Edwards and L. Ahamed, eds., *Economic Adjustment and Exchange Rates in Developing Countries.* Chicago: University of Chicago Press.

Buffie, E. F. 1986. "Devaluation, Investment and Growth in LDCs." *Journal of Development Economics* 20 (March):361-79.

Caballero, R., and V. Corbo. 1988. "Real Exchange Rate Uncertainty and Exports: Multi-Country Empirical Evidence." Working Paper 414.

Columbia University, Department of Economics, New York.

Calomiris, C. H., and R. G. Hubbard. 1989. "Price Flexibility, Credit Availability, and Economic Fluctuations: Evidence from the United States, 1894-1909." *Quarterly Journal of Economics* 104 (3):429-52.

Chenery, H., and M. Bruno. 1962. "Development Alternatives in an Open Economy: The Case of Israel." *Economic Journal* 72 (2):79-103.

Cooper, R., and A. John. 1988. "Coordinating Coordination Failures in Keynesian Models." *Quarterly Journal of Economics* 103 (3):441-64.

Dailami, M. 1987. "Expectations, Stock Market Volatility, and Private Investment Behavior: Theory and Empirical Evidence for Brazil." World Bank, Country Economics Department, Washington, D.C.

————. 1990. "Financial Policy and Corporate Investment in Imperfect Capital Markets: The Case of Korea." World Bank, Policy, Research, and External Affairs (PRE) Working Paper 409. Country Economics Department. Washington, D.C.

Dailami, M., and M. Walton. 1989. "Private Investment, Government Policy and Foreign Capital in Zimbabwe." World Bank, Policy, Research, and External Affairs (PRE) Working Paper 248. Country Economics Department. Washington, D.C.

de Melo, J., and J. Tybout. 1986. "The Effects of Financial Liberalization on Savings and Investment in Uruguay." *Economic Development and Cultural Change* 34 (2):561-88.

Dixit, A. 1987. "Entry and Exit Decisions of Firms under Fluctuating Real Exchange Rates." Princeton University, Department of Economics, Princeton, N.J.

Dornbusch, R. 1985. "Overborrowing: Three Case Studies," in G. W. Smith and J. T. Cuddington, eds., *International Debt and the Developing Countries*. Washington, D.C.: World Bank.

————. 1988. "Notes on Credibility and Stabilization." NBER Working Paper 2790. National Bureau of Economic Research, Cambridge, Mass.

————. 1991. "Policies to Move from Stabilization to Growth," in World Bank, *Proceedings of the World Bank Annual Conference on Development Economics 1990*. Washington, D.C.: World Bank.

Easterly, W. 1990. "Portfolio Effects in a CGE Model: Devaluation in a Dollarized Economy," in L. Taylor, ed., *Socially Relevant Policy Analysis for the Developing World: Structuralist Computable General Equilibrium Models*. Cambridge, Mass.: MIT Press.

Edwards, S. 1988. "Stabilization, Macroeconomic Policy and Trade Liberalization." World Bank, Country Economics Department, Washington, D.C.

Faini, R., and J. de Melo. 1990. "Adjustment, Investment, and the Real Exchange Rate in Developing Countries." *Economic Policy* 5 (October):492-519.

Fazzari, S., R. G. Hubbard, and B. C. Petersen. 1988a. "Financing Constraints and Corporate Investment." *Brookings Papers on Economic Activity* 1:141-206.

———. 1988b. "Investment, Financing Decisions, and Tax Policy." *American Economic Review* 78 (2):200-05.

Greene, J., and D. Villanueva. 1991. "Private Investment in Developing Countries: An Empirical Analysis." *IMF Staff Papers* 38 (1):33-58.

Hall, R., and D. W. Jorgenson. 1971. "Application of the Theory of Optimum Capital Accumulation," in G. Fromm, ed., *Tax Incentives and Capital Spending*. Washington, D.C.: Brookings Institution.

Hayashi, F. 1982. "Tobin's Marginal q and Average q: A Neoclassical Interpretation." *Econometrica* 50 (1):213-23.

Hubbard, G. 1990. *Asymmetric Information, Corporate Finance and Investment*. Chicago: University of Chicago Press.

Ingersoll, J., and S. Ross. 1988. "Waiting to Invest: Investment and Uncertainty." Yale University, Department of Economics, New Haven, Conn.

Jorgenson, D. W. 1967. "The Theory of Investment Behavior," in R. Ferber, ed., *Determinants of Investment Behavior*. Cambridge, Mass.: National Bureau of Economic Research.

Keynes, J. M. 1936. *The General Theory of Employment, Interest and Money*. San Diego: Harcourt Brace Jovanovich.

Khan, M., and C. Reinhart. 1990. "Private Investment and Economic Growth in Developing Countries." *World Development* 18 (January):19-27.

Kiyotaki, N. 1988. "Multiple Expectational Equilibria under Monopolistic Competition." *Quarterly Journal of Economics* 103 (November):695-713.

Krugman, P. 1988. *Exchange Rate Instability*. Cambridge, Mass.: MIT Press.

Krugman, P., and R. Baldwin. 1987. "The Persistence of the U.S. Trade Deficit." *Brookings Papers on Economic Activity* 1:1-43.

Krugman, P., and L. Taylor. 1978. "The Contractionary Effects of Devaluations." *Journal of International Economics* 8 (3):445-56.

Lim, Joseph Y. 1987. "The New Structuralist Critique of the Monetarist Theory of Inflation." *Journal of Development Economics* 25 (1):45-62.

Lizondo, J. S., and P. Montiel. 1989. "Contractionary Devaluation in Developing Countries: An Analytical Overview." *IMF Staff Papers* 36 (1):182-227.

Mackie-Mason, J. 1989. "Do Firms Care Who Provides Their Financing?" University of Michigan, Department of Economics, Ann Arbor, Michigan.

Malinvaud, E. 1980. *Profitability and Unemployment*. Cambridge: Cambridge University Press.

———. 1982. "Wages and Unemployment." *Economic Journal* 92 (1):1-12.

Mayer, C. P. 1989. "Financial Systems, Corporate Finance and Economic Development." City University of New York, Business School.

McDonald, R., and D. Siegel. 1986. "The Value of Waiting to Invest." *Quarterly Journal of Economics* 101 (November):707-27.

Musalem, A. R. 1989. "Private Investment in Mexico: An Empirical Analysis." World Bank, Policy, Research, and External Affairs (PRE)

Working Paper 183. Latin America and the Caribbean Country Department II. Washington, D.C.

Neary, J. P., and J. E. Stiglitz. 1983. "Towards a Reconstruction of Keynesian Economics: Expectations and Constrained Equilibria." *Quarterly Journal of Economics* 98 (suppl.):199-228.

Pindyck, R. 1988. "Irreversible Investment, Capacity Choice, and the Value of the Firm." *American Economic Review* 78 (5):969-85.

Precious, M. 1985. "Demand Constraints, Rational Expectations, and Investment Theory." *Oxford Economic Papers* 37 (December):576-605.

Risager, O. 1988. "Devaluation, Profitability and Investment: A Model with Anticipated Wage Adjustment." *Scandinavian Journal of Economics* 90 (2):125-40.

Rosensweig, J., and L. Taylor. 1990. "Devaluation, Capital Flows and Crowding Out: A CGE Model with Portfolio Choice for Thailand," in L. Taylor, ed., *Socially Relevant Policy Analysis for the Developing World: Structuralist Computable General Equilibrium Models*. Cambridge, Mass.: MIT Press.

Sachs, J. 1988. "The Debt Overhang of Developing Countries," in R. Findlay, ed., *Debt, Stabilization, and Development: Essays in Memory of Carlos Diaz Alejandro*. Oxford: Blackwell.

Schleifer, A., and R. Vishny. 1988. "The Efficiency of Investment in the Presence of Aggregate Demand Spillovers." *Journal of Political Economy* 96 (December):1221-31.

Servén, L. 1990. "Anticipated Real Exchange Rate Changes and the Dynamics of Investment." World Bank, Country Economics Department, Washington, D.C.

Servén, L., and A. Solimano. 1992. "Private Investment and Macroeconomic Adjustment: A Survey." *The World Bank Research Observer* 7(1) (January):95-114.

Shapiro, M. D. 1986. "Investment, Output and the Cost of Capital." *Brookings Papers on Economic Activity* 1:111-52.

Sneesens, H. R. 1987. "Investment and the Inflation-Unemployment Trade-Off in a Macroeconomic Rationing Model with Monopolistic Competition." *European Economic Review* 31 (3):781-815.

Solimano, A. 1986. "Contractionary Devaluation in the Southern Cone: The Case of Chile." *Journal of Development Economics* 23 (1):135-51.

_____. 1989. "How Private Investment Reacts to Changing Macroeconomic Conditions: The Case of Chile." World Bank, Policy, Research, and External Affairs (PRE) Working Paper 212. Country Economics Department. Washington, D.C. Also in A. Chhibber and others, *Reviving Private Investment in Developing Countries*. Amsterdam: North-Holland Publishing Company, 1992.

Stiglitz, J. E., and A. Weiss. 1981. "Credit Rationing in Markets with Imperfect Information." *American Economic Review* 71 (3):393-410.

Tobin, J. 1969. "A General Equilibrium Approach to Monetary Theory." *Journal of Money, Credit, and Banking* 1 (1):15-29.

Tornell, A. 1989. "Real vs. Financial Investment: Towards an Explanation of 'Short-Termism.'" Columbia University, Department of Economics, New York.

van Wijnbergen, S. 1982. "Stagflationary Effects of Monetary Stabilization Policies: A Quantitative Analysis." *Journal of Development Economics* 10 (April):133-70.

——. 1983a. "Credit Policy, Inflation and Growth in a Financially Repressed Economy." *Journal of Development Economics* 13 (April):45-65.

——. 1983b. "Interest Rate Management in LDC." *Journal of Monetary Economics* 12 (September):433-52.

——. 1985. "Trade Reform, Aggregate Investment and Capital Flight: On Credibility and the Value of Information." *Economic Letters* 19 (4):369-72.

# 3

## Irreversibility, Uncertainty, and Investment

### *Robert S. Pindyck*

The investment behavior of firms, industries, and countries is poorly understood, despite its importance to economic growth and market structure.[1] The success of econometric models in explaining and predicting changes in investment spending has been limited, and there is no clear explanation of why some countries or industries invest more than others.

One problem with existing models is that they ignore two important characteristics of most investment expenditures. First, these expenditures are largely irreversible—they involve mostly sunk costs that cannot be recovered. Second, because the investments can be delayed, a firm can wait for new information about prices, costs, and other market conditions before committing its resources.

As an emerging literature shows, the ability to delay an irreversible investment expenditure can profoundly affect the decision to invest. It also undermines the theoretical foundation of standard neoclassical investment models and invalidates the rule of net present value. In business school, students are usually taught to "invest in a project when the present value of its expected cash flows is at least as large as its cost." When investments are irreversible and decisions to invest can be postponed, this rule—and models based on it—are incorrect.

What makes an investment expenditure a sunk cost and thus irreversible? Usually the reason is that the capital is firm- or industry-specific; it cannot be used productively by a different firm or in a different industry. For example, most investments in marketing and advertising are firm-specific and hence are clearly sunk costs. A steel plant is industry-specific—it can only be used to produce steel. Although in principle the plant could be sold to another steel company, its cost should be viewed as mostly sunk, particularly if the industry is competitive. The reason is that the value of the plant will be about the same for all firms in the industry, so that little will likely be gained from selling it. (If the price of steel falls so that a plant turns

31

out to be a bad investment, other steel companies will also view it as a bad investment, and the ability to sell the plant will not be worth much.)

Even investments that are not firm- or industry-specific are often partly irreversible because of the "lemons" problem. For example, although office equipment, cars, trucks, and computers are not industry-specific, their resale value is well below their purchase cost, even if new. Government regulations or institutional arrangements can also create irreversibility. For example, capital controls may make it impossible for foreign (or domestic) investors to sell assets and reallocate their funds. Investments in new workers may be partly irreversible because of the high costs of hiring, training, and firing.

At the same time, firms do not always have an opportunity to delay investments. Strategic considerations may require that a firm invest quickly to preempt investment by existing or potential competitors (see Gilbert 1989 for a survey of the literature on strategic aspects of investment). In most cases, however, delay is feasible. It may carry a cost—the risk of entry by other firms or foregone cash flows—but this cost must be weighed against the benefits of waiting for new information.

An irreversible opportunity to invest is much like a financial call option. A call option gives the holder the right, for some specified period, to pay an exercise price and in return receive an asset (such as a share of stock) that has some value. Exercising the option is irreversible: although investors can sell the asset to other investors, they cannot retrieve the option or the money paid to exercise it. A firm with an investment opportunity likewise has the option to spend money (the "exercise price") now or in the future in return for an asset (an example being a project) of some value. Again, it can sell the asset to another firm, but it cannot reverse the investment. As with the financial call option, this option to invest is valuable because of the potential for a growing net payoff if the value of the asset rises. If the asset falls in value, the firm need not invest and will lose only what it spent to obtain the investment opportunity.

How do firms obtain investment opportunities? Sometimes they get them from patents or the ownership of land or natural resources. More generally, they arise from a firm's managerial resources, technological knowledge, reputation, market position, and possibly scale, which enable the firm to undertake investments that individuals or other firms cannot undertake.

The most important point is that these options to invest are valuable. A substantial part of the market value of most firms arises from their options to invest and grow, as opposed to the capital they have in place. (For discussions of growth options as sources of a firm's value, see Myers 1977; Kester 1984; Pindyck 1988.)

When a firm makes an irreversible investment expenditure, it exercises, or "kills," its option to invest. It gives up the possibility of waiting for new information that might affect the desirability or timing of the expenditure; it cannot disinvest should market conditions change adversely. The value of this lost option is an opportunity cost that must be included as part of the cost of the investment. As a result, the rule of net present value—"invest when the value of a unit of capital is at least as large as its purchase and installation cost"—must be modified. The value of the unit must *exceed* the cost of the purchase and installation by an amount equal to the value of keeping the investment option alive.

Recent studies have shown that the opportunity cost of investing can be large and that investment rules ignoring it can be grossly in error.[2] In addition, this opportunity cost is highly sensitive to uncertainty over the future value of the project, so that changing economic conditions affecting the perceived riskiness of future cash flows can have a large impact on investment spending, larger, say, than a change in interest rates. This point may help explain why neoclassical theory on investment has not provided good empirical models of investment behavior.

This chapter has several objectives. First, it reviews some basic models of irreversible investment to illustrate the option-like characteristics of investment opportunities and to show how optimal investment rules can be obtained from methods of option pricing or, alternatively, from dynamic programming. In addition to demonstrating a methodology for solving a class of investment problems, this chapter shows how the resulting rules on investment depend on various parameters that come from the market environment.

A second objective is to survey briefly some recent applications of this methodology to a variety of investment problems and to the analysis of the behavior of firms and industries. Examples include the effects of sunk costs of entry, exit, and temporary shutdowns and re-start-ups on decisions relating to investment and output, the implications of construction time (and the option to abandon construction) for the value of a project, and the determinants of a firm's choice of capacity. The chapter also shows how models of irreversible investment have helped explain the prevalence of "hysteresis," or the tendency for an effect (such as foreign sales in the United States) to persist well after the cause that brought it about (an appreciation of the dollar) has disappeared.

The next section uses a simple example involving two periods to illustrate how irreversibility can affect an investment decision and how option pricing methods can be used to value a firm's investment opportunity and determine whether the firm should invest. The following section works through a basic continuous time model of irreversible investment that was first examined by McDonald and Siegel (1986). The firm must decide when to invest in a project whose value follows a random walk. The problem is solved first using option pricing methods and then by dynamic programming, a procedure that reveals how the two approaches are related. This model is extended in the subsequent section such that the price of the firm's output follows a random walk and the firm can (temporarily) stop producing if the price falls below the variable cost. The section shows how to determine both the value of the project and the value of the firm's

option to invest in the project. It also derives the optimal investment rule
and examines its properties.

The above two sections use stochastic calculus. The basic techniques
and their application are described in the appendix. Readers who are less
technically inclined can skip directly to the fifth section, which surveys a
number of extensions that have appeared in the literature, as well as other
applications of the methodology, including the analysis of hysteresis.

The sixth section discusses some policy implications and suggests
future research. It is followed by a final section of conclusions.

## A simple two-period example

The implications of irreversibility and the option-like nature of an investment opportunity can be demonstrated most easily with a simple two-
period example. Consider a firm's decision to invest irreversibly in a widget
factory. The factory can be built instantly, at cost $I$, and will produce one
widget per year forever, with zero operating cost. Currently the price of
widgets is US$100, but next year the price will change. With probability $q$,
it will rise to $150; with probability $(1 - q)$ it will fall to $50 (figure 3-1). The
price will remain at this new level forever. It is assumed that this risk can
be diversified fully, so that the firm can discount future cash flows using the
risk-free rate, set here at 10 percent.

For the time being $I = \$800$ and $q = 0.5$. (How the investment decision
depends on $I$ and $q$ is discussed later.) Given these values for $I$ and $q$, is this
a good investment? Should the investment be made now, or is it better to
wait a year and see whether the price goes up or down? Suppose the

**Figure 3.1   Price of widgets**
          **(US$)**

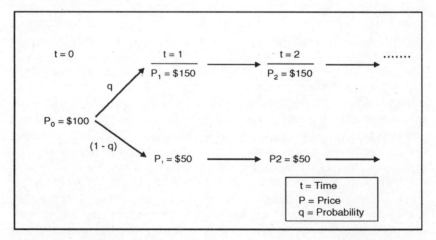

*Source:* Author's calculations.

investment is made now. Calculating the net present value (NPV) of this investment in the standard way,

$$NPV = -800 + \sum_{t=0}^{\infty} 100/(1.1)^t = -800 + 1,100 = \underline{\$300.}$$

The net present value is positive; the current value of the widget factory (that is, the present value of its expected cash flow) is $V_0 = 1,100 > 800$. It seems correct to make the investment now.

This conclusion is incorrect, however. The above calculations ignore a cost—the opportunity cost of investing now rather than waiting and keeping open the possibility of not investing should the price fall. To see this, calculate the net present value of this investment opportunity, assuming a wait of one year, after which the investment is made only if the price goes up:

$$NPV = (0.5)[-800/1.1 + \sum_{t=1}^{\infty} 150/(1.1)^t] = 425/1.1 = \underline{\$386.}$$

(Note that in year 0 there is no expenditure and no revenue. In year 1 the $800 are spent only if the price rises to $150. The probability that it will rise to that level is 0.5.) The net present value today is higher in the case of waiting a year, so that it is clearly better to wait than to invest now.

Note that if the only choices were to invest today or never, the choice would be to invest today. In that case the standard net present value rule would apply, given that there is no opportunity cost to killing the option of waiting since it is not an option. It would also be beneficial to invest today if a disinvestment were possible the next year that permitted recovery of the $800 should the price fall. In short, two things are needed to introduce an opportunity cost into the calculation of net present value—irreversibility and the ability to invest in the future as an alternative to investing today. There are situations in which a firm cannot wait at all or for very long. (One example is the anticipated entry of a competitor into a market that is large enough for only one firm. Another example is a patent or lease of mineral resources that is about to expire.) The less time there is to delay and the greater the cost of delaying, the less irreversibility will affect the investment decision. (This point is explored again in the third section in the context of a more general model.)

What is the value of the flexibility to make the investment decision next year, rather than having to invest either now or never? (This flexibility has some value, in that the best decision is to wait rather than invest now.) The value of this "flexibility option" is easy to calculate—it is the difference between the two net present values, or $386 - $300 = $86.

Finally, suppose there is a futures market for widgets, with the futures price for delivery one year from now equal to the expected future spot price, that is, $100.[3] Would the ability to hedge on the futures market change the investment decision? Specifically, would it be better to invest now rather than after a year? The answer is no. Note that if the investment were to be made now, the investor would hedge by selling short futures for five widgets; this sale would exactly offset any fluctuations in the net present value of the project next year. However, after the sale the net present value of the project today is $300, exactly what it is without hedging. Hence there is no gain from hedging, and it is still better to wait until next year to make the investment decision.

## Analogy to financial options

The above investment opportunity is analogous to a call option on a common stock. It gives the holder the right (which need not be exercised) to make an investment expenditure (the exercise price of the option) and receive an asset (a share of stock) whose value fluctuates stochastically. In the case of the above simple example, if next year the price rises to $150, the option can be exercised by paying $800, which obtains an asset that will be worth $V_1 = \$1,650 (= \sum_0^\infty 150/(1.1)^t)$, where $V_1$ is the value of the investment opportunity in the next year. If the price falls to $50, the asset would be worth only $550, and it would not pay to exercise the option.

It was calculated above that the value of the investment opportunity (assuming that the decision to invest can be made next year) is $386. It is helpful to recalculate this value using standard option pricing methods, because later such methods are used to analyze other investment problems. Let $F_0$ denote the value today of the investment opportunity, that is, what an investor should be willing to pay today to have the option to invest in the widget factory, and let $F_1$ denote its value next year. Note that $F_1$ is a random variable; it depends on what happens to the price of widgets. If the price rises to $150, then $F_1$ will equal $\sum_0^\infty 150/(1.1)^t - 800 = \$850$. If the price falls to $50, the option to invest will go unexercised, so that $F_1$ will equal 0. Thus all possible values for $F_1$ are known. The problem is to find $F_0$, the value of the option today.

To solve this problem, assume a portfolio that has two components: the investment opportunity itself; and a certain number of widgets. The number of widgets is set to make the portfolio risk-free—its value next year is independent of whether the price of widgets goes up or down. Since the portfolio is risk-free, the rate of return on the portfolio must be the risk-free rate. By setting the portfolio's return equal to that rate, it is possible to calculate the current value of the investment opportunity.

Specifically, consider a portfolio that includes the investment opportunity and a short position of n widgets. (If widgets were a traded commodity, such as oil, a short position could be obtained by borrowing from another producer or by going short in the futures market. For the moment, however, actual implementation of this portfolio is not a concern.) The value of this portfolio today is $\Phi_0 = F_0 - nP_0 = F_0 - 100n$. The value next year, $\Phi_1 = F_1 - nP_1$, depends on $P_1$. If $P_1 = \$150$ so that $F_1 = \$850$, $\Phi_1 = \$850 - \$150n$. If $P_1 = \$50$ so that $F_1 = 0$, $\Phi_1 = -\$50n$. Now, set n at a level that leaves the portfolio risk-free, that is, so that $\Phi_1$ is independent of what happens to price, as follows:

$850 - $150n = -$50n, or, n = 8.5. With n chosen this way, $\Phi_1 = -$425 whether the price goes up or down.

The return from holding this portfolio is the capital gain, $\Phi_1 - \Phi_0$, minus any payments that must be made to hold the short position. Since the expected rate of capital gain on a widget is zero (the expected price next year is $100, the same as this year's price), no rational investor would hold a long position unless the expected earning were at least 10 percent. Hence selling widgets short will require a payment of $0.1P_0 = $10 per widget per year.[4] The portfolio has a short position of 8.5 widgets, so that it would have to pay out a total of $85. Thus the return from holding this portfolio over the year is

$\Phi_1 - \Phi_0 - $85 = \Phi_1 - (F_0 - nP_0) - $85 = -$425 - F_0 + $850 - $85 = $340 - F_0$.

Because this return is risk-free, it must equal the risk-free rate, assumed here to be 10 percent, times the initial value of the portfolio, $\Phi_0 = F_0 - nP_0$: $340 - F_0 = 0.1(F_0 - $850). Thus $F_0 = $386$. Note that this value is the same as that obtained before by calculating the net present value of the investment opportunity under the assumption that the investor pursued the optimal strategy of waiting a year before deciding whether to invest.

The value of the investment opportunity—the value of the option to invest in this project—is $386. The payoff from investing (exercising the option) today is $1,100 - $800 = $300. Once the investment is made, however, the option is gone. The opportunity cost of investing is therefore $386. Hence the *full cost* of the investment is $800 + $386 = $1,186 > $1,100. As a result, the investor should wait and keep the option alive rather than investing today. This conclusion is the same as that which resulted from comparing net present values. This time, however, the value of the option to invest was also calculated and was taken explicitly into account as one of the costs of investing.

The calculation of the value of the option to invest was based on the construction of a risk-free portfolio, which requires that the holder can trade (hold a long or short position in) widgets. The portfolio could just as well have been constructed using another asset or combination of assets, whose price is perfectly correlated with the price of widgets.

What would happen if widgets could not be traded and there were no other assets that "spanned" the risk in a widget's price? The value of the option to invest could still be calculated as was done at the outset—by computing the net present value for each investment strategy (invest today versus wait a year and invest if the price goes up) and picking the strategy that yields the highest net present value. That is essentially the dynamic programming approach. In this case it gives exactly the same answer because all price risk can be diversified. (The third section explores this connection between option pricing and dynamic programming in more detail.)

*Changing the parameters*

So far the direct cost of the investment, $I$, has been fixed at $800. Changing this number and other parameters, and calculating the effects on the value of the investment opportunity and on the investment decision, yields further insight. For example, by going through the same steps as above, it is easy to see that the short position needed to obtain a risk-free portfolio depends on $I$ as follows: $n = 16.5 - 0.01I$. The current value of the option to invest is then given by $F_0 = 750 - 0.455I$.

The reader can check that as long as $I > \$642$, $F_0$ exceeds the net benefit from investing today (rather than waiting), which is $V_0 - I = \$1,100 - I$. Hence if $I > \$642$, the investor should wait rather than invest today. However, if $I = \$642$, $F_0 = \$458 = V_0 - I$, so that the investor would be indifferent between investing today and waiting until next year. (This outcome can also be seen by comparing the net present value of investing today with that of waiting until next year.) If $I < \$642$, it is better to invest today than to wait. The reason is that in this case the lost revenue from waiting exceeds the opportunity cost of closing off the option of waiting and not investing should the price fall. This point is illustrated in figure 3.2, which shows the value of the option, $F_0$, and the net payoff, $V_0 - I$, both as functions of $I$. When $I > \$642$, $F_0 = \$750 - 0.455I > V_0 - I$, so that the option should be kept alive. If, however, $I < \$642$, $\$750 - 0.455I < V_0 - I$, then the option should be exercised, and its value is just the net payoff, $V_0 - I$.

The way in which the value of the investment option depends on $q$—the probability that the price of widgets will rise next year—can also be calculated. Once again set $I = \$800$. The short position needed to obtain a risk-free portfolio is independent of $q$, or $n = 8.5$. The payment required for

**Figure 3.2  Option to invest in widget factory**

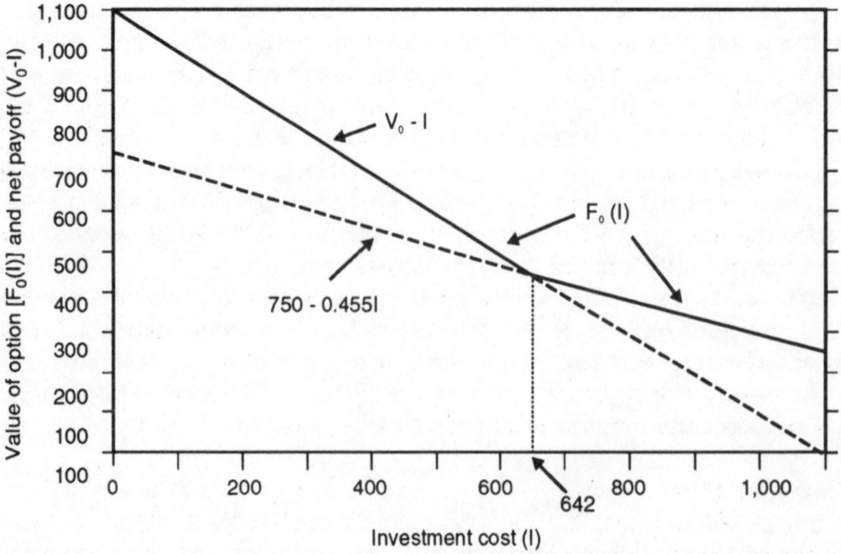

the short position does, however, depend on $q$, because the expected capital gain on a widget depends on $q$. The expected rate of capital gain is $[E(P_1) - P_0]/P_0 = q - 0.5$, so that the required payment per widget in the short position is $0.1 - (q - 0.5) = 0.6 - q$. By following the same steps as above, it is easy to see that the value today of the option to invest is $F_0 = 773q$. This value can also be written as a function of the current value of the project, $V_0$. With $V_0 = 100 + \sum_1^\infty (100q + 50)/(1.1)^t = 600 + 1{,}000q$, then $F_0 = 0.773V_0 - 464$. Finally, note that it is better to wait rather than invest today as long as $F_0 > V_0 - I$, or $q < 0.88$.

There is nothing special about the particular source of uncertainty in this problem. There will be a value to waiting (that is, an opportunity cost to investing today rather than waiting for information to arrive) whenever the investment is irreversible and the net payoff from the investment evolves stochastically over time. The example could have been constructed so that the uncertainty arises over future exchange rates, factor input costs, or government policy. For example, the payoff from investing, $V$, might rise or fall in the future depending on (unpredictable) changes in policy. Alternatively, the cost of the investment, $I$, might rise or fall in response to changes in the costs of materials or in policy variables, such as the granting or taking away of an investment subsidy or tax benefit.

In the example presented here, the unrealistic assumption was made that there is no longer any uncertainty after the second period. It is also possible to allow the price to change unpredictably *each period*. For example, posit that at $t = 2$ the price, which is now at $150, could increase to $225 with probability $q$ or fall to $75 with probability $(1 - q)$. If the price were $50, it could rise to $75 or fall to $25. Price could rise or fall in a similar way at $t = 3, 4$, and so on. The value of the option to invest and the optimal rule for exercising that option can be worked out. Although the algebra is messier, the method is essentially the same as for the simple two-period exercise carried out above. (The binomial option pricing model is based on this. See Cox, Ross, and Rubinstein 1979 and Cox and Rubinstein 1985 for detailed discussions.) In the next section the widget example is extended by allowing the payoff from the investment to fluctuate *continuously* over time.

The next two sections make use of continuous-time stochastic processes, as well as Ito's Lemma (which is essentially a rule for differentiating and integrating functions of such processes). These tools, which are becoming more and more widely used in economics and finance, provide a convenient way of analyzing problems involving the timing of investment and the valuation of options.[5]

## A more general problem of investment timing

McDonald and Siegel (1986) present one of the more basic models of irreversible investment. They considered the following problem: at what point is it optimal to pay a sunk cost $I$ in return for a project whose value is $V$, given that $V$ evolves according to a geometric Brownian motion:

(3-1)                                     $dV = \alpha V dt + \sigma V dz$

where $dz$ is the increment of a Wiener process, that is, $dz = \varepsilon(t)(dt)^{1/2}$, with $\varepsilon(t)$ a serially uncorrelated and normally distributed random variable. Equation (3-1) implies that the current value of the project is known but that future values are lognormally distributed with a variance that grows linearly with the time horizon. (See the appendix for an explanation of the Wiener process.) Thus, although information arrives over time (the firm observes V changing), the future value of the project is always uncertain.

McDonald and Siegel (1986) point out that the investment opportunity is equivalent to a perpetual call option and that deciding when to invest is equivalent to deciding when to exercise such an option. Thus, the investment decision can be viewed as a problem of option valuation (as illustrated by the simple example presented in the previous section). The solution to their problem is derived here again in two ways, first, using the methods of option pricing (contingent claims) and, second, using dynamic programming. These two approaches and the assumptions that each requires are then compared and the characteristics of the solution examined.

*The use of option pricing*

As noted, a firm's option to invest—to pay a sunk cost *I* and receive a project worth *V*—is analogous to a call option on a stock. Unlike most financial call options, however, it is *perpetual*—it has no expiration date. This option can be valued and the optimal exercise (investment) rule determined with the same methods used to value financial options. (For an overview of option pricing methods and their application, see Cox and Rubinstein 1985, Hull 1989, and Mason and Merton 1985.)

This approach requires one important assumption—that existing assets span stochastic changes in *V*. Specifically, it must be possible to find an asset or construct a dynamic portfolio of assets (a portfolio whose holdings are adjusted continuously as the prices of assets change), the price of which is perfectly correlated with *V*. In other words, the markets are sufficiently complete that the firm's decisions do not affect the set of opportunities available to investors. The assumption of spanning should hold for most commodities that are typically traded on both the spot and futures markets and for manufactured goods to the extent that prices are correlated with the values of shares or portfolios. There may, however, be cases in which this assumption will not hold; an example might be a new product unrelated to existing ones.

With the spanning assumption, the investment rule that maximizes the firm's market value can be determined without making any assumptions about risk preferences or discount rates, and with the investment problem involving only the valuation of contingent claims. (As will be seen shortly, it is possible to use dynamic programming to maximize the present value of the firm's expected flow of profits, subject to an arbitrary discount rate, even if spanning does not hold.)

Let $x$ be the price of an asset or dynamic portfolio of assets perfectly correlated with $V$, and denote by $\rho_{Vm}$ the correlation of $V$ with the market portfolio. Then $x$ evolves according to $dx = \mu x dt + \sigma x dz$. Further, according to the capital asset pricing model (CAPM), the expected return on $V$ is $\mu = r + \phi \rho_{Vm} \sigma$, where $r$ is the risk-free rate and $\phi$ is the market price of risk. Assume that $\alpha$, the expected percentage rate of change of $V$, is *less* than its risk-adjusted return, $\mu$. (As will become clear, the firm would never invest if this condition were not present. No matter what the current level of $V$, the firm would always be better off simply holding on to the option to invest.) The difference between $\mu$ and $\alpha$ is denoted by $\delta$, that is, $\delta = \mu - \alpha$.

A few words about the meaning of $\delta$ are in order, given the important role it plays in this model. The analogy with a financial call option is helpful here. If $V$ were the price of a share of common stock, $\delta$ would be the dividend rate on the stock. The total expected return on the stock would be $\mu = \delta + \alpha$, or the dividend rate plus the expected rate of capital gain.

If the dividend rate $\delta$ were zero, a call option on the stock would never be exercised prematurely but would always be held to maturity. The reason is that the entire return on the stock is captured in its price movements, and hence by the call option, so that there is no cost to keeping the option alive. If, however, the dividend rate is positive, keeping the option alive rather than exercising it carries an opportunity cost. That cost is the dividend stream that is foregone by holding the option rather than the stock. Since $\delta$ is a proportional dividend rate, the higher the price of the stock is, the greater the flow of dividends is. At some high enough price, the opportunity cost of foregone dividends becomes high enough to make it worthwhile to exercise the option.

For the present investment problem, $\mu$ is the expected rate of return from owning the completed project. It is the equilibrium rate established by the capital market, and it includes an appropriate risk premium. If $\delta > 0$, the expected rate of capital gain on the project is less than $\mu$. *Hence $\delta$ is an opportunity cost of delaying construction of the project, and instead keeping the option to invest alive.* If $\delta$ were zero, there would be no opportunity cost to keeping the option alive, and the investment would never be worthwhile, no matter how high the net present value of the project. For that reason $\delta$ is assumed to be greater than 0. On the other hand, if $\delta$ is very large, the value of the option will be very small because the opportunity cost of waiting is large. As $\delta$ approaches infinity, the value of the option goes to zero. In effect, the only choices are to invest now or never, and the standard net present value rule will again apply.

The parameter $\delta$ can be interpreted in different ways. For example, it could reflect competitors' entry and expansion of capacity. It could simply reflect the cash flows from the project. If the project is infinitely lived, then equation (3-1) can represent the evolution of $V$ during the operation of the project, and $\delta V$ is the rate of cash flow the project yields. Since $\delta$ is assumed to be constant, this interpretation is consistent with the point that future cash flows are a constant proportion of the project's market value.[6]

Equation (3-1) is an abstraction from most real projects. For example, if the variable cost is positive and a project can be shut down temporarily when price falls below the variable cost, $V$ will not follow a lognormal process, even if the price of the output does. Nonetheless, equation (3-1) is a useful simplification that will help clarify the main effects of irreversibility and uncertainty. More complicated—and hopefully more realistic—models are discussed later.

*Solving the investment problem*

As to the valuation of the investment opportunity and the optimal investment rule, let $F = F(V)$ be the value of the firm's option to invest. To find $F(V)$ and the optimal investment rule, consider the return on the following portfolio: hold the option, which is worth $F(V)$, and go short $dF/dV$ (denoted $F_v$ for brevity) units of the project (or, equivalently, of the asset or portfolio $x$). Using subscripts to denote derivatives, the value of this portfolio is $P = F - F_v V$. Note that this portfolio is dynamic; as $V$ changes, $F_v$ may change, in which case the composition of the portfolio will be changed.

The short position in this portfolio will require a payment of $\delta V F_v$ dollars per time period; otherwise no rational investor will enter into the long side of the transaction. (To see this assertion, note that an investor holding a long position in the project will demand the risk-adjusted return $\mu V$, which includes the capital gain *plus* the dividend stream $\delta V$. Since the short position includes $F_v$ units of the project, it will require paying $\delta V F_v$.) With this point taken into account, the total return from holding the portfolio over a short time interval $dt$ is $dF - F_v dV - \delta V F_v dt$. It will be seen shortly that this return is risk-free. Hence, to avoid arbitrage possibilities the return must equal $r(F - F_v V)dt$:

(3-2)              $$dF - F_v dV - \delta V F_v dt = r(F - F_v V)dt.$$

To obtain an expression for $dF$, use Ito's Lemma:

(3-3)              $$dF = F_v dV + (1/2)F_{vv}(dV)^2.$$

(Ito's Lemma is explained in the appendix. Note that higher order terms vanish.) Now substitute equation (3-1) for $dV$, with $\alpha$ replaced by $\mu-\delta$ and $(dV)^2 = \sigma^2 V^2 dt$ into equation (3-3):

(3-4)              $$dF = (\mu - \delta)V F_v dt + \sigma V F_v dz + (1/2)\sigma^2 V^2 F_{vv} dt.$$

Finally, substitute equation (3-4) into equation (3-2), rearrange the terms, and note that all the terms in $dz$ cancel out, so that the portfolio is indeed risk-free:

(3-5)              $$(1/2)\sigma^2 V^2 F_{vv} + (r - \delta)V F_v - rF = 0.$$

Equation (3-5) is a differential equation that $F(V)$ must satisfy. In addition, $F(V)$ must satisfy the following boundary conditions:

(3-6) $$F(0) = 0$$

(3-7) $$F(V^*) = V^* - I$$

(3-8) $$F_V(V^*) = 1.$$

Condition (3-6) says that if $V$ goes to zero, it will stay at zero (an implication of equation [3-1]), so that the option to invest will be of no value. $V^*$ is the price at which it is optimal to invest, and condition (3-7) just says that upon investing the firm receives a net payoff of $V^* - I$. Condition (3-8) is called the "smooth pasting" condition. If $F(V)$ were not continuous and smooth at the critical exercise point $V^*$, an investor could do better by exercising at a different point.[7]

To find $F(V)$, solve equation (3-5) subject to the boundary conditions (3-6)-(3-8). In this case it is possible to guess a functional form and to determine by substitution if it works. It is easy to see that the solution to equation (3-5), one that also satisfies condition (3-6), is:

(3-9) $$F(V) = aV^\beta$$

where $a$ is a constant and $\beta$ is given by:[8]

(3-10) $$\beta = 1/2 - (r - \delta)/\sigma^2 + \{[(r - \delta)/\sigma^2 - 1/2]^2 + 2r/\sigma^2\}^{1/2}.$$

The remaining boundary conditions, (3-7) and (3-8), can be used to solve for the two remaining unknowns: the constant $a$; and the critical value $V^*$ at which it is optimal to invest. By substituting equation (3-9) into conditions (3-7) and (3-8), it is easy to see that:

(3-11) $$V^* = \beta I/(\beta - 1)$$

and

(3-12) $$a = (V^* - I)/(V^*)^\beta.$$

Equations (3-9)-(3-12) give the value of the investment opportunity and the optimal investment rule, that is, the critical value $V^*$ at which it is optimal (in the sense of maximizing the firm's market value) to invest.

The characteristics of this solution will be examined below. The point here is that this solution was obtained by showing that a hedged (risk-free) portfolio could be constructed consisting of the option to invest and a short position in the project. However, $F(V)$ must be the solution to equation (3-5) even if the option to invest (or the project) does not exist and could not be included in the hedge portfolio. All that is required is spanning—it must be possible to find or construct an asset or dynamic portfolio of assets, $x$, that replicates the stochastic dynamics of $V$. As Merton (1977) has shown, the value function can be replicated with a portfolio consisting only of the asset $x$ and risk-free bonds. Since the value of this portfolio will have the same dynamics as $F(V)$, the solution to equation (3-5), $F(V)$ must be the value function to avoid dominance.

*Dynamic programming*

As discussed, spanning will not always hold. In that case, the investment problem can still be solved using dynamic programming. To solve the problem with this method, a rule is needed that maximizes the value of the investment opportunity, $F(V)$:

$$(3\text{-}13) \qquad F(V) = \max E_t[(V_T - I)e^{\mu T}]$$

where $E_t$ denotes the expectation at time $t$, $T$ is the (unknown) future time at which the investment is made, $\mu$ is the discount rate, and the maximization is subject to equation (3-1) for $V$. Assume, again, that $\mu > \alpha$, and denote $\delta = \mu - \alpha$.

Since the investment opportunity, $F(V)$, yields no cash flows up to time $T$ when the investment is made, the only return from holding it is its capital appreciation. As shown in the appendix, the Bellman equation for this problem is therefore:

$$(3\text{-}14) \qquad \mu F = (1/dt)E_t dF.$$

Equation (3-14) says that the total instantaneous return on the investment opportunity, $\mu F$, is equal to its expected rate of capital appreciation.

Ito's Lemma was used to obtain equation (3-3) for $dF$. Now substitute equation (3-1) for $dV$ and $(dV)^2$ into equation (3-3) to obtain the following expression for $dF$:

$$(3\text{-}15) \qquad dF = \alpha VF_V dt + \sigma VF_V dz + (1/2)\sigma^2 V^2 F_{VV} dt.$$

Since $E_t(dz) = 0$, then $(1/dt)E_t dF = \alpha VF_V + (1/2)\sigma^2 V^2 F_{VV}$. As such, equation (3-14) can be rewritten as:

$$(3\text{-}16) \qquad (1/2)\sigma^2 V^2 F_{VV} + \alpha VF_V - \mu F = 0$$

or, substituting $\alpha = \mu - \delta$,

$$(3\text{-}17) \qquad (1/2)\sigma^2 V^2 F_{VV} + (\mu - \delta)VF_V - \mu F = 0.$$

Observe that this equation is almost identical to equation (3-5); the only difference is that the discount rate $\mu$ replaces the risk-free rate, $r$. The boundary conditions (3-6)-(3-8) also apply here for the same reasons as before. (Note that condition [3-8] follows from the fact that $V^*$ is chosen to maximize the net payoff $V^* - I$.) Hence the contingent claims solution to the investment problem is equivalent to a dynamic programming solution, under the assumption of risk neutrality.[9]

Again, if spanning does not hold, the investment problem can still be solved subject to some discount rate. The solution will clearly be of the same form, and the effects of changes in $\sigma$ or $\delta$ will likewise be the same.

One point is worth noting, however. Without spanning, there is no theory for determining the "correct" value of the discount rate $\mu$ (unless restrictive assumptions are made about investors' or managers' utility functions). The CAPM, for example, would not hold and could not be used to calculate a risk-adjusted discount rate.

## Characteristics of the solution

Under the assumption that spanning holds, examine the optimal investment rule given by equations (3-9)-(3-12). A few numerical solutions will help illustrate the results and show how they depend on the values of the various parameters. As will be seen, these results are qualitatively the same as those that follow from standard option pricing models. Unless otherwise noted, in what follows $r = 0.04$, $\delta = 0.04$, and the cost of the investment, $I$, equals 1.

Figure 3-3 shows the value of the investment opportunity, $F(V)$, for $\sigma = 0.2$ and 0.3. (These values are conservative for many projects; in volatile markets, the standard deviation of the annual changes in a project's value can easily exceed 20 percent or 30 percent.) The tangency point of $F(V)$ with the line $V-I$ gives the critical value of $V$, $V^*$; the firm should invest only if $V \geq V^*$. For any positive $\sigma$, $V^* > I$. Thus the standard net present value rule, "invest when the value of a project is at least as great as its cost," must be modified to include the opportunity cost of investing now rather than waiting. That opportunity cost is exactly $F(V)$. When $V < V^*$, $V < I + F(V)$, that is, the value of the project is less than its *full* cost, the direct cost $I$ plus the opportunity cost of "killing" the investment option.

Note that $F(V)$ increases when $\sigma$ increases, as does the critical value $V^*$. Thus uncertainty increases the value of a firm's investment opportunities but decreases the amount of actual investing by a firm. As a result, when a firm's market or economic environment becomes more uncertain, the market value of the firm can go up, even though the firm does less investing and perhaps produces less.

This pattern should make it easier to understand the behavior of oil companies during the mid-1980s. During this period oil prices fell, but the perceived uncertainty over future oil prices rose. In response, oil companies paid more than ever for offshore leases and other oil-bearing lands, even though their development expenditures fell and they produced less.

Finally, note that the results regarding the effects of uncertainty involve no assumptions about risk preferences or the extent to which the riskiness

**Figure 3.3 Value of investment opportunity [F(V)]**
               (for σ = 0.2 and 0.3)

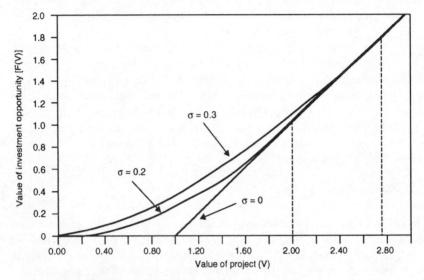

*Note:* σ = Standard deviaiton of V; δ = 0.04; r = 0.04; and I = 1.
*Source:* Author's calculations.

of *V* is correlated with the market. Firms can be risk-neutral, and stochastic changes in *V* can be completely diversifiable; an increase in σ will still increase *V** and hence tend to depress investment.

   Figures 3-4 and 3-5 show how *F(V)* and *V** depend on δ. Observe that an increase in δ from 0.04 to 0.08 results in a *decrease* in *F(V)* and therefore a decrease in the critical value *V**. (In the limit as δ → ∞, *F(V)* → 0 for *V < I* and *V** → *I*, as figure 3-5 shows.) The reason is that as δ becomes larger, the expected rate of growth of *V* falls, and the expected appreciation in the value of the option to invest and acquire *V* falls. In effect, it becomes costlier to wait rather than invest now. To see this conclusion, consider an investment in an apartment building, where δ*V* is the net flow of rental income. The total return on the building, which must equal the risk-adjusted market rate, has two components—this income flow plus the expected rate of capital gain. Hence the greater the income flow is relative to the total return on the building, the more an investor foregoes by holding an option to invest in the building rather than owning the building itself.

   If the risk-free rate, *r*, is increased, *F(V)* rises, as does *V**. The reason is that the present value of an investment expenditure *I* made at a future time *T* is $Ie^{-rT}$. The present value of the project that is received in return for that expenditure is, however, $Ve^{-δT}$. Hence, with δ fixed, an increase in *r* reduces the present value of the cost of the investment but does not reduce its payoff. At the same time, note that although an increase in *r* raises the value of a firm's investment options, it also results in fewer of those options being

## Figure 3.4 Value of investment opportunity [F(V)]
(for δ = 0.04 and 0.08)

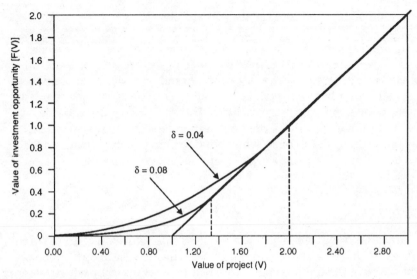

*Note:* σ = 0.2; r = 0.04; and I = 1.
*Source:* Author's calculations.

## Figure 3.5 Threshold value of project (V*) as a function of the rental rate (δ)

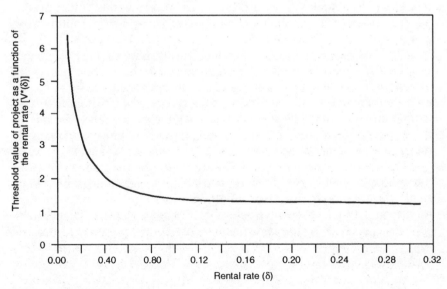

*Note:* σ = 0.2; r = 0.04; and I = 1.
*Source:* Author's calculations.

exercised.  Hence higher (real) interest rates reduce investment, but for a different reason than in the standard model.

## The value of a project and the decision to invest

As mentioned, equation (3-1) is an abstraction from most real projects.  A more realistic model would treat the price of the project's output, rather than the value of the project, as a geometric random walk (and possibly one or more factor input costs as well).  It would also allow the project to be shut down (permanently or temporarily) if prices fell below the variable cost. The model developed in the previous section can easily be extended in this way.  In so doing, it can be seen that option pricing methods can be used to find the value of the project and the optimal investment rule.

Suppose the output price, $P$, follows the stochastic process:

$$(3-18) \qquad\qquad dP = \alpha P dt + \sigma P dz.$$

Assume that $\alpha < \mu$, where $\mu$ is the expected rate return on $P$, adjusted for market risk, or an asset perfectly correlated with $P$, and let $\delta = \mu - \alpha$ as before. If the output is a storable commodity (such as oil or copper), $\delta$ will represent the *net marginal convenience yield* from storage, or the flow of benefits (less storage costs) that the marginal stored unit provides.  Assume for simplicity that $\delta$ is constant. (For most commodities, the marginal convenience yield fluctuates as the total amount of storage fluctuates.)  Also assume that: (a) the marginal and average cost of production is equal to a constant, $c$; (b) the project can be shut down with no cost if $P$ falls below $c$ and can later be restarted if $P$ rises above $c$; and (c) the project produces one unit of output per period and is infinitely lived, and the (sunk) cost of investing in the project is $I$.

There are now two problems to solve. The first is to find the value of this project, $V(P)$. To solve this problem, remember that the project itself is a set of options.[10]  Specifically, once the project has been built, the firm has, for each future time $t$, an option to produce a unit of output, that is, an option to pay $c$ and receive $P$. Hence the project is equivalent to a large number (in this case, an infinite number, because the project is assumed to last indefinitely) of operating options, and it can be valued accordingly.

The second problem is to find the value of the firm's option to invest in the project, given the project's value, and the optimal exercise (investment) rule.  The solution boils down to finding a critical $P^*$, at which the firm invests only if $P \geq P^*$. As shown below, the two steps of this problem can be solved sequentially by the same methods used in the previous section.[11]

### Valuing the project

If it is assumed that existing assets span the uncertainty over $P$, the project (as well as the option to invest) can be valued using contingent claim methods. Otherwise, a discount rate can be specified and dynamic programming can be used. Here spanning is assumed and the first approach used.

As before, construct a risk-free portfolio, one in which the project is held long and $V_P$ units of the output are held short. This portfolio has a value of $V(P) - V_P P$ and yields an instantaneous cash flow of $j(P-c)dt - \delta V_P P dt$, where $j = 1$ if $P \geq c$ so that the firm is producing, and $j = 0$ otherwise. (Recall that $\delta V_P P dt$ is the payment required to maintain the short position.) The total return on the portfolio is thus $dV - V_P dP + j(P-c)dt - \delta V_P P dt$. Since this return is risk-free, set it equal to $r(V - V_P P)dt$. Expanding $dV$ using Ito's Lemma, substituting equation (3-18) for $dP$, and rearranging yield the following differential equation for $V$:

(3-19) $$(1/2)\sigma^2 P^2 V_{PP} + (r - \delta)PV_P - rV + j(P - c) = 0.$$

This equation must be solved subject to the following boundary conditions:

(3-20) $$V(0) = 0$$

(3-21) $$V(c^-) = V(c^+)$$

(3-22) $$V_P(c^-) = V_P(c^+)$$

(3-23) $$\lim_{P \to \infty} V = P/\delta - c/r.$$

Condition (3-20) is an implication of equation (3-18): if $P$ is ever zero, it will remain zero, and the project has no value. Condition (3-23) says that as $P$ becomes very large, the probability that over any finite time period it will fall below cost and production will cease becomes very small. Hence the value of the project approaches the difference between two perpetuities: a flow of revenue, $P$, that is discounted at the risk-adjusted rate $\mu$ but is expected to grow at rate $\alpha$ and a flow of cost, $c$, which is constant and hence is discounted at rate $r$. Finally, conditions (3-19) and (3-20) say that the project's value is a continuous and smooth function of $P$.

The solution to equation (3-18) has two parts, one for $P < c$ and one for $P \geq c$. The reader can check by substitution that the following satisfies equation (3-18) as well as boundary conditions (3-21) and (3-23):

(3-24) $$V(P) = \begin{cases} A_1 P^{\beta_1} & ; P < c \\ A_2 P^{\beta_2} + P/\delta - c/r & ; P \geq c \end{cases}$$

where:[12]

$$\beta_1 = 1/2 - (r - \delta)/\sigma^2 + \{[(r - \delta)/\sigma^2 - 1/2]^2 + 2r/\sigma^2\}^{1/2}$$

and

$$\beta_2 = 1/2 - (r - \delta)/\sigma^2 - \{[(r - \delta)/\sigma^2 - 1/2]^2 + 2r/\sigma^2\}^{1/2}.$$

The constants $A_1$ and $A_2$ can be found by applying boundary conditions (3-21) and (3-22):

$$A_1 = \frac{r - \beta_2(r-\delta)\ c^{(1-\beta_1)}}{r\delta(\beta_1 - \beta_2)}$$

$$A_2 = \frac{r - \beta_1(r-\delta)\ c^{(1-\beta_2)}}{r\delta(\beta_1 - \beta_2)}.$$

The solution for $V(P)$ (equation [3-24]) can be interpreted as follows. When $P < c$, the project is not producing. Then $A_1 P^{\beta_1}$ is the value of the firm's options to produce in the future when $P$ increases. When $P \geq c$, the project is producing. If, irrespective of changes in $P$, the firm had no choice but to continue producing throughout the future, the present value of the future flow of profits would be given by $P/\delta - c/r$. However, should $P$ fall, the firm can stop producing and avoid losses. The value of its option to stop producing is $A_2 P^{\beta_2}$.

A numerical example helps illustrate this solution. Unless otherwise noted, $r = 0.04$, $\delta = 0.04$, and $c = 10$. Figure 3-6 shows $V(P)$ for $\sigma = 0, 0.2$, and $0.4$. When $\sigma = 0$, there is no possibility that $P$ will rise in the future, and the firm will not produce (and has no value) unless $P > 0$. If $P > 10$, $V(P) = (P - 10)/0.04 = 25P - 250$. However, if $\sigma > 0$, the firm always has some value as long as $P > 0$; although the firm may not be producing today, it is likely to produce in the future. Moreover, since the upside potential for future profit is unlimited while the downside is limited to zero, the greater $\sigma$ is, the greater the expected future flow of profits is and the higher $V$ is.

Figure 3-7 shows $V(P)$ for $\sigma = 0.2$ and $\delta = 0.02, 0.04$, and $0.08$. For any fixed discount rate adjusted for risk, a higher value of $\delta$ means a lower expected rate of appreciation of prices and hence a lower value for the firm.

*The investment decision*

With the value of the project known, the next step is to find the optimal investment rule. Specifically, what is the value of the firm's option to invest as a function of price $P$, and at what critical price $P^*$ should the firm exercise that option by spending an amount $I$ to purchase the project?

In the context of the same steps as above, the value of the firm's option to invest, $F(P)$, must satisfy the following differential equation:

(3-25)                              $(1/2)\sigma^2 P^2 F_{PP} + (r - \delta)PF_P - rF = 0.$

$F(P)$ must also satisfy the following boundary conditions:

**Figure 3.6 Value of project [V(P)]**
(for σ = 0, 0.02 and 0.4)

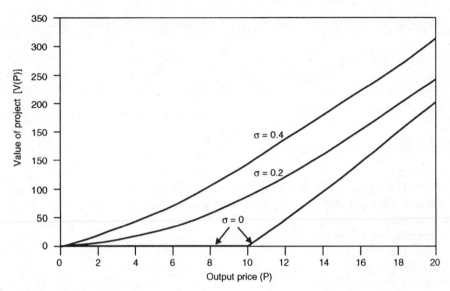

*Note:* δ = 0.04; r = 0.04; and c = 10.
*Source:* Author's calculations.

**Figure 3.7 Value of project [V(P)]**
(for δ = 0.02, 0.04 and 0.08)

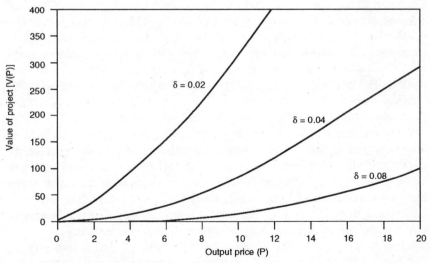

*Note:* σ = 0.2; r = 0.04; and c = 10.
*Source:* Author's calculations.

(3-26)                                         $F(0) = 0$

(3-27)                                         $F(P^*) = V(P^*) - I$

(3-28)                                         $F_P(P^*) = V_P(P^*).$

These conditions can be interpreted in the same way as conditions (3-6)-(3-8) for the model presented in the third section. The difference is that the payoff from investment $V$ is now a function of price $P$.

The solution to equation (3-25) and boundary condition (3-26) is:

(3-29)                             $F(P) = \begin{cases} aP^{\beta_1} & , P \le P^* \\ V(P) - I, & P > P^* \end{cases}$

where $\beta_1$ is given above under equation (3-24). To find the constant $a$ and the critical price $P^*$, boundary conditions (3-27) and (3-28) are used. If equation (3-29) for $F(P)$ and equation (3-24) for V(P) (for $P \ge c$) are substituted into boundary conditions (3-27) and (3-28), the constant $a$ is given by:

(3-30)                    $a = \dfrac{\beta_2 A_2}{\beta_1} (P^*)^{(\beta_2 - \beta_1)} + \dfrac{1}{\delta\beta_1} (P^*)^{(1-\beta_1)},$

and the critical price $P^*$ is the solution to

(3-31)          $\dfrac{A_2(\beta_1 - \beta_2)}{\beta_1} (P^*)^{\beta_2} + \dfrac{(\beta_1 - 1)}{\delta\beta_1} P^* - c/r - I = 0$

Equation (3-31), which is easily solved numerically, gives the optimal investment rule. (Note, first, that equation [3-31] has a unique positive solution for $P^*$ that is larger than $c$ and, second, that $V(P^*) > I$, so that the net present value of the project must exceed zero before it is optimal to invest.)

This solution is shown graphically in figure 3-8 for $\sigma = 0.2$, $\delta = 0.04$, and $I = 100$. The figure plots $F(P)$ and $V(P) - I$. From boundary condition (3-27) it can be seen that $P^*$ satisfies $F(P^*) = V(P^*) - I$, and from boundary condition (3-28) that $P^*$ is at a point of tangency of the two curves.

The comparative statics for changes in $\sigma$ or $\delta$ are of interest. As was seen, an increase in $\sigma$ results in an increase in $V(P)$ for any $P$. (The project is a set of call options on future production, and the greater the volatility of prices is, the greater the value of these options is.) Although an increase in $\sigma$ raises the value of the project, it also raises the critical price at which it is optimal to invest, that is, $\partial P^*/\partial\sigma > 0$. The reason is that for any $P$, the opportunity cost of investing, $F(P)$, increases even more than $V(P)$. Hence, as with the simpler model presented in the previous section, greater uncertainty reduces investment. This conclusion is illustrated in figure 3-9, which shows $F(P)$ and $V(P) - I$ for $\sigma = 0, 0.2$, and $0.4$. When $\sigma = 0$, the critical price is 14, which just makes the value of the project equal to its cost of 100. As $\sigma$ rises,

**Figure 3.8  Net payoff from project [V(P)-I] and value of investment opportunity [F(P)]**
(for σ = 0.2 and δ = 0.04)

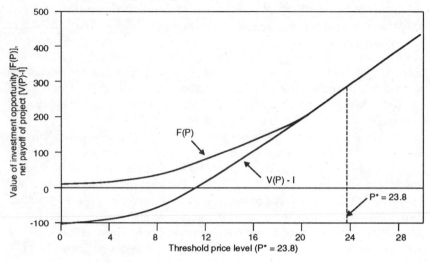

*Note:* r = 0.4, c = 10, and I = 1.
*Source:* Author's calculations.

**Figure 3.9  Net payoff from project [V(P)-I] and value of investment opportunity [F(P)]**
(for σ = 0.0, 0.2, and 0.4)

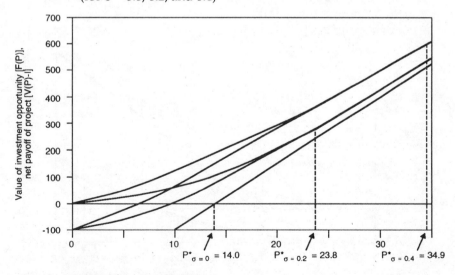

*Note:* δ = 0.04; r = 0.04; c = 10, and I = 100.
*Source:* Author's calculations.

both $V(P)$ and $F(P)$ increase; $P^*$ is 23.8 for $\sigma = 0.2$ and 34.9 for $\sigma = 0.4$.

An increase in $\delta$ also boosts the critical price $P^*$ at which the firm should invest. There are two opposing effects. If $\delta$ is larger, so that the expected rate of increase of $P$ is smaller, options on future production have a lower value, so that $V(P)$ is smaller. At the same time, the opportunity cost of waiting to invest rises (the expected rate of growth of $F[P]$ is smaller), so that there is more incentive to exercise the investment option than to keep it alive. The first effect dominates, however, so that a higher $\delta$ results in a higher $P^*$. This point is illustrated in figure 3-10, which shows $F(P)$ and $V(P) - I$ for $\delta = 0.04$ and 0.08. Note that when $\delta$ goes up, $V(P)$ and hence $F(P)$ fall sharply, and the tangency at $P^*$ moves to the right.

This result might at first seem to contradict what the simpler model in the third section says. Recall that in that model an increase in $\delta$ reduces the critical value of the *project*, $V^*$, at which the firm should invest. Although in this model $P^*$ is higher when $\delta$ is larger, the corresponding value of the project, $V(P^*)$, is lower. This outcome can be seen from figure 3-11, which shows $P^*$ as a function of $\sigma$ for $\delta = 0.04$ and 0.08, and in figure 3-12, which shows $V(P^*)$. If $\sigma$ is, say, 0.2 and $\delta$ is increased from 0.04 to 0.08, $P^*$ will rise from 23.8 to 29.2. Even at the higher $P^*$, however, $V$ is lower. Thus $V^* = V(P^*)$ is declining with $\delta$, just as in the simpler model.

This model shows how uncertainty over future prices affects both the value of a project and the decision to invest. As discussed in the next section, the model can easily be expanded to allow for the fixed costs of temporarily stopping and restarting production, if such costs are important. Expanded in this way, models such as this one can have practical application, espe-

**Figure 3.10  Net payoff from project [V(P)-I] and value of investment opportunity [F(P)]**
(for $\sigma = 0.04$ and 0.08)

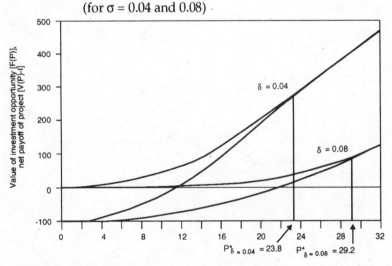

*Note:*  $\sigma = 0.2$, $r = 0.04$, $c = 10$, and $I = 100$.
*Source:* Author's calculations.

**Figure 3.11  Threshold price level (P\*) vs. standard deviation of value of project (σ)**
(for δ = 0.04 and 0.08)

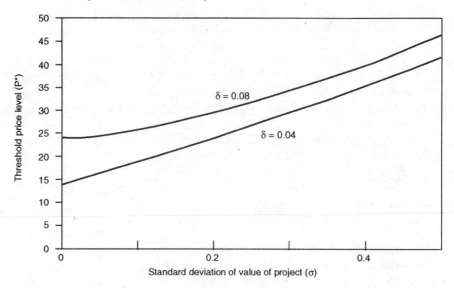

*Source:* Author's calculations.

**Figure 3.12  Threshold value of project [V(P\*)] vs. standard deviation of value of project (σ)**
(for δ = 0.04 and 0.08)

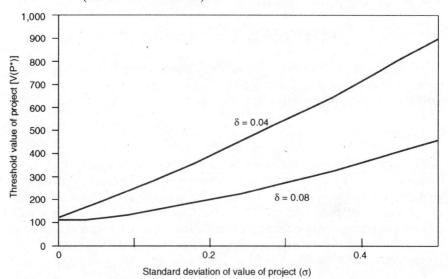

*Source:* Author's calculations.

cially if the project is one that produces a traded commodity, for example, copper or oil. In that case, σ and δ can be determined directly from data on the futures and spot markets.

## Alternative stochastic processes

The geometric random walk of equation (3-18) is convenient in that it permits an analytical solution. However, the price, $P$, might be better represented by a different stochastic process. For example, it could be argued that over the long run the price of a commodity will follow a mean-reverting process (with the mean reflecting the long-run marginal cost and perhaps varying over time). The model can be adapted to allow for this process or for alternative stochastic processes for $P$. In most cases, however, numerical methods will be necessary to obtain a solution.

As an example, suppose $P$ follows the mean-reverting process

$$(3\text{-}32) \qquad\qquad dP/P = \lambda\,(\overline{P}-P)dt + \sigma dz.$$

Here $P$ tends to revert back to a "normal" level, $\overline{P}$ (which might be the long-run marginal cost in the case of a commodity such as copper or coffee). With the same arguments as were applied earlier, it is easy to show that $V(P)$ must then satisfy the following differential equation:

$$(3\text{-}33) \qquad (1/2)\sigma^2 P^2 V_{PP} + [(r-\mu-\lambda)P + \lambda\overline{P}]PV_P - rV + j(P-c) = 0,$$

together with boundary conditions (3-20)-(3-22). The value of the investment option, $F(P)$, must satisfy:

$$(3\text{-}34) \qquad (1/2)\sigma^2 P^2 F_{PP} + [(r-\mu-\lambda)P + \lambda\,\overline{P}]PF_P - rF = 0$$

with boundary conditions (3-26)-(3-28). Equations (3-33) and (3-34) are ordinary differential equations, so that solution by numerical methods is relatively straightforward.

## Extensions

The models presented in the previous two sections, although fairly simple, illustrate how a project and an investment opportunity can be viewed as a set of options and valued accordingly. These insights have been extended to a variety of problems involving decisions related to investment and production under uncertainty. This section reviews some of the extensions.

## Sunk costs and hysteresis

The third and fourth sections examined models in which the investment expenditure is a sunk cost. Because the future value of the project is uncertain, there is an opportunity cost to investing that drives a wedge between the current value of the project and the direct cost of the investment.

In general, there may be a variety of sunk costs. For example, there may be a sunk cost of exiting an industry or abandoning a project. This cost could include such items as severance pay for workers and land reclamation in the case of a mine.[13] Because the value of the project might rise in the future, the sunk cost in turn creates an opportunity cost of shutting down. Sunk costs may also be associated with the operation of the project. In the fourth section it was assumed that the firm could stop and restart production with no cost. For most projects are, however, the sunk costs involved even in shutting down temporarily and restarting are likely to be substantial.

Brennan and Schwartz (1985) and Dixit (1989a) have studied the valuation of projects and the decision to invest when there are sunk costs of this sort. Brennan and Schwartz (1985) analyze the effects of sunk costs on the decision to open and close a mine (temporarily or permanently) when the price of the resource follows equation (3-17). Their model accounts for the fact that a mine is subject to cave-ins and flooding when not in use and that a temporary shutdown requires expenditures to avoid these possibilities. Likewise, re-opening a temporarily closed mine requires a substantial expenditure. Finally, a mine can be closed permanently. This decision will involve costs for land reclamation (but avoids the cost of a temporary shutdown).

Brennan and Schwartz obtain an analytical solution for the case of an infinite stock of resources. (Solutions can also be obtained for a finite stock of resources, but they require numerical methods.) Their solution gives the value of the mine as a function of the price of the resources and the current state of the mine (open or closed). It also gives the decision rule for changing the state of the mine (opening a closed mine or temporarily or permanently closing an open mine). Finally, given the value of the mine, Brennan and Schwartz show how (in principle) an option to invest in the mine can be valued and the optimal investment rule determined, using a contingent claim approach such as that in the fourth section.[14]

By working through a realistic example of a copper mine, Brennan and Schwartz show how the methods discussed in this paper can be applied in practice. Their work also shows, however, how the sunk costs of opening and closing a mine can explain the hysteresis (that is, effects that persist after the causes that brought them about have disappeared) often observed in extractive resource industries: during periods of low prices managers often continue to operate unprofitable mines that had been opened when prices were high; at other times managers fail to re-open seemingly profitable ones that had been closed when prices were low.

Dixit (1989a) develops this insight further. He studies a model with sunk costs $k$ and $l$, respectively, for entry and exit. The project produces one unit of output per period, with a variable cost of $w$. The output price, $P$, follows equation (3-18). If $\sigma = 0$, the standard result holds—enter (that is, spend $k$) if $P \geq w + \rho k$, and exit if $P \leq w - \rho l$, where $\rho$ is the firm's discount rate.[15]

However, if $\sigma > 0$, there are opportunity costs to entering or exiting. These costs raise the critical price above which it is optimal to enter and lower the critical price below which it is optimal to exit. (Furthermore, numerical simulations show that $\sigma$ need not be large to induce a significant effect.)

These models help explain the prevalence of hysteresis. In Dixit's model, firms that entered an industry when the price was high may remain there for an extended period even though the price has fallen below the variable cost, so that they are losing money. (The price may rise in the future, and to exit and later re-enter involves sunk costs.) In addition, firms that leave an industry after a protracted period of low prices may hesitate to re-enter, even after prices have risen enough to make entry seem profitable. Similarly, the Brennan and Schwartz model shows why many copper mines built during the 1970s, when copper prices were high, were kept open during the mid-1980s when copper prices had fallen to their lowest levels (in real terms) since the Great Depression.

The fact that the movement of exchange rates during the 1980s left the United States with a persistent trade deficit can also be seen as a result of hysteresis. Dixit (1989b), for example, models entry by Japanese firms into the U.S. market when the exchange rate follows a geometric Brownian motion. Again, there are sunk costs of entry and exit. The Japanese firms are ordered according to their variable costs, and all firms are price-takers. As with the models discussed above, the sunk costs combined with the uncertainty over the exchange rates create opportunity costs of entering or exiting the U.S. market. As a result, there is an exchange rate band within which Japanese firms neither enter nor exit, and the U.S. market price will not vary as long as the fluctuations in the exchange rates are within this band. Baldwin (1988) and Baldwin and Krugman (1989) develop related models that yield similar results. These models help explain the low rate at which changes in exchange rates are passed through, a phenomenon observed during the 1980s, and the persistence of the U.S. trade deficit even after the dollar depreciated. (Baldwin 1988 also provides empirical evidence that the overvaluation of the dollar during the early 1980s was indeed a shock that induced hysteresis.)

Sunk costs of entry and exit can also have hysteretic effects on the exchange rate itself and on prices. Baldwin and Krugman (1989), for example, show how the entry and exit decisions described above feed back to the exchange rate. In their model, a policy change (for example, a reduction in the supply of money) that causes the currency to appreciate sharply can lead to entry by foreign firms, which in turn will lead to an equilibrium exchange rate that is *below* the original one. (Krugman 1989 also discusses these ideas.) Similar effects occur with prices. In the case of copper, the reluctance of firms to close mines during the mid-1980s, when demand was weak, allowed the price to fall even more than it would have otherwise.

Finally, sunk costs may be important in explaining the dependence of consumer spending, particularly for durable goods, on income and wealth.

Most purchases of consumer durables are at least partly irreversible. Lam (1989) develops a model that accounts for this phenomenon and shows how irreversibility results in a sluggish adjustment of the stock of durables to changes in income. Grossman and Laroque (1990) study choices in consumption and portfolios when a durable good generates the consumption services and a transaction cost has to be paid when the good is sold. Unlike in standard models (for example, Merton 1971), optimal consumption is not a smooth function of wealth; a large change in wealth has to occur before consumers will change their holdings of durables and hence their consumption. As a result, the consumption-based CAPM fails to hold (although the market portfolio-based CAPM does hold).

*Sequential investment*

Many investments occur in stages that must be carried out sequentially, and sometimes the payoffs from or costs of completing each stage are uncertain. For example, investment in a new line of aircraft begins with engineering and continues with the production and testing of prototypes and the final tooling stages. An investment in a new drug by a pharmaceutical company begins with research that (with some probability) leads to a new compound, continues with extensive testing until the approval of the U.S. Food and Drug Administration is obtained, and concludes with the construction of a production facility and marketing of the product.

Sequential investment programs can take substantial time to complete (5-10 years for the above examples). In addition, they can be temporarily or permanently abandoned mid-stream if the value of the end product falls or the expected cost of completing the investment rises. Hence these investments can be viewed as compound options: each stage completed (or dollar invested) gives the firm an option to complete the next stage (or invest the next dollar).

The problem is finding a contingent plan for making these sequential and irreversible expenditures. Majd and Pindyck (1987) solve this problem in a model in which a firm invests continuously (each dollar spent brings an option to spend the next dollar) until the project is completed, investment can be stopped and later restarted at no cost, and there is a maximum rate at which outlays and construction can proceed (in other words, the project takes "time to build"). The payoff to the firm upon completion (that is, the value of the operating project) is $V$, which follows the geometric Brownian motion of equation (3-1). With $K$, the total remaining expenditure required to complete the project, the optimal rule is to keep investing at the maximum rate as long as $V$ exceeds a critical value $V^*(K)$, with $dV^*/dK < 0$. Based on the methods presented in the third and fourth sections, deriving a partial differential equation for $F(V,K)$, the value of the investment opportunity, is straightforward. Solutions to this equation and its associated boundary conditions, which are obtained by numerical methods, yield the optimal investment rule $V^*(K)$.[16]

These solutions show how time to build magnifies the effects of irreversibility and uncertainty. The lower the maximum rate of investment is (the longer it takes to complete the project), the higher the critical $V^*(K)$ required for construction to proceed is. The reasons are that the project's value upon completion is more uncertain, and the expected rate of growth of $V$ over the construction period is less than $\mu$, the risk-adjusted rate of return ($\delta$ is positive). Further, unlike the model in the third section where the critical value $V^*$ declines monotonically with $\delta$, with time to build, $V^*$ will increase with $\delta$ when $\delta$ is large. The reason is that while a higher $\delta$ increases the opportunity cost of waiting to begin construction, it also reduces the expected rate of growth of $V$ during the construction period, so that the (risk-adjusted) expected payoff from completing construction is reduced. Finally, by computing $F(V,K)$ for different maximum rates of investment, the value of flexibility in the construction time can be determined, that is, what an investor would be willing to pay to be able to build the project faster.[17]

In the Majd-Pindyck model investment occurs as a continuous flow—each dollar spent gives the firm an option to spend another dollar, up to the last dollar that gives the firm a completed project. Often, however, sequential investments occur in discrete stages, as with the aircraft and pharmaceutical examples. In these cases the optimal investment rule can be found by working backwards from the completed project, as was done with the model in the fourth section.

To see how to carry out this calculation, consider a two-stage investment in new capacity to produce oil. First, reserves of oil must be obtained through exploration or outright purchase at a cost of $I_1$. Second, development wells (and possibly pipelines) must be built at a cost of $I_2$. Let $P$ be the price of oil and assume it follows the geometric Brownian motion of equation (3-18). The firm thus begins with an option, worth $F_1(P)$, to invest in reserves. Doing so buys an option, worth $F_2(P)$, to invest in development wells. Making this investment yields a production capacity worth $V(P)$.

Working backwards to find the optimal investment rules, first note that, as in the model of the fourth section, $V(P)$ is the value of the firm's operating options and can be calculated accordingly. Next, $F_2(P)$ can be found; it is easy to show that it must satisfy equation (3-25) and boundary conditions (3-26)-(3-28), with $I_2$ replacing $I$, and $P^*$ the critical price at which the firm should invest in development wells. Finally, $F_1(P)$ can be found. It also satisfies equation (3-25) and conditions (3-26)-(3-28), but with $F_2(P)$ replacing $V(P)$ in conditions (3-27) and (3-28), $I_1$ replacing $I$, and $P^{**}$ replacing $P^*$. ($P^{**}$ is the critical price at which the firm should invest in reserves.) If the marginal cost of production is constant and there is no cost to stopping or restarting production, an analytical solution can be obtained.[18]

In this example there is no time to build; each stage (obtaining reserves and building development wells) can be completed instantly. For many projects each stage of the investment takes time, and the firm can stop investing in the middle of a stage. Then the problem must be solved numerically with a method such as the one in Majd and Pindyck (1987).[19]

In all the models discussed so far, no learning takes place, in the sense that future prices (or project values, $V$) are always uncertain, and the degree of uncertainty depends only on the time horizon. For some sequential investments, however, early stages provide information about costs or net payoffs in later stages. Synthetic fuels was a much debated example of this pattern; oil companies argued that demonstration plants were needed (and deserved funding by government) to determine production costs. The aircraft and pharmaceutical investments mentioned above also have these characteristics. The engineering, prototype production, and testing stages in the development of a new aircraft all provide information about the ultimate cost of production (as well as the aircraft's flight characteristics, which will help determine its market value). Likewise, the research and development and testing stages of the development of a new drug determine its efficacy and side effects, and hence its value.

Roberts and Weitzman (1981) develop a model of sequential investment that stresses this role of information-gathering. In their model each stage of investment yields information that reduces the uncertainty over the value of the completed project. Since the project can be stopped mid-stream, it may pay to go ahead with the early stages of the investment even though ex ante the net present value of the entire project is negative. Hence a simple net present value rule can lead to the *rejection* of projects that should be undertaken. This is just the opposite of the finding noted earlier that the simple net present value rule can *accept* projects that should be rejected. The crucial assumption in the Roberts-Weitzman model is that prices and costs do not evolve stochastically. The value of the completed project may not be known (at least until the early stages are completed), but that value does not change over time, so that there is no gain from waiting and no opportunity cost to investing now. Instead, information-gathering adds a shadow value to the early stages of the investment.[20]

This result applies whenever information-gathering rather than waiting yields information. The basic principle is easily seen by modifying the simple two-period example presented in the second section. Suppose the widget factory can only be built this year, at a cost of $1,200. By first spending $50 to research the widget market, however, it is possible to determine whether widget prices will rise or fall next year. Clearly it is worth spending the $50, even though the net present value of the entire project (the research plus the construction of the factory) is negative. The factory will be built only if the research shows that widget prices will rise.

## Incremental investment and choice of capacity

So far this chapter has examined decisions to invest in single, discrete projects, such as building a new factory or developing a new aircraft. Much of the economics literature on investment, however, focuses on *incremental* investment: firms invest to the point at which the cost of the marginal unit of capital just equals the present value of the revenues it is expected to generate. The cost of the unit can include adjustment costs (related to the time and expense of installing and learning to use new capital) in addition to purchase cost. In most models adjustment costs are a convex function of the rate of investment and are thus a crucial determinant of that rate. (For an overview, see Nickell 1978 or the more recent survey by Abel 1990.)

Except for work by Arrow (1968) and Nickell (1974), which is in a deterministic context, the literature generally ignores the effects of irreversibility. As with discrete projects, irreversibility and the ability to delay investment decisions change the fundamental rule for investing. The firm must include as part of the total cost of an incremental unit of capital the opportunity cost of investing in that unit now rather than waiting.

Bertola (1989) and Pindyck (1988) developed models of incremental investment and capacity choice that account for irreversibility. In Pindyck's model, the firm faces a linear inverse demand function, $P = \theta(t) - \gamma Q$, where $\theta$ follows a geometric Brownian motion and has a Leontief production technology. The firm can invest at any time at a cost of $k$ per unit of capital, and each unit of capital gives it the capacity to produce up to one unit of output per period. The investment problem is solved first by determining the value of an incremental unit of capital, given $\theta$ and an existing capital stock, $K$, and then finding the value of the option to invest in this unit and the optimal exercise rule. This rule is a function $K^*(\theta)$ (invest whenever $K < K^*[\theta]$), which determines the firm's optimal capital stock. Pindyck shows that an increase in the variance of $\theta$ increases the value of an incremental unit of capital (that unit represents a set of call options on future production) but raises the value of the option to invest in the unit even more, so that investment requires a higher value of $\theta$. Hence a more volatile demand implies that a firm should hold less capital but have a higher market value.[21]

In Bertola's model the firm's net revenue function is of the form $AK^{1-\beta}Z$, with $0 < \beta < 1$. (This form would follow from a Cobb-Douglas production function and an isoelastic demand curve.) The demand shift variable $Z$ and the purchase price of capital follow correlated geometric Brownian motions. Bertola solves for the optimal investment rule and shows that the marginal profitability of capital that triggers investment is higher than the user cost of capital as conventionally measured. The capital stock, $K$, is nonstationary, but Bertola finds the steady-state distribution for the ratio of the marginal profitability of capital to its price. Irreversibility and uncertainty reduce the mean of this ratio—on average capital intensity is higher. Although the firm has a higher threshold for investment, this situation is outweighed on average by low outcomes for $Z$.

The finding that uncertainty over future demand can increase the value of a marginal unit of capital is not new. The only requirement is that the marginal revenue product of capital be convex in price. This situation holds when the unit of capital can go unutilized (so that it represents a set of operating options). As Hartman (1972) points out, however, it is also the case for a competitive firm that combines capital and labor with a linear homogeneous production function. Hartman shows that, as a result, price uncertainty increases the firm's investment and capital stock.

Abel (1983) extends Hartman's result to a dynamic model in which price follows a geometric Brownian motion and there are convex costs of adjusting the capital stock. Again the result is that uncertainty increases the firm's rate of investment. Finally, Caballero (1990) introduces asymmetric costs of adjustment to allow for irreversibility (it can be costlier to reduce $K$ than to increase it). He shows again that price uncertainty increases the rate of investment. However, the Abel and Caballero results hinge on assumptions of constant returns and perfect competition, which make the marginal revenue product of capital independent of the capital stock. Then the firm could ignore its future capital stock (and hence irreversibility) when deciding how much to invest today. As Caballero shows, decreasing returns or imperfect competition link the marginal revenue products of capital across time, so that the basic result in Pindyck (1988) and Bertola (1989) holds.[22]

The assumption that a firm can invest incrementally is extreme. In most industries expansion of capacity is lumpy, and there are economies of scale (a 400-room hotel usually costs less to build and operate than two 200-room hotels). Hence firms must decide when to add capacity and how large an addition to make.

This problem was first studied in a stochastic setting by Manne (1961). He considers a firm that must always have enough capacity to satisfy demand; that demand grows according to a simple Brownian motion with drift. The cost of adding an amount of capacity $x$ is $kx^a$, with $0<a<1$; the firm must choose $x$ to minimize the present value of the expected capital costs. Manne shows that, with economies of scale, uncertainty over the growth of demand leads a firm to add capacity in larger increments, and increases the present value of expected costs.

In Manne's model (which might apply to an electric utility that must always satisfy demand) the firm does not choose when to invest, only how much. Most firms must choose both. Pindyck (1988) determines the effects of uncertainty on these decisions when there are no scale economies in construction by extending his model to a firm that must decide when to build a single plant and how large it should be.[23] As with Manne's model, uncertainty increases the optimal plant size. However, it also raises the critical demand threshold at which the plant is built. Thus uncertainty over demand should lead firms to delay additions to capacity but to make those additions larger when they occur.

Sometimes a choice of technology accompanies a choice of capacity. Consider a firm that produces two products, A and B, with interdependent demands that vary stochastically. It can produce these products by (irreversibly) installing and utilizing product-specific capital or by (irreversibly) installing a more costly flexible type of capital that can be used to produce either or both products. The problem is to decide which type and how much capital to install. He and Pindyck (1992) solve this problem for a model with linear demands by first valuing incremental units of capital (output-specific and flexible) and then finding the optimal investment rule and hence the optimal amounts of capacity. By integrating the value of incremental units of specific and flexible capital, the preferred type of capital, as well as the value (if any) of flexibility, can be determined.

In all of the studies cited so far, the stochastic state variable (the value of the project, the price of the firm's output, or a demand or cost shift variable) is specified exogenously. In a competitive equilibrium, firms' decisions about investment and output depend on the price process but also collectively generate that process. It is desirable to know whether firms' decisions are consistent with the price processes specified.

At least two studies address this issue. Lippman and Rumelt (1985) model a competitive industry where firms face sunk costs of entry and exit and the market demand curve fluctuates stochastically. They find an equilibrium consisting of optimal investment and production rules for firms (with uncertainty they hold less capacity) and a corresponding process for the market price. Leahy (1989) extends Dixit's (1989a) model of entry and exit to an industry setting in which price is endogenous. He shows that price will be driven by demand shocks until an entry or exit barrier is reached, at which point entry or exit prevent it from moving further. Hence price follows a regulated Brownian motion. Surprisingly, it makes no difference whether firms take entry and exit into account or simply assume that price will follow a geometric Brownian motion; the same entry and exit barriers result. This finding suggests that models in which price is exogenous may provide a reasonable description of investment and capacity for an industry.

## Investment behavior and economic policy

Nondiversifiable risk plays a role in even the simplest models of investment by affecting the cost of capital. The findings summarized in this paper suggest, however, that risk may be a truly crucial determinant of investment. This conclusion is likely to have implications for the explanation and prediction of investment behavior at the industry- or economy-wide level and for the design of policy.

As detailed in chapter 2, "Private Investment and Macroeconomic Adjustment: A Survey," investment spending on an aggregate level may be highly sensitive to risk in various forms: uncertainties over the future prices of products and costs of inputs that directly determine cash flows; uncertainty over exchange rates; and uncertainty over future tax and regulatory policies. It is therefore important to understand how investment might depend on risk factors that are at least partly under government control, such as price, wage, and exchange rate stability, the threat of price controls or expropriation, and changes in trade regimes.

Irreversibility is also likely to have policy implications for specific industries. The energy industry is an example. Stability and credibility arise as issues because of the possibility of price controls, "windfall" profit taxes, or related policies that might be imposed should prices rise substantially. Investment decisions must take into account that price is evolving stochastically, but must also consider the probability that prices may be capped at some level or otherwise regulated.

A more fundamental problem is the volatility of market prices themselves. For many raw commodities (oil is an example) the volatility of prices rose substantially in the early 1970s and has remained high. Other things being equal, this greater volatility should increase the value of the land and other resources needed to produce the commodity, and have a depressing effect on expenditures for construction and on production capacity. Most studies of the gains from price stabilization focus on adjustment costs and the curvature of demand and (static) supply curves. (See Newbery and Stiglitz 1981 for an overview.) The irreversibility of investment creates an additional gain that must be accounted for.

The literature on these effects of uncertainty and instability is largely theoretical. The reason may be that models of irreversible investment under uncertainty are relatively complicated and are therefore difficult to translate into well-specified empirical models. In any case the gap between theory and empiricism is disturbing. While it is clear from the theory that increases in the volatility of, say, interest rates or exchange rates should depress investment, it is not at all clear how large these effects should be. Nor is it clear how important these factors have been in explaining investment across countries and over time. Most econometric models of aggregate economic activity ignore the role of risk or deal with it only implicitly. A more explicit treatment of risk may help explain economic fluctuations, especially investment spending, better.[24] Substantial empirical work is needed to determine whether the theoretical models discussed in this paper have predictive power.[25]

One step in this direction is the paper by Bertola and Caballero (1990). They solve the problem of optimal irreversible accumulation of capital for an individual firm with a Cobb-Douglas production function and then characterize the behavior of *aggregate* investment when there are both firm-specific and aggregate sources of uncertainty. Their model does well in replicating the behavior of postwar U.S. investment.

Simulation models may provide another vehicle for testing the implications of irreversibility and uncertainty. The structure of such a model might be similar to the model presented in the fourth section, parameterized to "fit" a particular industry. The predicted effects of observed changes in, say, price volatility could be determined and compared with the predicted effects of changes in interest or tax rates. Models of this sort could likewise be used to predict the effect of such factors as a perceived possible shift in the tax regime or the imposition of price controls. Such models may also be a good way to study the uncertainty of the "peso problem" sort.

## Conclusions

The focus of this chapter was largely on investment in capital goods. The principles, however, apply to a broad variety of problems involving irreversibility. For example, as Dornbusch (1987) points out, the same issues arise in labor markets, where firms face high (sunk) costs of hiring, training, and sometimes firing workers. (Bentolila and Bertola 1990 developed a formal model that explains how hiring and firing costs affect employment decisions.)

Another important set of applications arises in the context of natural resources and the environment. If the future values of wilderness areas and parking lots are uncertain, it may be better to wait before irreversibly paving over a wilderness area. Here the option value of waiting creates an opportunity cost, which must be added to the current direct cost of destroying the wilderness area when doing a cost-benefit analysis of the parking lot. Arrow and Fisher (1974) and Henry (1974) first made this point, one that has been elaborated upon in the environmental economics literature.[26] It has become especially germane in recent years because of concern over possible irreversible long-term environmental changes such as ozone depletion and global warming.

While this insight is important, actually measuring these opportunity costs can be difficult. In the case of a well-defined project (a widget factory), it is possible to construct a model like the one in the fourth section. It is not always clear, however, what the correct stochastic process is for, say, the price of outputs. Even if equation (3-18) is accepted, the opportunity cost of investing now (and the investment rule) will depend on parameters such as $\alpha$ and $\sigma$ that may not be easy to measure. The problem is much greater when applying these methods to investment decisions involving resources and the environment. Then the model must address, for example, the stochastic evolution of society's valuation of wilderness areas.

On the other hand, models such as the ones discussed in this chapter can be solved (by numerical methods) with alternative stochastic processes for the relevant state variables, and it is easy to determine the sensitivity of the solution to alternative parameter values, as was done in the third and fourth sections. These models at least provide some insight into the importance of irreversibility and the ranges of opportunity costs that might be implied. Obtaining such insight is clearly better than ignoring irreversibility.

# Appendix 3A

This appendix provides a brief introduction to the tools of stochastic calculus and dynamic programming that are used in the third and fourth sections. (For more detailed introductory discussions see Dreyfus 1965, Merton 1971, Chow 1979, Malliaris and Brock 1982, or Hull 1989. For more rigorous treatments see Kushner 1967 or Fleming and Rishel 1975.) This discussion begins with the Wiener process, then covers Ito's Lemma, and finally reviews stochastic dynamic programming.

## *Wiener processes*

A Wiener process (also called a Brownian motion) is a continuous-time Markov stochastic process whose increments are independent no matter how small the time interval. Specifically, if $z(t)$ is a Wiener process, then any change in $z$, $\Delta z$, corresponding to a time interval, $\Delta t$, satisfies the following conditions:

(a) The relationship between $\Delta z$ and $\Delta t$ is given by $\Delta z = \varepsilon_t \sqrt{\Delta t}$ where $\varepsilon_t$ is a normally distributed random variable with a mean of zero and a standard deviation of 1.

(b) $\varepsilon_t$ is serially uncorrelated, that is, $E(\varepsilon_t \varepsilon_s) = 0$ for $t \neq s$. Thus the values of $\Delta z$ for any two different intervals of time are independent (so that $z[t]$ follows a Markov process).

Examine what these two conditions imply for the change in $z$ over some finite interval of time, $T$. This interval can be broken up into $n$ units of length, $\Delta t$, each, with $n = T/\Delta t$. Then the change in $z$ over this interval is given by:

$$z(s + T) - z(s) = \sum_{i=1}^{n} \varepsilon_i (\Delta t)^{1/2}.$$

Since the $\varepsilon_i$'s are independent of each other, the change $z(s + T) - z(s)$ is normally distributed with a mean of 0 and a variance of $n\Delta t = T$. This last point, which follows from the fact that $\Delta z$ depends on $\sqrt{\Delta t}$ and not on $\Delta t$, is particularly important: *the variance of the change in a Wiener process grows linearly with the time interval*.

Letting the $\Delta t$'s become infinitesimally small, the increment of the Wiener process can be written as $dz = \varepsilon(t)(dt)^{1/2}$. Since $\varepsilon(t)$ has zero mean and unit standard deviation, $E(dz) = 0$ and $E[(dz)^2] = dt$. Finally, consider two Wiener processes, $z_1(t)$ and $z_2(t)$. It is possible to write $E(dz_1 dz_2) = \rho_{12} dt$, where $\rho_{12}$ is the coefficient of correlation between the two processes.

The following generalization of the Wiener process is often employed:

(3-A-1) $$dx = a(x,t)dt + b(x,t)dz.$$

The continuous-time stochastic process $x(t)$ represented by equation (3-A-1) is called an *Ito process*. Consider the mean and variance of the increments of this process. Since $E(dz) = 0$, $E(dx) = a(x,t)dt$. The variance of $dx$ is equal to $E\{[dx - E(dx)]^2\} = b^2(x,t)dt$. Hence $a(x,t)$ is referred to as the expected rate of drift of the Ito process, and $b^2(x,t)$ as the rate of variance.

An important special case of equation (3-A-1) is the *geometric Brownian motion with drift*. Here $a(x,t) = \alpha x$, and $b(x,t) = \sigma x$, where $\alpha$ and s are constants. In this case equation (3-A-1) becomes:

$$(3\text{-}A\text{-}2) \qquad\qquad dx = \alpha xdt + \sigma xdz.$$

(This expression is identical to equation [3-1] in the third section but with $V$ replaced by $x$.) From the above discussion of the Wiener process, it follows that over any finite interval of time *percentage* changes in $x$, $\Delta x/x$, are normally distributed. Hence absolute changes in $x$, $\Delta x$, are *lognormally* distributed. The expected value of $\Delta x$ will be derived shortly.

An important property of the Ito process (equation [3-A-1]) is that while it is continuous in time, it is not differentiable. To see this characteristic, note that $dx/dt$ includes a term with $dz/dt = \varepsilon(t)(dt)^{-1/2}$, which becomes infinitely large as dt becomes infinitesimally small. However, it is often desirable to work with functions of $x$ (or $z$), and it is necessary to find the differentials of such functions. Doing so requires using Ito's Lemma.

*Ito's Lemma*

Ito's Lemma is most easily understood as a Taylor series expansion. Suppose $x$ follows the Ito process (equation [3-A-1]), and consider a function $F(x,t)$ that is at least twice differentiable. The objective is to find the total differential of this function, $dF$. The usual rules of calculus define this differential in terms of first-order changes in $x$ and $t$: $dF = F_x dx + F_t dt$, where subscripts denote partial derivatives, that is, $F_x = \partial F/\partial x$, and so on. Suppose, however, that higher order terms for changes in $x$ are also included:

$$(3\text{-}A\text{-}3) \qquad dF = F_x dx + F_t dt + (1/2)F_{xx}(dx)^2 + (1/6)F_{xxx}(dx)^3 + \dots.$$

In ordinary calculus, these higher order terms all vanish in the limit. To see whether that outcome pertains here, expand the third and fourth terms on the right-hand side of equation (3-A-3). First, substitute equation (3-A-1) for $dx$ to determine $(dx)^2$:

$$(3\text{-}A\text{-}4) \qquad (dx)^2 = a^2(x,t)(dt)^2 + 2a(x,t)b(x,t)(dt)^{3/2} + b^2(x,t)dt.$$

Terms in $(dt)^{3/2}$ and $(dt)^2$ vanish as dt becomes infinitesimal and can therefore be ignored. Now write $(dx)^2 = 1/2b^2(x,t)dt$. As for the fourth term on the right-hand side of equation (3-A-3), every term in the expansion of $(dx)^3$ will include dt raised to a power greater than 1 and will vanish in the limit. This condition holds for any higher order terms in equation (3-A-3).

Hence Ito's Lemma gives the differential dF as:

(3-A-5) $$dF = F_x dx + F_t dt + (1/2)F_{xx}(dx)^2,$$

or, substituting from equation (3-1-1) for $dx$,

(3-A-6) $$dF = [F_t + a(x,t)F_x + 1/2b^2(x,t)F_{xx}]dt + b(x,t)F_x dz.$$

This procedure can easily be extended to functions of several Ito processes. Suppose that $F = F(x_1,...,x_m,t)$ is a function of time and the $\mu$ Ito processes, $x_1, ..., x_m$, where

(3-A-7) $$dx_i = a_i(x_1,...x_m,t)dt + b_i(x_1,...,x_m,t)dz_i,\ i = 1,...,m$$

and $E(dz_i dz_j) = \rho_{ij} dt$. Then, letting $F_i$ denote $\partial F/\partial x_i$ and $F_{ij}$ denote $\partial^2 F/\partial x_i \partial x_j$, Ito's Lemma gives the differential $dF$ as:

(3-A-8) $$dF = F_t dt + \sum_i F_i dx_i + 1/2\sum_i\sum_j F_{ij} dx_i dx_j$$

or, substituting for $dx_i$:

(3-A-9) $$dF = [F_t + \sum_i a_i(x_1,...,t)F_i + 1/2\sum_i b_i^2(x_1,...,t)F_{ii}$$

$$+ \sum_{i \neq j}\rho_{ij}b_i(x_1,...,t)b_j(x_1,...,t)F_{ij}]dt + \sum_i b(x_1,...,t)F_i dz_i$$

**Example: Geometric Brownian motion.** Return to the process given by equation (3-A-2). Ito's Lemma can be used to find the process followed by $F(x) = \log x$. Since $F_t = 0$, $F_x = 1/x$, and $F_{xx} = -1/x^2$, from equation (3-1-5):

(3-A-10) $$dF = (1/x)dx - (1/2x^2)(dx)^2$$

$$= \alpha dt + \sigma dz - 1/2\sigma^2 dt = (\alpha - 1/2\sigma^2)dt + \sigma dz.$$

Hence, over any finite time interval $T$, the change in $\log x$ is normally distributed with mean $(\alpha - 1/2\sigma^2)T$ and variance $\sigma^2 T$.

The geometric Brownian motion is often used to model the prices of stocks and other assets. It says returns are normally distributed, with a standard deviation that grows with the square root of the holding period.

**Example: Correlated Brownian motions.** As a second example of the use of Ito's Lemma, consider a function $F(x,y) = xy$, where $x$ and $y$ each follow geometric Brownian motions:

(3-A-11) $$dx = \alpha_x x dt + \sigma_x x dz_x$$

(3-A-12)                                    $dy = \alpha_y y dt + \sigma_y y dz_y$

with $E(dz_x dz_y) = \rho$. The objective is to find the process followed by $F(x,y)$ and the process followed by $G = \log F$.

Since $F_{xx} = F_{yy} = 0$ and $F_{xy} = 1$, from equation (3-A-8):

(3-A-13)                                    $dF = x dy + y dx + (dx)(dy)$.

Now substitute for $dx$ and $dy$ and rearrange:

(3-A-14)               $dF = (\alpha_x + \alpha_y + \rho\sigma_x\sigma_y)F dt + (\sigma_x dz_x + \sigma_y dz_y)F$.

Hence $F$ also follows a geometric Brownian motion. What about $G = \log F$? With the same steps as in the previous example,

(3-A-15)           $dG = (\alpha_x + \alpha_y - 1/2\sigma^2_x - 1/2\sigma^2_y)dt + \sigma_x dz_x + \sigma_y dz_y$.

From equation (3-A-15) it can be seen see that over any time interval $T$ the change in $\log F$ is normally distributed with mean $(\alpha_x + \alpha_y - 1/2\sigma^2_x - 1/2\sigma^2_y)T$ and variance $(\sigma^2_x + \sigma^2_y + 2\rho\sigma_x + \sigma_y)T$.

## Stochastic dynamic programming

Ito's Lemma also allows dynamic programming to be applied to optimization problems in which one or more of the state variables follow Ito processes. Consider the following problem of choosing u(t) over time to maximize the value of an asset that yields a flow of income, $\Pi$:

(3-A-16)                          $\max_u E_0 \int_0^\infty \Pi[x(t)u(t)]e^{-\mu t}dt$,

where $x(t)$ follows the Ito process given by:

(3-A-17)                                    $dx = a(x,u)dt + b(x,u)dz$.

Let $J$ be the value of the asset, assuming $u(t)$ is chosen optimally, that is,

(3-A-18)                     $J(x) = \max_u E_0 \int_0^\infty \Pi[x(\tau)u(\tau)]e^{-\mu\tau}d\tau$.

Since time appears in the maximand only through the discount factor, the Bellman equation (the fundamental equation of optimality) for this problem can be written as:

(3-A-19)                          $\mu J = \max_u[\Pi(x,u) + (1/dt)E_t dJ]$.

Equation (3-A-19) says that the total return on this asset, $\mu J$, has two components, the income flow, $\Pi(x,u)$, and the expected rate of capital gain,

$(1/dt)E_t dJ$. (Note that in writing the expected capital gain the expectation operator $E_t$ is applied, a step that eliminates terms in $dz$, *before* taking the time derivative.) The optimal $u(t)$ balances current income against expected capital gains to maximize the sum of the two components.

To solve this problem, it is necessary to take the differential $dJ$. Since $J$ is a function of the Ito process $x(t)$, Ito's Lemma is applied. From equation (3-A-5),

$$(3\text{-}A\text{-}20) \qquad\qquad dJ = J_x dx + 1/2 J_{xx}(dx)^2.$$

Now substitute equation (3-A-17) for $dx$ into equation (3-A-20):

$$(3\text{-}A\text{-}21) \qquad dJ = [a(x,u)J_x + 1/2 b^2(x,u)J_{xx}]dt + b(x,u)J_x dz.$$

Given this expression for $dJ$ and with $E(dz) = 0$, it is possible to rewrite the Bellman equation (3-A-19) as:

$$(3\text{-}A\text{-}22) \qquad \mu J = \max_u [\Pi(x,u) + a(x,u)J_x + 1/2 b^2(x,u)J_{xx}).$$

In principle, a solution can be obtained by going through the following steps. First, maximize the expression in curly brackets with respect to $u$ to obtain an optimal $u^* = u^*(x, J_x, J_{xx})$. Second, substitute this $u^*$ back into equation (3-A-22) to eliminate $u$. The resulting differential equation can then be solved for the value function $J(x)$, from which the optimal feedback rule $U^*(x)$ can be found.

**Example: Bellman equation for investment problems.** The third section examined an investment timing problem in which a firm had to decide when it should pay a sunk cost, $I$, to receive a project worth, $V$, given that $V$ follows the geometric Brownian motion of equation (3-1). To apply dynamic programming, the maximization problem was written as equation (3-13), in which $F(V)$ is the value function, or the value of the investment opportunity, based on the assumption that it is optimally exercised.

It should now be clear why the Bellman equation for this problem is given by equation (3-14). Since the investment opportunity yields no cash flow, the only return from holding it is its expected capital appreciation, $(1/dt)E_t dF$, which must equal the total return $\mu F$, from which equation (3-14) follows. Expanding $dF$ using Ito's Lemma results in equation (3-17), a differential equation for $F(V)$. This equation is quite general and could apply to a variety of different problems. To get a solution $F(V)$ and investment rule $V^*$ for the problem presented here, boundary conditions (3-6)-(3-8) are also applied.

**Example: Value of a project.** The fourth section examined a model of investment in which the value of the project had first to be calculated as a function of the output price, $P$. Differential equation (3-19) was derived for

$V(P)$ by treating the project as a contingent claim. Here this equation is rederived using dynamic programming.

The dynamic programming problem is to choose an operating policy ($j$ = 0 or 1) to maximize the expected sum of discounted profits. If the firm is risk-neutral, the problem is:

(3-A-23) $$\max_{j=0,1} E_0 \int_0^\infty j[P(t) - c]e^{-rt}dt,$$

given that $P$ follows the geometric Brownian motion of equation (3-18). The Bellman equation for the value function $V(P)$ is then:

(3-A-24) $$rV = \max_{j=0,1} [j(P - c) + (1/dt)E_t dV].$$

By Ito's Lemma, $(1/dt)E_t dV = 1/2\sigma^2 P^2 V_{PP} + \alpha P V_P$. Maximizing with respect to $j$ gives the optimal operating policy, $j = 1$ (that is, do operate) if $P>c$, and $j = 0$ (that is, do not operate) otherwise. Substituting $\alpha = r - \delta$ and rearranging gives equation (3-19).

## Notes

1.  This chapter is a slightly modified version of the article originally published in the *Journal of Economic Literature*, September 1991. The author thanks Prabhat Mehta for his research assistance and to Ben Bernanke, Vittorio Corbo, Nalin Kulatilaka, Robert McDonald, John Pencavel, Luis Servén, Andrés Solimano, and two anonymous referees for helpful comments and suggestions. Financial support was provided by the Center for Energy Policy Research of the Massachusetts Institute of Technology, the World Bank, and the National Science Foundation under Grant No. SES-8318990. Any errors are the author's.

2.  See, for example, McDonald and Siegel (1986), Brennan and Schwartz (1985), Majd and Pindyck (1987), and Pindyck (1988). Bernanke (1983) and Cukierman (1980) have developed related models in which firms have an incentive to postpone irreversible investments so that they can wait for new information. However, in their models this information makes the future value of an investment less uncertain. In this chapter the focus is on situations in which the future is always uncertain even though information arrives over time.

3.  In this example, the futures price equals the expected future price given the assumption that the risk can be fully diversified. (If the price of widgets were positively correlated with the market portfolio, the futures price would be less than the expected future spot price.) Note that if widgets were storable and aggregate storage was positive, the marginal convenience yield from holding inventory would be 10 percent. The reason is that since the futures price equals the current spot price, the net holding cost (the interest cost of 10 percent less the marginal convenience yield) must be zero.

4.  This transaction is analogous to selling a dividend-paying stock short. The short position requires payment of the dividend, because no rational investor would hold the offsetting long position without receiving that dividend.
5.  The appendix describes the use of these tools for readers unfamiliar with them. Those readers might want to review the appendix before proceeding. Introductory treatments can also be found in Merton (1971), Chow (1979), Hull (1989), and Malliaris and Brock (1982).) Readers who prefer to avoid this technical material altogether can skip directly to the fifth section, although they will miss some insights by doing so.
6.  A constant payout rate, $\delta$, and required return, $\mu$, imply an infinite project life. With $CF$ denoting the cash flow from the project,

$$V_0 = \int_0^T CF_t e^{\mu t} dt = \int_0^T \delta V_0 e^{(\mu-\delta)t} e^{\mu t} dt.$$

The implication is that $T = \infty$. If the project has a finite life, equation (3-1) cannot represent the evolution of $V$ during the operating period. However, it can represent its evolution prior to construction of the project, the only information that matters for the investment decision. See Majd and Pindyck (1987, 11-13) for a detailed discussion of this point.
7.  Dixit (1988) provides a heuristic derivation of this condition.
8.  The general solution to equation (3-5) is

$$F(V) = a_1 V^{\beta_1} + a_2 V^{\beta_2},$$

where

$$\beta_1 = 1/2 - (r - \delta)/\sigma^2 + \{[(r - \delta)/\sigma^2 - 1/2]^2 + 2r/\sigma^2\}^{1/2} > 1$$

and

$$\beta_2 = 1/2 - (r - \delta)/\sigma^2 - \{[(r - \delta)/\sigma^2 - 1/2]^2 + 2r/\sigma^2\}^{1/2} < 0.$$

Boundary condition (3-6) implies that $a_2 = 0$, so that the solution can be written as in equation (3-9).
9.  This result was first demonstrated by Cox and Ross (1976). Note also that equation (3-5) is the Bellman equation for maximization of the net payoff to the hedge portfolio. Since the portfolio is risk-free, the Bellman equation for that problem is:

$$rP = - \delta VF_V + (1/dt)E_t dP,$$

that is, the return on the portfolio, $rP$, equals the per period cash flow that it pays out (which is negative, since $\delta VF_V$ must be paid in to maintain the short position) plus the expected rate of capital gain. By substituting $P = F - F_V V$ and expanding $dF$ as before, it can be seen that equation (3-5) follows from the above equation.

10. This point and its implications are discussed in detail in McDonald and Siegel (1985).

11. Note that the option to invest is an option to purchase a package of call options (because the project is just a set of options to pay $c$ and receive $P$ at each future time $t$). Hence the valuation involves a compound option. For examples of the valuation of compound financial options, see Geske (1979) and Carr (1988). The present problem can be treated in a simpler manner.

12. By substituting equation (3-24) for $V(P)$ into (3-19), the reader can check that $ß_1$ and $ß_2$ are the solutions to the following quadratic equation:

$$(1/2)\sigma^2 ß_1(ß_1 - 1) + (r - \delta)ß_1 - r = 0.$$

Since $V(0) = 0$, the positive solution $(ß_1 > 1)$ must apply when $P < c$, and the negative solution $(ß_2 < 0)$ must apply when $P > c$. Note that $ß_1$ is the same as $ß$ in equation (3-10).

13. The scrap value of the project could exceed these costs. In this case the owner of the project holds a *put option* (an option to "sell" the project for the net scrap value), which raises the project's value. This situation has been analyzed by Myers and Majd (1985).

14. MacKie-Mason (1990) developed a related model of a mine that shows how nonlinear tax rules (such as a percentage depletion allowance) affect the value of operating options as well as the decision whether to invest.

15. As Dixit points out, hysteresis would occur if, for example, the price began at a level between $w$ and $w + \rho k$, rose above $w + \rho k$ so that entry occurred, but then fell to its original level, which is too high to induce exit. The firm's price expectations would then, however, be irrational (since the price is in fact varying stochastically).

16. With $k$ denoting the maximum rate of investment, this equation is:

$$1/2\sigma^2 V^2 F_{VV} + (r - \delta)VF_V - rF - x(kF_K + k) = 0$$

where $x = 1$ when the firm is investing and 0 otherwise. $F(V,K)$ must also satisfy the following boundary conditions:

$$F(V,0) = V,$$
$$\lim_{V \to \infty} F_V(V,K) = e^{-\delta K/k}, \text{ and}$$
$$F(0,K) = 0,$$

with $F(V,K)$ and $F_V(V,K)$ continuous at the boundary $V^*(K)$. For an overview of the numerical methods for solving partial differential equations of this kind, see Geske and Shastri (1985).

17. The production decision of a firm facing a learning curve and stochastically shifting demand is another example of this kind of sequential investment. Here, part of the firm's cost of production is actually an (irreversible) investment that yields a reduction in future costs. Because demand fluctuates, the future payoffs from this investment are uncertain. Majd and Pindyck (1989) introduce stochastic demand into a learning curve model and derive the optimal production rule. They show how uncertainty over future demand reduces the shadow value of cumulative production generated by learning and thus raises the critical price at which it is optimal for the firm to produce.

18. Paddock, Siegel, and Smith (1988) value oil reserves as options to produce oil but ignore the development stage. Tourinho (1979) first suggested that reserves of natural resources can be valued as options.

19. In a related paper, Baldwin (1982) analyzes sequential investment decisions when investment opportunities arrive randomly and the firm has limited resources to invest. She values the sequence of opportunities and shows that a simple net present value rule will lead to overinvestment.

20. Weitzman, Newey, and Rabin (1981) use this model to evaluate the case for building demonstration plants for synthetic fuel production. They find that learning about costs could justify these early investments. Much of the debate over synthetic fuels has had to do with the role of government, and in particular whether subsidies (for demonstration plants or for actual production) can be justified. These issues are discussed in Joskow and Pindyck (1979) and Schmalensee (1980).

21. The ratio of a firm's market value to the value of its capital in place should always exceed one (because part of its market value is the value of its growth options), and this ratio should be higher for firms selling in more volatile markets. Kester's (1984) study suggests that this rule is indeed the case.

22. Even if firms are perfectly competitive and have constant returns, stochastic fluctuations in demand will depress irreversible investment if new firms can enter in response to increases in prices (see Pindyck 1990b for a discussion of this point). Abel, Bertola, Caballero, and Pindyck also examine the effects that increased demand or price uncertainty have on holding the discount rate fixed. As Craine (1989) points out, an increase in the uncertainty of demand is likely to be accompanied by an increase in the systematic riskiness of the firm's capital and hence in an increase in its risk-adjusted discount rate.

23. The firm has an option, worth $G(K,\theta)$, to build a plant of arbitrary size $K$. Once built, the plant has a value $V(K,\theta)$ (the value of the firm's operating options), which can be found using the methods presented in the fourth section. $G(K,\theta)$ will satisfy equation (3-25), but with boundary conditions $G(K^*,\theta^*) = V(K^*,\theta^*) - kK^*$ and $G_\theta(K^*,\theta^*) = V_\theta(K^*,\theta^*)$, where $\theta^*$ is the critical $\theta$ at which the plant should be built, and $K^*$ is its optimal size. See Pindyck (1988, appendix).

24. The sharp jumps in energy prices in 1974 and 1979-80 clearly contributed to the 1975 and 1980-82 recessions. They reduced the real incomes of oil-importing countries and caused adjustment problems—inflation and further drops in income that resulted from the rigidities that prevented wages and non-energy prices from quickly equilibrating. However, energy shocks also raised uncertainty over future economic conditions. For example, it was unclear whether energy prices would fall or keep rising, what impact higher energy prices would have on the marginal products of various types of capital, and how long-lived the inflationary impact of the shocks would be. Much more volatile exchange rates and interest rates also made the economic environment more uncertain, especially in 1979-82. This uncertainty may have contributed to the decline in investment spending that occurred, a point made by Bernanke (1983) with respect to changes in oil prices. See also Evans (1984) and Tatom (1984) for discussions of the effects of the increased volatility of interest rates.
25. See Pindyck (1990) for a more detailed discussion of this issue.
26. Recent examples are Fisher and Hanemann (1987) and Hanemann (1989). This concept of an option value should be distinguished from that of Schmalensee (1972), which is more like a risk premium that is needed to compensate risk-averse consumers because of uncertainty over future valuations of an environmental amenity. For a recent discussion of this latter concept see Plummer and Hartman (1986).

## References

Abel, A. B. 1983. "Optimal Investment under Uncertainty." *American Economic Review* 73 (March):228-33.
———.1990. "Consumption and Investment," in B. Friedman and F. Hahn, eds., *Handbook of Monetary Economics*. New York: North-Holland Publishing.
Arrow, K. J. 1968. "Optimal Capital Policy with Irreversible Investment," in J. N. Wolfe. ed., *Value, Capital and Growth,* Essays in Honor of Sir John Hicks. Edinburgh: Edinburgh University Press.
Arrow, K. J., and A. C. Fisher. 1974. "Environmental Preservation, Uncertainty, and Irreversibility." *Quarterly Journal of Economics* 88 (2)(May):312-19.
Baldwin, R. 1988. "Hysteresis in Import Prices: The Beachhead Effect." *American Economic Review* 78 (September):773-85.
Baldwin, R., and P. Krugman. 1989. "Persistent Trade Effects of Large Exchange Rate Shocks. *Quarterly Journal of Economics* 104 (November):635-54.
Bentolila, S., and G. Bertola. 1990. "Firing Costs and Labor Demand: How Bad Is Eurosclerosis?" *Review of Economic Studies* 57 (July):381-402.
Bernanke, B. S. 1983. "Irreversibility, Uncertainty, and Cyclical Investment." *Quarterly Journal of Economics* 98 (February):85-106.

Bertola, G. 1989. "Irreversible Investment." Department of Economics, Princeton University, Princeton, N.J.

Bertola, G., and R. J. Caballero. 1991. "Irreversibility and Aggregate Investment." National Bureau of Economic Research (NBER) Working Paper Series no. 3865 (October):1-31.

Brennan, M. J., and E. S. Schwartz. 1985. "Evaluating Natural Resource Investments." *Journal of Business* 58 (January):135-57.

Caballero, R. J. 1991. "On the Sign of the Investment-Uncertainty Relationship." *American Economic Review* 81 (1):279-88.

Carr, P. 1988. "The Valuation of Sequential Exchange Opportunities." *Journal of Finance* 43 (December):1235-56.

Chow, G. C. 1979. "Optimal Control of Stochastic Differential Equation Systems." *Journal of Economic Dynamics and Control* 1 (May):143-75.

Cox, J. C., and S. A. Ross. 1976. "The Valuation of Options for Alternative Stochastic Processes." *Journal of Financial Economics* 3 (1/2)(January/March):145-66.

Cox, J. C., and M. Rubinstein. 1985. *Options Markets*. Englewood Cliffs, N.J.: Prentice-Hall.

Cox, J. C., S. A. Ross, and M. Rubinstein. 1979. "Option Pricing: A Simplified Approach." *Journal of Financial Economics* 7 (3)(September):229-63.

Craine, R. 1989. "Risky Business: The Allocation of Capital." *Journal of Monetary Economics* 23 (March):201-18.

Cukierman, A. 1980. "The Effects of Uncertainty on Investment under Risk Neutrality with Endogenous Information." *Journal of Political Economy* 88 (June):462-75.

Dixit, A. 1988. "A Heuristic Argument for the Smooth Pasting Condition." Department of Economics, Princeton University, Princeton, N.J. March.

———. 1989a. "Entry and Exit Decisions under Uncertainty." *Journal of Political Economy* 97 (June):620-38.

———. 1989b. "Hysteresis, Import Penetration, and Exchange Rate Pass-Through." *Quarterly Journal of Economics* 104 (May):205-28.

Dornbusch, R. 1987. "Open Economy Macroeconomics: New Directions." National Bureau of Economic Research (NBER) Working Paper Series no. 2372 (August):1-13.

Dreyfus, S. E. 1965. *Dynamic Programming and the Calculus of Variations*. New York: Academic Press.

Evans, P. 1984. "The Effects on Output of Money Growth and Interest Rate Volatility in the United States. *Journal of Political Economy* 92 (April):204-22.

Fisher, A. C., and W. M. Hanemann. 1987. "Quasi-Option Value: Some Misconceptions Dispelled." *Journal of Environmental Economics and Management* 14 (July):183-90.

Fleming, W. H., and R. W. Rishel. 1975. *Deterministic and Stochastic Optimal Control*. New York: Springer-Verlag.

Geske, R. 1979. "The Valuation of Compound Options." *Journal of Financial Economics* 7 (March):63-81.

Geske, R., and K. Shastri. 1985. "Valuation by Approximation: A Comparison of Alternative Option Valuation Techniques." *Journal of Financial and Quantitative Analysis* 20 (March):45-71.

Gilbert, R. J. 1989. "Mobility Barriers and the Value of Incumbency." *Handbook of Industrial Organization*. Vol. I. New York: North-Holland Publishing.

Grossman, G. M., and C. Shapiro. 1986. "Optimal Dynamic R&D Programs." *RAND Journal of Economics* 17 (Winter):581-93.

Grossman, S. J., and G. Laroque. 1990. "Asset Pricing and Optimal Portfolio Choice in the Presence of Illiquid Durable Consumption Goods." *Econometrica* 58 (January):25-52.

Hanemann, W. M. 1989. "Information and the Concept of Option Value." *Journal of Environmental Economics and Management* 16 (January):23-37.

Hartman, R. 1972. "The Effects of Price and Cost Uncertainty on Investment." *Journal of Economic Theory* 5 (October):258-66.

He, H., and R. S. Pindyck. 1992. "Investments in Flexible Production Capacity." *Journal of Economic Dynamics and Control* 16 (July-October):575-99.

Henry, C. 1974. "Investment Decisions under Uncertainty: The Irreversibility Effect." *American Economic Review* 64 (December):1006-12.

Hull, J. 1989. *Options, Futures, and Other Derivative Securities*. Englewood Cliffs, N.J.: Prentice-Hall.

Joskow, P. L., and R. S. Pindyck. 1979. "Synthetic Fuels: Should the Government Subsidize Nonconventional Energy Supplies?" *Regulation* 3 (September):18-24.

Kester, W. C. 1984. "Today's Options for Tomorrow's Growth." *Harvard Business Review* 62 (March/April):153-60.

Krugman, P. R. 1989. *Exchange Rate Instability*. Cambridge, Mass.: MIT Press.

Kushner, H. J. 1967. *Stochastic Stability and Control*. New York: Academic Press.

Lam, P-S. 1989. "Irreversibility and Consumer Durables Expenditures." *Journal of Monetary Economics* 23 (January):135-50.

Leahy, J. 1989. "Notes on an Industry Equilibrium Model of Entry and Exit." Department of Economics, Princeton University, Princeton, N.J. November.

Lippman, S. A., and R. P. Rumelt. 1985. "Industry-Specific Capital and Uncertainty." Department of Economics, University of California—Los Angeles, September.

MacKie-Mason, J. K. 1990. "Some Nonlinear Tax Effects on Asset Values and Investment Decisions under Uncertainty." *Journal of Public Economics* 42 (August):301-27.

Majd, S., and R. S. Pindyck. 1987. "Time to Build, Option Value, and Investment Decisions." *Journal of Financial Economics* 18 (March):7-27.

———. 1989. "The Learning Curve and Optimal Production under Uncertainty." *RAND Journal of Economics* 20 (Autumn):331-43.

Malliaris, A. G., and W. A. Brock. 1982. *Stochastic Methods in Economics and Finance.* New York: North-Holland Publishing.

Manne, Alan S. 1961. "Capacity Expansion and Probabilistic Growth." *Econometrica* 29 (October):632-49.

Mason, S., and R. C. Merton. 1985. "The Role of Contingent Claims Analysis in Corporate Finance," in E.Altman and M. Subrahmanyam, eds., *Recent Advances in Corporate Finance.* Homewood, Ill.: Richard D. Irwin.

McDonald, R., and D. R.Siegel. 1985. "Investment and the Valuation of Firms When There Is an Option to Shut Down." *International Economic Review* 26 (June):331-49.

———. 1986. "The Value of Waiting to Invest." *Quarterly Journal of Economics* 101 (November):707-28.

Merton, R. C. 1971. "Optimum Consumption and Portfolio Rules in a Continuous-Time Model." *Journal of Economic Theory* 3 (4)(December):373-413.

———. 1977. "On the Pricing of Contingent Claims and the Modigliani Miller Theorem." *Journal of Financial Economics* 5 (November):241-49.

Myers, S. C. 1977. "Determinants of Corporate Borrowing." *Journal of Financial Economics* 5 (November):147-75.

Myers, S. C., and S. Majd. 1985. "Calculating Abandonment Value Using Option Pricing Theory." MIT Sloan School of Management Working Paper No.1462-83. Massachusetts Institute of Technology, Cambridge, Mass. January.

Newbery, D., and J. Stiglitz. 1981. *The Theory of Commodity Price Stabilization.* New York: Oxford University Press.

Nickell, S. J. 1974. "On the Role of Expectations in the Pure Theory of Investment." *Review of Economic Studies* 41 (January):1-20.

———. 1978. *The Investment Decisions of Firms.* New York: Cambridge University Press.

Paddock, J. L., D. R. Siegel, and J. L. Smith. 1988. "Option Valuation of Claims on Real Assets: The Case of Offshore Petroleum Leases." *Quarterly Journal of Economics* 103 (August):479-508.

Pindyck, R. S. 1988. "Irreversible Investment, Capacity Choice, and the Value of the Firm." *American Economic Review* 78 (December):965-85.

———. 1990a. "Irreversibility and the Explanation of Investment Behavior," in D. Lund and B. K. Øksendal, eds., *Stochastic Models and Option Values.* Amsterdam: North-Holland Publishing.

———. 1993. "A Note on Competitive Investment under Uncertainty." *American Economic Review* vol 83, No. 1, pp. 273-277.

Plummer, M. L., and R. C. Hartman. 1986. "Option Value: A General Approach." *Economic Inquiry* 24 (July):455-71.

Roberts, K., and M. L.Weitzman. 1981. "Funding Criteria for Research, Development, and Exploration Projects." *Econometrica* 49 (5)(September):1261-88.

Schmalensee, R. 1972. "Option Demand and Consumer's Surplus: Valuing

Price Changes under Uncertainty." *American Economic Review* 62 (December):813-24.
———. 1980. "Appropriate Government Policy Toward Commercialization of New Energy Supply Technologies." *The Energy Journal* 1 (July):1-40.
Tatom, J. A. 1984. "Interest Rate Variability: Its Link to the Variability of Monetary Growth and Economic Performance." Federal Reserve Bank of St. Louis *Review* 66 (November):31-47.
Tourinho, O. A. 1979. "The Valuation of Reserves of Natural Resources: An Option Pricing Approach." Unpublished Ph.D. dissertation. Department of Economics, University of California-Berkeley, Berkeley, Calif.
Weitzman, M., W. Newey, and M. Rabin. 1981. "Sequential R&D Strategy for Synfuels." *Bell Journal of Economics* 12 (2)(Autumn):574-90.

# 4

# On the Dynamics of Aggregate Investment

*Ricardo J. Caballero*

Few economists question the crucial role of capital accumulation in deter-mining countries' economic performance.[1] Unfortunately, fewer econo-mists (perhaps none?) would be confident in explaining the behavior of actual aggregate investment. It has been known for some time that the simple neoclassical specification of Jorgenson (1963) has little to do with actual investment at the firm level—firms do not adjust continuously to satisfy some frictionless static first-order condition—and even less to do with aggregate investment, since the cost of capital fluctuates too much to be consistent with the behavior of actual investment. Adding intertemporal considerations together with simple forms of adjustment costs has not improved things much; the empirical success of the renown dynamic $q$-theory model (see Tobin 1969, Hayashi 1982, and Abel 1983 for the different stages of this theory) has been at least as bad, if not worse, than that of the simple frictionless model (Abel and Blanchard 1986). Moreover, up to now the best-fitting specification seems to have been the ad hoc accelerator model.

It is not entirely surprising that these theories fail to explain investment, since their microeconomic foundation is clearly unrealistic.[2] The neoclassi-cal model assumes no adjustment cost at all, while the $q$-theory implicitly assumes that adjustment costs are such[3] that firms adjust continuously—although only partially—by small amounts. Even casual empiricism, however, suggests that actual microeconomic investment decisions are infrequent and many times far from infinitesimal (from the firm's perspec-tive). Furthermore, researchers have noticed that investments at the firm level are close to irreversible and that this characteristic conveys distinctive implications for microeconomic investment (Arrow 1968; Nickell 1974), especially in an uncertain environment (Bernanke 1983; McDonald and Siegel 1986; Ingersoll and Ross 1987; Majd and Pindyck 1987; Pindyck 1988; chapter 3, "Irreversibility, Uncertainty, and Investment," in this volume; Bertola 1988; and Bertola and Caballero 1990a).

One of the implications of the irreversibility of investment decisions is that firms alternate between periods of inaction in which gross investment is nil and their capital stock is eroded by depreciation, and periods of positive gross investment. Aggregate investment does not, however, match this description of action-inaction, so that it is necessary to abandon the representative agent framework and face a difficult aggregation problem. At each point in time the question is not only how much individual firms are investing but also how many firms are doing it. Answering that question requires some understanding of the dynamic behavior of the cross-sectional distribution of firms' marginal profitability of capital. Caballero and Engel (1991, 1993) provide the basic principles and methodology to track a cross-sectional distribution when firms face both idiosyncratic and aggregate shocks. Bertola and Caballero (1990b) and Caballero (1992, 1993) generalize these results to include models with implications similar to those of the irreversible investment model, and develop procedures to implement these models empirically. Bertola and Caballero (1990a) study precisely the problem of aggregate investment in the presence of constraints of micro-economic irreversibility. This chapter borrows heavily from the latter paper.

Three sections follow. The next one presents the theory of aggregate investment in the presence of irreversibility constraints and other forms of realistic adjustment costs. In so doing, it discusses several fallacies arising from both the use of conditional statements to explain long-run average results and the direct extrapolation of microeconomic arguments to the aggregate. The subsequent section outlines an econometric methodology to estimate these new models and presents examples based on the recent investment experiences of several developing countries. The chapter ends with some concluding remarks and directions for future research.

## The theory

### Frictionless investment: The firm

If capital could be rented in a perfect spot market and there were no costs for installing and removing equipment and structures, investment by firm $i \in [0,1]$ would be determined at each point in time by the simple static condition:

(4-1) $$\Pi_k(K_{it}^f, \Theta_{it}) = c_{it}$$

where $\Pi(.,.)$ = the firm's flow profit function
$\quad\quad K^f$ = the firm's "frictionless" stock of capital
$\quad\quad \Theta$ = exogenous stochastic component summarizing such things as wages and productivity, and
$\quad\quad c_t$ = rental cost of capital (real interest rate plus the physical rate of depreciation minus the expected appreciation of a unit of capital times the price of capital).

For expository simplicity assume that $c_{it} = c$, and for tractability that the firm's profit function takes a simple isoelastic form:[4]

$$(4-2) \qquad \Pi(K_{it}, \Theta_{it}) = K_{it}{}^{\alpha}\Theta_{it} \qquad 0 \le \alpha \le 1$$

where K is the firm's actual stock of capital.

With equations (4-1) and (4-2), it is easy to obtain a simple expression for the frictionless stock of capital at the firm level:

$$(4-3) \qquad K_{it}^{f} = \left[ \frac{\alpha\Theta_{it}}{c} \right]^{1/1-\alpha}$$

Investment is entirely determined by this equation. Investment (net) or disinvestment occurs only when the conditions the firm faces (as relates, for example, to productivity, wages, and demand) change. The rate of growth of a firm's capital stock—the ratio of investment to capital—is given by:

$$(4-4) \qquad N_{it}^{f} = [1/1-\alpha] \, d\theta_{it},$$

where $N_{if}^{f}$ is the frictionless ratio of net investment to capital and $\theta$ is the logarithm of $\Theta$.

Figure 4-1(A) illustrates a sample path of the log of the stock of capital—hence investment—for a given path of $\theta$. Positive changes in $\theta$, perhaps as a result of increases in productivity or demand or a reduction in wages, lead to positive net investment, while negative changes in $\theta$ yield negative net investment. The expression for the firm's frictionless stock of capital is obtained from the first-order condition given in equation (4-1), which says that at all points in time the marginal profitability of capital must equal the cost of capital, in this case a constant, as shown in figure 4-1(B).

*Irreversible investment: the firm*

In reality, especially that of developing countries, rental and secondary markets are far from perfect, and there are many types of adjustment costs. In particular, once installed, capital has alternative uses only at a substantial discount. At the extreme, when there is no alternative use for capital, investment is said to be *irreversible*. This case is the base one studied in this chapter. To make things simple, assume that adjustment in the opposite direction, that is, positive gross investment, is costless and that there are no indivisibilities or advantages to bunching adjustments. This case permits the most important aspects of aggregation to be highlighted in the context of realistic nonconvex adjustment cost functions, while keeping the model as simple as possible. (Other forms of nonconvexities and their distinctive implications are discussed later.)

Suppose for a moment that the firm chooses to disregard the irreversibility constraint, so that condition (4-3) in which gross investment is positive is met at all times. There will be times, however, in which the firm

**Figure 4.1    Frictionless behavior**
           (path of the log of the capital stock)

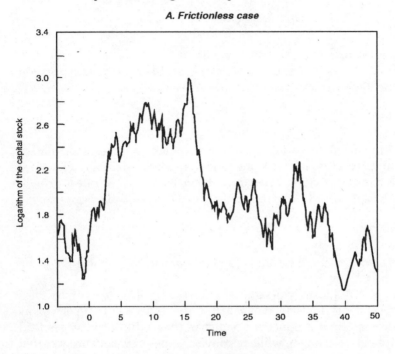

*A. Frictionless case*

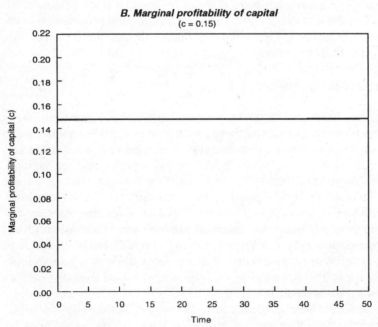

*B. Marginal profitability of capital*
(c = 0.15)

*Source:* Author's elaboration.

would like to disinvest at a rate faster than depreciation but cannot. At those times, $\Pi_k(K_{it}, \Theta_{it}) < c$. In these situations the firm "gets stuck" with too much capital. Figure 4-2 depicts this situation: the dashed line in figure 4-2(A) denotes the path of frictionless (log of) capital, which is identical to that of figure 4-1. The solid line depicts the corresponding path of actual (log of) capital. All those periods in which the dashed line is below the solid line represent times in which there is "too much" capital. Since in this case the firm never has "too little" capital, it ends up holding, on average, too much capital. The dual of this situation can be seen in figure 4-2(B), where the dashed line represents the cost of capital and the marginal profitability of frictionless capital and the solid line illustrates the path of the marginal profitability of actual capital. It is apparent that in this case the marginal profitability of capital is, on average, below its cost. Thus the firm is overinvesting.

An optimizing firm will try to remedy the excessive accumulation of capital, at least in part. This tendency leads, under assumptions standard to this literature, to a modification of condition (4-1) for good times. If $K^d$ denotes the desired stock of capital at each point in time when there is a positive probability of facing binding irreversibility constraints in the future, then:

(4-5)
$$\Pi_k(K_{it}^d, \Theta_{it}) = c + h$$

where $h$ is a positive constant that depends on the parameters of the profit function as well as on the characteristics of the stochastic process that generates $\theta$. In particular, it is increasing on the variance of shock $\theta$.

Comparing equations (4-1) and (4-5) yields the relation $K^d_{it} < K^f_{it}$. This relation does not say that investment—and therefore capital—is less in the (partial equilibrium) firm facing irreversibility constraints than in an equivalent firm that does not face them; it just says that the firm will be more reluctant to invest in good times. What is often forgotten, however, is that the reason for this reluctance is those occasions when the firm gets stuck with too much capital.

This situation is portrayed in figure 4-3(A), where the dashed, dotted, and solid lines represent one possible sample path of the (log of) the frictionless, the desired, and the actual stock of capital, respectively. Three types of situations can be observed. The first one corresponds to periods in which gross investment is positive, so that desired and actual capital are the same and below the frictionless level. The second one occurs when gross investment is zero, so that the actual stock is above the desired stock but the actual stock is still below the frictionless level. Finally, there are periods in which not only is gross investment zero, but actual stock exceeds the frictionless level. These regimes have a counterpart in the marginal profitability of capital, as revealed in figure 4-3(B). The marginal profitability of capital never exceeds the modified cost of capital, $c + h$, that is, the cost of capital that determines the desired stock of capital. Regime 1 corresponds

**Figure 4.2    Suboptimal constrained behavior**
            (path of the log of the capital stock)

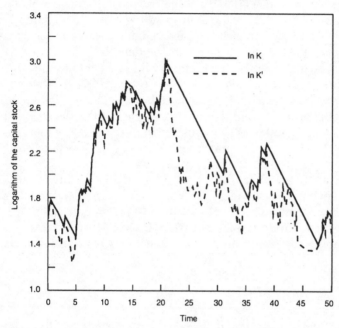

*A. Constrained case (suboptimal)*

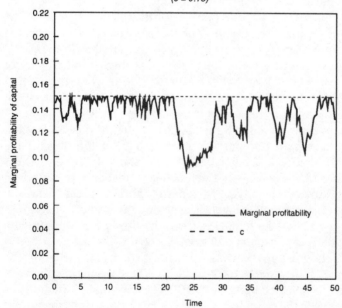

*B. Marginal profitability of capital*
            *(c = 0.15)*

**Figure 4.3    Irreversible investment**
(path of the log of the capital stock)

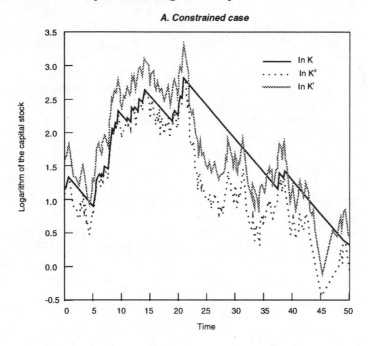

*A. Constrained case*

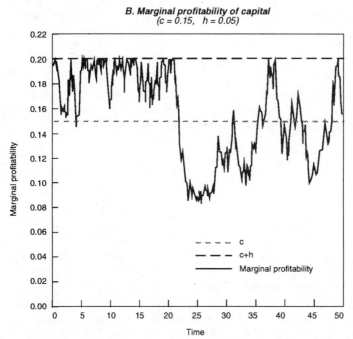

*B. Marginal profitability of capital*
(c = 0.15,   h = 0.05)

to the times in which the marginal profitability of capital ($\Pi_k$) equals $c + h$; regime 2 occurs when $\Pi_k$ is between $c + h$ and $c$, and regime 3 when $\Pi_k$ is below $c$.

When investment is irreversible, the firm will adjust its behavior in good times. It will try to limit both the number of periods when it has too much capital and the magnitude of the excesses. It can do so only by holding less capital in good periods than at times when investment is fully reversible. Whether the firm holds more or less capital on average than in a frictionless framework is ambiguous. The outcome depends on the specific parametric assumptions made (see, for example, Bertola and Caballero 1990b).[5]

Similarly, an implication of the irreversible investment literature is often said to be that an increase in uncertainty about $\theta$ lowers the capital stock. Once more, there is more reluctance to invest in good times, but the reasons are an increase in the frequency of bad times, that is, of periods in which the stock of capital is excessive, and an increase in their magnitude. As before, what happens to average capital accumulation when uncertainty is larger is ambiguous.

The main purpose of the chapter, however, is to explain the implications of these results for the *dynamic* behavior of *aggregate* investment, as discussed below.

*Frictionless and desired investment: The aggregate*

With the net frictionless investment of firm $i$ at time $t$ denoted by $I_{it}^f$, and with the identity $I_i^f \equiv N_i^f K_i^f$ it is possible to construct a measure of aggregate net frictionless investment, $I^f$, by integrating equation (4-5) over the continuum of firms' $i \ \varepsilon[0,1]$:

$$(4\text{-}6) \qquad\qquad I_t^f = [1/1 - \alpha] \int_0^1 K_{it}^f \, d\theta_{it} di.$$

Assuming that the rate of change in shocks $\theta_i$ is approximately independent of the initial stock of (frictionless) capital held by firms yields a simple expression for the frictionless (net) aggregate investment/capital ratio,

$$(4\text{-}7) \qquad\qquad N_t^f = [1/1 - \alpha] \int_0^1 d\theta_{it} di.,$$

or simply

$$(4\text{-}8) \qquad\qquad N_t^f = [1/1 - \alpha] d\theta_t,$$

where $d\theta_t \equiv \int_0^1 d\theta_{it} di$ is the "aggregate" shock. This terminology seems particularly appropriate in the context of this chapter—the existence of a large number of firms—since $d\theta_t$ is different from zero only because of the nondissipating correlation of shocks across sectors. The result is an equation similar to that of a single firm, with the sole exception that the aggregate shock replaces firm-specific shocks and therefore may have important stochastic differences with any particular firm.[6]

An expression for the desired (in the presence of future irreversibility constraints) aggregate investment/capital ratio can be obtained from an identical derivation:

(4-9) $$N_t^d = [1/1 - \alpha]d\theta_t.$$

Hence, the dynamic behavior of $N_t^d$ is indistinguishable from that of $N_t^f$. Alternatively, $I_t^d$ is at all times proportional to $I_t^f$, with a constant of proportionality that is less than one and monotonic with respect to $c/(c+h)$.

*Irreversible investment: The aggregate*

Unfortunately, the representative agent framework does not carry over to the case where firms face irreversibility constraints. As seen in figure 4-3, individual firms alternate between periods in which they invest and periods in which they let depreciation erode their stock of capital. This description of aggregate investment is clearly not a good one. Most likely, aggregate gross investment is almost never equal to zero, not even when high frequency observations are available.[7]

In general, regardless of the realization of the aggregate shock, there will be active (that is, investing) and inactive (that is, depreciating) firms at all times. The problem of aggregation is that of determining the fraction of firms doing one or the other, and the dynamic problem is that of tracking down the endogenous change in these fractions.

Recall that $K_{it} = K_{it}^d$ whenever the firm is investing, while at all other times $K_{it} > K_{it}^d$. It is therefore convenient to define a variable $Z_{it}$ that captures the gap between actual and desired capital:

(4-10) $$Z_{it} \equiv lnK_{it} - lnK_{it}^d.$$

Rearranging equation (4-10) shows that the dynamic behavior of the actual stock of capital at the firm level can be described in terms of the dynamic behavior of its desired stock of capital and that of the gap variable, $Z_{it}$.

The equivalent statement at the aggregate level is that the dynamic behavior of the aggregate stock of capital—when the firms face irreversibility constraints—can be described in terms of the dynamic behavior of the aggregate desired stock of capital, $N_t^d$, and the evolution of the *mean* of the *cross-sectional distribution* of gaps (measured by the log-distance of actual desired capital), $Z_t$. The implication is that the aggregate investment/capital ratio, $N_t$, is approximately described by

(4-11) $$N_t = N_t^d + dZ_t.$$

Since the dynamic behavior of $N_t^d$ is identical to that of $N_t^f$, the above equation can be rewritten as

(4-12)                                    $N_t = N_t^f + dZ_t$ .

At each point in time there exist given values of $Z_{it}$; thus, at each point
in time, a histogram of these quantities can be constructed. This histogram,
or *cross-sectional density*, denoted by $f(z,t)$, depends on the history of the
realizations of $\theta_i$'s up to time $t$ and on the nature of the depreciation affecting
the stocks of capital held by firms. The importance of this density is that it
permits the dynamic behavior of $Z_t$ to be tracked down and, with it, the
dynamic behavior of $N_t$, provided that $N_t^f$, which typically can be constructed from simple economic principles, as seen earlier, is known.

Under fairly reasonable assumptions, this density will, at any point in
time, take the shape shown in figure 4-4. The exponential-like form of this
density, with large concentrations of firms near point $Z_{it} = 0$ (the investment
point), is the result of the positive depreciation rate and drift in the driving
forces of capital formation (for example, growth in productivity). If these
parameters are large, firms will often invest, and f(z,t) will on average have
a high concentration of units with small disequilibria. If, on the other hand,
idiosyncratic uncertainty is large, $f(z,t)$ will look flatter, since at any point in
time there will be a significant number of firms whose negative shocks more
than offset the depreciation of their capital.

**Figure 4.4    Cross-sectional density**

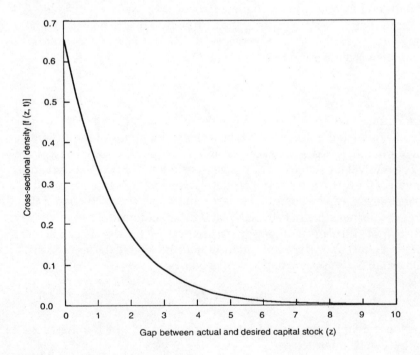

Aggregate shocks, on the other hand, are the main reason for the index $t$ in the cross-sectional density. If they were not present, $f(z,t)$ would eventually converge to a stable density, where $dZ_t \equiv 0$; hence $N_t = N_t^f$. The presence of aggregate shocks, however, prevents the cross-sectional density from ever converging and therefore introduces a breach in the dynamic behavior of the investment/capital ratios in economies where individual firms face and do not face irreversibility constraints.

When firms are affected by positive aggregate shocks (that is, on average the firm-level shocks are positive), the disequilibrium gaps tend to shrink, and more firms actually invest. The result is illustrated in figure 4-5 by the gradual shift in the cross-sectional density from the solid to the outermost dashed curve. In contrast, if a sequence of bad aggregate shocks hits the economy, the cross-sectional density gradually moves from the solid to the inmost dotted line, as the average gap increases and the fraction of firms actually investing falls.

Figure 4-5 and equation (4-12) permit the main impact of microeconomic irreversibility constraints on the dynamic behavior of aggregate investment to be isolated. In good times $N_t^f$ rises while the mean of the cross-sectional density falls, a pattern that smooths the responsiveness of investment to exogenous positive shocks. Put differently, the cross-sectional density

**Figure 4.5    Cross-sectional density**

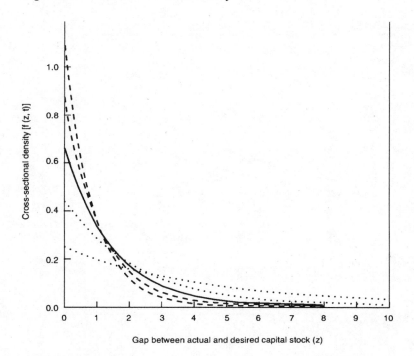

Gap between actual and desired capital stock (z)

*Source:* Author's elaboration.

siphons off part of the energy of the exogenous shocks. This energy, however, is not lost but is released slowly over time when good times cease. Exactly the opposite happens in bad times.

Interestingly, contrary to what the literature typically argues, nothing in the previous paragraph suggests an asymmetric response of aggregate investment to aggregate shocks. It can be shown (see Caballero 1992) that this pattern is not an accident but the work of very powerful underlying laws of probability: properly aggregated systems have a natural tendency not only to dampen but also to erase microeconomic asymmetries. The condition does not mean that a model of this nature cannot generate aggregate asymmetries; it only means that the sources of these asymmetries are quite different from what direct microeconomic extrapolations suggest.

Figure 4-6 shows the response of the actual investment/capital ratio ($y$ axis) to shocks leading to changes in the frictionless investment/capital ratio ($x$ axis). The different lines correspond to different initial conditions (before the current shock). The solid line starts from a situation in which the stock of capital has been growing at a rate of 9 percent a year for a long time, so that the initial cross-sectional density is very concentrated near the investment barrier. Conversely, the line of short dashes corresponds to a case in which the net investment/capital ratio has been a negative 9 percent

**Figure 4.6    Smoothness-fully irreversibility case**
         **($\sigma = 0.4$, $\delta = 0.1$)**

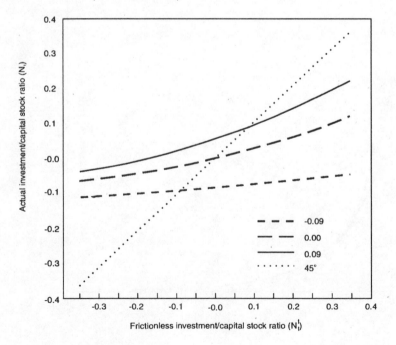

for a long time, so that gross investment has been very low for a long time, and the cross-sectional density is still exponential but very spread out. The line of long dashes corresponds to an intermediate case. The distribution of shocks has been assumed to lead to a standard deviation of the frictionless stock at the microeconomic level of 40 percent a year, and the depreciation rate is 10 percent a year.

This figure confirms several of the issues discussed above. First, and most important, the irreversibility constraints at the microeconomic level lead to pronounced "excess smoothness" in the way capital responds to aggregate shocks. Second, even though there is an extreme form of asymmetry in the adjustment cost at the microeconomic level, there is no evidence of first-order asymmetry at the aggregate level. (The slight asymmetry observed for large [although continuous] shocks in good times is discussed extensively below.) Third, the first-order serial correlation (approximately measured by the distance of each of the lines from the zero line when $N_t^f = 0$) is larger when the economy is in a bad state (this "asymmetry" is the result of the positive rate of depreciation).

The irreversible investment case, as stated, is an extreme form of adjustment cost. It may be more realistic to assume that it is very costly to reduce the stock of capital but not infinitely costly. Figure 4-7 repeats the

**Figure 4.7 Smoothness-partial irreversibility**
($\sigma = 0.4$, $\delta = 0.1$)

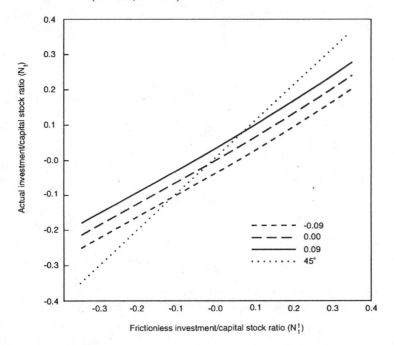

Source: Author's elaboration.

experiment in figure 4-6 under this new structure for the cost of adjustment. For this purpose a large proportional cost for downgrading the capital stock is used that leads firms to wait until their capital stocks are twice as large as their desired stocks before implementing marginal sales of stocks. The conclusions of figure 4-6 hold, although now the degree of excess smoothness is much milder. The reason is complex and lies in the large amount of uncertainty (mostly idiosyncratic) individual firms face (see Caballero 1993 and Bertola and Caballero 1990b). When the support of $Z_i$ is bounded, a substantial increase in uncertainty reduces the ability of aggregate shocks to alter the shape of the cross-sectional density and therefore to alter $Z_t$, the reason for the "smoothing" effect.

Figure 4-8 corresponds to the same case as in figure 4-7 but with the total uncertainty firms face reduced to 10 percent a year (given that the size of the aggregate shocks has been kept constant, this level corresponds to an increase in the relative importance of aggregate uncertainty), and the initial conditions even more spread out than before.

This figure shows interesting asymmetries. The direction of the asymmetries depends not on whether the shocks are positive or negative but on initial conditions. If the initial conditions are good—in the sense that the mean cross-sectional distribution is very low—there is little smoothness

**Figure 4.8    Smoothness-partial irreversibility**
            $(\sigma = 0.1, \delta = 0.1)$

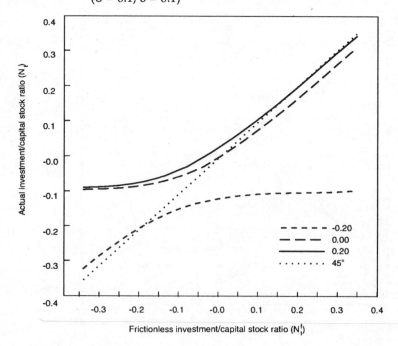

Frictionless investment/capital stock ratio ($N_t^i$)

*Source:* Author's elaboration.

with respect to further positive shocks, since there is very little space for downward movements in $Zt$, the reason for the smoothing of positive shocks. Conversely, there is plenty of space for upward shifts in $Z_t$, so that in good times negative changes produce substantial smoothness.

Up to this point the asymmetry goes in the direction of the microeconomic asymmetry. In contrast, the "bad" initial conditions case yields exactly the opposite type of asymmetry, since there is more room for $Z_t$ to move downward than upward.

It is also interesting to note that the intermediate case shows the former type of asymmetry; this shift in the center of gravity is caused by the positive depreciation rate. A strong positive drift in the economy would play a similar role. Thus, the presence and type of macroeconomic asymmetries depend on things far more complex than the asymmetry of adjustment costs at the microeconomic level (Caballero 1990).

These conclusions, including the impulse responses, extend to more general models of realistic nonconvex adjustment costs. For example, figure 4-9 depicts the cross-sectional density that is typical when there are fixed (as opposed to proportional) costs of both upgrading and downgrading capital stock at the firm level, a situation that yields inaction and investment of a finite size.

**Figure 4.9    Cross-sectional densities, fixed costs**
($\sigma = 0.2$, $\delta = 0.1$)

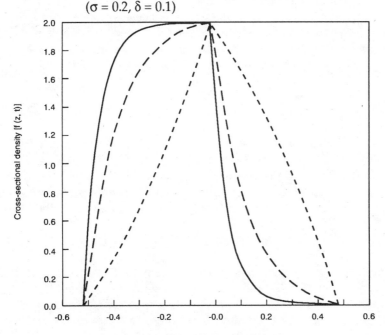

Gap between actual and desired capital stock (z)

*Source:* Author's elaboration.

## Econometrics

This section outlines a procedure for implementing the new theoretical developments described above. The method involves the use of examples constructed from private investment data for four developing countries: Brazil, Korea, Mexico, and Turkey. The results presented below are only illustrative of the procedures suggested and should by no means be taken as careful descriptions of the investment behavior of these countries.

### The long-run determinants (frictionless capital)

Estimating these models requires—at least conceptually—two distinct steps. First, the path of the frictionless (or desired) series must be estimated, and from this calculation (see equation 4-3) the path of aggregate shocks must be recovered. The latter are the impulses that feed the cross-sectional density in the second step, where the dynamic behavior of the model is estimated. The first step is addressed here first.[8]

Economic theory typically provides clear insights into the determinants of the frictionless aggregate stock of capital. Let this stock be

$$(4\text{-}13) \qquad\qquad lnK_t^f = \beta X_t,$$

where $\beta$ is the vector of coefficients and $X_t$ is the set of observable variables.[9] The task of this section is to find values for $\beta$. This task is not easy, since in the presence of adjustment costs the left-hand side variable is a non-observable theoretical construct. With the definition of $Z_t$, however, equation (4-13) can be rewritten in terms of the actual stock of capital:

$$(4\text{-}14) \qquad\qquad lnK_t = \beta_0 + \beta X_t + Z_t,$$

where $\beta_0 = lnK_t^d - lnK_t^f$.

$Z_t$ is—by construction—a stationary variable. It reveals that if the variables in $X_t$ are integrated (and not co-integrated among them), $\beta$ can be estimated from a conventional co-integrating regression.

Although theoretically correct, the previous procedure is likely to yield misleading results because of severe small-sample problems. Recall that

$$(4\text{-}15) \qquad\qquad lnK_t = \beta_0 + lnK_t^f + Z_t$$

and that, because of the adjustment costs, $lnK_t$ is a smoothed version of $lnK_t^f$. The implication is that $lnK_t^f$ and $Z_t$ must be negatively correlated. The normal equations of the simple co-integrating regression (ordinary least squares, or OLS) disregard this negative correlation; thus, the only way OLS can match the smooth behavior of $lnK_t$ is by biasing the coefficients in $\beta$ toward zero (Caballero 1993).

The small-sample problem can be reduced by using a Stock and Watson

(1989)–type correction. This correction involves expanding the regression in equation (4-14) by adding a set of auxiliary variables:

$$(4\text{-}16) \qquad lnK_t = \beta X_t + \gamma[\Delta X_t] + \varepsilon_t,$$

where $[\Delta X_t]$ is the vector of lags (and possibly leads) of the first difference of $X$, and $\varepsilon_t$ is the stationary disturbance that is ideally orthogonal to $X_t$. Put differently, $[\Delta X_t]$ is included to "clean" the correlation between $X_t$ and $Z_t$. One problem with this correction is that it requires significant degrees of freedom (40 or 50) to work properly, a potentially serious limitation when using data on developing countries. On the other hand, an advantage of concentrating on small-sample issues is that it does not really matter whether $X_t$ is integrated or not. All that matters is the variance of $X_t$ relative to its covariance with $Z_t$. This point is important when estimating investment equations, since the cost of capital is typically a stationary variable.

To illustrate some of these issues, a neoclassical model is used where $X_t$ is formed by the logarithm of gross national product (GNP), a proxy for the cost of capital, and a linear time trend. The proxy for the cost of capital is formed by the projection of a measure of the ex-post real interest rate (plus depreciation) on its own lag and the output measure lagged once. The coefficient of output is fixed so as to be equal to one, and the response of the frictionless capital/output ratio to changes in the cost of capital is estimated.

The data were obtained from the World Bank Macroeconomic Adjustment and Growth Division's CECMG data base. They contain annual observations from 1970 to 1985. Table 4-1 shows that despite the extremely small sample size and the consequent large standard errors, the correction does play an important role in yielding more reasonable point estimates of the parameter of primary concern. When no correction is implemented, the cost of capital elasticities not only is small but also has the wrong sign in three of the four countries considered. On the other hand, when a Stock and

**Table 4.1 Long-run cost of capital elasticity—Stock and Watson correction**

|  | Brazil | Korea | Mexico | Turkey |
|---|---|---|---|---|
| $\beta_r$ | 0.089 | 0.329 | 0.118 | -0.022 |
| OLS | (0.056) | (0.307) | (0.110) | (0.021) |
| $\beta_r$ | -0.722 | -3.770 | -0.565 | -0.102 |
| SW | (0.445) | (2.052) | (0.253) | (0.022) |

*Note:* The standard errors are in parentheses; the OLS standard errors are incorrect (as in most co-integrating regressions). OLS corresponds to the standard co-integrating regression, while SW is OLS on a system expanded with three lags of the first difference of the cost of capital measure. All equations include a linear time trend and a constant (not reported).
*Source:* Author's calculations.

**Figure 4.10   Actual and frictionless investment to capital stock ratios for
Brazil, Korea, Mexico, and Turkey**

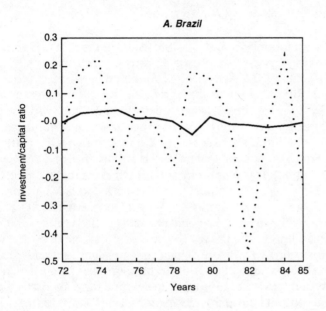

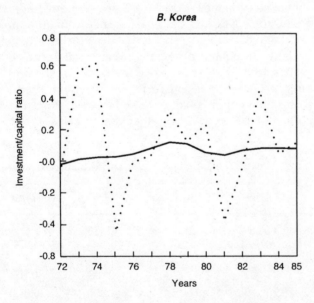

———————  Actual investment to capital stock ratio (N)

· · · · · ·  Frictionless investment to capital stock ratio (N$^f$)

Source: Author's elaboration.

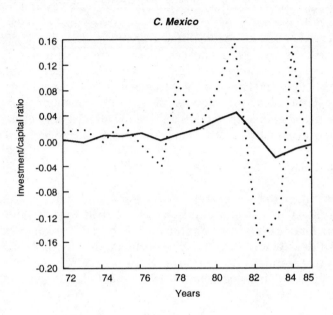

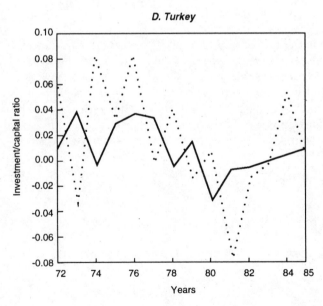

Watson-type correction is implemented by including three lags of the first difference of the cost of capital measure, the coefficients become large and negative, as expected for the long-run relation between capital and its cost.

The different panels of figure 4-10 depict the estimated paths of $N_t^f$ and the observed paths of $N_t$ for the different countries. It is apparent from these figures that the actual series are considerably smoother than a frictionless model implies. It is important to note, nonetheless, that adjustment costs affect both good and bad times; it is true that the response of investment to positive stimuli seems to be slow, consistent with conventional wisdom, but it is also true that investment falls more slowly than it does in an economy without irreversibility or other adjustment costs during bad times.

## Distributional dynamics

The dynamic part of the model—that is, estimation of the evolution of the cross-sectional density—is addressed next. Caballero (1993) shows that if the behavior of each $N_t^f$ can be approximated by a Brownian motion with a standard deviation $\sigma$, then the cross-sectional density of $Z_i$—when individual units are subject to nonconvex adjustment costs—can be characterized by the following stochastic partial differential equation:

$$(4\text{-}17) \qquad df(z,t) = (\delta dt + N_t^f)\, \frac{\partial f(z,t)}{\partial z} + \frac{\sigma^2}{2} \frac{\partial^2 f(z,t)}{\partial z^2}\, dt,$$

where $\delta$ is the rate of depreciation of the capital stock and the boundary conditions are to be determined once the particular type of prevalent adjustment cost is specified.

With the estimates of $N_t^f$ from the previous section, a discrete time approximation of the path of the cross-sectional density can be computed. Bertola and Caballero (1990a) show that in the case of irreversible investment being discussed here, the following system results:

$$(4\text{-}18)\; f(z, j) = \xi_j e^{-\xi_j z} + \int_{0+}^{\infty} A(\beta; j)\, e^{-\lambda_j(\beta)t} e^{-\xi_j z/2} \left[\cos(\beta z) - \frac{\xi_j}{2\beta}\sin(\beta z)\right] d\beta$$

$$(4\text{-}19)\; A(\beta; j) = \frac{2}{\pi(1 + \xi_j^2/4\beta^2)} \int_0^\infty f(z, j-1) e^{\xi_j z/2} \left[\cos(\beta z) - \frac{\xi_j}{2\beta}\sin(\beta z)\right] dz$$

where $j$ is the discrete time index (measured in years), $\lambda_j(\beta) \equiv (-\beta^2 + \xi_j^2/4)\,\theta/\xi_j$, and

$$\xi_j \equiv \frac{2(\delta + N_j^f)}{\sigma^2}.$$

Starting this system from an arbitrary density (chosen to match the ergodic probability density of an individual $Z_i$), and feeding the output of this system into a squared errors objective function, allows the only parameter that is left free at this stage, $\sigma$, to be estimated, and an estimated path

**Table 4.2: General statistics and second stage results**

|              | Brazil | Korea | Mexico | Turkey |
|--------------|--------|-------|--------|--------|
| $\sigma_a$   | 0.203  | 0.310 | 0.100  | 0.045  |
| $\sigma$     | 0.600  | 0.800 | 0.600  | 0.600  |
|              |        |       |        |        |
| $\sigma_{\hat{n}}$ | 0.033 | 0.089 | 0.017 | 0.011 |
| $\sigma_n$   | 0.030  | 0.033 | 0.018  | 0.020  |
| $\sigma_{nf}$ | 0.203 | 0.310 | 0.101  | 0.045  |

Note: All values are annual percents. $\sigma_a = \sigma_{nf}$ is the standard deviation of the frictionless aggregate. $\sigma_{\hat{n}}$ is the standard deviation of the fitted investment/capital ratio. $\sigma_n$ is the standard deviation of the actual investment/capital ratio.
Source: Author's calculations.

of the mean of the cross-sectional density to be recovered. The unbounded support nature of the irreversible investment case presents numerical problems, however, that yield an extremely flat objective function after a certain level of $\sigma$; for this reason a grid search approach is used in which the search is stopped at the minimum value of $\sigma$ within the flat region of the objective function. Table 4.2 presents the basic results. The first row shows that aggregate uncertainty—the standard deviation of $Nf$—ranges from a low of 5 percent a year for Turkey (about the same as that for the United States) to a high of 31 percent for Korea. The second row, on the other hand, shows that total uncertainty at the microeconomic level—as seen by the econometrician—is in the range of 60-80 percent a year. This combination of parameters yields a standard deviation of the fitted values of $Nt$, as indicated in the third row, that is not far from the observed standard deviation shown in the fourth row and that is considerably lower than the standard deviation of the frictionless series, shown in the bottom row. The model is therefore very successful in smoothing out aggregate shocks to approximate the behavior of actual investment.

The panels of figure 4-11 are more revealing than this table. They are identical to the panels of figure 4-10 but with the addition of the path of the investment/capital ratio implied by the model (dashed line). The results are fairly good, especially for Mexico.[10] Although far from perfect, these results are promising, particularly when taking into account all the short-comings of the data and the substantial scope for improvement, especially in the modelling of frictionless investment.

**Final remarks**

This chapter surveyed new developments in the theory and implementa-tion of models of aggregate investment in the presence of irreversibility

**Figure 4.11   Actual, frictionless, and predicted investment to capital
stock ratios for Brazil, Korea, Mexico, and Turkey**

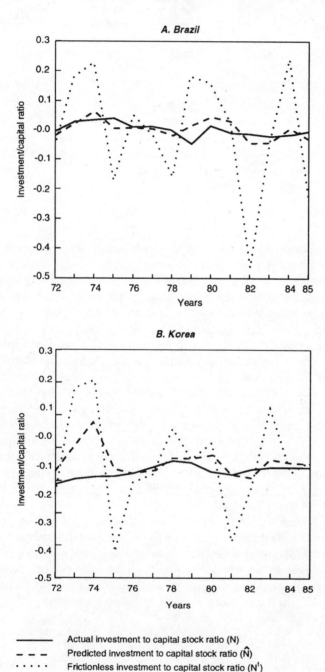

Source: Author's elaboration.

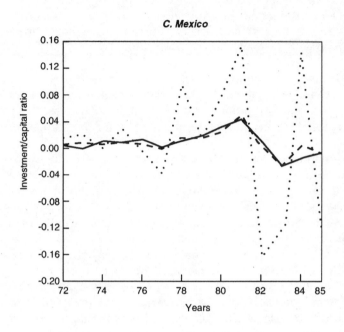

**C. Mexico**

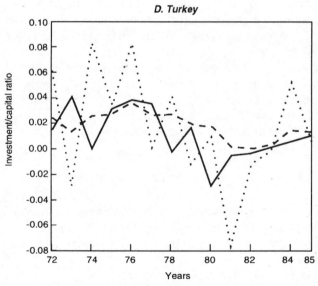

**D. Turkey**

constraints at the microeconomic level. From the aggregate point of view, other nonconvexities in adjustment cost technology behave quite similarly except for very large shocks. In developing countries, however, large events may be more common than rare, and the researcher should be particularly concerned with the main sources of adjustment costs at the microeconomic level.

The discussion omitted many realistic elements, two of which seem salient: changes in the level of uncertainty (either aggregate or idiosyncratic); and general equilibrium considerations. The reason for the omissions is technical, but at least partial remedy for the problems is close at hand.

As mentioned, the empirical evidence was used only to illustrate the basic procedures involved in the empirical implementation of these models. Nevertheless, the fit is surprisingly good for some of the countries. Although much work remains to be done, this result is encouraging.

One of the priorities of the empirical agenda should be a detailed description of the target model (that is, the model without adjustment costs). In particular, much effort should be put into the construction of measures of the cost of capital, particularly because of the significant imperfections in the capital markets in most developing countries. The likely complementarity between private and public capital should also be modelled at this stage. Efforts on these fronts should prove useful even if the adjustment cost models discussed here are not empirically relevant since, as shown, it is possible to recover medium- and long-run responses of capital to changes in its cost that are robust to the type of adjustment frictions firms face.

The theory reviewed here also suggests that microeconomic data may help in understanding aggregate dynamics to a degree beyond that of conventional representative agent theory. Any clue to the shape of the cross-sectional density at any point in time may considerably improve forecasting. Census data may soon become a more direct need for modern macroeconomists.

## Notes

1. I am grateful to Luis Servén, Andrés Solimano, and especially Sweder van Wijnbergen for their very useful comments.
2. However, this point holds true for most representative agent-type models.
3. Convex and differentiable at zero.
4. See Caballero (1991) and Bertola and Caballero (1990a) for a derivation of a profit function of this nature. Relaxing the log-linearity (on capital) assumption on the profit function makes the aggregation part of the problem much harder.
5. What is unambiguous, however, is that, relative to the frictionless case, the firm has too little capital in good times and too much in bad times.

Not surprisingly, the value of the firm is reduced by the presence of an irreversibility constraint.

6. It is important to note, however, that this similarity does not mean the higher moments of the shocks affecting firms can be recovered from the aggregate frictionless equation. These moments are important in assessing the effect of irreversibility constraints on firms' investment decisions.
7. The argument that aggregate gross investment is never equal to zero has been used on occasion to discredit the relevance of irreversibility constraints for macroeconomic phenomena. This criticism is, however, mostly the result of a misapplication of the representative agent framework.
8. This discussion is germane to any model in which adjustment costs play a role, convex or nonconvex.
9. The presence of non-observables adds all the problems of signal extraction; these issues are omitted here.
10. Note that the model does not have much chance of fitting well in the early periods, since the initial cross-sectional density (the ergodic one) is arbitrarily chosen. With larger sample sizes it is convenient to drop the first 10 percent or 15 percent of the observations from the likelihood (but not from the dynamic generation of the cross-sectional density).

## References

Abel, A. B. 1983. "Optimal Investment under Uncertainty." *American Economic Review* 73 (1):228-33.

Abel, A. B., and O. J. Blanchard. 1986. "The Present Value of Profits and Cyclical Movements in Investment." *Econometrica* 54 (2):249-73.

Arrow, K. J. 1968. "Optimal Capital Policy with Irreversible Investment," in J. N. Wolfe, ed., *Value, Capital and Growth. Papers in Honour of Sir John Hicks*. Edinburgh: Edinburgh University Press.

Bernanke, B. H. S. 1983. "Irreversibility, Uncertainty, and Cyclical Investment." *Quarterly Journal of Economics* 98 (1) (February): 85-106.

Bertola, G. 1988. "Adjustment Costs and Dynamic Factor Demands: Investment and Employment under Uncertainty." Ph.D. dissertation. Massachusetts Institute of Technology, Department of Economics, Cambridge, Mass.

Bertola, G., and R. J. Caballero. 1990a. "Irreversibility and Aggregate Investment." Columbia University Working Paper no. 488. New York City, New York.

———. 1990b. "Kinked Adjustment Costs and Aggregate Dynamics," in O. J. Blanchard and S. Fischer, eds., *NBER Macroeconomic Annual 1990*. Cambridge, Mass.: The MIT Press.

Caballero, R. J. 1990. "Adjustment Costs and Stock Elasticities: Small Sample Problems." Columbia University, Department of Economics, New York City, New York.

———. 1991. "On the Sign of the Investment-Uncertainty Relationship."
    *American Economic Review* 81 (1):279-88.
———. 1992. "A Fallacy of Composition." *American Economic Review* 82
    (5):1279-92.
———. 1993. "Expenditure on Durable Goods: An Explanation for Their
    Slow Adjustment." *Journal of Political Economy*, April.
Caballero, R. J., and E. M. R. A. Engel. 1991. "Dynamic S-s Economics."
    *Econometrica* 5 (6):1659-86.
———. 1993. "Heterogeneity and Output Fluctuations in a Dynamic Menu
    Cost Economy." *Review of Economic Studies* 60 (1):95-120.
Hayashi, F. 1982. "Tobin's Marginal q and Average q: A Neoclassical
    Interpretation." *Econometrica* 50 (1):213-24.
Ingersoll, J. E., Jr., and S. A. Ross. 1987. "Waiting to Invest: Investment and
    Uncertainty." Yale University, Department of Economics, New Haven,
    Conn.
Jorgenson, D. W. 1963. "Capital Theory and Investment Behavior."
    *American Economic Review Papers and Proceedings* 53:247-59.
Majd, S., and R. S. Pindyck. 1987. "Time to Build, Option Value, and
    Investment Decisions." *Journal of Financial Economics* 18 (1):7-27.
McDonald, R., and D. Siegel. 1986. "The Value of Waiting to Invest."
    *Quarterly Journal of Economics* 101 (4):707-27.
Nickell, S. 1974. "On the Role of Expectations in the Pure Theory of
    Investment." *Review of Economic Studies* 41 (1):1-19.
Pindyck, R. S. 1988. "Irreversible Investment, Capacity Choice, and the
    Value of the Firm." *American Economic Review* 78 (5):969-85.
Stock, J. H., and M. W. Watson. 1989. "A Simple MLE of Cointegrating
    Vectors in Higher Order Integrated Systems." NBER Working Paper
    no. 83. National Bureau of Economic Research, Cambridge, Mass.
    December.
Tobin, J. 1969. "A General Equilibrium Approach to Monetary Theory."
    *Journal of Money, Credit and Banking* 1 (1):15-29.

# 5

# Empirical Investment Equations for Developing Countries

## Martin Rama

Since the debt crisis, there has been increasing interest in the determinants of private investment in developing countries.[1] For industrialized countries, the literature on this topic is plentiful for both theoretical models (see the surveys by Nickell 1978 or Artus and Muet 1986) and empirical results with different specifications (see Abel 1980 or Artus and Muet 1984, among others). In contrast, studies on developing countries are partial and scattered.

Two main questions about private investment decisions in developing countries need to be addressed. The first, a theoretical one, concerns the variables on which decisions depend: are they the same as in industrialized countries, or should specific factors, arising from the different macroeconomic settings, be considered? The second question is empirical, having to do with available estimates: what can be learned from the applied research on the determinants of private investment in developing countries?

This paper provides a preliminary answer to both questions. The next section revisits the theoretical debate on the specific factors that should be taken into account in developing countries. The subsequent section introduces the main outcomes of that debate into a single analytical framework, which gives rise to different empirical equations depending on the assumptions made concerning some key features of the economy (such as market structure and credit rationing). The following section presents a classification of 31 empirical studies on investment in developing countries according to their chosen specification, and compares their estimates. A methodological proposal for further research, particularly as regards the impact that the economic instability characterizing most developing countries has on private investment, is discussed in the final section.

## Some specific issues

The literature on investment decisions in industrialized countries puts forward basically two arguments. The first one, which relates to changes in aggregate demand, gives rise to the "income accelerator." The second one concerns the relative prices of capital and labor (or more generally, variable inputs) and therefore profitability. The literature on private investment in developing countries considers not only these two arguments, but typically four others that arise from the specific features of these countries.

### Financial repression

Since the work of McKinnon (1973) and Shaw (1973), it has been widely accepted that a significant share of the firms in developing countries face credit rationing. This kind of quantity constraint may be relevant in industrialized countries also, as a result of the different information available to creditors and debtors. However, in addition to the information problem, developing countries are often characterized by administered interest rates that are set at "low" levels and by direct allocation of credit for the benefit of some firms. The impact of these policy choices on private investment is amplified by the weakness of the capital markets in developing countries, a situation that restrains the access of firms to additional equity capital.

According to this approach, in developing countries ceilings are more relevant than spreads for credit allocation. For this reason the individual firm does not face unlimited supplies of credit at a given interest rate, as would be the case in a Modigliani-Miller world. Moreover, unlimited supplies of credit with interest rates increasing in line with the firm's debt-to-equity ratio do not seem likely either. Instead, a firm has access (at best) to a given credit ceiling, but the interest rate does not depend on the amount borrowed.[2]

At the macroeconomic level, this possible constraint on the level of investment had been already considered by the two-gap model, developed in the 1960s by McKinnon (1964) and Chenery and Strout (1966), among others. This model assumes that domestic saving, the world demand for exports, and foreign financing are given. The sum of domestic saving and foreign financing puts an upper bound on total investment (thus giving rise to a saving gap), whereas the sum of exports and foreign financing sets up the maximum level of imports (leading to a foreign exchange gap). Since the first of these two gaps is related to interest rates that do not clear the market, its effects are quite similar to those arising from credit rationing.

Financial repression has an important consequence from the viewpoint of research. Despite the existence of an investment function, in some periods the observed capital accumulation could be determined by the amount of saving forthcoming at the prevailing interest rate. Therefore, the microeconomic foundations of investment decisions should be analyzed by means of an equilibrium-with-rationing approach, such as the one that characterizes disequilibrium models (see Malinvaud 1977).[3]

## Foreign exchange shortage

Since developing countries must import most capital goods, the kind of foreign exchange shortage considered by the two-gap model can be an additional constraint on private investment. This outcome would apply if balance-of-payment difficulties (associated, for instance, with the debt crisis) lead to the use of direct exchange allocation or to the establishment of import quotas. Such policy devices would introduce an upper bound on purchases of machinery and equipment, which are usually made abroad and cannot easily be replaced by domestic substitutes.[4]

The discussion on the determinants of private investment in developing countries would not be complete if such a potential constraint were not explicitly taken into account. From the point of view of empirical research, its consequences are similar to those of credit rationing. In both cases, the investment equation to be used must arise from an optimization problem that explicitly includes the possibility of quantity rationing.

## Lack of infrastructure

It is usually accepted that private investment can fall as a result of higher public investment when the latter rests on scarce financial resources. In industrialized countries, this crowding-out effect is induced by higher interest rates. In developing countries in which financial repression prevails, it can arise from a tight credit rationing at the prevailing administered interest rate. However, public investment could also impose a positive externality on private investment in countries characterized by a lack of infrastructure or by weaknesses in the provision of public goods. In this case, the accumulation of public capital would be complementary to private investment.

This ambiguous relationship between public and private investment presents a challenge to applied research. On the one hand, empirical estimates should provide an answer on whether or not the lack of infrastructure is important enough to give rise to a significant externality. On the other hand, these estimates should help decide whether the crowding-out effect dominates the positive externality, or the opposite.

## Economic instability

Some of the variables relevant for investment decisions fluctuate more in developing countries than in industrialized ones. In part the reason is their different economic structures, particularly as regards sectoral diversification. For instance, there may be important variations in the real exchange rate in countries whose exports are concentrated in a few raw materials or agricultural products. However, most of the instability that characterizes developing countries results from political and institutional factors. In fact, the larger changes in the real exchange rate often result from policy-induced over- or undervaluation of the domestic currency. The same holds true for the availability of credit, aggregate demand, and other variables whose level depends on sudden (and sometimes dramatic) changes in economic policy.

If firm owners are risk-averse, that instability will result in lower levels of investment because of the larger variance in expected profits. This outcome would also hold if investment were irreversible (at least partly), so as to give rise to sunk costs whenever capacity utilization fell (Pindyck 1988). Even if firm owners were risk-neutral and capital goods could be resold, however, there would be important consequences for empirical research. Dramatic changes in economic policy (such as the adoption of adjustment programs) put forward the Lucas critique. As such, different specifications should be used for the investment function, depending on prevailing macroeconomic conditions.

**An integrative framework**

Three of the issues discussed—financial repression, shortage of foreign exchange, and lack of infrastructure—can be introduced in a rigorous manner into the investment equations usually considered for empirical research. Here a single analytical model from which different specifications can be drawn is used for this purpose. As regards economic instability, the fourth issue, its consequences on the specification of empirical investment equations are discussed in the next to last section.

*Objective function and constraints*

Consider the investment decisions of a single representative firm that seeks to maximize the sum of its discounted dividends, or, tantamount, to maximize the rise in its market value, $\Delta V$, over a finite horizon. This dynamic feature of the investment decision can be taken into account by considering just two periods: present ($t$) and future ($t + 1$):

(5-1)    $\Delta V = (p_t.Q_t - w_t.L_t) + [v_t.KP_t - v_{t-1}.(1 + r_{t-1}).KP_{t-1}]$

$$- v_t.KP_t.(u_t + \frac{\Gamma}{2}.u_t^2)$$

$$+ \frac{1}{1 + r_t}.(p_{t+1}.Q_{t+1} - w_{t+1}.L_{t+1})$$

$$+ \frac{v_{t+1}.KP_{t-1}}{1 + r_t} - v_t.KP_t$$

where   $V$   = the market value of the firm
          $Q$   = output

$KP$ = capital stock
$L$ = employment level
$p$ = nominal price of output
$v$ = nominal market price of capital goods
$w$ = nominal wage
$r$ = discount rate (or nominal interest rate), which is treated as given,[5] and
$u$ = investment rate.

The first term on the right-hand side of equation (5-1) represents current profits in period t. The second one measures capital gains or losses during the first period that arise from changes in the market price of the firm's machinery and equipment. Since neither of these two terms depends on the level of investment, they are hereafter replaced by $Z_t$ and treated as given. The third term is a convex function of the investment rate, $u_t$, which is the ratio between gross investment, $IP_t$, and the capital stock, $KP_t$. The whole third term is equal to (larger than) $IP_t$ when the parameter $\Gamma$ is null (strictly positive).[6] The fourth term stands for the discounted value of future current profits, whereas the last one corresponds to capital gains or losses in the second period.

The firm's optimization problem includes a set of technological and economic constraints. Among the former is the motion law of capital stock, which depends on the investment level and the depreciation rate, $\delta$:

$$(5\text{-}2) \qquad KP_{t+1} = \frac{KP_t + IP_t}{1 + \delta} = KP_t \cdot \frac{1 + u_t}{1 + \delta} \quad , 0 \le \delta < 1.$$

The production function is the second technological constraint on investment decisions. Assume, for simplicity's sake, that

$$(5\text{-}3) \qquad Q_{t+1} = f(KG_{t-1}, KP_{t+1}, L_{t+1}) = KG^{\tau}_{t+1} \cdot KP^{\alpha}_{t+1} \cdot L^{\beta}_{t+1}$$

$$\tau \ge 0, \ 0 < \alpha < 1, \ 0 < \beta < 1$$

where $KG$ is the public sector's capital stock. $KG$ measures the level of development reached by the country's infrastructure. A larger $KG$ imposes a positive externality on private production whenever $\tau > 0$. To the contrary, where $\tau = 0$, equation (5-3) is just a standard Cobb-Douglas production function. Note, further, that $\beta = 0$ corresponds to the fixed coefficients case, with private capital stock as the scarce production factor.[7]

Economic constraints arise from the structure of the markets in which the firm operates. A quite general specification of the demand curve faced by the firm is the following:

$$(5\text{-}4) \qquad Q_{t+1} = (\frac{Y_{t+1}}{J}) \cdot (\frac{p_{t+1}}{P_{t+1}})^{-\sigma}$$

where $Y$ is aggregate demand, $J$ is the number of firms in the whole economy, $p$ is the nominal price of output and $P$ is the general price index. Therefore, $p/P$ is the relative price of the firm's output.[8]

Depending on the value of $\sigma$, different market structures are obtained. The firm operates in monopolistic competition when $\sigma > 1$, in which case $p_{t+1}$ is one of its control variables. Besides, it operates in a perfectly competitive market when $\sigma \to +\infty$, whereas it faces a sales constraint such as those considered by disequilibrium models when $\sigma = 0$. In these two cases, the price is given at the level $p_{t+1} = P_{t+1}$, so that it does not represent a control variable of the firm anymore.

Concerning the other markets, the discussion in the second section points out that credit and foreign exchange shortages are likely in developing countries. If the firm is unable to borrow beyond a certain limit, investment expenditures are bounded by:

$$(5\text{-}5) \qquad v_t.KP_t.(u_t + \frac{\Gamma}{2}.u_t^2) \le P_t.F_t$$

where $F$ is the financial resources available to the firm (the sum, measured in real terms, of internal financing, net credit, and additional equity capital).

The second possible quantity constraint relates to using the direct allocation of foreign exchange as a way to reduce purchases abroad. Assuming that a given share $\Phi$ of total investment must be imported, the rationing scheme implies:

$$(5\text{-}6) \qquad \Phi.IP_t \le \frac{x_t.A_t}{v_t}, 0 < \Phi \le 1$$

where $x$ is the nominal exchange rate and $A$ is the foreign currency available to the firm.[9] If quantity restrictions were used instead of an administered allocation of foreign exchange, $x_t.A_t/v_t$ would directly measure the allowed import quota.

*Monopolistic competition*

Assume that monopolistic competition prevails in the goods market ($\sigma > 1$) and that there are no investment costs ($\Gamma = 0$). By replacing equation (5-2) in (5-1), the firm's objective function can be rewritten as:

$$(5\text{-}7) \qquad \Delta V = Z_t + \frac{1}{1+r_t}.(p_{t+1}.Q_{t+1} - c_{t+1}.KP_{t+1} - w_{t+1}.L_{t+1})$$

with: $c_{t+1} \approx v_t.(\delta + r_t - (v_{t+1} - v_t)/v_t)$ since $\delta.r_t \approx 0$.

Here, $c_{t+1}$ is the standard analytical expression for the user cost of capital, that is, for the flow price of capital services. Indeed, $\delta$ is the depreciation charge per unit of capital, whereas $r_t - (v_{t+1} - v_t)/v_t$ can be seen as a real interest rate evaluated with respect to the market price of capital goods. The $c_{t+1}$ variable allows the intertemporal optimization problem to be transformed into a traditional static one.

The firm maximizes $\Delta V$ with respect to its future price $p_{t+1}$ and its future capital stock $KP_{t+1}$. Taking into account equations (5-3) and (5-4), the objective function becomes:

(5-8)
$$\Delta V = Z_t + \frac{1}{1+r_t} \cdot [p_{t+1}^{1-\sigma} \cdot (Y_{t+1}/J) \cdot P_{t+1}^{\sigma} - c_{t+1} \cdot KP_{t+1}$$
$$-w_{t+1} \cdot (Y_{t+1}/J)^{1/\beta} \cdot p_{t+1}^{-\sigma/\beta} \cdot P_{t+1}^{\sigma/\beta} \cdot KG_{t+1}^{-\tau/\beta} \cdot KP_{t+1}^{-\alpha/\beta}].$$

The first-order condition with respect to $p_{t+1}$ gives rise to a standard mark-up equation on labor costs:

(5-9)
$$\frac{p_{t+1}}{P_{t+1}} = (\frac{\sigma}{\sigma-\theta})^{\beta/\theta} \cdot (Y_{t+1}/J)^{(1-\beta)/\theta} \cdot KG_{t+1}^{-\tau/\theta} \cdot KP_{t+1}^{\alpha/\theta} \cdot (\frac{w_{t+1}}{P_{t+1}})^{\beta/\theta}$$

with $\Theta = \beta + (1-\beta)\sigma$. The mark-up ratio rises in line with aggregate demand and declines in line with both capital stock and (assuming $\tau > 0$) the country's infrastructure.

The firm's optimal capital stock is obtained by replacing this result in the first-order condition associated with $KP_{t+1}$:

(5-10)
$$KP_{t+1}^{(\alpha+\beta)+(1-\alpha-\beta)\sigma} = (\frac{\alpha}{\beta})^{\theta} \cdot (\frac{\sigma-\theta}{\sigma})^{\sigma} \cdot (\frac{Y_{t+1}}{J}) \cdot KG_{t+1}^{\tau(\sigma-1)} \cdot (\frac{c_{t+1}}{P_{t+1}})^{-\theta} \cdot (\frac{w_{t+1}}{P_{t+1}})^{-(\sigma-\theta)}.$$

For $KP_{t+1}$ to correspond to the maximum $\Delta V$, the second-order condition must also be fulfilled. Intuitively, where $\sigma > 1$, it is necessary to verify $\alpha + \beta < \sigma/(\sigma-1)$. Otherwise, the exponent of $KP_{t+1}$ in equation (5-10) would be negative, so that the optimal capital stock would increase with the user cost of capital, decrease with aggregate demand, and so forth.

The optimal investment rule under monopolistic competition is obtained by rewriting equation (5-10) in growth rates, hereafter indicated by a hat, ^. Provided that

(5-11)
$$K\hat{P}_{t+1} \approx \frac{IP_t}{KP_t} - \delta$$

(see equation 5-2), and replacing $\Theta$ by its analytical expression,

(5-12)
$$\frac{IP_t}{KP_t} = \delta + \phi_{R1} \cdot (\frac{\hat{Y}_{t+1}}{J}) + \phi_{R2} \cdot K\hat{G}_{t+1} + \phi_{R3} \cdot (\frac{\hat{c}_{t+1}}{P_{t+1}})$$
$$+ \phi_{R4} \cdot (\frac{\hat{w}_{t+1}}{P_{t+1}})$$

with: $\phi_{R1} = \dfrac{1}{(\alpha+\beta)+(1-\alpha-\beta)\sigma} > 0, \quad \phi_{R2} = \dfrac{\tau(\sigma-1)}{(\alpha+\beta)+(1-\alpha-\beta)\sigma} \geq 0,$

$$\phi_{R3} = \frac{\beta + (1 - \beta)\sigma}{(\alpha + \beta) + (1 - \alpha - \beta)\sigma} < 0, \quad \phi_{R4} \frac{\beta(\sigma - 1)}{(\alpha + \beta) + (1 - \alpha - \beta)\sigma} < 0.$$

The subscript *R* indicates that the coefficients correspond to the monopolistic competition model.

Equation (5-12) is the kind of analytical expression developed for industrialized countries by Blanchard (1988) or, in a more elaborate framework, by Sneessens (1987). Its main aim is to provide a microfoundation for the arguments usually considered when dealing with data. Indeed, the first term on the right-hand side of equation (5-12) can be seen as an income accelerator. Concerning the last two terms, they capture the effects of changes in relative factor prices.

What is added by equation (5-12) is the effect of a larger infrastructure on private investment (the second term). Thus, the equation captures one of the arguments of the literature on investment in developing countries discussed above. Such an effect arises from the specification of the production function and is embodied in coefficient $\phi_{R2}$, which is positive whenever $\tau > 0$.

Finally, notice that the structural parameters $\alpha$, $\beta$, $\tau$, and $\sigma$ can be drawn from the $\phi$ coefficients in equation (5-12):

(5-13)
$$\alpha = \frac{1 + \phi_{R3}}{\phi_{R1} + \phi_{R3} + \phi_{R4}}, \quad \beta = \frac{\phi_{R4}}{\phi_{R1} + \phi_{R3} + \phi_{R4}}$$

$$\tau = \frac{\phi_{R2}}{\phi_{R1} + \phi_{R3} + \phi_{R4}}, \quad \sigma = \frac{\phi_{R3} + \phi_{R4}}{\phi_{R1}}$$

Concerning $\delta$, no additional calculations are required.

*The "true" neoclassical case*

Deriving the optimal investment rule under perfect competition from equation (5-12) is straightforward. In this case, the firm faces an infinitely elastic demand curve ($\sigma \to +\infty$) at a given price ($p_{t+1} = P_{t+1}$). By using limits, equation (5-12) yields:

(5-14)
$$\frac{IP_t}{KP_t} = \delta + \phi_{N2} \cdot K\hat{G}_{t+1} + \phi_{N3} \cdot (\frac{\hat{c}_{t+1}}{P_{t+1}}) + \phi_{N4} \cdot (\frac{\hat{w}_{t+1}}{P_{t+1}})$$

with: $\phi_{N2} = \frac{\tau}{1 - \alpha - \beta} \geq 0, \quad \phi_{N3} = -\frac{1 - \beta}{1 - \alpha - \beta} < 0, \quad \phi_{N4} = -\frac{\beta}{1 - \alpha - \beta} < 0.$

The subscript $N$ indicates that the coefficients correspond to the "true" neoclassical model.

The restriction required on the production function parameters to fulfill the second-order condition is now $\alpha + \beta < 1$. These parameters verify:

$$(5\text{-}15) \qquad \alpha = \frac{1 + \phi_{N3}}{\phi_{N3} + \phi_{N4}} \,, \quad \beta = \frac{\phi_{N4}}{\phi_{N3} + \phi_{N4}} \,, \quad \tau = \frac{\phi_{N2}}{\phi_{N3} + \phi_{N4}} \,.$$

Investment rules such as the one represented by equation (5-14) have seldom been used in industrialized countries (an exception is the paper by Schramm 1972). One possible explanation is that the omission of an income accelerator effect leads to disappointing empirical results. In addition, what has usually been identified as the "neoclassical" investment function is a specification quite different from equation (5-14).

*Effective demand (the so-called "neoclassical model")*

At the opposite of perfect competition, it can be assumed that the firm faces quantity rationing in the goods market. This situation is likely to occur when prices are set by the government or when they result from prior contracts. In terms of equation (5-4), demand is fully inelastic with respect to relative prices ($\sigma = 0$) so that sales have to be taken as given at the level $Y_{t+1}/J$. Replacing $\sigma = 0$ in the $\phi$ coefficients of equation (5-12) yields the following investment rule:

$$(5\text{-}16) \qquad \frac{IP_t}{KP_t} = \delta + \phi_{K1} \cdot \left( \frac{\hat{Y}_{t+1}}{J} \right) + \phi_{K2} \cdot K\hat{G}_{t+1} + \phi_{K5} \cdot \left( \frac{\hat{c}_{t+1}}{w_{t+1}} \right)$$

with: $\quad \phi_{K1} = \dfrac{1}{\alpha + \beta} > 0, \ \phi_{K2} = -\dfrac{\tau}{\alpha + \beta} \leq 0, \ \phi_{K5} = -\dfrac{\beta}{\alpha + \beta} < 0$

and structural parameters $\alpha$, $\beta$, and $\tau$ given by:

$$\alpha = \frac{1 + \phi_{K5}}{\phi_{K1}} \,, \quad \beta = -\frac{\phi_{K5}}{\phi_{K1}} \,, \quad \tau = -\frac{\phi_{K2}}{\phi_{K1}} \,.$$

The subscript $K$ indicates that the coefficients correspond to the effective demand model. In this case, no restrictions are required on the returns to scale $\alpha + \beta$.

According to equation (5-16), if the firm faces a sales constraint, its investment rate is a decreasing function of the growth of the country's infrastructure ($\phi_{K2} \leq 0$). This Keynesian feature is in sharp contrast with the results arising from the market structures analyzed above. Therefore, it can be used to check whether the sales constraint is binding (a significantly positive estimate for $\phi_{K2}$ would suggest that actual $\sigma$ is not null).

Except for the role of the public sector's capital stock, equation (5-16) is quite similar to Jorgenson's (1963) investment rule. The latter, which has been widely used for empirical research in industrialized countries, is known as the "neoclassical model." The reason is that, unlike the "naive" income accelerator, it takes relative factor prices into account. However, equation (5-16) is also close to the investment rules arising from disequilibrium models (see, particularly, the analysis developed by Grossman 1972).

*The implicit approach (Tobin's q)*

Now assume there are significant investment costs, so that $\Gamma > 0$. Since the expected user cost of capital cannot be calculated anymore, the optimal investment rule will not depend on $c_{t+1}$. Instead, consider the following Lagrangian:

$$(5\text{-}17) \quad \mathcal{L} = Z_t + \frac{1}{1+r_t} \cdot (p_{t+1} \cdot Q_{t+1} - w_{t+1} \cdot L_{t+1}) - v_t \cdot KP_t \cdot (u_t + \frac{\Gamma}{2} \cdot u_t^2)$$

$$+ \frac{v_{t+1} \cdot KP_{t+1}}{1+r_t} - v_t \cdot KP_t + v_t^* \cdot (KP_t \cdot \frac{1+u_t}{1+\delta} - KP_{t+1})$$

where $v_t^*$ is the multiplier associated with the motion law of capital stock. The control variables are now $u_t$, $KP_{t+1}$, and $L_{t+1}$, which leads to the following first-order conditions:

$$(5\text{-}18) \quad 1 + \Gamma \cdot u_t = \frac{v_t^*}{v_t \cdot (1+\delta)}$$

$$(5\text{-}19) \quad v_t^* = \frac{1}{1+r_t} \cdot [p_{t+1} \cdot f'_{KP}(KG_{t+1}, KP_{t+1}, L_{t+1}) + v_{t+1}]$$

$$(5\text{-}20) \quad f'_L(KG_{t+1}, KP_{t+1}, L_{t+1}) = \frac{w_{t+1}}{p_{t+1}}$$

where ' is the first derivative with respect to the variable indicated in the subscript.

According to equation (5-19), the multiplier $v_t^*$ gathers the discounted effects of a larger capital stock on future current profits, but also on the resale price of the firm. Therefore, $v_t^*$ must be seen as the shadow price of additional capital. The right-hand side of equation (5-18) in turn is nothing but the *marginal* value of the q variable defined by Tobin (1969), since it measures the ratio between the shadow price of additional capital, $v_t^*$ (here, adjusted for depreciation), and its market price, $v_t$.

Replacing equation (5-19) into (5-18) leads to the following investment rule:

(5-21)     $$1 + \Gamma \cdot u_t = q_t = \frac{p_{t+1} \cdot f'_{KP}(KG_{t+1}, KP_{t+1}, L_{t+1}) + v_{t+1}}{v_t \cdot (1 + \delta) \cdot (1 + r_t)}$$

where $q$ is the marginal Tobin's ratio. The problem with equation (5-21) is that only *average* $q$ is statistically observable. Indeed, the value of the firm on the stock market provides information on the shadow price of existing capital goods, that is, on the sum of total discounted profits plus the resale price of total capital. It does not, however, necessarily provide information on the shadow price of investments to be made. This point can be seen by replacing the analytical expression of the demand curve (equation [5-4]) and the last first-order condition (equation [5-20]) into the right-hand side of equation (5-21), which yields, for marginal $q$:

(5-22)     $$q_t = \frac{1}{v_t \cdot (1 + \delta) \cdot (1 + r_t)} \cdot [\alpha \cdot \beta^{(\sigma - \theta)/\theta} \cdot KP_{t+1}^{-[(\alpha + \beta) + (1 - \alpha - \beta)\sigma]/\theta}$$

$$\cdot (\frac{Y_{t+1}}{J})^{1/\theta} \cdot KG_{t+1}^{\tau(\sigma - 1)/\theta} \cdot P_{t+1}^{\sigma/\theta} \cdot w_{t+1}^{-(\sigma - \theta)/\theta} + v_{t+1}].$$

Marginal $q$ is equal to the statistically observable $q$ only if the exponent of $KP$ in equation (5-22) is zero. This condition occurs when $\alpha + \beta = \sigma/(\sigma - 1)$, that is, when increasing returns to scale are exactly offset by the price decrease resulting from more output. This situation is, of course, very unlikely. However, the assumption $\alpha + \beta = \sigma/(\sigma - 1)$ has been widely used in the literature in the hypothesis of perfect competition in the goods market ($\sigma \to +\infty$). In this case, the required restriction on the production function parameters is $\alpha + \beta = 1$ (Hayashi 1982).[10]

For a given capital stock, $KP$, the average Tobin's ratio can be written, by definition, as:

(5-23)     $$\bar{q}_t(KP) = \int_0^{KP} (\frac{1}{KP}) \cdot q_t(k) \, dk$$

where $\bar{q}$ is the average Tobin's ratio. Replacing the analytical expression of marginal $q_t$ in equation (5-23) yields:

(5-24)     $$\bar{q}_t = q_t + \frac{(\alpha + \beta) + (1 - \alpha - \beta) \cdot \sigma}{(\sigma - 1) \cdot (1 + \delta)} \cdot \frac{p_{t+1} \cdot Q_{t+1}}{v_t \cdot (1 + r_t) \cdot KP_{t+1}}.$$

It is worth noting that this result does not hold when $\sigma = 0$, that is, when the firm faces quantity rationing in the goods market. Indeed, for any given price $p_{t+1} = P_{t+1}$, there exists a capital stock $KP_m$ such that the firm would no longer face a sales constraint if $KP$ were lower than $KP_m$. Hence, to discuss the case $\sigma = 0$, a more complicated relationship between average and marginal $q$ must be considered, in which the relevant demand curve is different depending on whether $KP$ is lower or higher than $KP_m$ (Precious 1985).

In equilibrium, all firms set the same price, since they all face the same optimization problem. Hence, $p_{t+1} = P_{t+1}$ and $Q_{t+1} = Y_{t+1}/J$. By replacing these two equalities into the analytical expression of average $q$, equation (5-21) leads to the following investment rule:

$$(5\text{-}25) \qquad\qquad \frac{IP_t}{KP_t} = \phi_{T6} \cdot (\bar{q}_{t+1}) + \phi_{T7} \cdot y_{t+1}$$

with:  $y_{t+1} = \dfrac{P_{t+1} \cdot (Y_{t+1}/J)}{v_t \cdot (1 + r_t) \cdot KP_{t+1}}$ , $\phi_{T6} = 1/\Gamma > 0$, $\phi_{T7} = -\dfrac{(\alpha + \beta) + (1 - \alpha - \beta) \cdot \sigma}{\Gamma \cdot (\sigma - 1) \cdot (1 + \delta)}$

where $y$ is the discounted average productivity of capital. The subscript $T$ indicates that the coefficients correspond to the implicit approach model.

Coefficient $\phi_{T7}$ is positive when $\alpha + \beta > \sigma/(\sigma - 1)$, that is, when increasing returns to scale more than offset the decrease in prices resulting from more output. Unfortunately, $\Gamma$ is the only structural parameter of the model that can be drawn from the $\phi$ coefficients in equation (5-25).

The investment rule represented by equation (5-25) is similar to the one discussed by Schiantarelli and Georgoutsos (1990). In both cases, the empirical equation bridges the gap between the statistically observable average $q$ and the relevant marginal $q$ by means of a variable or set of variables related to the business cycle. Indeed, the ratio $y_{t+1}$ can be seen as an indicator of the discounted average productivity of capital. In the case of a fixed coefficients technology ($\beta = 0$), it represents a proxy for capacity utilization (Licandro 1992). Thus, the inclusion of $y_{t+1}$ in the investment rule provides a rationale for a current practice in empirical Tobin's q studies for industrialized countries (see, for instance, von Furstenberg 1977; Malkiel, von Furstenberg, and Watson 1979; and Chan-Lee and Torres 1987).

*Credit rationing*

When a firm faces credit rationing, the constraint represented by equation (5-5) is binding. This equation can be rewritten as a polynomial of degree two in $u_t$:

$$(5\text{-}26) \qquad\qquad \frac{\Gamma}{2} \cdot u_t^2 + u_t - \frac{P_t \cdot F_t}{v_t \cdot KP_t} = 0$$

with the only positive root given by:

$$u_t = -\frac{1}{\Gamma} + \frac{1}{\Gamma} \cdot (1 + 2\Gamma \cdot \frac{P_t \cdot F_t}{v_t \cdot KP_t})^{1/2}$$

Taking a second-order Taylor expansion around $F_t = 0$, the following investment rule is obtained:

$$(5\text{-}27) \qquad \frac{IP_t}{KP_t} = \frac{P_t \cdot F_t}{v_t \cdot KP_t} + \phi_{F8} \cdot (\frac{P_t \cdot F_t}{v_t \cdot KP_t})^2$$

with: $\phi_{F8} = -\Gamma$. The subscript $F$ indicates that the coefficients correspond to the financial repression model.

The second term on the right-hand side of equation (5-27) is approximately zero when investment costs are not large, but strictly negative otherwise. Notice that no restriction is required on the parameters of the model. However, as in the implicit approach, the latter cannot be directly drawn from the coefficients of the reduced form.

Equations such as (5-27) are used in industrialized countries to account for the adjustment toward the optimal capital stock. The idea is that the fundamentals of investment decisions are aggregate demand and factor prices, whereas financial conditions affect the speed at which investment can be undertaken (see, for example, Gardner and Sheldon 1975). Consequently, there should be a positive coefficient for contemporary $F_t$ values but negative coefficients for lagged $F_t$ values, and credit rationing would not modify the investment level in the long run. This outcome would not necessarily hold in developing countries, if financial repression actually were a long-lasting obstacle to capital accumulation.

## Foreign exchange shortage

Finally, the firm can be rationed by the availability of foreign exchange. Provided that a given share $\Phi$ of total investment must be imported, this rationing sets the upper limit for purchases of machinery and equipment. Hence, equation (5-7) is binding and gives rise to the following investment rule:

$$(5\text{-}28) \qquad \frac{IP_t}{KP_t} = \phi_{x9} \cdot \frac{x_t \cdot A_t}{v_t \cdot KP_t}$$

with: $\phi_{x9} = 1/\Phi$. The subscript $X$ indicates that the coefficients correspond to the foreign exchange shortage model.

Once again, the main structural parameters of the model cannot be drawn from this equation.

## Main empirical findings

The discussion above shows that there are many competing specifications for the investment function depending on the values of some key parameters of the economy and on whether some quantity constraints are binding. Now the empirical performance of such equations must be considered.

### From theory to estimation

Table 5-1 summarizes the relationship between the theoretical models discussed above and the restrictions on the optimization problem of the representative firm. Each of the models is identified with a capital letter: $R$ for monopolistic competition without investment costs; $N$ for the "true" neoclassical case; $K$ for quantity rationing in the goods market; $T$ for the Tobin's $q$ approach; $F$ for credit rationing; and $X$ for a foreign exchange shortage. These letters are the same as in the $\phi$ coefficients of the corresponding investment rules, represented by equations (5-12), (5-14), (5-16), (5-25), (5-27), and (5-28).

The six theoretical models combine in different ways nine exogenous variables. Each of them is identified by a number, ranging from 1 (for the growth rate of demand) to 9 (for the availability of foreign exchange). Notice that these are the numbers associated with the $\phi$ coefficients in the six investment rules. For instance, the coefficient multiplying the growth rate of infrastructure is $\phi_{R2}$ in the monopolistic competition model, $\phi_{N2}$ in the neoclassical model, and $\phi_{K2}$ in the Keynesian model.

The theoretical investment rules are not used in their pure form for the empirical task. A first set of adjustments concerns time lags.[11] For instance, "time to build" has to be taken into account. Indeed, the theoretical models explain the decision to invest, whereas the data measure actual investment. The lag between both, which may be different from one investment project to another, arises because of delays required to choose, buy, receive, and install new capital goods. Therefore, aggregate $IP/KP_t$ should be related not only to the current values of the exogenous variables but also to their lagged values. An additional "timing" problem with the investment rules discussed above concerns expectations, which are not statistically observable. For this reason, variables such as $Y_{t+1}$, $KG_{t+1}$, and $w_{t+1}/P_{t+1}$ are replaced by distributed-lag functions relating their future level to their current and past values.

When time lags are considered, the six investment equations can be rewritten as in table 5-1.[12] In the latter, each of the $\phi$ coefficients is replaced by $\phi(L)$, with $L$ being an operator such that $Lx_t = x_{t-1}$ and $\phi(L)$ representing a polynomial expression of degree $k$ in $L$. It follows that $\phi(L).x_t$ is equal to $a_0.x_t + a_1.x_{t-1} + ... + a_k.x_{t-k}$. The long-term coefficient of $x_t$ in turn is the sum of the effects arising from $x_t, x_{t-1}, ..., x_{t-k}$, that is: $a_0 + a_1 + ... + a_k$, or, in a more compact notation, $\phi(1)$. Such a long-term coefficient should be equal to the $\phi$ coefficient of the theoretical model. This point is stated in the last column of table 5-1.

A second type of adjustment arises from aggregation. Each of the six investment equations is derived from the optimization problem of a single firm. However, it is intuitively clear that they can be combined to get mixed investment equations at the macroeconomic level. For instance, it could be assumed that a fraction $\mu$ of the firms does not face quantity rationing, either in the financial market or in the foreign exchange market. The investment rate, $u_t$, of these firms would therefore result from the theoretical models $R$, $N$, $K$, or $T$ depending on the values of parameters $\Gamma$ and $\sigma$ (say, $u_t = u_{it}$, with $i = R, N, K,$ or $T$). It could also be assumed that for a fraction $\Omega$ of the firms, the investment rate is bounded by the availability of credit ($u_t = u_{Ft}$). Finally, in the remaining firms, the foreign exchange shortage would be the binding constraint ($u_t = u_{Xt}$). Hence, the macroeconomic investment equation would be:

$$(5\text{-}29) \qquad u_t = \mu \cdot u_{it} + \Omega \cdot u_{Ft} + (1 - \mu - \Omega) \cdot u_{Xt}$$

with the analytical expressions of $u_{it}$, $u_{Ft}$, and $u_{Xt}$ given by table 5-1 and with $\mu$ and $\Omega$ possibly set equal to either 0 or 1 based on prior information, where $u_i$, $u_F$, and $u_X$ are investment rates.

The coefficients in equation (5-29) can be written as $\mu.\phi_i$ (with $i = R, N, K,$ or $T$), $\Omega.\phi_F$, and $(1 - \mu - \Omega).\phi_X$, with the same analytical expression for $\phi_i$, $\phi_F$, and $\phi_X$ as in table 5-1. In models $R$, $N$, and $K$, the structural parameters $\alpha$, $\beta$, $\tau$, and $\sigma$ could be drawn from the $\phi$ coefficients. This possibility is also true for parameter $\Gamma$ in both the $T$ and $F$ models and for parameter $\Phi$ in the $X$ model. In equation (5-29), however, the number of structural parameters is higher than the number of coefficients. Therefore, this second type of adjustment to the theoretical rules implies a significant loss of information on the key features of the economy.

Finally, the third type of adjustment is an ad-hoc attempt to take into account the economic instability characterizing most developing countries. Often, an additional variable is included in the chosen specification to measure the variance of some relevant macroeconomic aggregate, such as total output or returns on financial assets. Since increased economic instability should depress private investment, the expected sign of the $\phi$ coefficient associated with this tenth variable would be negative whatever the chosen specification.

*An overview of applied research*

The empirical studies on private investment in developing countries are not very numerous. It must be granted that standard macroeconometric models have been estimated in many countries to produce short-run forecasts. However, their investment equations are often specified in a rather ad-hoc way. For this reason the approach used in this study was to survey a set of 31 recent studies that deal specifically with the determinants of private investment in developing countries.[13] Their results are presented

**Table 5.1 Competing specifications for the investment equation**

| Model | Restrictions on the parameters | Quantity Constraints | | Empirical investment equation | Long-run coefficients |
|---|---|---|---|---|---|
| | | Credit | Exchange | | |
| R | $\Gamma = 0$ $\sigma = 1$ $\alpha + \beta < \dfrac{\sigma}{\sigma - 1}$ | No | No | $\dfrac{IP}{KP} = \delta + \phi_{R1}(L) \cdot \hat{Y} + \phi_{R2}(L) \cdot \hat{K}G +$ $+ \phi_{R3}(L) \cdot (\dfrac{\hat{C}}{P}) + \phi_{R4}(L) \cdot (\dfrac{\hat{W}}{P})$ | $\phi_{R1}(1) = \dfrac{1}{(\alpha+\beta)+(1-\alpha-\beta)\sigma}$ $\phi_{R2}(1) = \dfrac{\tau(\sigma-1)}{(\alpha+\beta)+(1-\alpha-\beta)\sigma}$ $\phi_{R3}(1) = \dfrac{-\beta-(1-\beta)\sigma}{(\alpha+\beta)+(1-\alpha-\beta)\sigma}$ $\phi_{R4}(1) = \dfrac{\beta-\beta\sigma}{(\alpha+\beta)+(1-\alpha-\beta)\sigma}$ |
| N | $\Gamma = 0$ $\sigma \to +\infty$ $\alpha + \beta < 1$ | No | No | $\dfrac{IP}{KP} = \delta + \phi_{N2}(L) \cdot \hat{K}G +$ $+ \phi_{N3}(L) \cdot (\dfrac{\hat{C}}{P}) + \phi_{N4}(L) \cdot (\dfrac{\hat{W}}{P})$ | $\phi_{N2}(1) = \dfrac{\tau}{1-\alpha-\beta}$ $\phi_{N3}(1) = -\dfrac{\beta}{1-\alpha-\beta}$ $\phi_{N4}(1) = -\dfrac{\beta}{1-\alpha-\beta}$ |

| Model | Restriction | | | Equation | Coefficients |
|---|---|---|---|---|---|
| K | $\Gamma = 0$ <br> $\sigma = 0$ | No | No | $\dfrac{IP}{KP} = \delta + \phi_{K1}(L)\cdot\hat{Y} +$ <br> $+\ \phi_{K2}(L)\cdot\dot{K}G + \phi_{KS}(L)\cdot\left(\dfrac{\hat{c}}{w}\right)$ | $\phi_{K1}(1) = \dfrac{1}{\alpha+\beta}$ <br> $\phi_{K2}(1) = -\dfrac{\tau}{\alpha+\beta}$ <br> $\phi_{KS}(1) = -\dfrac{\beta}{\alpha+\beta}$ |
| T | $\Gamma > 0$ <br> $\sigma > 1$ | No | No | $\dfrac{IP}{KP} = \phi_{T6}(L)\cdot(\bar{q}-1) + \phi_{T7}(L)\cdot y$ | $\phi_{T6}(1) = 1/\Gamma$ <br> $\phi_{T7}(1) = -\dfrac{(\alpha+\beta)+(1-\alpha-\beta)\sigma}{\Gamma(\sigma-1)(1+\sigma)}$ |
| F | No Restrictions | Yes | No | $\dfrac{IP}{KP} = \dfrac{P.F}{v.KP} + \phi_{F8}(L)\cdot\left(\dfrac{P.F}{v.KP}\right)^2$ | $\phi_{F8}(1) = -\Gamma$ |
| X | No Restrictions | No | Yes | $\dfrac{IP}{KP} = \phi_{X9}(L)\cdot\left(\dfrac{x.A}{v.KP}\right)$ | $\phi_{X9}(1) = 1/\Phi$ |

*Note:*

| | | |
|---|---|---|
| IP | = | Gross private investment |
| KP | = | Capital stock |
| Y | = | Aggregate demand |
| KG | = | Public sector's capital stock |
| c | = | Nominal user cost of capital |
| P | = | General price index |
| w | = | Nominal wage |
| $\bar{q}$ | = | Average Tobin's ratio |
| y | = | Average productivity of capital |
| F | = | Financial resources available for investment |
| v | = | Nominal market price of capital goods |
| x | = | Nominal exchange rate |
| A | = | foreign currency available for investment |
| $\hat{}$ | = | Growth rate |
| (L) | = | Lag operator |

Models:

| | | |
|---|---|---|
| R | = | Monopolistic competition |
| N | = | "True" neoclassical |
| K | = | Effective demand |
| T | = | Implicit approach |
| F | = | Financial repression |
| X | = | Foreign exchange shortage. |

*Source:* The author.

in table 5A.1 (at the end of the chapter), whose first column identifies the corresponding authors and dates. While this set of studies is not exhaustive, it includes a large variety of specifications, countries, and data sources and therefore provides a rather accurate picture of the state of the art.

As regards the countries, they are indicated in the second column of table 5A.1.[14] A look at the list suggests that the sample has some regional bias: the share of Latin American countries seems excessively high, whereas just a few African countries are considered. Such a bias could arise from the unavailability of data. Lack of data could also account for the fact that only two estimates are based on microeconomic information (see the third column). Nevertheless, the level of disaggregation in the remaining studies is sometimes significant. For instance, one of them uses information at the three-digit level, whereas two others distinguish between small and large firms. Concerning the frequency of the series, only three of the studies employ quarterly information; the others are based on annual data.

The fifth column indicates the specification of the investment equation. Although the theoretical grounds provided by the authors may be different from those presented in the third section of this paper, in comparing the results table 5A.1 is only concerned with the exogenous variables considered in each case (1 to 9 in terms of the $\phi$ coefficients).[15] Depending on the studies, these variables are sometimes lagged one period. More frequently, the investment equation includes a partial adjustment process (this is true in 11 cases).

In eight of the studies, the chosen specification corresponds to a "pure" model ($R, N, K, T, F,$ or $X$ in terms of table 5-1), the "pure" effective demand specification being the only one not represented in the sample. In the remaining cases, instead of a single model, linear combinations of two or more specifications are used, as in equation (5-29). Most of them include credit as an argument, a fact that shows the wide acceptance of the $F$ model for developing countries.

The fit of the estimated equations, measured by the adjusted coefficient of determination, can be found in the last column of table 5A.1.[16] Whereas the average coefficient is quite low (about 0.7), there are large differences between studies, ranging from 0.08 to 0.99. However, care is needed when assessing these results. On the one hand, low coefficients are quite common when using panel data, the case with the lowest reported value. On the other hand, some of the best fits correspond to estimates in which the endogenous variable (fourth column) is not scaled, so that a high coefficient of determination could just reflect a spurious correlation between trending variables.[17]

*Estimated coefficients*

The columns numbered 1 through 10 in table 5A.1 embody the exogenous variables that may affect private investment decisions in developing countries. The estimated sign of the corresponding $\phi$ coefficients in each of the studies is indicated by "+" or "-" when they are not statistically significant, and by "++" or "--" when they are significant at the 5 percent level.[18] Since 23 of the studies are based on mixed investment rules (such as equation [5-29]), there is almost no information on the structural parameters of the model. An attempt was made to draw their values from the $\phi$ coefficients of the remaining seven studies, but the results were rather discouraging and are not discussed here. Instead, some regularities in the sign and significance of the estimated coefficients are noteworthy.

Aggregate demand appears as an important variable in explaining private investment. Included in all but eight of the studies, its coefficient is always positive and almost always statistically significant. The implication is that the pure neoclassical model (in which there is no income accelerator) may not be appropriate for developing countries. However, these results need to be treated with care because of the spurious correlation problem mentioned above: if investment is not scaled (by the capital stock, for instance), aggregate output could just be acting as a trend.

Concerning public investment, although most of the studies discuss its crowding-out effects, only 11 account for the possibility of an externality on private investment.[19] The corresponding coefficient has the "right" sign in seven cases, a reflection of a positive value of parameter $\tau$. In the study by Gupta (1984), the coefficient is negative even though the model is not based on the $K$ specification (it does not consider the rental/wage ratio as an argument). The opposite is true for the study by Sundararajan and Thakur (1980), in which the empirical investment equation includes model $K$ but leads to a positive coefficient for public investment. In both cases, this point would mean that the development of infrastructure gives rise to a negative externality ($\tau < 0$), a rather surprising outcome.[20] In fact, the results could reflect a wrong appraisal of the structure of the goods market.

As regards relative factor prices, table 5A.1 depicts a more disappointing panorama. Very often, they are not even taken into account in the empirical investment equations. Besides, in most cases they are not measured as required. In particular, this problem occurs with the user cost of capital, which is defined in the proper way only in five cases. In the remaining studies, it is replaced by a large variety of proxies, such as the ex-post real interest rate, the actual or expected inflation rate, the relative price of capital goods, and the ratio of assets to liabilities. The corresponding coefficients generally have the "right" sign, although they are not always statistically significant.

Four studies avoid taking factor prices explicitly into account, choosing instead the implicit approach, either in its pure form or combined with the $F$ model. In all the cases, the coefficient of the q variable is positive and highly significant. Two of the studies also include a business-cycle indicator, which "corrects" the observable average $q$ and leads to the (relevant) marginal $q$. The corresponding coefficients are positive and statistically significant, evidence that increasing returns to scale more than offset the effect of a downward-sloping demand curve. These results suggest that the implicit approach may be a useful device in developing countries, in spite of the weakness of their capital markets.

The availability of credit also emerges from table 5A.1 as one of the decisive arguments for private investment in many developing countries. Indeed, financial variables are included in 21 of the studies, and the corresponding coefficients almost always have the right sign and are generally significant. However, as was the case with relative factor prices, financial variables are sometimes measured in quite misleading ways. In particular, instead of credit availability (which is related to savings, banking system regulations, and other factors), most of the studies consider actual credit, which represents just the "short side" of the financial market. In this case, the estimated coefficients do not convey information on whether investment decisions are determined by actual credit or the opposite. Therefore, care is needed when assessing the financial repression hypothesis from the results reported in table 5A.1.

Eight of the studies take the availability of foreign exchange into account by means of a large variety of statistical indicators, among them exports, international reserves, and the real exchange rate. The corresponding coefficients always have the right sign and are almost always significantly positive. However, a rise in the chosen statistical indicators could reflect sound and sustainable domestic economic policies. Expected profitability should therefore increase, even though aggregate demand, current factor prices, and other factors remain unchanged in the short run. If this situation pertained, the chosen balance-of-payment variables could account for the "investment climate," but not necessarily for quantity rationing.

Finally, seven studies include additional indicators for economic instability. In some cases, these are dummy variables that reflect economic policy changes or uncertainties. Other studies measure instability through the standard deviations of either relative prices, aggregate output, or stock market yields. In all the cases, the corresponding coefficients have the expected sign and are statistically significant.

## Dealing with economic instability

The results reported in table 5A.1 provide some support to the theoretical arguments discussed in the second and third sections concerning the determinants of private investment in developing countries. In particular, the estimated coefficients often have the right sign and are generally significant. The fit of the equations is not, however, fully satisfactory. One of the reasons could be the aggregation criteria used to get a single equation from many different investment rules. Aggregation raises specific problems in the context of economic instability, such as that characterizing most developing countries.

The most general specification (equation [5-29]) was obtained by assuming that a share, $\mu$, of the firms did not face quantity rationing, whereas for shares $\Omega$ and $1 - \mu - \Omega$, investment was determined by the availability of credit and foreign exchange, respectively. Parameters $\mu$ and $\Omega$ could possibly be set equal to zero or one based on prior information, but they had to be constant for the whole period studied. However, it is intuitively clear that $\mu$ and $\Omega$ could rise or fall significantly if economic policy were sharply modified. For example, monetary tightness could increase the share of firms that face credit rationing, while the adoption of exchange rate controls could increase the share of firms constrained by available foreign currency. In this section, a rigorous aggregation procedure is used to deal with these changes.

The theoretical analysis presented in the third section holds at the level of any single firm $j$, with $j = 1, 2, ..., J$. Thus, the firm's investment rate is $u_{jt} = (u_i)_{jt}$, with $i = R, N, K$, or $T$ if no quantity constraint is binding. If, to the contrary, firm $j$ is rationed in the credit market, its investment rate is $u_{jt} = (u_F)_{jt}$. Finally, $u_{jt} = (u_X)_{jt}$ if firm $j$ faces a foreign exchange shortage.[21] This can be written as:

$$(5\text{-}30) \qquad u_{jt} = \text{Min}\,[(u_i)_{jt}, (u_F)_{jt}, (u_X)_{jt}]$$

where Min is the minimum operator.

The investment rates $(u_i)_{jt}, (u_F)_{jt}$, and $(u_X)_{jt}$ will generally differ from one firm to another, depending on their capital stock and their access to financial resources and foreign currency. This heterogeneity is captured by the following multiplicative model:

$$(5\text{-}31) \qquad (u_i)_{jt} = (u_i)_t . s_{ij}, \, (u_F)_{jt} = u_{Ft} . s_{Fj}, \, (u_X)_{jt} = u_{Xt} . s_{Xj}$$

where $s$ is firm-specific stochastic disturbances. In equation (5-31), $u_{it}, u_{Ft}$, and $u_{Xt}$ are aggregate investment functions such as those considered in table 5-1. Hence, they only depend on macroeconomic variables, such as aggregate demand and average factor prices (the reason that the "$j$" index is set aside). Concerning $s_i, s_{Fj}$, and $s_{Xj}$, they represent positive disturbances that differ from one firm to another but that do not change over time (therefore, the "$t$" index can be omitted). Depending on their specific disturbances, some firms will be able to attain their desired investment rates, whereas others will be constrained either by credit or by foreign exchange.

Assume that $s_i, s_F$, and $s_X$ can be treated as independent stochastic variables, and let $h_i(s), h_F(s)$, and $h_X(s)$ be their corresponding density functions. In this case, the aggregate investment rate is given by the following mean of equation (5-30):

$$(5\text{-}32) \quad u_t = \int_0^{+\infty} \int_0^{+\infty} \int_0^{+\infty} \text{Min}\,\{u_{it}s_{ij}, u_{Ft}s_{Fj}, u_{Xt}s_{Xj}\} . h_i(s_i)h_F(s_F)h_X(s_X)ds_ids_Fds_X$$

where $h$ are the density functions. If, in addition, $h_i(s), h_F(s)$, and $h_X(s)$ can be approximated by the same Weibull law with unit mean, it can be shown that equation (5-32) becomes:

(5-33)                         $$u_t = [u_{it}^{-\pi} + u_{Ft}^{-\pi} + u_{Xt}^{-\pi}]^{-1/\pi}$$

(see Gouriéroux, Laffont, and Monfort 1984, p. 28).

In equation (5-33), the $\pi$ parameter ($\pi > 0$) arises from the Weibull law and is higher the lower the variance of disturbances $s_i$, $s_F$, and $s_X$. Notice that for $\pi \to +\infty$, the right-hand side of equation (5-33) becomes a minimum condition. In economic terms, the variance of the $s_i$, $s_F$, and $s_X$ disturbances is zero, so that for given levels of $u_{it}$, $u_{Ft}$, and $u_{Xt}$, all the firms are in the same situation. Consequently, there are no aggregation problems, and the investment rate for the whole economy is just the lowest of three different rates arising from competing specifications, which can all be expressed in the same way as for a single representative firm.[22]

Equation (5-33) is close to the investment rule developed by Lambert (1986). In his model, the optimal capital stock can be explained by two competing specifications, while an error correction mechanism leads to the investment equation to be estimated. However, the Lambert model is only concerned with shortages in the goods market (in terms of the third section, the competing specifications would be models $K$ and $N$). Equation (5-33), to the contrary, allows for a wider range of constraints on the optimization problem of firms.

Equation (5-33) is also close to the kind of weighted average represented by equation (5-29), on which stands most of the applied research discussed in the fourth section. However, there are two important differences between these two specifications. First, in equation (5-33) parameter $\pi$ is estimated simultaneously with the $\phi$ coefficients in $u_{it}$, $u_{Ft}$, and $u_{Xt}$. Since the values of the structural parameters of the model are to be drawn from these coefficients, equation (5-33) avoids the loss of information that characterized equation (5-29).

The second difference concerns the $\mu$ share of nonconstrained firms and the $\Omega$ share of firms facing credit rationing. In equation (5-29) these shares are constant. In equation (5-33), in contrast, they both change over time, their optimal estimates for period t being:

(5-34)                    $$\mu_t = [\frac{u_{it}}{u_t^*}], \Omega_t = [\frac{U_{Ft}}{u_t^*}]^{-\pi}$$

where $u_i$ and $u_F$ are investment rates and $u_t^*$ is the forecast of the aggregate investment rate (see Sneessens and Drèze 1986). Once the parameter $\pi$ and the $\phi$ coefficients in $u_{it}$, $u_{Ft}$, and $u_{Xt}$ have been estimated, these shares can be easily calculated. Therefore, equation (5-33) allows a more accurate analysis of the determinants of private investment. For example, there could be a depressed investment rate in some periods because of generalized credit rationing (that is, because of a low $u_{Ft}$), while in other periods the same outcome could arise because of low profitability (low $u_{it}$). Such shifts are not observable when equation (5-29) is used for empirical research.

As a result, equation (5-33) allows an analysis of the changing effects of economic policy measures depending on the current situation. For instance, when an important share of the firms face credit rationing ($\Omega_t$ is large), higher public investment could lead to a significant crowding-out of private investment. On the contrary, when private investment is low because of depressed profitability ($\mu_t$ is large), development of the country's infrastructure would have a positive impact because it imposes an externality on private profits.

## Concluding remarks

The determinants of decisions on private investment in developing countries are not necessarily the same as in industrialized countries. The discussion above points out issues specific to developing countries that arise from their different macroeconomic and institutional setting, such as financial repression, shortages of foreign exchange, lack of infrastructure, and a significant economic instability. The empirical studies provide some support for these arguments. Hence, their careful introduction into the theoretical models from which investment equations are drawn deserves further research. This conclusion pertains in particular to the intertemporal dimension of the analysis, restrained in this paper to a simple two-period framework.

With a few exceptions, the empirical studies are not fully satisfactory. The endogenous variable is seldom scaled, as the theoretical models require, so that it probably contains a time trend. Moreover, some key exogenous variables, such as the user cost of capital, are measured in misleading ways. The same holds true for the upper bounds on the availability of credit and foreign exchange, which define two quantity constraints particularly relevant in developing countries. This measurement issue also deserves further research.

Finally, the paper stresses the importance of the aggregation procedure in the context of significant economic instability. Sudden and dramatic policy changes give relevance to the Lucas critique, since they modify the investment rule. By raising or decreasing the share of firms that face a rationing of credit or foreign exchange, these changes preclude the representative firm approach. The paper includes a methodological proposal to deal with this problem. Applied research would help decide whether the suggested procedure improves the econometric performance of empirical investment equations in developing countries.

# Appendix 5A.

The following table compares results of empirical studies on investment in developing countries.

## Table 5A.1  Empirical studies on investment in developing countries

| Study | Countries | Data | Endogenous variable | Model specification | Aggregate demand (1) | Public capital stock (2) | Relative factor prices (3),(4),(5) |
|---|---|---|---|---|---|---|---|
| Behrman (1972) | Chi | Macro (6 sectors) Annual 1945-65 | $IP_t$ | R One equation for each sector | VAR.: $YP_t^*/YP_t$ (Omitted for manufacturing sector) | Omitted | VAR.: $YP_t \cdot \dfrac{d(c/P)_t}{dt}$ COEF.: -- |
| Bilsborrow (1977) | Col | Micro (22 manuf. firms) Annual 1950-64 | $\hat{KP}_t$ | R,F,X Variables are means across the 22 firms | VAR.: $\hat{YP}_{t-1}$ COEF.: ++ | Omitted | VAR.: Minus the assets-to-liabilities ratio in t-1. Estimates for individual firms only. COEF.: - |
| Blejer & Khan (1984) | Arg Bar Bol Bra Chi Col Cos Dom Ecu Gua Hai Hon Ins Kor Mal Mex Pan Par Sin Sri T&T Tha Tur Ven | Macro Annual 1971-79 | $IP_t$ | K,F With a lagged IP + a dummy for each country | VAR.: $Y_{t-1}$ COEF.: ++ | VAR.: $IG_t$ COEF.: -- | Omitted |
| Chhibber & Shafik (1992) | Ins | Macro Annual 1974-87 | $IP_t$ | R,X With a lagged KP | VAR.: $Y_{t-1}$ COEF.: ++ | Omitted | VAR.: $\hat{r}_t - P_t$ COEF.: -- VAR.: $v_{t-1}/P_{t-1}$ COEF.: -- |
| Chhibber & van Wijnbergen (1992) | Tur | Macro Annual 1970-86 | $IP_t$ | R,F | VAR.: $Y_{t-1}$ COEF.: ++ | VAR.: Share of infrastructure investment in public investment in t-3 COEF.: + | VAR.: $\hat{r}_t - P_t$ COEF.: -- |
| Dailami (1987a) | Bra | Macro Annual 1958-84 | $dIP_t/dt$ | R With a lagged endogenous variable | VAR.: $dY_t/dt$ COEF.: ++ | Omitted | VAR.: $d(c/P)_t/dt$ COEF.: - VAR.: $d(w/P)_t/dt$ COEF.: + |
| Dailami (1987b) | Kor | Macro Annual 1963-83 | $\dfrac{IP_t}{KP_t}$ | T,F | Omitted | Omitted | Omitted |
| Dailami (1992) | Col | Macro Annual 1971-86 | $IP_t$ | R,F With a lagged endogenous variable | VAR.: $\hat{Y}_t$ COEF.: ++ | Omitted | Omitted |

| Average Tobin's $\bar{q}$ (6) | Business-cycle indicators (7) | Credit availability (8) | Foreign exchange availability (9) | Economic instability (10) | Source, fit and technique |
|---|---|---|---|---|---|
| Omitted | Omitted | Omitted | Omitted | VAR.: Standard deviation of relative output price over three years COEF.: -- | Reported coefficients are for the manufacturing sector (equation Man 3) $\bar{R}^2 = 0.59$ (ML + Hall & Sutch for lags). |
| Omitted | Omitted | VAR:$(P.F/v.KP)_{t-1}$ With F = firms' internal funds COEF.: ++ | VAR.: $A_t$ With A = international reserves in t-1 + exports in t COEF.: ++ | Omitted | From equation (7): time-series. $\bar{R}^2 = 0.50$ (OLS) |
| Omitted | Omitted | VAR.: $dF_t/dt$ Change in actual credit + net capital inflows to private sector COEF.: ++ | Omitted | VAR.: $Y_t - Y_t^*$ (Intended to capture cyclical fluctuations) COEF.: -- | From equation (21). $\bar{R}^2 = 0.93$ (OLS; grid search for AR parameter) |
| Omitted | Omitted | Omitted | VAR.: Real exchange rate in t-1 COEF.: ++ | Omitted | From table (2). $\bar{R}^2$ not reported. (OLS) Coefficients from the cointegrating vector. |
| Omitted | Omitted | VAR.: $F_t/Y_t$ With F = credit to private sector COEF.: ++ | Omitted | Omitted | From equation (2.2) in Table 2. $\bar{R}^2 = 0.68$ (2SLS) |
| Omitted | Omitted | Omitted | Omitted | VAR.: Risk premium (stock market volatility) COEF.: -- | From equat. (20) (unconstr. estimates, Table 2) $\bar{R}^2 = 0.39$ (ML; grid search for AR parameter) |
| VAR.: $\bar{q}_t$ COEF.: ++ | Omitted | VAR.: Estimated shadow price of additional credit COEF.: ++ | Omitted | Omitted | From equation (15). $\bar{R}^2$ not reported. (ML) |
| Omitted | Omitted | VAR.: $F_t$ With F = total loans from financial institutions COEF.: ++ | Omitted | Omitted | From equation (4) in Table 2. $\bar{R}^2 = 0.49$ (OLS) |

## Table 5A.1   Empirical studies on investment in developing countries (continued)

| Study | Countries | Data | Endo-genous variable | Model specifi-cation | Aggregate demand (1) | Public capital stock (2) | Relative factor prices (3),(4),(5) |
|---|---|---|---|---|---|---|---|
| Dailami & Walton (1992) | Zim | Macro Annual 1970-87 | $IP_t$ | R | VAR.: $\hat{Y}_t$ COEF.: ++ | Omitted | VAR.: $v_t/P_t$ COEF.: -- <br> VAR.: $r_t - \hat{P}_t$ COEF.: -- |
| de Melo & Tybout (1986) | Uru | Macro Annual 1962-83 | $IP_t$ / $Y_t$ | R,F,X With a lagged endogenous variable | VAR.: $\hat{Y}_t$ COEF.: + <br> VAR.: $Y_{t-1}$ COEF.: ++ | Omitted | VAR.: $r_t - \hat{P}_t$ COEF.: - |
| Fry (1980) | 61 developing countries | Macro Annual 1964-76 | $IP_t + IG_t$ / $Y_t$ | R,F,X A lagged endogenous variable + a dummy for each country | VAR.: $\hat{Y}_t$ COEF.: ++ | Omitted | VAR.: $- P_t/P_t^e$ COEF.: -- |
| Galbis (1979) | Arg Bol Bra Col Cos Dom Ecu Gua Hon Mex Nic Pan Par Per Sal Uru | Macro Annual 1961-73 | $IP_t$ / $Y_t$ | N One equation for each country | Omitted | VAR.: $IG_t/Y_t$ COEF.: + | VAR.: $- \hat{P}_t$ COEF.: - |
| García (1987) | Bra Uru Ven | Macro Annual 1970-85 | $IP_t$ | R,F One equation for each country | VAR.: $Y_t/Y_t^*$ COEF.: ++ | Omitted | Omitted |
| Green & Villanueva (1990) | Arg Bol Bra Chi Col Cos Ecu Gua Ind Ken Kor Mex Pak Per Phi Sin Sri Tha Tun Tur Uru Ven Zim | Macro Annual 1975-87 | $IP_t$ / $Y_t$ | R,X With a dummy intercept for each country | VAR.: $\hat{Y}_{t-1}$ COEF.: ++ | VAR.: $IG_t/Y_t$ COEF.: ++ | VAR.: $r_t - \hat{P}_{t+1}$ COEF.: -- |
| Gupta (1984) | Arg Bol Col Cos Dom Ecu Gua Hon Ind Ins Kor Mal Mex Pak Pan Par Per Phi Sal Sin Sri Tai Tha Uru Ven | Macro Annual 1967-77 | $IP_t$ | R,F Estimated for full sample and 3 country groups | VAR.: $Y_t$ COEF.: ++ | VAR.: $IG_t$ COEF.: -- | VAR.: $r_t$ COEF.: -- <br> VAR.: $- \hat{P}_t^e$ COEF.: -- |
| Leff & Sato (1988) | Arg Bol Bra Chi Col Cos Dom Gua Guy Hai Hon Jam Mex Nic Pan Par Per Sal T&T Uru Ven | Macro Annual 1955-83 | $IP_t + IG_t$ | R,F One equation for each country | VAR.: $dY_t/dt$ COEF.: ++ | Omitted | VAR.: $- \hat{P}_t^e$ COEF.: -- |

| Average Tobin's $\bar{q}$ (6) | Business-cycle indicators (7) | Credit availability (8) | Foreign exchange availability (9) | Economic instability (10) | Source, fit and technique |
|---|---|---|---|---|---|
| Omitted | Omitted | Omitted | Omitted | Omitted | From equation (1)<br><br>$\bar{R}^2 = 0.82$<br><br>(OLS) |
| Omitted | Omitted | VAR.: Real money growth<br>COEF.: + (t)<br>COEF.: ++ (t-1) | VAR.: Real exchange rate<br>COEF.: + | Omitted | Includes a significant dummy for financial liberalization. From Table 7, column 4<br>$\bar{R}^2 = 0.82$<br>(IV) |
| Omitted | Omitted | VAR.: $F_t/Y_t$<br>COEF.: +<br>VAR.: $F_t/Y_t$<br>COEF.: ++<br>With F = domestic credit | VAR.: $A_t/Y_t$<br>With A = foreign exchange receipts<br>COEF.: ++<br>VAR.: purchasing power of exports<br>COEF.: ++ | Omitted | From equation (4) in Table 3.<br>$\bar{R}^2 = 0.68$<br>(2SLS) |
| Omitted | Omitted | Omitted | Omitted | Omitted | From equation (2) Reported coefficients are averages for the 16 countries.<br>$\bar{R}^2 = 0.23$<br>(OLS) |
| Omitted | Omitted | VAR.: $F_{t-1}$<br>With F = real non wage income.<br>COEF.: ++ | Omitted | Omitted | From equation (7) (reported coefficients correspond to Brazil).<br>$\bar{R}^2 = 0.94$<br>(OLS) |
| Omitted | Omitted | Omitted | VAR.: Foreign debt service/exports.<br>COEF.: -- | VAR.: Foreign debt/output<br>COEF.: --<br>VAR.: $P_t$<br>COEF.: -- | From equation (1) in Table 4.<br>$\bar{R}^2 = 0.81$<br>(IV) |
| Omitted | Omitted | VAR.: $F_t$<br>With F = private savings in financial assets.<br>COEF.: ++ | Omitted | Omitted | Coefficients correspond to 8 low-inflation countries.<br>$\bar{R}^2$ not reported.<br>(2SLS) |
| Omitted | Omitted | VAR.: $dF_t/dt$<br>With F = stock of real credit.<br>COEF.: ++ | Omitted | Omitted | From equation (5) Reported coefficients are averages for the 21 countries.<br>$\bar{R}^2$ not reported.<br>(3SLS) |

## Table 5A.1   Empirical studies on investment in developing countries (continued)

| Study | Countries | Data | Endo-genous variable | Model specifi-cation | Aggregate demand (1) | Public capital stock (2) | Relative factor prices (3),(4),(5) |
|---|---|---|---|---|---|---|---|
| Love (1989) | Bra Col Cos Eth Gha Gua Hon Mex Mor Nic Phi Sal | Macro Annual 1960-84 | $\dfrac{d(IP_t+IG_t)}{dt}$ | X One equation for each country | Omitted | Omitted | Omitted |
| Musalem (1989) | Mex | Macro Annual 1962-87 | $IP_t$ | R With a lagged KP | VAR.: $Y_t/KP_t$ COEF.: ++ | VAR.: $IG_t$ COEF.: ++ | VAR.: $r_{t-1}-P_{t-1}$ COEF.: -- VAR.: $v_t/P_t$ COEF.: - |
| Ocampo, Londono & Villar (1988) | Col | Macro Annual 1950-80 | $\dfrac{IP_t+IG_t}{Y_t}$ Machinery and equipment only | R,X | VAR.: $dY_t/dt$ COEF.: + | Omitted | VAR.: $v_t/P_t$ COEF.: -- |
| Pereira-Leite & Vaez-Zadeh (1986) | Kor | Macro (manufact. sector) Annual 1970-81 | $IP_t$ | R,F With a lagged KP | VAR.: $YP_t$ (manufacturing sector only) COEF.: ++ | Omitted | VAR.: $r_t-\hat{P}_t$ COEF.: - |
| Rama (1987) | Uru | Macro Quarterly 1976-85 | $IP_t$ (Machinery only) | T,F With variable weights (disequil. estimates) | Omitted | Omitted | Omitted |
| Scmhidt-Hebbel & Müller (1992) | Mor | Macro Annual 1970-88 | $\dfrac{IP_t}{Y_t}$ | R,F,X With a lagged endogenous variable | VAR.: $Y_t^*/Y_t$ COEF.: ++ | VAR.: $KG_t/Y_t$ COEF.: ++ | VAR.: $c_t/P_t$ COEF.: -- |
| Schwartzman (1984) | Mex | Micro (23 manuf. firms) Annual 1966-82 | $\dfrac{IP_t}{KP_t}$ | T | Omitted | Omitted | Omitted |
| Shafik (1992) | Egy | Macro Annual 1960-86 | $IP_t$ | R,F | VAR.: $Y_t$ COEF.: ++ | VAR.: $IG_t$ COEF.: + | VAR.: $v_t/P_t$ COEF.: -- VAR.: $P_t/W_t$ COEF.: ++ |

| Average Tobin's $\bar{q}$ (6) | Business-cycle indicators (7) | Credit availability (8) | Foreign exchange availability (9) | Economic instability (10) | Source, fit and technique |
|---|---|---|---|---|---|
| Omitted | Omitted | Omitted | VAR.: Exports (deviations from time trend) COEF.: ++ VAR.: International reserves (dev. from trend) COEF.: + | Omitted | From equation (7). Reported coefficients are averages for the 12 countries. $\bar{R}^2 = 0.35$ (OLS) |
| Omitted | Omitted | Omitted | Omitted | Omitted | From equation (10). $\bar{R}^2 = 0.95$ (OLS) |
| Omitted | Omitted | Omitted | VAR.: A dummy accounts for years with import controls. COEF.: -- | Omitted | From Table 8, 6th equation. $\bar{R}^2 = 0.77$ (OLS) |
| Omitted | Omitted | VAR.: $F_t$ With F = internal financing (small firms) or bonds + foreign finance (large firms). COEF.: ++ | Omitted | Omitted | Last equation for small firms. $\bar{R}^2 = 0.97$ Fourth equation for large firms. $\bar{R}^2 = 0.93$ (OLS) |
| VAR.: $\bar{q}_t . v_t / P_t$ COEF.: ++ | VAR.: $y_t$ With y = excess demand arising from a disequilibrium model. COEF.: ++ | VAR.: current profits (COEF.: ++), accumulated liabilities, (COEF.: --) foreign saving (COEF.: +), and government saving (COEF.:--). | Omitted | Omitted | From eq. (21). Reported coefficients are averages on 3 and 11 quarters lags. $\bar{R}^2 = 0.84$ (ML) |
| Omitted | Omitted | VAR.: $F_t / Y_t$ With F = banking sector credit to private firms. COEF.: ++ | VAR.: Terms-of-trade effect/ output. COEF.: ++ | VAR.: Foreign debt/output COEF.: -- | From equation (1.4) in Table 1. $\bar{R}^2 = 0.94$ (OLS) Includes a significant dummy for high-investment years. |
| VAR.: $\bar{q}_t$ COEF.: ++ | Omitted | Omitted | Omitted | Omitted | From equat. (23) (estimates in Table VII). $\bar{R}^2 = 0.08$ (OLS) |
| Omitted | Omitted | VAR.: $F_t$ With F = credit to the private sector. COEF.: ++ | Omitted | Omitted | From equation (2.4) in Table 2. $\bar{R}^2 = 0.96$ (OLS) Coefficients from the cointegrating vector. |

## Table 5A.1  Empirical studies on investment in developing countries (continued)

| Study | Countries | Data | Endo-genous variable | Model specifi-cation | Aggregate demand (1) | Public capital stock (2) | Relative factor prices (3),(4),(5) |
|---|---|---|---|---|---|---|---|
| Solimano (1992) | Chi | Macro Quarterly 1977-87 | $IP_t$ | T,F With a lagged endogenous variable | Omitted | Omitted | Omitted |
| Sundararajan (1987) | Kor | Macro Annual 1963-81 | $IP_t$ | K,F With a lagged KP | VAR.: $YP_t$ COEF.: ++ | VAR.: $KG_t$ Not significant. COEF. not reported. | VAR.: $c_t/w_t$ With c depending on the debt-to-equity ratio. COEF.: - |
| Sundararajan & Thakur (1980) | Ind Kor | Macro Annual 1960-76 | $IP_t$ | K,F With a lagged KP. One equat. for each country. | VAR.: $YP_t$ COEF.: ++ VAR.: $YP_{t-1}$ COEF.: ++ | VAR.: $KG_t$ COEF.: + | VAR.: $c_{t-1}/w_{t-1}$ COEF.: - VAR.: $c_{t-2}/w_{t-2}$ COEF.: -- |
| Tun Wai & Wong (1982) | Gre Kor Mal Mex Tha | Macro Annual 1960-76 | $IP_t$ | K,F With a lagged KP. One equat. for each country. | VAR.: $YP_t$ COEF.: ++ | VAR.: $IG_t$ But IG replaces YP, so that the coefficient captures the income accele-rator effect | Omitted |
| Tybout (1983) | Col | Macro 25 3-digit industries (2 sizes) Annual 1973-76 | $\dfrac{(IP_{ij})_t}{(KP_{ij})_{t-1}}$ (size i, indus-try j) | K,F With a lagged endogenous variable | VAR.: $\dfrac{d(YP_{ij})/dt}{(KP_{ij})_{t-1}}$ COEF.: ++ | Omitted | Omitted |
| van Wijnbergen (1982) | Kor | Macro Quarterly 1966-79 | $IP_t$ | N,F With a lagged endogenous variable | Omitted | Omitted | VAR.: $r_{t-1} - \hat{P}_{t-1}$ COEF.: -- |
| Vogel & Buser (1976) | Arg Bol Bra Chi Col Cos Ecu Gua Hon Mex Nic Par Per Sal Uru Ven | Macro Annual 1950-71 | $\dfrac{IP_t + IG_t}{Y_t}$ | F With a dummy in-tercept for each country. | Omitted | Omitted | Omitted |

| Average Tobin's $\bar{q}$ (6) | Business-cycle indicators (7) | Credit availability (8) | Foreign exchange availability (9) | Economic instability (10) | Source, fit and technique |
|---|---|---|---|---|---|
| VAR.: $\bar{q}_t .v_t /P_t$ COEF.: ++ | VAR.: $Y_t$ COEF.: ++ | VAR.: $F_t$ With F = stock of real credit. COEF.: ++ | Omitted | VAR.: Variance of Y over 4 quarters. COEF.: -- | $\bar{R}^2 = 0.79$ (3SLS) Stability examined by the Kalman-filter method. |
| Omitted | Omitted | VAR.: $P_t .F_t /v_t$ With F = gross savings - public investment. COEF.: ++ | Omitted | Two signifi-cant dummy variables ac-count for eco-nomic policy changes and uncertainties. | From equation (11) (estimates in Table 3, equation 2). $\bar{R}^2 = 0.99$ (2SLS) |
| Omitted | Omitted | VAR.: $P_t .F_t /v_t$ With F = gross savings - public investment. COEF.: ++ | Omitted | Omitted | From equation (20). Reported coefficients are for India. $\bar{R}^2 = 0.95$ (OLS) |
| Omitted | Omitted | VAR.: $F_t$ With F = change in bank credit or net capital in-flow to the private sector. COEF.: + | Omitted | Omitted | From equation (3) (reported coefficients are averages for the five countries). $\bar{R}^2 = 0.95$ (OLS) |
| Omitted | Omitted | VAR.: $\dfrac{dF/dt}{(KP_{ij})_{t-1}}$ For class i, j with F = non dis-tributed profits (lag distribut.). COEF.: + | Omitted | Omitted | From equation (7) $\bar{R}^2$ not reported. (FIML, because of simultaneous esti-mates for small and large firms). |
| Omitted | Omitted | VAR.: $(dF/dt)_{t-1}$ With F = real credit to the private sector. COEF.: ++ | Omitted | Omitted | From equat.(10). $\bar{R}^2 = 0.80$ (2SLS, with sea-sonal dummies). |
| Omitted | Omitted | For F = cur-rency outside banks, or de-mand deposits, coefficients were not significant. | Omitted | Omitted | From equation (12). $\bar{R}^2 = 0.62$ (OLS) |

## Notes

1.  The comments by the late Bela Balassa, Eduardo Borensztein, Luis Servén, and Andrés Solimano, and by participants at the 6th World Congress of the Econometric Society (Barcelona), are gratefully acknowledged.
2.  However, if there was a spillover of the credit demand to the curb markets, the average interest rate would rise in line with the amount borrowed by the firm.
3.  Other disequilibria considered by these models do not seem relevant to explaining private investment in developing countries. This is the case with manpower shortages in particular.
4.  Note, however, that in many developing countries such devices aim at restraining purchases of sumptuary consumption, rather than at input and investment imports.
5.  Steigum (1983) and Chirinko (1987) analyze the case in which the interest rate, $r$ (and therefore investment decisions themselves), depends on the debt-to-equity ratio of the firm.
6.  Note that the price of capital, $v_t$, is the same in this term as in the previous one, a reflection of the assumption that capital goods can be resold.
7.  A third technological constraint would be $IP_t \geq 0$. However, throughout the paper it is assumed that the determinants of investment are such as to avoid the corner solution $IP_t = 0$.
8.  The microfoundation for this kind of demand function is provided by Dixit and Stiglitz (1977).
9.  Equation (5-6) is written as if the price of capital goods were the same no matter what their origin (imported or domestically produced).
10. If $\sigma = 0$, to the contrary, verifying that marginal $q$ is a decreasing function of $KP$ is straightforward (Blanchard and Sachs 1982).
11. Although the model considered just two periods (present and future), it is possible to proceed as if both of them included many years or quarters (say, $t, t-1, t-2, \ldots$ and $t+1, t+2, \ldots$ respectively).
12. For simplicity's sake, in table 5-1 the number of firms ($J$) is treated as given.
13. An additional study by Lim (1987) was not used because it is only incidentally concerned with investment and the corresponding empirical equation does not lead to significant coefficients.
14. The meaning of all the abbreviations used in table 5A.1 (for countries, variables, and econometric technique) can be found in the appendix.
15. For instance, a specification including the income accelerator and relative factor prices is seen as arising from model $R$, unless it takes into account the rental/wage ratio (model $K$) or omits aggregate demand (model N).
16. Note that in some cases the endogenous variable is the overall investment, so that it includes the accumulation of capital by the government. Studies dealing with public sector investment only (such as those by

Heller 1975 and Chow 1985) were not considered.

17. In fact, only two of the studies (Chhibber and Shafik 1992 and Shafik 1992) test for co-integration of the regressions in levels.

18. In table 5A.1 the exogenous variables are multiplied by -1 whenever necessary to obtain coefficients whose expected signs are the same as in table 5-1.

19. The study by Tun Wai and Wong (1982) is not included among these because the accumulation of government capital replaces aggregate output, so that it probably captures an income accelerator effect.

20. Here crowding-out is not the issue, since the empirical investment equations used by both Gupta and by Sundararajan and Thakur take financial repression into account by including the availability of savings among their arguments.

21. Models F and X do not entail restrictions on the structural parameters of the model (see table 5-1). Therefore, they are both compatible with any of the four other specifications (R, N, K, or T).

22. This point leads to a specific econometric problem, since there is no information on whether an observation $u_t$ arises from the $u_{it}$ model, from the $u_{Ft}$ model, or from the $u_{Xt}$ model. Quandt (1988) provides useful tools to deal with such a problem.

## References

Abel, A. 1980. "Empirical Investment Equations: An Integrative Framework." *Carnegie-Rochester Conference Series on Public Policy* 12 (Spring):39-91.

Artus, P., and P.-A. Muet. 1984. "Un panorama des développements récents de l'économétrie de l'investissement" [An Overview of Recent Developments in the Econometrics of Investment]. *Revue Economique* 35 (5)(September):791-830.

———. 1986. *Investissement et emploi* [Investment and Employment]. Paris: Economica.

Behrman, J. 1972. "Sectoral Investment Determination in a Developing Economy." *American Economic Review* 62 (5)(December):825-41.

Bilsborrow, R. 1977. "The Determinants of Fixed Investment by Manufacturing Firms in a Developing Country." *International Economic Review* 18 (3)(October):697-717.

Blanchard, O. 1988. "Unemployment: Getting the Questions Right and Some of the Answers." NBER Working Paper 2698. National Bureau of Economic Research, Cambridge, Mass., September.

Blanchard, O., and J. Sachs. 1982. "Anticipations, Recessions and Policy: An Intertemporal Disequilibrium Model." NBER Working Paper 971. National Bureau of Economic Research, Cambridge, Mass., August.

Blejer, M., and M. Khan. 1984. "Government Policy and Private Investment in Developing Countries." *IMF Staff Papers* 31 (2)(June):379-403.

Chan-Lee, J., and R. Torres. 1987. "q de Tobin et taux d'accumulation en

France" [Tobin's q and the Accumulation Rate in France]. *Annales d'Economie et de Statistique* 5 (January-March):37-48.

Chenery, H., and A. Strout. 1966. "Foreign Assistance and Economic Development." *American Economic Review* 56 (4)(September):681-733.

Chhibber, A., and N. Shafik. 1992. "Does Devaluation Hurt Private Investment? The Indonesian Case," in A. Chhibber, M. Dailami, and N. Shafik, eds., *Reviving Private Investment in Developing Countries: Empirical Studies and Policy Lessons.* Amsterdam: North-Holland Publishing.

Chhibber, A., and S. van Wijnbergen. 1992. "Public Policy and Private Investment in Turkey," in A. Chhibber, M. Dailami, and N. Shafik, eds., *Reviving Private Investment in Developing Countries: Empirical Studies and Policy Lessons.* Amsterdam: North-Holland Publishing.

Chirinko, R. 1987. "Tobin's q and Financial Policy." *Journal of Monetary Economics* 19 (January):69-87.

Chow, G. 1985. "A Model of Chinese National Income Determination." *Journal of Political Economy* 93 (4)(August):782-92.

Dailami, M. 1987a. "Expectations, Stock Market Volatility, and Private Investment Behavior: Theory and Empirical Evidence for Brazil." Unpublished. World Bank, Country Economics Department, Washington, D.C. August.

———. 1987b. "Optimal Corporate Debt Financing and Real Investment Decisions under Controlled Banking Systems." Unpublished. World Bank, Country Economics Department, Washington, D.C. December.

———. 1992. "Government Policy and Private Investment Recovery in Colombia," in A. Chhibber, M. Dailami, and N. Shafik, eds., *Reviving Private Investment in Developing Countries: Empirical Studies and Policy Lessons.* Amsterdam: North-Holland Publishing.

Dailami, M., and M. Walton. 1992. "Private Investment, Government Policy, and Foreign Capital: A Study of the Zimbabwean Experience," in A. Chhibber, M. Dailami, and N. Shafik, eds., *Reviving Private Investment in Developing Countries: Empirical Studies and Policy Lessons.* Amsterdam: North-Holland Publishing.

de Melo, J., and J. Tybout. 1986. "The Effects of Financial Liberalization on Savings and Investment in Uruguay." *Economic Development and Cultural Change* 34 (3):561-87.

Dixit, A., and J. Stiglitz. 1977. "Monopolistic Competition and Optimum Product Diversity." *American Economic Review* 67 (3)(June):297-308.

Fry, M. 1980. "Saving, Investment, Growth and the Cost of Financial Repression." *World Development* 8 (4)(April):317-27.

Galbis, V. 1979. "Money, Investment and Growth in Latin America, 1961-1973." *Economic Development and Cultural Change* 27 (3)(March):423-43.

Garcia, E. 1987. "Neo-Keynesian Models in Planning and Macroeconomic Policies: The Experience of ILPES." Unpublished. Economic Commission for Latin America and the Caribbean (ECLAC), Santiago de Chile, August.

Gardner, R., and R. Sheldon. 1975. "Financial Conditions and the Time Path of Equipment Expenditures." *Review of Economics and Statistics* 57 (2)(May):164-70.

Gouriéroux, C., J.-J. Laffont, and A. Monfort. 1984. "Econométrie des modèles d'équilibre avec rationnement: une mise à jour" [The Econometrics of Equilibrium-with-Rationing Models: An Update]. *Annales de l'INSEE* 55-56 (July-December):5-37.

Greene, J., and D. Villanueva. 1990. "Private Investment in Developing Countries: An Empirical Analysis." Working Paper 90/40. International Monetary Fund, Washington, D.C., April.

Grossman, H. 1972. "A Choice-Theoretic Model of an Income-Investment Accelerator." *American Economic Review* 62 (4) (September):630-41.

Gupta, K. 1984. *Finance and Economic Growth in Developing Countries.* London: Croom Helm.

Hayashi, F. 1982. "Tobin's Marginal q and Average q: A Neoclassical Interpretation." *Econometrica* 50 (1)(January):213-24.

Heller, P. 1975. "A Model of Public Fiscal Behavior in Developing Countries: Investment, Aid and Taxation." *American Economic Review* 65 (June):429-45.

Jorgenson, D. 1963. "Capital Theory and Investment Behaviour." *American Economic Review* 53 (2) Papers and Proceedings (May):247-59.

Lambert, J.-P. 1986. "Conflicting Specifications for Investment Functions in Rationing Models: A Reconciliation." CORE Discussion Paper, 8629. Center for Operations Research and Econometrics, Louvain, October.

Leff, N., and K. Sato. 1988. "Estimating Investment and Savings Functions for Developing Countries, with an Application to Latin America." *International Economic Journal* 2 (3)(Autumn):1-17.

Licandro, O. 1992. "Q Investment Models, Factor Complementarity and Monopolistic Competition." *Recherches Economiques de Louvain* 58 (1):51-73.

Lim, D. 1987. "Export Instability, Investment and Economic Growth in Developing Countries." *Australian Economic Papers* 26 (49)(December):318-27.

Love, J. 1989. "Export Instability, Imports and Investment in Developing Countries." *Journal of Development Studies* 25 (2)(January):183-91.

Malinvaud, E. 1977. *The Theory of Unemployment Reconsidered.* London: Basil Blackwell.

Malkiel, B., G. von Furstenberg, and H. Watson. 1979. "Expectations, Tobin's q and Industry Investment." *Journal of Finance* 34 (2):549-64.

McKinnon, R. 1964. "Foreign Exchange Constraints in Economic Development and Efficient Aid Allocation." *Economic Journal* 74 (June):388-409.

————. 1973. *Money and Capital in Economic Development.* Washington, D.C.: The Brookings Institution.

Musalem, A. 1989. "Private Investment in Mexico: An Empirical Analysis." World Bank, Working Paper WPS 183, Country Economics Department. Washington, D.C., April.

Nickell, S. 1978. *The Investment Decisions of Firms.* Cambridge: Cambridge

University Press.

Ocampo, J. A., J. L. Londoño, and L. Villar. 1988. "Ahorro e inversión en Colombia" [Saving and Investment in Colombia]. In R. Werneck, ed., *Ahorro e inversión en Latinoamérica* [Saving and Investment in Latin America]. Report 207. Ottawa: International Development Research Center.

Pereira-Leite, S., and R. Vaez-Zadeh. 1986. "Credit Allocation and Investment Decisions: The Case of the Manufacturing Sector in Korea." *World Development* 14 (1)(January):115-26.

Pindyck, R. 1988. "Irreversible Investment, Capacity Choice and the Value of the Firm." *American Economic Review* 78 (December):969-85.

Precious, M. 1985. "Demand Constraints, Rational Expectations and Investment Theory." *Oxford Economic Papers* 37 (4)(December):576-605.

Quandt, R. 1988. *The Econometrics of Disequilibrium*. London: Basil Blackwell.

Rama, M. 1987. "Inversión privada: teoría q y enfoque de desequilibrio" [Private Investment: Q Theory and the Disequilibrium Approach], in *7th Latin American Meeting of the Econometric Society: Papers and Abstracts* 4 (August). Sao Paulo: Universidade de Sao Paulo.

Schiantarelli, F., and D. Georgoutsos. 1990. "Monopolistic Competition and the Q Theory of Investment." *European Economic Review* 34 (5)(July):1061-78.

Schmidt-Hebbel, K., and T. Müller. 1992. "Private Investment under Macroeconomic Adjustment in Morocco," in A. Chhibber, M. Dailami, and N. Shafik, eds., *Reviving Private Investment in Developing Countries: Empirical Studies and Policy Lessons*. Amsterdam: North-Holland Publishing.

Schramm, R. 1972. "Neoclassical Investment Models and French Private Manufacturing Investment." *American Economic Review* 62 (4)(September):553-63.

Schwartzman, A. 1984. "Investment, Exchange Rates, and Q in the Mexican Economy." Unpublished. Ph.D. dissertation, Massachusetts Institute of Technology, Cambridge, Mass.

Shafik, N. 1992. "Private Investment and Public Policy: The Egyptian Case," 69-98. In A. Chhibber, M. Dailami, and N. Shafik, eds., *Reviving Private Investment in Developing Countries: Empirical Studies and Policy Lessons*. Amsterdam: North-Holland Publishing.

Shaw, E. 1973. *Financial Deepening in Economic Development*. New York: Oxford University Press.

Sneessens, H. 1987. "Investment and the Inflation-Unemployment Tradeoff in a Macroeconomic Rationing Model with Monopolistic Competition." *European Economic Review* 31 (3)(April):781-815.

Sneessens, H., and J. Drèze. 1986. "A Discussion of Belgian Unemployment, Combining Traditional Concepts and Disequilibrium Econometrics." *Economica* 53 (Supplement):S89-120.

Solimano, A. 1992. "How Private Investment Reacts to Changing Macroeconomic Conditions: The Case of Chile in the 1980s," in A.

Chhibber, M. Dailami, and N. Shafik, eds., *Reviving Private Investment in Developing Countries: Empirical Studies and Policy Lessons.* Amsterdam: North-Holland Publishing.

Steigum, E. 1983. "A Financial Theory of Investment Behavior." *Econometrica* 51 (3)(May):637-45.

Sundararajan, V. 1987. "The Debt-Equity Ratio of Firms and the Effectiveness of Interest Rate Policy: Analysis with a Dynamic Model of Saving, Investment and Growth in Korea." *IMF Staff Papers* 34 (2)(June):260-310.

Sundararajan, V., and S. Thakur. 1980. "Public Investment, Crowding Out and Growth: A Dynamic Model Applied to India and Korea." *IMF Staff Papers* 27 (4)(December):814-55.

Tobin, J. 1969. "A General Equilibrium Approach to Monetary Theory." *Journal of Money, Credit and Banking* 1 (February):15-29.

Tun Wai, U., and C. Wong. 1982. "Determinants of Private Investment in Developing Countries." *Journal of Development Studies* 19 (October):19-36.

Tybout, J. 1983. "Credit Rationing and Investment Behavior in a Developing Country." *Review of Economics and Statistics* 65 (65)(November):598-607.

van Wijnbergen, S. 1982. "Stagflationary Effects of Monetary Stabilization Policies: A Quantitative Analysis of South Korea." *Journal of Development Economics* 10 (April):133-69.

Vogel, R., and S. Buser. 1976. "Inflation, Financial Repression and Capital Formation in Latin America," in R. McKinnon, ed., *Money and Finance in Economic Development: Essays in Honor of Edward S. Shaw.* New York: Marcel Dekker.

von Furstenberg, G. 1977. "Corporate Investment: Does Market Valuation Matter in the Aggregate?" *Brookings Papers on Economic Activity* 2:347-97.

# Part B.  Adjustment and Investment Performance

# 6

## Economic Adjustment and Investment Performance in Developing Countries: The Experience of the 1980s

*Luis Servén*
*and*
*Andrés Solimano*

Developing countries experienced a significant decline in investment rates and a parallel slowdown in growth in the eighties.[1] Investment fell following the decline in the availability of external financing after the debt crisis, a decline that was not compensated for by an adequate increase in domestic savings. However, the drop in external financing was not the only factor behind the slowdown in investment. In some instances, the adjustment measures themselves were a factor. For example, the required fiscal adjustment, which was oriented to cut domestic absorption, correcting external imbalances and reducing inflation, often took the form of a decrease in public investment—in particular, in public projects complementary to private investment. The large resource transfer required to service the foreign debt of most developing countries also discouraged private investment, as part of the future returns on new investment projects would effectively accrue to creditors in the form of debt repayments (see chapter 2 "Private Investment and Macroeconomic Adjustment: A Survey", in this volume).

In many countries adjustment policies involved changes in economic incentives. However, very often they did not produce a sizable investment response, thus preventing an effective transition from adjustment to resumed growth. The recovery of private investment probably was slowed by a lack of confidence in the permanence of the policy measures and a high level of uncertainty about the future macroeconomic environment.

This chapter investigates the role domestic and external factors played in the investment performance of developing countries in the eighties, drawing on the experience of selected countries and on an econometric analysis of investment using panel data for a group of 15 developing countries. The chapter draws some lessons that can be applied to the design of growth—enhancing adjustment policies so as to bridge the gap between adjustment and growth.

The chapter is organized as follows. The next section presents the empirical record of investment in developing countries in the 1970s and 1980s. It explores the response of private and public investment to external shocks, macroeconomic adjustment, and structural reform by comparing three groups of selected countries: Latin American ones that pursued structural reform and liberalization (Chile, Mexico, and Bolivia); countries that did not pursue such ambitious reforms and that suffered severe macroeconomic instability (Argentina and Brazil); and the outward-oriented East Asian countries that adjusted to the adverse external shocks of the 1980s while maintaining high growth, low inflation, and, in general, a remarkable degree of macroeconomic stability (Korea, Singapore, and Thailand).

An econometric analysis of the determinants of private investment in developing countries using cross-country data for the period 1975-87 for a selected group of developing countries is presented next. The empirical estimates are used to evaluate the contribution of different factors to the slowdown in investment after 1982.

The conclusions appear in the final section.

## Investment in developing countries, 1970-88

Between 1970 and 1988 investment rates in developing countries exhibited two distinct stages, with the turning point in 1981-82 (figure 6-1). For 78 developing countries, the average share of investment in gross domestic product (GDP) in constant prices increased from about 22 percent in 1970 to 25 percent in 1981, and for most of this period the investment rates were historically high. With the rise in international real interest rates in 1981 and the onset of the debt crisis in 1982, however, the rate of investment fell sharply. The decline started earlier in the highly indebted countries than it did in other developing countries, and in the former the decline was larger. For most developing countries, with the exception of those in Asia, a slowdown in growth accompanied the decline in investment (tables 6-1 and 6-2).

The fall in investment was so severe that some countries may not even have been able fully to replace depreciating capital. For example, in Africa the minimum investment needed to replace depreciated capital was estimated at roughly 13 percent of GDP; in 1987, seven countries in sub-Saharan Africa had investment rates below that level. Similarly, the minimum rate of investment needed to replace capital in Latin America was estimated at 14 percent; in 1987, three countries were below that level (Easterly 1989).

**Figure 6.1   Share of investment in GDP for developing countries**
(unweighted averages)

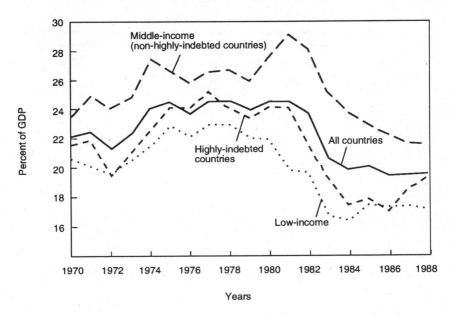

*Source:* World Bank data.

The deficit in the resource balance (that is, the difference between domestic investment and domestic savings) in developing countries was considerably smaller after the 1982 debt crisis as a result of the decline in external financing (table 6-1). However, the decrease in the external deficit was not matched by an offsetting increase in domestic savings, so that it was reflected almost entirely in reduced investment.

The empirical evidence from data for a set of 29 developing countries for which a breakdown between public and private investment was available shows that the share of private investment in GDP in current prices was relatively stable until 1980 and then declined, followed by a modest recovery after 1985 (figure 6-2).[2] The decline was larger in the highly indebted countries than in other countries (figure 6-3). Public investment as a share of GDP rose until 1982 and then fell after 1982, two years later than private investment (figure 6-1 and table 6-3). Unlike private investment, the rates of public investment declined steadily until 1988.

**Private investment and macroeconomic adjustment:**
**Selected country experiences**

The discussion in this section is organized around the behavior of private investment during adjustment in three stylized groups of countries in Latin

**Table 6.1  Investment, saving, and growth in developing countries, 1970-88**

| Indicator | Group | 1970-80 | 1981-82 | 1983-84 | 1985-88 |
|---|---|---|---|---|---|
| Gross domestic investment | All | 22.4 | 24.0 | 20.2 | 19.6 |
| (percentage of GDP | Highly-indebted | 22.8 | 23.0 | 18.0 | 18.4 |
| at current prices) | Middle-income | 25.5 | 28.6 | 24.4 | 21.9 |
|  | Low-income | 19.7 | 20.3 | 17.0 | 17.4 |
| Gross domestic saving | All | 16.1 | 13.7 | 13.9 | 14.9 |
| (percentage of GDP | Highly-indebted | 20.3 | 20.1 | 19.8 | 20.2 |
| at current prices) | Middle-income | 18.3 | 17.5 | 17.7 | 17.8 |
|  | Low-income | 12.5 | 7.6 | 8.0 | 9.9 |
| Resource balance deficit | All | 6.4 | 10.3 | 6.2 | 4.6 |
| (percentage of GDP | Highly-indebted | 2.5 | 2.9 | 4.7 | 4.8 |
| at current prices) | Middle-income | 7.2 | 11.1 | 6.7 | 4.8 |
|  | Low-income | 7.2 | 12.7 | 8.9 | 7.5 |
| Gross domestic investment | All | 23.4 | 24.1 | 20.6 | 19.6 |
| (percentage of GDP | Highly-indebted | 23.1 | 22.3 | 17.1 | 16.8 |
| at constant prices) | Middle-income | 25.7 | 28.6 | 24.9 | 22.1 |
|  | Low-income | 21.5 | 20.7 | 17.8 | 18.0 |
| Rate of growth of real GDP | All | 4.7 | 2.7 | 1.8 | 3.3 |
| (percentage per year) | Highly-indebted | 5.0 | -0.3 | -0.4 | 2.7 |
|  | Middle-income | 6.1 | 4.5 | 3.9 | 3.2 |
|  | Low-income | 3.5 | 2.5 | 0.5 | 3.5 |

*Source*:  World Bank data base.

**Table 6.2  Growth and investment**

| Region | Real GDP growth | | Investment ratio | |
|---|---|---|---|---|
|  | 1965-88 | 1980-88 | 1965-88 | 1980-88 |
| Sub-Saharan Africa | 3.3 | 0.5 | 17.6 | 15.9 |
| Asia | 6.3 | 7.4 | 27.7 | 31.1 |
| Europe/Middle East/ North Africa | 4.6 | 2.8 | 28.4 | 27.3 |
| Latin America and Caribbean | 4.5 | 1.6 | 19.7 | 17.9 |

*Source*:  International Monetary Fund (1989, table 15).

**Figure 6.2 Public and private investment for 29 countries**
(unweighted average, percent of GDP)

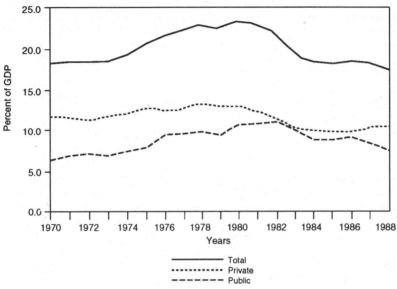

Source: World Bank data.

**Figure 6.3 Public and private investment for 13 highly-indebted
 countries**
(unweighted average, percent of GDP)

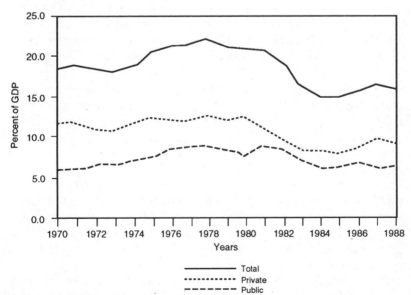

Source: World Bank data.

**Table 6.3  Public and private investment for a group of 29 developing countries, 1970-88**
(percentage of GDP at current prices)

| Group | 1970-80 | 1981-82 | 1983-84 | 1985-88 |
|---|---|---|---|---|
| 29 countries | | | | |
| Total | 20.3 | 22.2 | 18.8 | 17.6 |
| Private | 12.2 | 11.7 | 9.7 | 9.6 |
| Public | 8.2 | 10.5 | 9.0 | 8.0 |
| | | | | |
| 13 highly-indebted countries | | | | |
| Total | 20.1 | 20.2 | 15.1 | 15.2 |
| Private | 12.3 | 10.9 | 8.1 | 8.7 |
| Public | 7.8 | 9.2 | 7.0 | 6.5 |

*Note:*    Sample includes Argentina*, Bangladesh, Bolivia*, Brazil*, Chile*, Colombia*, Costa Rica*, Ecuador*, Guatemala, Hungary, India, Indonesia, Kenya, Korea, Malaysia, Mexico*, Nigeria*, Pakistan, Peru*, Philippines*, Portugal, Sri Lanka, Thailand, Tunisia, Turkey, Uruguay*, Venezuela*, Zambia, Zimbabwe. Countries marked with an (*) are highly-indebted.
*Source:*  World Bank (1992).

America and East Asia. The first group, composed of Chile, Mexico, and Bolivia, adopted decisive stabilization policies oriented toward elimination of the basic macroeconomic imbalances, together with policies of structural reform, including the liberalization of foreign trade and deregulation of the credit and labor markets along free-market lines. The second group was made up of Argentina and Brazil, two countries that in the 1980s were unable to stabilize their economies and correct the basic macroeconomic imbalances in a sustainable way. They did not attempt comprehensive structural reforms and liberalization of the type adopted by the countries in the first group. The third group, consisting of three East Asian economies—Korea, Singapore, and Thailand—adjusted primarily through macro policies and managed to deal with the external shocks and debt crisis of the eighties without sacrificing growth and domestic macroeconomic stability.

*Adjusting cum liberalizing countries in Latin America*

Chile, Mexico, and Bolivia. These Latin American countries had several features of their macroeconomic policies and structural reforms in common. Their macroeconomic policies entailed both real depreciation of the exchange rate and restrictive fiscal and monetary policies to reduce the large current account deficits and high rates of inflation existing at the time the reforms started to be applied.[3]

The structural reforms the three countries implemented were trade liberalization, financial deregulation, privatization, and development of greater flexibility in the labor market. The degree, timing, and results of these policy reforms varied in each country, although all three shared a general free-market orientation.

Following the swings in the world economy in the 1980s, the three countries suffered the cycle of overborrowing, a sharp cutoff in foreign lending, and the onset of the debt crisis. The pattern of investment followed the "debt cycle" (figure 6-4). Public investment in Mexico and private investment in Chile increased sharply during the boom of the late seventies and early eighties that was led by external borrowing. In 1982, when access to external lending was abruptly cut off and countries were forced to reduce their current account deficit rapidly, investment fell sharply. Thus, basically the adjustment was carried out by cutting the demand for investment rather than by increasing domestic savings.

**Investment in Chile: The "mature" reformer.** The experience of Chile is particularly interesting in several respects. First, it started its reforms earlier—in the mid-1970s—than the countries in the other two groups did, and it therefore provides a better "laboratory experiment" for assessing the impact of liberalization on private investment. Second, at the time the reforms started to be applied, the Chilean economy exhibited large macroeconomic imbalances in the form of high rates of inflation (over three digits by the mid-1970s) and a large fiscal deficit. Achievement and maintenance of low and stable inflation remained a top priority in economic policy. In addition, the commitment to structural reforms along free-market lines remained quite strong,[4] and the democratic administration that took office in early 1990 reiterated a commitment to reform.

The response of private investment to the stabilization cum liberalization program of the mid-1970s was strong. The share of private investment in GDP rose from 5.3 percent in 1971-75 to 11.2 percent in 1976-81. In contrast, public investment fell from 10.6 percent in 1971-75 to 5.8 percent in 1976-81.

Several hypotheses (and some puzzles) can be offered to explain the response of private investment. One is the importance of political economy factors. The country went from the "Chilean Road to Socialism" program of President Salvador Allende in 1970-73, which involved large-scale na-tionalization and deeper land reform, to a radical free-market experiment launched in 1975 under the military regime. The new economic program assured full respect for private property, deregulation of the markets, and tight political control of the defeated left and of a militant working class very active under Allende. The private sector responded forcefully to the new program. The reduction in public investment apparently crowded-in private investment because a large part of the increase in public investment in the period 1971-75 corresponded to enterprises that had just been nationalized.

One of the puzzles in the strong response of private investment is that it coincided with a period of very high real interest rates—over 25 percent per year in the second half of the 1970s. Ex-post, however, given the massive

**Figure 6.4   Public and private investment rates in Chile, Mexico, and Bolivia**
(unweighted average, percent of GDP)

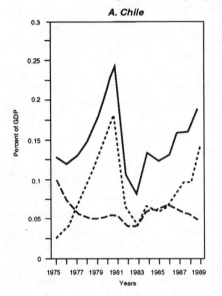

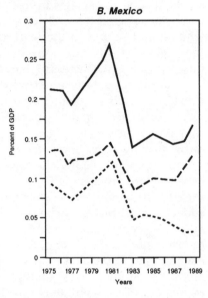

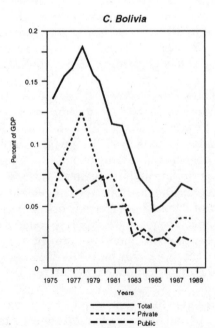

*Source:* World Bank data.

rescue operation the government undertook in 1982-83 with respect to the internal and external debt the private sector had acquired, the private sector ended up paying an effective real interest rate that was much lower.

In the 1980s private investment followed closely the cycles of economic activity. It boomed in the early eighties, although its composition tilted heavily toward the nontraded sectors—housing, structures, and commercial buildings—following the real appreciation of the peso that developed at the time. During the crisis of 1982-83, investment fell by more than 10 percentage points of GDP with respect to 1980-81. The subsequent recovery was relatively forceful, and by 1989 private investment had reached its 1980 level. Given the strong performance of the export sector and the very large real depreciation of the exchange rate after 1982 (on the order of 70 percent), it seems that private investment shifted toward the traded goods sector in contrast with the trend in the early 1980s.[5]

**Investment in Mexico and Bolivia.** Total investment in Mexico fell by 8 percentage points of GDP in the period 1982-89 compared with 1978-81. However, the bulk of the cut involved public investment: the ratio of public investment to GDP fell by nearly 5 percentage points in 1982-89 over 1978-81. Nevertheless, it is important to recognize that the level of public investment during the period 1978-81 had reached a high—and probably unsustainable—level following the oil boom.[6] Private investment fell moderately between 1982-85 and then, despite the high real interest rates, started to recover, a shift that coincided with the implementation of the main structural reforms.[7]

In Bolivia, investment declined steadily during the 1980s. The first half of the decade was characterized by macroeconomic turbulence that ended in the hyperinflation of 1984-85. Then, in August 1985 the government introduced a sharp and successful program to stabilize inflation, which went from the five-digit level of hyperinflation to an average of about 20 percent in the second half of the 1980s. The main problem Bolivia experienced in its stabilization cum liberalization effort was a lack of per capita growth and any significant response by private investment in the aftermath of the stabilization (table 6-4).[8]

**Lessons from the three experiences.** What can be concluded about the effects of adjustment and the implementation of the reforms on the performance of private investment in these economies? The first point is that of diversity. In Chile, private investment reacted forcefully to the reforms in the mid-1970s and recovered relatively fast in the second half of the 1980s after the restoration of macroeconomic stability and the government's reassurance that it was committed to the reforms. In Mexico, the response of private investment to the reforms launched in the mid- to late 1980s was moderate. In Bolivia, private investment remained stagnant, and so did growth in the aftermath of the stabilization and reform.

Second, the experience of these countries in the 1980s shows clearly that reforms may enhance private investment if they are accompanied by a stable macro environment. Chile in the second half of the 1980s is a good

**Table 6.4 Public and private investment and macroeconomic indicators** (annual averages, percent)

| A. Chile | | | | |
| --- | --- | --- | --- | --- |
| *Variable* | *1978-81* | *1982-84* | *1985-88* | *1989* |
| Total investment (percent of GDP), real | 19.3 | 10.5 | 14.3 | 19.2 |
| Public investment (percent of GDP), real | 5.3 | 4.8 | 6.2 | 4.7 |
| Private investment (percent of GDP), real | 14.0 | 2.7 | 8.1 | 14.5 |
| Real GDP growth (percent) | 7.5 | -2.9 | 5.3 | 9.9 |
| Inflation (GDP deflator) | 36.0 | 18.1 | 23.6 | 12.6 |
| Current account balance (percent of GDP) | -8.6 | -8.1 | -5.0 | -3.6 |
| Foreign debt (percent of GDP) | 46.2 | 88.2 | 113.9 | 72.3 |
| Real exchange rate (1980=100) | 102.8 | 107.6 | 172.8 | 193.7 |

| B. Mexico | | | | |
| --- | --- | --- | --- | --- |
| *Variable* | *1978-81* | *1982-84* | *1985-88* | *1989* |
| Total investment (percent of GDP), real | 24.3 | 17.2 | 15.4 | 17.2 |
| Public investment (percent of GDP), real | 10.5 | 6.9 | 4.7 | 3.6 |
| Private investment (percent of GDP), real | 13.3 | 10.3 | 10.7 | 13.6 |
| Real GDP growth (percent) | 8.7 | -0.4 | 0.5 | 2.9 |

(continued)

Table 6.4 (continuation)

| | | | | |
|---|---|---|---|---|
| Inflation (GDP deflator) | 22.3 | 70.2 | 92.7 | 17.2 |
| Current account balance (percent of GDP) | -4.7 | 0.8 | 0.1 | 2.8 |
| Foreign debt (percent of GDP) | 30.8 | 55.0 | 66.3 | 43.9 |
| Real exchange rate (1980=100) | 103.4 | 126.5 | 147.7 | 135.6 |

### C. Bolivia

| Variable | 1978-81 | 1982-84 | 1985-88 | 1989 |
|---|---|---|---|---|
| Total investment (percent of GDP), real | 15.7 | 9.6 | 4.5 | 6.7 |
| Public investment (percent of GDP), real | 9.4 | 4.9 | 2.5 | 2.4 |
| Private investment (percent of GDP), real | 6.3 | 4.7 | 1.9 | 4.2 |
| Real GDP growth (percent) | 0.8 | -3.7 | 0.4 | 2.8 |
| Inflation (GDP deflator) | 24.1 | 561.7 | 2,938.8 | 14.5 |
| Current account balance (percent of GDP) | -10.8 | -5.5 | -9.2 | -5.9 |
| Foreign debt (percent of GDP) | 93.0 | 133.6 | 147.1 | 97.4 |
| Real exchange rate (1980 =100) | 98.8 | 70.7 | 77.9 | 138.9 |

*Source*: Investment—elaboration based on Pfeffermann and Madarassy (1991); other variables—World Bank data.

example of how fiscal balance, moderately positive real interest rates, and competitive real exchange rates provide a suitable framework for private investment to respond to the incentives generated by the structural reforms.[9] To the contrary, in the case of Bolivia, where disinflation was consolidated but the fiscal deficit was still high (near 5 percent in 1986-90) and the economy highly dollarized (Morales 1991), the macroeconomic environment was not entirely supportive of a strong recovery of private investment.

A third point is that a favorable private investment response is associated with adequate external financing. All three countries experienced a debt overhang, and they carried out a sizable resource transfer abroad. From simple savings—investment identities it can be concluded that without a corresponding increase in domestic savings, a high level of investment can hardly be achieved. In addition, the foreign debt service acts like an implicit tax on investment.

A fourth point, generally downplayed in the academic literature but one that investors in the real world seem to pay a lot of attention to, is the favorable "business climate" generated by the liberalization.[10] In fact, the privatization measures as well as other liberalizing policies adopted in these countries reflected a renewed faith in free markets and private initiative. The distinctive feature is that governments had come to perceive these principles as the "new engine to growth."

## Two non-adjusting cases in Latin America: Argentina and Brazil

Brazil and Argentina stood out in Latin America in the eighties[11] as clearcut examples of countries that were unable to stabilize their high inflation, which in several cases slid into outright hyperinflation. Brazil managed to grow at an impressive 7 percent a year between 1940 and 1980, and its development strategy at the time was that of a dirigiste state, supported, in the sixties and seventies, by foreign direct investment and abundant external credits. Brazil used the external borrowing of the seventies largely to finance its ambitious development plans, which required high rates of investment to speed growth. In contrast, Argentina started to experience a noticeable economic decline after the early seventies, a reflection of the slowdown in growth and mounting economic and political instability.

The adverse external shocks of the early eighties and the onset of the debt crisis hit Argentina and Brazil severely. Correction of the external and fiscal imbalances took the form of an acceleration in inflation and slowdown in growth. In contrast with Mexico and Bolivia (Chile had undertaken its structural reforms in the mid-1970s), domestic authorities in Argentina and Brazil did not seize the opportunity of the crisis to attempt *comprehensive* structural reforms in the public sector, the trade regime, or other areas. The governments devoted the bulk of their energy to fighting inflation and managing their large external debt.[12]

It is not surprising to find that the investment record of countries such as Argentina and Brazil was poor in the 1980s. However, there are some

**Table 6.5  Public and private investment and macroeconomic indicators**
(annual averages, percent)

| A. Argentina | | | | |
|---|---|---|---|---|
| *Variable* | *1978-81* | *1982-84* | *1985-88* | *1989* |
| Total investment (percent of GDP), real | 20.3 | 14.9 | 12.9 | 6.9 |
| Public investment (percent of GDP), real | 8.0 | 6.0 | 5.3 | 3.2 |
| Private investment (percent of GDP), real | 12.3 | 8.9 | 7.6 | 3.7 |
| Real GDP growth (percent) | -0.3 | -0.0 | 0.2 | -3.1 |
| Inflation (GDP deflator) | 128.9 | 396.6 | 319.6 | 3,449.9 |
| Current account balance (percent of GDP) | -3.3 | -3.7 | -3.0 | -2.4 |
| Foreign debt (percent of GDP) | 45.4 | 70.0 | 69.8 | 76.3 |
| Real exchange rate (1980=100) | 124.1 | 210.0 | 239.8 | 296.3 |

| B. Brazil | | | | |
|---|---|---|---|---|
| *Variable* | *1978-81* | *1982-84* | *1985-88* | *1989* |
| Total investment (percent of GDP), real | 23.1 | 18.7 | 17.6 | 18.0 |
| Public investment (percent of GDP), real | 8.9 | 7.0 | 5.8 | n.a. |
| Private investment (percent of GDP), real | 14.2 | 11.7 | 11.8 | n.a. |
| Real GDP growth (percent) | 3.7 | 0.8 | 4.8 | 5.3 |

(continued)

Table 6.5 (continuation)

| | | | | |
|---|---|---|---|---|
| Inflation (GDP deflator) | 73.0 | 154.1 | 317.6 | 2,629.7 |
| Current account balance (percent of GDP) | -4.5 | -3.1 | -0.8 | 2.2 |
| Foreign debt (percent of GDP) | 28.5 | 43.5 | 39.7 | 23.2 |
| Real exchange rate (1980=100) | 87.6 | 89.1 | 101.9 | 78.7 |

n.a.  Not available.
*Source*: Investment—elaboration based on Pfeffermann and Madarassy (1991); other variables—World Bank data.

differences in their experiences.  As table 6-5 illustrates, investment rates dropped far more in Argentina than in Brazil.  In fact, total investment in Argentina in the period 1985-89 was 8.6 percentage points of GDP lower than in 1978-81; this drop in total investment decomposes into a reduction in private investment of 5.5 percentage points of GDP and a cut in public investment of 3.1 percentage points.  Moreover, the decline in investment persisted (on average) in the second half of the 1980s, in contrast to the experience of other Latin American countries.  In Brazil the drop in total investment was less serious than that in Argentina—its share in GDP was 5.4 percentage points lower in 1985-89 than in 1978-81—while private investment started to recover after 1984, although public investment was still below its pre-crisis level.

Argentina provides almost a textbook (and dramatic) case study of protracted economic instability acting as a powerful deterrent to private investment.  As figure 6-5 shows, the downward trend in private investment—as well as in public investment—had already started in Argentina in the mid-seventies.  Clearly, the preference for taking resources abroad rather than investing them at home was at work before the debt crisis, and to a large extent that factor was responsible for the absence of recovery afterwards.  On top of that lack of private investment, the data show a decline in public investment in the 1980s, a phenomenon tied to the fiscal crisis that Argentina was suffering.[13]

Brazil experienced the same downward trend in public investment starting in the early eighties.  That reduction was part of the fiscal response to the reduced external financing as well as to the enlarged burden posed by the internal public debt.

**Figure 6.5 Public and private investment rates in Argentina and Brazil**
(percent of GDP)

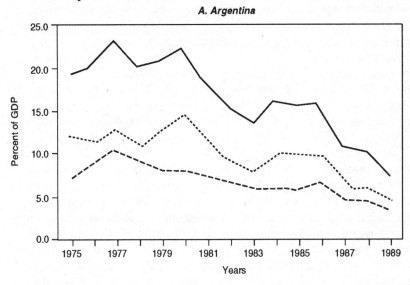

A. Argentina

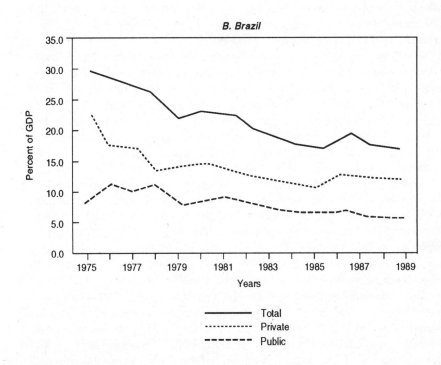

B. Brazil

Total
Private
Public

*Source:* World Bank data.

*Macroeconomic stability in Southeast Asia: Korea, Singapore, and Thailand*

In stark contrast to several of the Latin American countries, Korea, Singapore, and Thailand have had remarkable records of macroeconomic stability (table 6-6). In addition, they have had high-growth, outward-oriented but not laissez-faire economies. Finally, the distribution of income has been much more equitable in East Asia than in Latin America.[14]

Since the mid-sixties Korea has been a high-growth country, strongly oriented toward the expansion of manufacturing exports. The distribution of income has been relatively egalitarian,[15] although at the political level authoritarian military regimes governed the country from the sixties until 1987.

The high rates of investment in Korea were guided by a series of five-year economic plans. The government intervened actively to control, among other things, the allocation of credit to firms, with an overwhelming focus on exports. The close link between government and business in turn created large conglomerates and a high degree of industrial concentration.[16] The trade regime was far from liberal, with both tariffs and quantitative restrictions in place, although in the eighties the government relaxed these barriers. Exchange rate policy was oriented to maintaining the external competitiveness of Korean exports, although some episodes of real appreciation took place (for example, in the late 1970s). Korea recovered quickly from the impact of the debt crisis in 1979-82. In contrast with most highly indebted countries,[17] it was able to reduce its current account deficit after 1982 while restoring a high level of growth, maintaining a low level of inflation, and avoiding fiscal imbalances.

The case of Singapore is unique. It is a city-state, with a high-growth economy completely open to foreign trade and with (almost) unrestricted capital mobility operating under a fixed exchange rate regime. Its per capita income is comparable with that of low-income OECD countries, and the distribution of income is considered to be relatively even. Singapore did not suffer a debt crisis in the eighties and has been running current account surpluses since the mid-1980s in the context of its high growth and very low inflation.

Thailand borrowed in the late seventies and adjusted gradually afterwards, taking advantage of its good record of creditworthiness (Corden 1990). In the eighties, it reduced the deficit on the current account within a macro environment of sustained growth, while maintaining inflation at low levels and holding the fiscal budget in check. Thailand's performance is certainly a case of successful handling of the adverse foreign shocks without experiencing a macroeconomic crisis and domestic instability.

What about investment in these economies? Figure 6-6 illustrates two main features. First, Korea and Singapore in particular were high-investment, high-growth economies. In the period 1978-88, Korea sustained an average rate of investment near 30 percent of GDP and grew at an annual average rate of 6.5 percent. Singapore invested, on average, around 40 percent of GDP over the same period and grew at an average annual rate of

## Table 6.6 Public and private investment and macroeconomic indicators
(annual averages, percent)

### A. Korea

| Variable | 1978-81 | 1982-84 | 1985-88 | 1989 |
|---|---|---|---|---|
| Total investment (percent of GDP), real | 32.6 | 32.1 | 30.8 | 31.5 |
| Public investment (percent of GDP), real | 7.6 | 7.6 | 7.1 | 5.6 |
| Private investment (percent of GDP), real | 25.0 | 24.5 | 23.7 | 25.9 |
| Real GDP growth (percent) | 5.5 | 9.7 | 10.7 | 6.2 |
| Inflation (GDP deflator) | 21.0 | 5.1 | 3.6 | 6.5 |
| Current account balance (percent of GDP) | -5.9 | -2.3 | 4.8 | 2.4 |
| Foreign debt (percent of GDP) | 41.1 | 48.7 | 36.8 | 15.8 |
| Real exchange rate (1980=100) | 97.7 | 96.5 | 115.9 | 98.6 |

### B. Singapore

| Variable | 1978-81 | 1982-84 | 1985-88 | 1989 |
|---|---|---|---|---|
| Total investment (percent of GDP), real | 39.3 | 49.4 | 39.3 | 83.3 |
| Public investment (percent of GDP), real | 10.1 | 15.6 | 13.6 | 6.9 |
| Private investment (percent of GDP), real | 29.1 | 33.9 | 25.8 | 31.4 |
| Real GDP growth (percent) | 9.3 | 7.8 | 5.2 | 8.8 |

(continued)

Table 6.6 (continuation)

| | | | | |
|---|---|---|---|---|
| Inflation (GDP deflator) | 6.5 | 2.9 | 0.3 | 2.5 |
| Current account balance (percent of GDP) | -9.4 | -4.7 | 3.1 | n.a. |
| Foreign debt (percent of GDP) | 12.7 | 9.4 | 11.6 | n.a. |
| Real exchange rate (1980=100) | 98.6 | 89.1 | 104.8 | 110.2 |

## C. Thailand

| Variable | 1978-81 | 1982-84 | 1985-88 | 1989 |
|---|---|---|---|---|
| Total investment (percent of GDP), real | 25.9 | 25.0 | 23.6 | 25.6 |
| Public investment (percent of GDP), real | 8.5 | 8.5 | 7.0 | 4.4 |
| Private investment (percent of GDP), real | 17.5 | 16.5 | 16.7 | 21.2 |
| Real GDP growth (percent) | 6.6 | 6.1 | 6.8 | 9.9 |
| Inflation (GDP deflator) | 9.9 | 2.4 | 3.8 | 6.0 |
| Current account balance (percent of GDP) | -6.6 | -5.1 | -1.8 | -3.6 |
| Foreign debt (percent of GDP) | 25.5 | 35.2 | 42.5 | 24.0 |
| Real exchange rate (1980=100) | 103.5 | 93.3 | 118.5 | 126.1 |

n.a. Not available.
*Source*: Investment—elaboration based on Pfeffermann and Madarassy (1991); other variables—World Bank data.

## Figure 6.6  Public and private investment rates in Korea, Singapore, and Thailand
(percent of GDP)

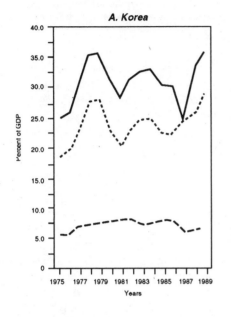

A. Korea

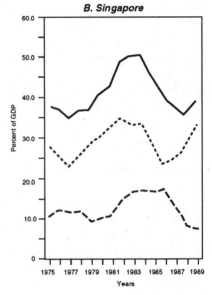

B. Singapore

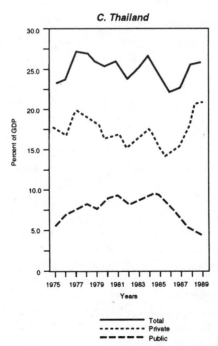

C. Thailand

———— Total
·········· Private
— — — Public

*Source:* World Bank data.

7.5 percent. Investment was not immune to the cycles of economic activity experienced in these economies in the eighties, however, and the data show some volatility in investment. A judgment on the relative efficiency of capital in these countries requires some difficult international comparisons, although the implied incremental capital/output ratios (ICORs) do not look particularly low (see chapter 8, "Investment and Macroeconomic Adjustment: The Case of East Asia", this volume).

Second, the data show that in these countries private investment was more important by far than public investment as a share of total investment (table 6-6). In Korea, around three-fourths of total investment was private; in Singapore and Thailand, the share of private investment in total capital formation was around two-thirds. These countries offer interesting examples of strong private sectors backed by active, growth-oriented governments.

*An overall assessment*

Some conclusions emerge from the diversity of experiences examined above:
• There are some clear differences in the level and composition of investment between the Latin American and East Asian countries. During the 1980s (and also earlier), rates of investment on the order of 30 percent of GDP and more (for example, 40 percent on average in Singapore) were not unusual in the East Asian countries.[18] Their growth record was also remarkable for the 1980s, with annual average rates on the order of 6.5-7.5 percent. In Latin America, historically the rates of investment were on the order of 20-25 percent, supporting rates of GDP growth of 5.5-6.0 percent a year.[19] In the 1980s, the average annual rate of growth of GDP decelerated sharply to around 1.5 percent, and the rates of investment centered in the range of 15-18 percent of GDP.[20]
• The analysis suggests that a high degree of macroeconomic stability—defined as low and predictable inflation and external and internal balances—is of paramount importance to ensuring a strong response by private investment to economic incentives. The East Asian cases are good examples. In contrast, in some Latin American countries there is evidence that macroeconomic instability has been largely responsible for the poor performance of private investment in the 1980s.
• The evidence from Chile, Mexico, and Bolivia on the effects of structural reforms (trade liberalization, fiscal reform, and privatization) on private investment is mixed. Chile experienced a rapid recovery of private investment in both the late 1970s, following the inception of the reforms, and in the late 1980s, a period when macroeconomic balance was restored, the terms of trade turned favorable, and the government affirmed its commitment to the reforms. Mexico also saw a revival of private investment in the late 1980s in spite of high domestic real interest rates. Bolivia, however, which had also adopted liberalization policies after eliminating the hyperinflation of the mid-1980s, did not witness an upsurge in private investment, and per-capita growth remained stagnant.

- Several Latin American countries (adjusting and non-adjusting) experienced a decline in public investment during the 1980s. Chile was an exception, although public investment also declined sharply in the 1970s when the structural reforms were adopted. The implication is that public investment tends to be squeezed in the process of balancing the fiscal and external accounts.

### Determinants of investment performance: An empirical investigation

The preceding discussion examined the overall investment record of developing countries and selected country experiences. An immediate question is to what extent this performance can be explained by the external environment and the economic polices these countries faced in the last decade.

Chapter 2, "Private Investment and Macroeconomic Adjustment: A Survey," discussed at length, from the theoretical viewpoint, the determinants of private investment. It identified two key sets of factors as affecting investment performance: first, standard macroeconomic factors, such as real output growth and macroeconomic policies; and, second, the perceived degree of uncertainty and credibility surrounding the macroeconomic framework. On the first group of variables, chapter 2 concluded that output growth typically has a strong effect on investment. In contrast, the level of the real exchange rate was found to play an ambiguous role, as it affects investment through several channels that operate in different directions (adversely through the cost of imports of capital goods and its financial repercussions, and positively through its impact on exports). Likewise, public investment can crowd private investment in or out, depending on the extent to which it involves projects complementary to or substitutive for private investment. Finally, chapter 2 also concluded that uncertainty could have a very adverse effect on private investment.

What was the role of each of these factors in the observed investment performance of developing countries? To investigate this question, a simple investment equation was estimated using pooled cross-section—time series data for a group of 15 developing countries. Based on the discussion in chapter 2, it is postulated that real private investment is a function of real growth in output, the real exchange rate, real public investment, the foreign debt burden, and the degree of macroeconomic uncertainty/instability (inflation, volatility of inflation and the variability of the real exchange rate), as follows:

(6-1) $$IP/Y = F(\Delta Y, e, IG/Y, D^*/Y, \sigma)$$
where $IP$ = real private investment
$Y$ = real GDP
$e$ = real exchange rate
$IG$ = real public investment
$D^*/Y$ = ratio of foreign debt to GDP
$\sigma$ = appropriate measure of instability.

According to the discussion in chapter 2, it is expected that the growth of real output will exert a positive effect on the rate of private investment. In turn, the effect of the real exchange rate is uncertain, since it affects investment through several channels that operate in opposite directions, as discussed in chapter 2. The sign of the coefficient of public investment depends on whether public investment is primarily complementary to or substitutive for private investment. Last, an increase in the degree of economic instability or in the burden of foreign debt should reduce investment.[21] Finally, a dummy variable is introduced into the regressions that takes a value of one after 1982 to capture a possible shift in the empirical equation as a result of the reduction in the availability of external financing after the debt crisis.[22]

To estimate the investment equation, data for the years 1976-88 for 15 developing countries were used; hence, the sample consisted of 195 observations. The choice of countries and time period was dictated by the availability and reliability of the data. The countries in the study were Argentina, Bolivia, Brazil, Chile, Colombia, Costa Rica, Kenya, Korea, Mexico, Peru, Singapore, Thailand, Turkey, Uruguay, and Zimbabwe.

### Table 6.7  Macroeconomic and investment indicators

| Country group | Period | Real GDP growth | Total invest. GDP | Private invest. GDP | Public invest. GDP | Debt GDP | Real exchange rate | Inflat. instab. index | R.E.R.[a] instab. index |
|---|---|---|---|---|---|---|---|---|---|
| All | 1975-88 | 0.036 | 0.206 | 0.131 | 0.075 | 0.487 | 113.6 | 1.000 | 1.000 |
|  | 1975-81 | 0.044 | 0.226 | 0.144 | 0.082 | 0.344 | 104.6 | 0.406 | 0.897 |
|  | 1982-88 | 0.028 | 0.185 | 0.117 | 0.068 | 0.629 | 122.6 | 1.593 | 1.103 |
| Latin America | | | | | | | | | |
|  | 1975-88 | 0.023 | 0.171 | 0.106 | 0.065 | 0.589 | 125.2 | 1.585 | 1.167 |
|  | 1975-81 | 0.037 | 0.200 | 0.123 | 0.077 | 0.409 | 113.1 | 0.585 | 1.040 |
|  | 1982-88 | 0.009 | 0.143 | 0.089 | 0.054 | 0.769 | 138.1 | 2.584 | 1.286 |
| East Asia | 1975-88 | 0.073 | 0.320 | 0.230 | 0.090 | 0.269 | 99.3 | 0.068 | 0.643 |
|  | 1975-81 | 0.073 | 0.312 | 0.228 | 0.084 | 0.232 | 93.8 | 0.101 | 0.754 |
|  | 1982-88 | 0.073 | 0.325 | 0.230 | 0.095 | 0.307 | 104.9 | 0.035 | 1.532 |
| Africa | 1975-88 | 0.036 | 0.184 | 0.104 | 0.080 | 0.414 | 98.8 | 0.091 | 1.234 |
|  | 1975-81 | 0.036 | 0.217 | 0.128 | 0.089 | 0.270 | 94.7 | 0.094 | 1.230 |
|  | 1982-88 | 0.036 | 0.154 | 0.081 | 0.073 | 0.558 | 102.9 | 1.089 | 1.226 |

*Note*:    The sample covers the years 1975-88 and includes Argentina, Bolivia, Brazil, Chile, Colombia, Costa Rica, Kenya, Korea, Mexico, Peru, Singapore, Thailand, Turkey, Uruguay, and Zimbabwe.
a.  R.E.R. = real exchange rate.
*Source*: World Bank data base and authors' calculations.

To measure uncertainty, σ, the sample variability of some key macroeconomic variables was used. In particular, the variabilities of the real exchange rate and the inflation rate were considered. In each case, uncertainty is summarized by the coefficient of variation of the relevant variable over the last three years;[23] however, using longer or shorter time horizons did not significantly affect the estimated parameters.

The sample averages of the explanatory variables are summarized in table 6-7 for all the countries in the sample and for some regional subsamples. It should be emphasized that the regional groupings are "unbalanced," in that the Latin American group consists of nine countries, while the East Asian and African regions only include three and two countries, respectively. Nevertheless, the information in the table reveals a number of interesting differences across time periods and country groups.

For the overall sample, there was a decline in all the investment indicators between the pre- and post-debt crisis years. The fall in total investment exceeded 4 percentage points of GDP. When looked at regionally, however, the decline was concentrated in the Latin American and African country groups, for which the fall was about 6 percent of GDP. In contrast, the East Asia region actually showed a small increase in investment in the second half of the sample period—in addition to a consistently higher rate of investment than the other groups had in all periods. It can also be seen that the rates of both private and public investment declined in the Latin America and Africa country groups, while they both rose in East Asia.

On average, real GDP growth also declined after 1982. However, the regional disaggregation again shows that the slowdown was concentrated in the Latin American countries, with the other groups in the sample showing no significant change in their growth pattern.

All country groups experienced an increase in their average debt ratios between the pre- and post-1982 periods. The increase was, however, much larger in the Latin American and African countries in the sample (it almost doubled for both groups after the debt crisis) than it was in the East Asian group. Similarly, the real exchange rate depreciated on average in all three country groups, although the extent of the depreciation was much larger in Latin America (in excess of 20 percent) than in the other two country groups (around 10 percent).

The pattern of the indicators of instability over time and across regions also deserves comment. The last two columns of table 6-7 show two interesting facts. First, the East Asian country group was clearly "more stable" in terms of either of the instability measures than were the other two regions. Second, for the overall sample, after 1982 there was a spectacular increase in the variability (and the level) of inflation, along with a more moderate rise in the instability of the real exchange rate. However, the regional grouping reveals that the increase in instability was concentrated in the Latin American countries, while the East Asian group actually showed an improvement in terms of both indicators, and the African countries in the sample did not register any significant change in macroeconomic instability.

**Table 6.8  Estimation results, 1976-88**
(dependent variable: log of the private investment/GDP ratio)

| Variable | Model I | Model II |
|---|---|---|
| Real GDP growth[a] (lagged) | 1.166 | 1.149 |
| | (3.50) | (3.56) |
| Real public investment[b] | 0.160 | 0.147 |
| as percentage of real GDP | (2.55) | (2.31) |
| Foreign debt[b] | -0.230 | -0.240 |
| as percentage of GDP | (-3.50) | (-3.56) |
| Real exchange rate[b] | 0.101 | —— |
| | (0.98) | |
| Inflation instability[c] | -0.006 | -0.008 |
| index | (-1.69) | (-2.03) |
| R.E.R. instability[c] | -0.043 | -0.027 |
| index | (-1.92) | (-1.61) |
| Post-1982 dummy | -0.107 | -0.095 |
| | (-3.09) | (-2.89) |
| $R^2$ | 0.974 | 0.978 |
| Autocorrelation coefficient | 0.400 | 0.402 |
| SEE | 0.068 | 0.068 |
| Standard deviation of dep. variable | 0.530 | 0.530 |
| Number of observations | 195 | 195 |

*Note:* t-statistics appear in brackets. The regressions include 15 country dummies.
a. First differences of the log of real GDP.
b. Expressed in logs.
c. Measured by the coefficient of variation.
*Source:* Authors' calculations.

The investment equation was estimated using the "fixed effects" panel data specification (see, for example, Hsiao 1986). Since preliminary experiments indicated the presence of moderate but significant first-order serial correlation in the residuals, the two-stage estimation procedure proposed by Bhargava, Franzini, and Narendranathan (1982) was used. The second round estimates do not show any symptoms of auto-correlation. Finally, both linear and logarithmic specifications were tested; the latter were adopted in view of their superior performance in terms of explanatory power and overall significance.

The empirical estimates appear in table 6-8. Since the level of the real exchange rate always failed to be statistically significant at any reasonable level of confidence, both the specifications with and without it are reported. As can be seen from the table, deleting the real exchange rate has only a negligible effect on the remaining coefficients.

Overall, the results for either specification are quite good: the parameter estimates carry their theoretically correct signs, and the explanatory power of the equations is extremely high.

As in most empirical studies, it was found here that (lagged) growth in real output had a strong positive impact on private investment. Public investment also had a positive effect on private investment. In short, the complementarity relationships between both investment categories dominated the sample. As expected, the foreign debt burden had a strong negative effect on the private investment ratio; as argued, this result may reflect a combination of the increased macroeconomic uncertainty arising from the need to carry out an increased resource transfer abroad and the effects of credit rationing on the world capital markets. In contrast, the effect of the real exchange rate reported in the first column of table 6-8 is not significant;[24] this result is in accordance with the theoretical discussion in which several channels were identified through which the real exchange rate may affect investment in opposite directions.[25]

The two measures of instability carry a negative sign, as expected. Although their individual significance is not always above the 5 percent level, taken together they are strongly significant: for example, using model II, the null hypothesis that they are jointly insignificant can be rejected (the computed value of the chi-square statistic with two degrees of freedom is 6.70, well above the 5 percent limit of 5.99). This result is probably attributable to the fact that both variables contain some common information (for example, greater variability in inflation will often be reflected in greater variability in the real exchange rate).

Finally, the post-1982 dummy is negative and strongly significant, clear evidence of a downward shift in investment as a result of the worsened international environment and the reduction in external financing after the debt crisis.

Since the parameter estimates in table 6-8 correspond to a logarithmic specification of the determinants of the ratio of private investment to GDP, it may be useful to restate them in a manner that provides a more direct measure of the impact of the different variables on the investment ratio. Table 6-9 provides that information: it details the impact on the share of private investment in GDP of a 1 percentage point increase in each of the right-hand side variables, using the second specification in the previous table.[26]

According to the figures in the table, the largest effect corresponds to the public investment ratio: an increase in the ratio of public investment to GDP of 1 percentage point raises the private investment ratio by over one-fourth

## Table 6.9 Determinants of real private investment
(percentage of GDP)

| *Effect on the private investment/GDP ratio of a 1 percentage point increase in* | *Percentage points* |
|---|---|
| Public investment/GDP | 0.257 |
| Foreign debt/GDP | -0.065 |
| Real GDP growth | 0.151 |
| Inflation instability | -0.001 |
| Real exchange rate instability | -0.003 |

*Note*: The figures were obtained using the "all countries" sample mean of each variable (presented in Table 6.7).
*Source*: Authors' calculations based on tables 6.7 and 6.8.

## Table 6.10 Contribution of explanatory variables to the change in private investment, 1982-88 vs. 1975-81

| | All countries | Latin America[a] | East Asia[b] | Africa[c] |
|---|---|---|---|---|
| Change in private investment (percent of GDP) | -2.7 | -3.4 | 0.5 | -4.7 |
| Explained by changes in: | | | | |
| Foreign debt/GDP | -1.8 | -2.3 | -0.5 | -1.9 |
| GDP growth rate | -0.2 | -0.4 | 0.0 | 0.0 |
| Public investment/GDP | -0.4 | -0.6 | 0.3 | -0.4 |
| Instability | -0.2 | -0.3 | 0.1 | 0.0 |
| Post-1982 dummy | -1.2 | -1.2 | -1.2 | -1.2 |
| Explained change | -3.8 | -4.8 | -1.3 | -3.5 |
| Residual[d] | 1.1 | 1.4 | 1.8 | -1.2 |

a. The countries are Argentina, Bolivia, Brazil, Chile, Colombia, Costa Rica, Mexico, Peru, and Uruguay.
b. The East Asia group includes Korea, Singapore, and Thailand.
c. The Africa group includes Kenya and Zimbabwe.
d. Residual = actual change minus explained change.
*Source*: Authors' calculations based on tables 6.7 and 6.8.

of a point. Similarly, a 1 percentage point increase in the growth rate of real GDP increases the investment ratio by 0.15 percentage points; in turn, an increase in foreign debt of 1 percentage point of GDP reduces investment by about 0.07 percentage point of GDP. Finally, a 1 percent increase in the instability of inflation and the real exchange rate results in declines in the investment ratio of 0.001 and 0.003 percentage points, respectively.

An important practical question that follows from the empirical results is: what has been the relative contribution of each of the explanatory variables to the actual variation of investment in developing countries in recent years? Identifying the variables that have made the greatest contributions is a task of more than scholarly interest: if some of the variables can be affected in a systematic manner by economic policy, then the exercise may provide guidance as to what the main policy priorities should be to revive private investment.

Table 6-10 presents the contribution of each of the determinants of investment to the observed evolution of the ratio of private investment to GDP between the pre- and post-debt crisis periods.[27] The calculations for the overall sample of countries and for the three regional groupings defined above are both reported.

For all country groups, the estimated equation predicts a fall in the investment share between both subperiods. For the overall sample, all variables contribute to the adverse investment performance. However, the largest contribution corresponds to the debt burden, which is responsible for a decline in the share of private investment in GDP of almost 2 percentage points; moreover, this variable contributes about half of the explained change for all country groups. Similarly, the post-crisis dummy also has a large impact: it explains a reduction in the investment share of more than 1 percentage point.

In turn, the evolution of public investment played a significant role: its reduction contributed to a deterioration in the private investment ratio of about 0.5 percentage point in both the overall sample and the Latin American and African country groups; however, its increase in the East Asian countries helped *raise* their private investment ratio by about 0.3 percentage point of GDP.

According to table 6-7, real GDP growth in the sample countries slowed only in the Latin American countries, while it was practically unchanged in the rest. Hence, in table 6-10 its contribution to the decline in investment is only 0.2 percentage points in the overall sample. However, in the case of the Latin America region, the deterioration in growth contributes a fall of 0.4 percentage points in the investment ratio.

Finally, the change in macroeconomic uncertainty, which combines the two instability measures, also contributed to the change in the private investment ratio. Its pattern differed widely across regions: it led to a 0.3 percentage point decline in investment in Latin America but to a 0.1 percent increase in East Asia; in the African country group, its contribution was nil. It should be remembered, however, that these figures probably represent a lower bound for the effects of instability, since a significant portion of the adverse contribution of the external debt burden to the investment performance reported above is likely to be related to the macroeconomic uncertainty associated with servicing the foreign debt.

To conclude, it should be emphasized that these computed contributions of the different explanatory variables to the observed investment performance should be viewed with some caution. Interpreting the contributions in terms of "causality" may be misleading, as in general the different variables are not mutually independent. For example, in a context of external credit rationing, an increased foreign debt burden is likely (or almost certain) to be associated with reduced public investment; in this sense, the adverse effect of the external debt burden on private investment would be understated by simple calculations such as the ones reported above—which consider only the *direct* effect of each variable on investment.

## Conclusions and policy implications

This chapter investigated the macroeconomic determinants of the recent investment performance of developing countries, drawing on the experience of selected countries and on an econometric analysis of a sample of developing countries.

The comparison of the experience of several Latin American and East Asian countries suggests some lessons regarding the performance of investment following adjustment and reform. First, the investment and growth performance of the Latin American and East Asian countries in the 1980s differed markedly. In the latter, the adjustment to the external shocks was relatively mild, and after an initial decline in investment and growth, both returned to pre-shock levels fairly rapidly. In contrast, in several Latin American economies the adverse external shocks of the early 1980s and the debt crisis led to a protracted period of macroeconomic instability, with large drops in investment and growth. Moreover, recovering a path of sustained growth has proved slow and complicated. The maintenance of macroeconomic stability and predictable policy, in addition to a more rapid resumption of foreign financing in East Asia relative to Latin America, to a large extent explain the differences in the performance of investment in both regions.

Second, the evidence from Chile, Mexico, and Bolivia on the effects of structural reforms (trade liberalization, fiscal reform, and privatization) on private investment is mixed. In the late 1970s and 1980s in Chile and in the late 1980s in Mexico, the response of private investment to the reforms was considerable. However, Bolivia, which adopted liberalization policies after eliminating the hyperinflation of the mid-1980s, did not see an upsurge in private investment, and per-capita growth remained stagnant.

Third, the decline in public investment is a disturbing factor in the investment response to adjustment and reform. That trend was observed in Chile in the mid- to late 1970s and in Mexico in the late 1980s. In addition, this feature was also present in non-adjusting economies such as Argentina and Brazil in the 1980s. While in some instances the cut in public investment was unavoidable (because it had reached unsustainable levels, as, for example, in Mexico in the late 1970s), in others the across-the-board contraction in the accumulation of public capital probably affected many projects that were complementary with private investment.

The determinants of private investment were analyzed econometrically using panel data for 15 developing countries. Overall, the specification presented here had a high explanatory power, accounting for more than 90 percent of the observed variation in the ratio of private investment to GDP. The results indicate that, in the sample, growth in output and public investment had a significantly positive impact on private investment. In contrast, the foreign debt burden, macroeconomic instability (measured by the variability of both inflation and the real exchange rate), and the deterioration in the external environment after 1982 exerted a significantly adverse effect on private investment. Finally, the effect of the real exchange rate was found to be insignificant.

Given the econometric estimates, the contributions of the different explanatory variables to the decline in the average ratio of private investment to GDP after 1982 were analyzed. All the variables contributed to some extent to the fall in investment, but the external debt burden and credit rationing may have played relatively the largest roles in the slowdown in investment. However, the contributions of the different variables differed widely across the regions represented in the sample; for example, increased macroeconomic instability and reduced public investment helped push the private investment ratio in Latin America down, while reduced instability and higher public investment had the opposite effect in East Asia. These regional patterns are in broad agreement with the conclusions derived from the country experiences reviewed above.

This analysis has some important implications for the design of growth-enhancing macroeconomic adjustment programs. First, macroeconomic stability and policy credibility are key ingredients for the achievement of a strong investment response. In a context of high macroeconomic uncertainty, the reaction of investment to changes in incentives is likely to be very limited. The same will happen if the policy measures are perceived to be inconsistent or temporary. In such circumstances, investors will prefer to wait and see before committing resources to irreversible fixed investments.

Second, even if the policy changes are perceived as permanent, insufficient public investment (particularly in infrastructure) in projects complementary with private investment may hamper the recovery of the latter. The protection of well-targeted public investment projects in infrastructure during the course of macroeconomic and, particularly, fiscal adjustment can play an important role in stimulating the private sector's response to adjustment measures.

Third, the availability of sufficient external resources may be a key ingredient for the recovery of private investment, not only because it contributes directly to an easing of the financing constraints on investment, but also because it may raise the private sector's confidence in the viability of the adjustment effort. In particular, the empirical findings suggest that debt relief measures could go a long way toward helping revive investment by liberating investible resources currently committed to service the debt burden, and also by reducing the disincentive effects on investment caused by the debt overhang.

## Notes

1.  The authors appreciate the comments by Bela Balassa, Max Corden, Stanley Fischer, Felipe Larrain, and Dani Rodrik on an earlier version of this chapter. Raimundo Soto provided efficient research assistance.
2.  The breakdown of investment into private and public components draws on Pfeffermann and Madarassy (1991). Private investment was obtained from the national accounts data as the difference between total investment and investment by the consolidated public sector.
3.  Mexico used incomes policy for stabilization purposes after late 1987; Chile and Bolivia used some form of exchange rate stabilization and/ or wage controls to help disinflation at different times during stabilization. For the Chilean experience with stabilization in the last two decades, see Corbo and Solimano (1991). Bolivia's experience with stabilization and reform is described in Morales (1991).
4.  The crisis of 1982-83 placed some of Chile's policies under heavy stress. Some reversals took place, such as increases in tariffs and direct government intervention in the financial system. However, as the crisis receded, the government lowered tariffs again and gradually deregulated the financial system.
5.  An econometric analysis of the behavior of private investment in Chile in the 1980s appears in Solimano (1989).
6.  The share of public investment in GDP in Mexico rose from 7.7 percent in the period 1971-77 to 10.5 percent in 1978-81.
7.  See Ortiz (1990) for a discussion of the Mexican case and the behavior of private investment in the late 1980s.
8.  See Morales (1991) for a discussion of the Bolivian plan.
9.  The development plans of the late sixties in forestry and agro-industrial activities, and the new land-property structure following the agrarian reform, also were elements in the strong export response of agricultural goods in Chile in the mid- to late-1980s.
10. Keynes (1936, chapter 12), referred to it as "...the state of confidence...a matter to which practical men always pay the closest and most anxious attention. But economists have not analyzed it carefully...."
11. Peru and Nicaragua are other cases of extreme macroeconomic instability in Latin America in the 1980s.
12. Argentina was the pioneer with heterodox stabilization, launching the Austral plan in mid-1985; Brazil followed with the Cruzado plan in

early 1986. After some initial success, those plans were undercut by a resumption of inflation and the repeated use of price controls and emergency fiscal measures to curb (transitorily) the escalating inflation. The situation in both economies worsened in 1989 as the rate of inflation approached hyperinflationary levels in the context of domestic recession and political disarray. See Heymann (1991), Kiguel and Liviatan (1991), Cardoso (1991), and Solimano (1989) on the experience of these two countries and other countries with stabilization.

13. It is well-known that the quality of public services has deteriorated sharply in Argentina in recent years. No doubt this situation is related to the inability of the state to improve the collection of the fiscal revenues from the tax system.

14. See chapter 8, "Investment and Macroeconomic Adjustment: The Case of East Asia, " in this volume for some comparative figures on international patterns of income distribution in East Asia, Latin America, and the countries in the Organization for Economic Co-operation and Development (OECD).

15. The aragrian reform is credited with being an important factor in the relatively even distribution of income in Korea (Collins and Park).

16. See Collins and Park (1989) for good description of the Korean case.

17. Chile is perhaps an exception in this respect.

18. In terms of composition of total investment, private investment was overwhelmingly dominant, representing between two-thirds and three-quarters of total capital accumulation in these East Asian economies.

19. The average annual rate of growth of GDP in 19 Latin American countries for the period 1950-80 was 5.8 percent, with output measured in terms of adjusting purchasing power. Per capita GDP grew in the same period at an annual rate of 3 percent. See Cardoso and Fishlow (1992).

20. This range is an unweighted average for Argentina, Bolivia, Brazil, Chile, and Mexico for the period 1978-88.

21. It is important to emphasize that, as discussed, the ratio of debt to GDP may affect investment negatively through more than one channel, as it constitutes a summary measure of anticipated taxation, external liquidity problems, and the macroeconomic uncertainty associated with servicing the foreign debt.

22. The empirical equation does not include the real interest rate among the explanatory variables. Experiments by authors with alternative measures of the ex-ante rate of interest proved unsuccessful. The usual difficulties in measuring such a variable are likely to be compounded here by the wide differences in financial market arrangements across the countries in the sample and across time periods. Thus, a decision was made to exclude the interest rate from the final specification.

23. The measure thus obtained rescaled so that its sample mean equaled 1.

24. This result was not altered in other specifications that allowed for one- or two year lags in the effect of the real exchange rate .

25. Time-series studies of private investment tell a somewhat different

story. In Solimano(1989), which examines the case of Chile, a real appreciation of the exchange rate raises(aggregate) private investment, but the outburst of investment is unsustainable: conversely, a real depreciation reduces investment in the short term. Musalem(1989) also finds a significant negative effect of depreciation on investment for Mexico. For further discussion of this issue, see Fischer (1991).

26. Thus, the calculations in table 7-9 involve a linearization of the logarithmic equation around the sample means of the variables.

27. The figures in table 7-10 follow directly from tables 7-7 and 7-9. Because for each subperiod and/or region the residuals need not add up to zero, and because table 7-9 is based on a linear approximation, there is in general a discrepancy between the observed and actual changes in the ratio of investment to GDP. This discrepancy is the figure reported at the bottom of table 7-10.

## References

Bhargava, A., L. Franzini, and W. Narendranathan. 1982. "Serial Correlation and the Fixed Effects Model." *Review of Economic Studies* 49:533-49.

Cardoso, E. 1991. "From Inertial Inflation to Megainflation: Brazil in the 1980s." In M. Bruno, et al., eds., *Lessons of Economic Stabilization and Its Aftermath*. Cambridge, Mass.: MIT Press.

Cardoso, E., and A. Fishlow. 1992. "Latin American Economic Development: 1950-1980." *Journal of Latin American Studies* 24:197-218.

Collins, S., and W. A. Park. 1989. "External Debt and Macroeconomic Performance in South Korea," In J. Sachs, ed., *Developing Country Debt and the World Economy*. Chicago: University of Chicago Press.

Corbo, V., and A. Solimano. 1991. "Stabilization Policies in Chile Revisited," in M. Bruno, et al., eds., *Lessons from Stabilization and Its Aftermath*. Cambridge, Mass.: MIT Press.

Corden, M. 1990. "Macroeconomic Policy and Growth: Some Lessons of Experience." Prepared for the World Bank Conference on Development Economics, Washington, D.C., April 26 and 27, 1990.

Easterly, W. 1989. "Fiscal Adjustment and Deficit Financing during the Debt Crisis," in I. Husain and I. Diwan, eds., *Dealing with the Debt Crisis*. Washington, D.C.: World Bank.

Fischer, S. 1991. "Growth, Macroeconomics and Development." National Bureau of Economic Research (NBER) Working Paper Series no. 3702 (May):1-53.

Heymann, D. 1991. "From Sharp Disinflation and Hyper and Back: The Argentine Experience, 1985-89," in M. Bruno, et al., eds., *Lessons from Stabilization and Its Aftermath*. Cambridge, Mass.: MIT Press.

Hsiao, C. 1986. *Analysis of Panel Data*. Cambridge: Cambridge University Press.

International Monetary Fund (IMF). 1989. *Short-Term Economic Outlook*. Washington, D.C.: IMF.

Keynes, J. M. 1936. *The General Theory of Employment, Interest, and Money.* New York: A Harvest BHJ Book.

Kiguel, M., and N. Liviatan. 1991. "The Inflation-Stabilization Cycles in Argentina and Brazil," in M. Bruno, et al., eds., *Lessons from Stabilization and Its Aftermath.* Cambridge, Mass.: MIT Press.

Larrain, F., and R. Vergara. 1991. "Investment and Macroeconomic Adjustment in East Asia." Mimeo. World Bank, Washington, D.C.

Morales, J. A. 1991. "The Transition from Stabilization to Sustained Growth in Bolivia," in M. Bruno, et al., eds., *Lessons from Stabilization and Its Aftermath.* Cambridge, Mass.: MIT Press.

Musalem, A. 1989. "Private Investment in Mexico: An Empirical Analysis." World Bank, Policy, Planning and Research (PPR) Working Paper no. 183. Washington, D.C.

Ortiz, G. 1990. "Mexico Beyond the Debt Crises. Towards Sustainable Growth with Price Stability," in M. Bruno, et al., eds., *Lessons from Stabilization and Its Aftermath.* Cambridge, Mass.: MIT Press.

Pfefferman, G., and A. Madarassy. 1991. "Trends in Private Investment in Developing Countries." International Finance Corporation Discussion Paper. Washington, D.C.

Solimano, A. 1989. "How Private Investment Reacts to Changing Macroeconomic Conditions. The Chilean Experience in the 1980s." World Bank, Policy, Research, and External Affairs (PRE) Working Paper Series no. 212. Washington, D.C. Also in A. Chhibber, M. Dailami, and N. Shafik, eds., *Reviving Private Investment in Developing Countries: Empirical Studies and Policy Lessons.* Amsterdam: North-Holland Publishing, 1992.

———. 1990. "Inflation and the Costs of Stabilization. Historical and Recent Experiences and Policy Lessons." *The World Bank Research Observer* 5 (2)(July):167-86.

World Bank. 1992. "Adjustment Lending Policies for Sustainable Growth." World Bank, Policy, Planning and Research (PPR) Working Paper no. 14. Washington, D.C.

# 7

# Macroeconomic Environment and Capital Formation in Latin America

## *Eliana Cardoso*

This chapter discusses the macroeconomic climate affecting investment in Latin America and explores the relationships between investment and growth, exchange rates, and the terms of trade.[1]

The next section summarizes the macroeconomic background of Latin America and discusses the contrasting experiences of Argentina, Brazil, Chile, and Mexico. Real per capita gross domestic product (GDP) in Latin America more than doubled between 1950 and 1980. By 1989, however, per capita GDP had fallen below its 1980 level in all the countries of Latin America except Brazil, Chile, Colombia, and the Dominican Republic.

GDP depends on the quantity and quality of investment. Figure 7-1 shows the shares of investment in GDP in different developing regions. The economies of East Asia have been investing some 30 percent of GDP each year during the 1970s, a proportion that held roughly constant through the 1980s. In contrast, the share of investment in GDP in Latin America has been well below the levels in East Asia: it was 24 percent at the end of the 1970s and fell to a debt-stricken plateau of roughly 17 percent in the mid-1980s. In 1989 the region still suffered a deep crisis, although, between 1987 and 1989, Latin America's investment increased to more than 20 percent of GDP, even with continuing capital flight.

Part of Latin America's plight has undoubtedly originated from the unfavorable external environment in which private loans were suspended and the terms of trade worsened. Although these factors have been important, they do not provide a complete picture of what went wrong there during the 1980s. Many of the problems derive from errors in domestic policy.[2] Since 1982 Latin American countries have faced the choice between adjustment or accommodation. Chile and Mexico chose adjustment, suffered a large recession, and reformed their economies. After 1984, Chile recovered quickly because of an aggressive policy of depreciation of the real exchange rate and revival of both public and private investment.

**Figure 7.1  Gross domestic investment in developing countries, 1980-89**

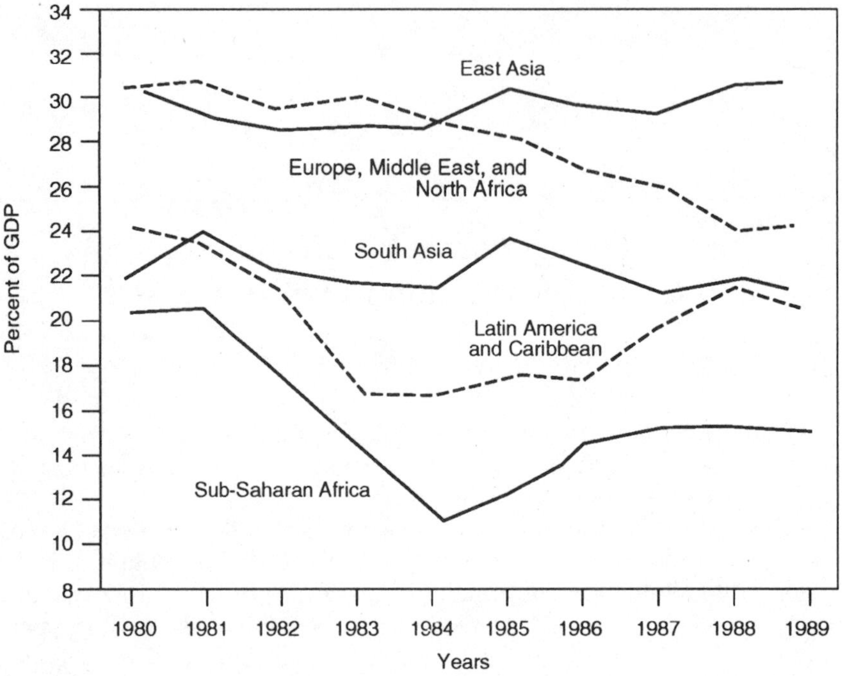

Source:  World Bank.

Mexico's recovery is still in progress.  Argentina and Brazil, in contrast, chose accommodation.  By 1990 the lack of adjustment in both countries had resulted in inflation and recession.  The effects of the financial instability on investment were clearly visible in Argentina but were much less apparent in Brazil.

After the 1982 debt shock, the real exchange rate in Brazil depreciated only slightly compared with the preceding period, and the share of investment in GDP fell much less than it did in Argentina, Chile, Mexico, and Venezuela, where the real depreciation was large (table 7-1). Servén and Solimano (1990) surveyed empirical studies that showed the adverse impact of real depreciation on investment (appendix 7-1 reports on other empirical studies of investment). This chapter shows that, once the relevant variables (for instance, the terms of trade) are taken into account, the effect of a real depreciation on investment is not significant.

The third section looks at the theoretical issue of the relationship between the real exchange rate and the real price of capital. A model of a small open economy with a crawling peg is used to discuss the dynamics of both the real price of capital and the real exchange rate in response to a deterioration in the terms of trade. With a nominal exchange rate rule fixed

**Table 7.1  Real depreciation and changes in real investment shares, selected countries, 1982-88 relative to 1980-81**
(percent)

|  | Change in effective real exchange rates[a] | Change in investment share in GDP |
|---|---|---|
| Argentina | -39.3 | -29.5 |
| Brazil | -8.4 | -14.0 |
| Chile | -22.2 | -36.6 |
| Colombia | -13.3 | -2.6 |
| Mexico | -26.5 | -24.9 |
| Venezuela | -4.4 | -23.2 |

a. Morgan Guaranty defines the real exchange rate as domestic prices divided by foreign prices. A minus sign thus indicates a depreciation.
*Source:* Morgan Guaranty and World Bank.

**Table 7.2  Share of gross domestic output in regional output and growth rates of Latin American countries**

| Countries | Share in total GDP, 1980 (percent) | Growth rate of per capita GDP (percent per year) | |
|---|---|---|---|
| | | 1950-80 | 1981-89[a] |
| Brazil | 34.2 | 4.2 | 0.0 |
| Mexico | 23.1 | 3.0 | -1.0 |
| Argentina | 11.8 | 1.8 | -2.6 |
| Colombia | 6.3 | 2.3 | 1.5 |
| Venezuela | 7.1 | 1.5 | -2.8 |
| Peru | 3.9 | 2.1 | -2.7 |
| Chile | 3.4 | 1.8 | 1.1 |
| Uruguay | 1.2 | 1.4 | -0.8 |
| Ecuador | 1.6 | 3.1 | -0.1 |
| Guatemala | 1.2 | 1.8 | -2.0 |
| Dominican Republic | 1.1 | 2.6 | 0.2 |
| Bolivia | 0.8 | 1.3 | -2.9 |
| El Salvador | 0.5 | 1.3 | -1.9 |
| Paraguay | 0.7 | 2.4 | 0.0 |
| Costa Rica | 0.6 | 3.3 | -0.7 |
| Panama | 0.5 | 2.9 | -1.9 |
| Nicaragua | 0.4 | 2.3 | -3.7 |
| Honduras | 0.4 | 1.4 | -1.3 |
| Haiti | 0.2 | 0.7 | -2.1 |
| Latin America[b] | | 2.7 | -0.8 |

Note:  Countries are in order of their average share in regional GDP between 1950 and 1985.
a. Preliminary.
b. Except Cuba.
*Sources:* Summers and Heston (1984); and ECLAC.

by the central bank, a deterioration in the terms of trade leads to an immediate decline in the real price of capital, followed by a depreciating real exchange rate while the real price of capital slowly recovers.

The fourth section further explores the role of the terms of trade in determining investment.[3]

The determinants of investment in Latin America are the focus of the fifth section. The regressions use quadrennial panel data for the period 1970-85 in Argentina, Brazil, Chile, Colombia, Mexico, and Venezuela. Together, these six countries accounted for 86 percent of total GDP in the region in 1980 (table 7-2). The decline in the shares of private investment in Latin America during the 1980s seems to have resulted from the deterioration in the terms of trade, decline in growth (the result of adjustment programs designed to reduce current account deficits), reduction in complementary public investment, increased macroeconomic instability, and large stock of foreign debt. The real exchange rate and the real rate of depreciation had no significant role in determining private investment in the regressions presented here.

Four appendices present more detailed information on some empirical studies of investment in Latin America (appendix 7-1), the price of capital and the real exchange rate (appendix 7-2), the data used in the regressions presented in this chapter (appendix 7-3), and investment shares in GDP (appendix 7-4).

## Macroeconomic background

Between 1950 and 1980 real per capita GDP in Latin America grew at 2.7 percent a year because of the expanding world economy, strong demand for primary products, and rapid capital accumulation in the industrial sector. As a result of its stellar performance, Brazil increased its share of regional GDP from less than 25 percent to more than 33 percent. Not all Latin American countries did as well as Brazil and Mexico, however. The Southern Cone countries of Argentina, Chile, and Uruguay experienced subpar performance that eroded the positions they held in 1950. A number of smaller countries also lagged, including several in Central America. In most countries, however, the growth rate of employment exceeded that of the working age population, with a marked transformation in the structure of production. Latin America evolved from a rural to a predominantly urban society, experiencing dramatic changes in occupational and social mobility.

The impressive growth from 1950 to 1980 in Latin America seems less positive when two factors are considered. The first is the overall dramatic economic reversal in the 1980s (table 7-2). The second is the surging performance of the Asian countries. The contrast between the performance of the two regions is now widely interpreted as proving the errors of the import-substitution strategy favored by Latin America in most of the post-War period.

## Economic policies and growth before the 1980s

During the 1950s most Latin American countries moved toward an import-substitution strategy. Policymakers saw it as the pragmatic response to the problems following the Great Depression of the 1930s and the disruption of the Second World War. Later, structuralists, reformists, and developmentalists conceived economic models that justified the import-substitution strategy, pointing to the inadequacy of market mechanisms alone to achieve industrialization. They built their arguments on two pillars: the foreign exchange constraint as an important determinant of growth; and market imperfections. These conditions supported a strong presence by the state.

While this model made sense, it was far from perfect. It downplayed the role of the market and did not address three issues:

• Protection led to overvalued exchange rates and hence to an eventual reduction in the supply of exports. Industrialization in turn required increased inputs of capital goods and intermediate imports.

• In sectoral terms, import-substitution policies excessively promoted industrial growth at the expense of agriculture. Moreover, relatively capital-intensive manufactures absorbed only a fraction of the increase in the labor force, a situation that put pressure on the government to serve as the employer of last resort.

• Finally, as the resources taxed away from primary exports failed to increase, subsidies for industrial investment and growing government responsibilities put new pressure on the budget. Monetization of the deficit led to persistent inflation.

In the 1960s some countries recognized the limits of the import-substitution strategy and modified their commercial policy. Exchange rate systems with crawling pegs accommodated high rates of domestic inflation and averted the overvaluation so predominant in earlier periods. Explicit concern for the promotion of nontraditional exports produced special programs of export subsidies in many countries after 1965. This period of adaptation and relatively successful adjustment of the earlier model came to an end in 1973 when the rise in oil prices created international disequilibrium. Mounting indebtedness and deteriorating domestic policy in the more difficult external environment characterized the economic shock that followed the rise in oil prices. To reduce inflation, the Southern Cone countries resorted to international monetarism that led to a substantial increase in external liabilities. Mexico and Venezuela, confident that the value of their national oil reserves would increase, vastly expanded their borrowing. Brazil tried to sustain its pace of industrial expansion as its debt service payments were growing larger and domestic pressures were mounting. For the region as a whole, growth in output slowed in the 1970s but remained at satisfactory levels.

Cardoso and Fishlow (1992) provide a synthetic view of the period 1950-80. Their regression analysis used quinquennial panel data for 18

Latin American countries. A key finding was that growth in Latin America required more than an increase in capital formation. It also varied systematically with trade performance. Both the expansion of exports and the rate of growth of imports mattered. Exports were significant not only for their contribution to productive efficiency, but also because higher export earnings could avert recurrent crises with stabilization and their adverse effects on the growth of output. More novel is the finding that the availability of imports exerted an independent influence. Import substitution, successfully pursued, required imported inputs. Countries suffered when forced to curtail their foreign purchases excessively. This access to imports, both through export earnings and foreign finance, differentiated the successes from the failures. On this issue Brazil and Mexico diverged from the countries of the Southern Cone.

## The 1980s: External shocks and inflation

Even in Brazil and Mexico, the prospects for accelerating progress dimmed in the early 1980s. The precariousness of the Latin American economies became fully apparent when a new oil price rise, an abrupt increase in real interest rates, and a recession in the countries of the Organisation for Economic Co-operation and Development (OECD) coincided in the early 1980s. Countries in Latin America chose their adjustment style poorly after 1973. In addition to the original import-substitution bias of the 1950s, they suffered from an asymmetric opening to the world economy that featured vast financial flows with limited trade penetration. At the same time, fiscal distortions reduced the room for maneuver. To foster continued growth in the late 1970s, governments incurred deficits that in the 1980s they could no longer finance abroad. Starting in 1982, the supply of capital dried up. Interest payments on the debt became an enormous drain on export earnings and savings.

Table 7-3 shows that investment in the period 1983-88 fell on average by 6.8 percent of GDP compared with the period 1970-82, almost exactly equal to the increase in the surplus in the non-interest current account. While investment ratios dropped immediately in 1983 to accommodate the switch

**Table 7.3  Investment and the non-interest current account in Latin America, 1960-88**
(percent of GDP)

| Years | Investment | Non-interest current account |
|-------|------------|------------------------------|
| 1960-69 | 18.6 | 5.3 |
| 1970-82 | 23.2 | -0.4 |
| 1983-88 | 16.4 | 6.1 |

*Source*: Inter-American Development Bank (1989).

in net international transfers, they stabilized thereafter on a modest upward trend (figure 7-1).

Relative to the 1970s, while income growth and investment declined, real wages fell and inflation accelerated. Recent analyses of the inflation can be divided into a "fiscal" view and a "balance-of-payments" view (Montiel 1989). Followers of the fiscal view point to movements in the budget deficit as the fundamental source of monetary emission that pushes the economy to higher rates of inflation. Supporters of the balance-of-payments view link inflation to depreciation of the exchange rate triggered by balance-of-payments crises.

Consider, for example, a country that has a large external debt and is suddenly deprived of inflows of foreign capital. The government has to finance domestically the purchase of the foreign exchange needed to service the external debt. In the absence of a cut in the primary budget deficit, it will create more credit. At the same time it also undertakes devaluations of the exchange rate to balance the external payments. Devaluations increase the debt service when measured in domestic currency and thus increase the budget deficit when measured in that currency. This situation in turn raises the amount of money that needs to be created and hence inflation. Under these circumstances, to avoid an acceleration in inflation the government needs to create a primary surplus large enough to counterbalance the financial impact of the debt shock. Mexico and Chile moved in this direction, and their answer to forced debt service has been to increase taxes and reduce expenditures. The response in Argentina and Brazil, however, has been to finance the purchase of foreign exchange by issuing debt or printing money. Figure 7-2 shows the results of these contrasting policies

**Figure 7.2 Adjustment and accommodation in the 1980s**

| | | Inflation | |
|---|---|---|---|
| | | Reduced Inflation in 1989 | Hyperinflation in 1989 |
| Per capita income | 1989 > 1980 | Chile | Brazil |
| | 1989 < 1980 | Mexico | Argentina |

*Source:* Author's elaboration.

in 1989. Chile appears as the success story of adjustment while Argentina is the basket case. Brazil and Mexico are less clearcut cases.

*The experience with accommodation: Argentina and Brazil*

The rapid acceleration of inflation in Argentina and Brazil after 1987 cannot be directly attributed to the debt crisis. At different times their governments have run imposed moratoria on the external debt service and have allowed the real exchange rate to appreciate (figures 7-3 and 7-4). In both countries the acceleration in inflation resulted from the lack of domestic adjustment and the consequent flight from money. Here the similarities between the two countries end, however. Slow growth and reduced investment were not new for Argentina. In contrast, the financial instability in Brazil did not affect the country's performance until 1990, except for a short period between 1981 and 1983.

Two facts are worth emphasizing. First, to judge from its faster rate of growth in real per capita GDP since the 1920s, Brazil appears to have been

**Figure 7.3  Brazil: The real exchange rate**
(1980-82=100)

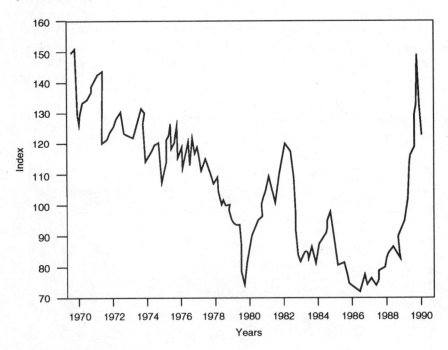

*Note:* Morgan Guaranty defines the effective real exchange rate as domestic prices divided by foreign prices. A movement upwards indicates a real appreciation.

*Source:* Morgan Guaranty.

more dynamic than Argentina. Between 1920 and 1988 the average rate of per capita growth in GDP in Brazil was 3.4 percent, compared with 1 percent in Argentina. Second, the Argentinean GDP figures show much greater instability than do Brazil's (Cardoso 1990). Between 1920 and 1988 the coefficient of variation of the growth rate of per capita GDP in Argentina was 4.5, whereas in Brazil it was 1.3. The extreme oscillations of Argentina's real exchange rate, whose extraordinary swings reflect economic policy mistakes, further illustrate the instability of its economy. The outstanding episode is the appreciation of 1979-81, which was followed by the collapse of the peso. In contrast, in Brazil until recently a pragmatic exchange rate policy prevented any comparable episodes.[4]

Recurrent patterns of inflation and stabilization in Argentina reflect a tense struggle between the interests of different groups, each with sufficient political resources to defend its share of national income. Labor leaders struggle with authorities over macro policies as fiercely as they bargain at the plant level. This conflict is unavoidable because wages are greatly affected by government intervention in the economy and by the successive

**Figure 7.4  Argentina:  The real exchange rate**
(1980-82=100)

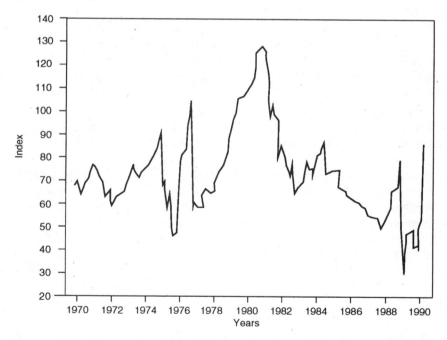

*Note:* Morgan Guaranty defines the effective real exchange rate as domestic prices divided by foreign prices. A movement upwards indicates a real appreciation.

*Source:* Morgan Guaranty.

anti-inflation stabilization programs. Each change of regime brings about major shifts in policy. Among industrialist and agro-exporting sectors the uncertainty about the future compresses time horizons and diverts resources from production to short-term speculative activities.

When a military coup overthrew the Peronist regime in 1976, Argentina was on the verge of hyperinflation. The first priority of the new regime was to stabilize inflation. Because inflation failed to decline below the 150 percent range, policymakers opted for an "expectations-managed approach." Beginning in 1979 they fixed the rate of depreciation of the exchange rate in advance using a *tablita*, which set forth gradually declining rates of depreciation.[5] Inflation gradually fell below 100 percent, but since that level continually exceeded the rate of depreciation, the real exchange rate appreciated. By 1980 overvaluation and colossal capital flight forced a large devaluation. Over the next few years depreciation and inflation became rampant. The budget deficit increased with the growing external interest payments at the same time that the deterioration in the terms of trade and the Malvinas war only amplified the devastation of the economy. The rate of inflation reached 600 percent by the time President Raul Alfonsín came to power in 1983. In 1985, his administration introduced the Austral Plan, which used a price freeze to achieve disinflation. By 1987, however, the acceleration of inflation was once more the central feature of the economy. Inflation had proved impossible to stop, the external debt remained a harrowing problem, and Argentina faced growing poverty.

In the same way as Argentina, Brazil traditionally has lived with high rates of inflation. Between 1980 and 1985 the government's failure to absorb the debt and oil shocks in a non-inflationary manner pushed inflation from 50 percent to 220 percent and beyond. In February 1986 Brazil embarked on a major stabilization effort—the notorious Cruzado Plan. Among the factors that led to the failure of the Cruzado Plan, the most prominent was the overheating of the economy through loose fiscal and monetary policies, as well as through an overly generous wage policy. Very low interest rates and increasing real wages produced a consumers' boom. When the government removed the freeze a year later, prices exploded. The government made new efforts to control inflation—the Bresser Plan in mid-1987 and the Summer Plan in January 1989. Because President José Sarney lacked the political will to implement measures of fiscal consolidation, the government did not keep its promises to eliminate the budget deficits. Sarney also lacked credibility, determination, and allies in Congress. With the budget deficit left untouched all three plans merely amounted to attempts to stop inflation by decree.

While in other high-inflation countries in Latin America flight from money has meant capital flight into deposits in Miami or cash dollars, in Brazil it has led to the creation of an even more perfect domestic money market. A real rate of return on government securities in excess of the economy's growth rate created, however, a rapidly growing stock of real government interest-bearing debt per capita. By the end of 1989, the ratio of domestic debt to GDP in Brazil was 0.83, but more significantly the maturity of this debt was explosively short. Debt maturity shrank as the government avoided paying even higher risk premia, a stance that gave people illusory liquidity. Debt repudiation seemed to be around the corner. There was also the plausible alternative of a forced consolidation of the debt into long-term bonds or into public enterprise ownership. The March 1990 Collor Plan presented a third alternative: blocking financial assets for 18 months.

The government achieved a temporary consolidation of the domestic debt by postponing debt service. It closed the banks for five days, blocked part of the *cruzados novos* in bank accounts, and introduced a new currency, the *cruzeiro*, to be exchanged on a one-to-one basis for the *cruzado novo*. The plan initially set an 18-month freeze on savings accounts of more than 50,000 cruzeiros (US$1,200) and limited withdrawals from bank deposits and money market funds. The measure was to be temporary—either the government would unfreeze the assets, write them off, or convert them into interest-bearing nonmarketable loans.

The blocking of assets reduced government spending on the debt service, so that the budget deficit was lowered, at least for a while. It also limited the extent to which the desired substitution of monetary wealth into commodities could take place. As a result of this process, production, sales, fuel consumption, and employment plunged, and in April 1990 the economy came to a halt. By July, despite pockets of recession, production in many sectors was again approaching the levels before the plan, and most economic indicators were pointing to a recovery. By then rapid remonetization had spread fears that inflation would take off again. The extreme financial instability of Brazil and Argentina at the end of the 1980s stands in radical contrast to the stability Chile and Mexico recently achieved.

## The Experience with adjustment: Chile and Mexico

The great instability of copper prices has traditionally harmed Chile's economic performance. Between 1900 and 1985 the average deviation of real copper prices from their trend was greater than 25 percent—an average deviation higher than that of any other commodity. The three most serious recessions in Chile (the 1930s, 1974-75, and 1982-83) all coincided with declining copper prices. At the same time, Chile's poor economic performance during the 1950s and 1960s derived in good measure from the combination of growing protectionism and state intervention as a development strategy. As prices lost their role as a guide to investment, fiscal and credit subsidies increased, a trend that multiplied the distortions and inefficiencies. At the same time budget deficits, inflation, and payments crises became intermittent. Inward-looking growth led to overdiversification of production for domestic markets and a concentration of exports in a few primary activities such as copper.

In the early 1970s the Allende regime, unable to finance its programs with taxes, did so with massive deficit spending. Although the government managed to repress inflation for a while with price controls, by August 1973 inflation had reached 300 percent a year. In the last quarter of that year a military junta took over. It freed all prices, devalued the exchange rate, controlled wages, and imposed restrictive fiscal and monetary policies. The result was a hyperstagflation.

To maintain the disinflation achieved in 1974, in mid-1975 the government tightened fiscal policy. This move brought the fiscal deficit down to 3 percent of GDP, and Chile's gross national product (GNP) fell by 13 percent. Inflation was only partially reduced. Meanwhile, the government undertook important economic reforms. It returned most activities in the public sector to private hands. It opened up trade: it reduced the tariffs from an average rate of 94 percent in 1973 to an average rate of 33 percent in 1976, and by mid-1979 it had lowered all tariff rates to 10 percent. Stubborn inflation finally convinced policymakers that the answer was global monetarism. By 1980 the public sector surplus exceeded 3 percent of GDP, seignorage revenue was negative, and inflation was on its way down. The real exchange rate appreciated dramatically, however, and in 1982 external disequilibria finally forced a reversal of the exchange rate policy.

During the exchange rate-based stabilization a debt-led boom developed. It was followed by a financial crisis and a severe recession that occasioned a 15 percent drop in GDP in 1982. The fragile condition of financial institutions forced massive rescue operations and liquidations. Starting in June 1982, the government undertook a number of discrete devaluations to correct the accumulated overvaluation. From then on a crawling peg continued to depreciate the exchange rate in real terms. Fiscal and monetary policies were restrictive.

Since 1984 Chile has experienced six years of expansion with moderate inflation and a reduction of the debt ratios. The annual growth rate of GDP of 6.3 percent between 1984 and 1989, with inflation of only 20 percent a year, occurred in the context of reduced current account deficits. In contrast to other Latin American countries, Chile was able to run a primary surplus big enough to transfer resources to the central bank to cover the quasi-fiscal budget deficit.

It took 15 years of reforms to cure Chile of both its accumulated past policy mistakes and the mega-inflation of the mid-1970s. During the last five years a pragmatic exchange rate policy has supported a recovery driven by export growth and the revival of public sector investment. The transition to democracy without capital flight indicates that Chile might finally be on a stable development path.

The same cannot yet be said of Mexico. Despite major economic reforms in the 1980s Mexico still seems politically and economically far from the Chilean miracle. Compared with Chile, Argentina, and Brazil, Mexico enjoyed extremely low inflation until the mid-1970s. Between 1960 and 1973 the average for Mexico was around 3 percent. In the mid-1970s inflation jumped to 15 percent and during the late 1970s rose further in large measure as a result of the budget deficits of President Jose Lopez Portillo's government.  Although public revenues from oil exports increased twelvefold from 1977 to 1981, they lagged behind government expenditures. To prevent further inflation, the government postponed increases in the prices and tariffs of goods and services provided by the public sector.  It financed the government deficits by external borrowing.  Continuing deterioration of the balance of payments, despite devaluations in 1981 and 1982, gave rise to the expectation that gradual depreciation of the exchange rate would be insufficient to correct imbalances in the current account; as a result, capital flight reached unprecedented levels.

Stabilization came at the end of 1982, and by late 1983 most of the fears of financial disaster that had prevailed the year before had vanished.  Large trade and current accounts surpluses were generated and the foreign debt renegotiated.  The debt service burden caused inflation to increase because resources had to be extracted from the private sector to finance the external debt of the public sector.

Between 1983 and 1988 the government implemented remarkable reforms on the fiscal and trade fronts.  There has been a dramatic turnaround in the budget, with a consistent surplus on the primary balance since 1983.  The improvement, amounting to 15 percent of GDP between 1982 and 1988, came mainly from cuts in expenditures, which fell by 11 percent of GDP.  The remaining gains resulted from a stronger effort to collect internal revenue, including corrections of public prices, reform of the income tax code, improvements in tax administration, and reduction of public enterprises.  Between 1982 and 1988 the government privatized over 700 enterprises.  The budget improved with the yearly return on sales of assets and the reduction in subsidies.  Trade reform followed the fiscal reform, especially since 1985, when the government reduced quantitative restrictions to 25 percent of imports.  It also reduced the maximum tariff, which was 100 percent in 1982, to 20 percent in 1988; the average effective protection also decreased substantially.

Despite these reforms and a falling per capita income over five years, the orthodox program did not stop inflation.  In October 1987 the collapse of the stock market exposed the precariousness of Mexico's economic situation.  The increased interest rates were not enough to stop the capital flight and fall in reserves.  The government allowed the exchange rate to depreciate, and inflation picked up again.  In 1988 it introduced a new program, the Pacto Social, which used a fixed exchange rate supported by price controls and a wage freeze to halt inflation.  As a result of the Pacto, monthly rates of inflation dropped from an average of about 15 percent in January 1988 to only 1 percent in the second half of the year.  Of additional help was Mexico's 1989 agreement with commercial bank creditors on a multiyear financing package and two alternative debt-exchange options. This development meant that debt amounting to about $22.5 billion would be subject to reduced interest rates and that additional gross claims of about $7 billion would be extinguished.  The 1989 rate of per capita GDP growth was 1 percent, the first real improvement since the onset of the debt crisis.

**Figure 7.5  Chile: The real exchange rate**
(1980-82=100)

Note: Morgan Guaranty defines the effective real exchange rate as domestic prices
divided by foreign prices. A movement upwards indicates a real appreciation.

Source: Morgan Guaranty.

Capital, after having flown abroad for years, began to return to Mexico.

The picture is not yet perfect. Although modernization and the prospect of free trade with the United States have improved expectations, investment has not increased sufficiently to generate sustainable growth while inflation is again rising. The 1990 increase in the oil price is good news for Mexico and could provide the bridge to sustained growth. Nevertheless, despite this rise in oil prices, Mexico still has balance-of-payments problems.

Mexico differs from Chile in two important areas. One is the exchange rate policy it followed in the last four years (figures 7-5 and 7-6). The other is in the realm of politics. While Chile has pursued an aggressive devaluation policy since the mid-1980s, Mexico has maneuvered its exchange rate very carefully to avoid any inflationary impact. After a 20 percent devaluation, the government fixed the peso's exchange rate against the dollar in February 1988. Later it began to devalue daily, but at a rate equivalent to only 14 percent a year, well below the economy's rate of inflation. Since May 1990 the rate of devaluation has been even slower.

**Figure 7.6  Mexico: The real exchange rate**
(1980-82=100)

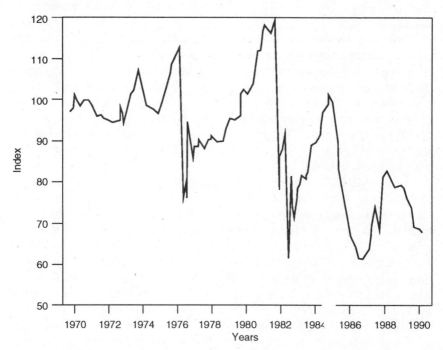

*Note:* Morgan Guaranty defines the effective real exchange rate as domestic prices
divided by foreign prices.  A movement upwards indicates a real appreciation.
*Source:* Morgan Guaranty.

Mexico also differs from Chile in its political development.  The
transition to democracy in Chile owes much to the tradition of strong,
competitive political parties.  By contrast, this tradition is absent in Mexico.
President Carlos Salinas is increasingly popular, but it is unclear how much
popular support the undemocratic government actually has.  Most Mexi-
cans are worse off than they were in 1981, and if politics go wrong, capital
flight could resume and scare prospective investors.

### Exchange rate dynamics and the stock market

This section focuses on a simple model of the real exchange rate and the real
price of capital to understand the mechanisms that affect these two variables.  It is argued that the negative correlation between investment and real
exchange rates observed in the 1980s derives from shocks that simultaneously reduce the real price of capital and generate a real depreciation,
rather than from a causal relationship running from real devaluations to

desired lower levels of investment. This section develops the argument in the context of economies where the central bank chooses the nominal exchange rate. (Appendix 7-2 examines the case of flexible exchange rates.)

There are two separate strands of literature on monetary policy. The closed economy models emphasize the impact of monetary policy on yields from and prices of assets and the resulting link to investment and aggregate demand. By contrast, the open economy literature shows that, under conditions of capital mobility and flexible exchange rates, changes in net exports, not investment, are the chief result of monetary policy. Cardoso (1983) and Gavin (1989) integrate the two approaches by introducing the real price of capital as an additional key variable in the open economy macroeconomic model.[6]

In the Mundell-Fleming model, monetary expansion leads to an increase in aggregate demand. The expansion in income is entirely attributable to depreciation of the exchange rate, induced by incipient outflows of capital. As long as foreign interest rates remain fixed, the monetary expansion has no effects on investment spending. Dornbusch (1976) extends the Mundell-Fleming model to expectations about exchange rates and price flexibility in the long run. In this model, given the differential speeds of adjustment in the markets for goods and assets, a monetary expansion leads to an initial overshooting of exchange rates. Similar to the Mundell-Fleming model, however, the effects of monetary expansion derive entirely from the change in the relative price of domestic goods, and investment spending is not emphasized as a transmission channel of monetary policy.

These results contrast with the conclusions of the closed economy models, where the main channel of transmission from monetary expansion to aggregate demand is the stock market and investment (as, for example, in Tobin's analysis). In closed economy IS/LM models, a monetary expansion increases aggregate demand because it reduces interest rates, raises the price of capital, and thus induces more investment.

The model developed in this section reconciles the two views, showing that in an open economy with flexible exchange rates a monetary expansion affects exchange rates and the price of stocks, so that both investment and net exports expand.

*The model*

Consider a small open economy with flexible exchange rates and four assets—money, stocks, short-term domestic bonds, and foreign bonds. Nonmoney assets are assumed to be perfect substitutes, and arbitrage ensures they have the same expected short-run rate of return. Therefore the expected real interest rate on domestic bonds, $r^*$, must equal the given real interest rate on foreign bonds, $\bar{r}$, plus the expected real depreciation rate, $\dot{e}^*/e - \dot{p}^*/p$:

(7-1) $$r^* = \bar{r} + \dot{e}^*/e - \dot{p}^*/p,$$

where  $r^*$ = expected real interest rate on domestic bonds
$\bar{r}$ = real interest rate on foreign bonds
$e$ = nominal exchange rate
$p$ = level of prices
$\cdot$ = a time derivative
$*$ = an expectation.

It is assumed in equation (7-1) that the rate of foreign inflation is zero, so that the real interest rate on foreign bonds is equal to its nominal interest rate.

Arbitrage also ensures that the expected real interest on bonds equals the real profit rate, $\rho/q$, plus expected capital gains, $\dot{q}^*/q$:

(7-2) $$r^* = \rho/q + \dot{q}^*/q$$

where $\rho$ is profits per unit of physical capital and $q$ is the real price of stocks in terms of domestic goods. Under the assumption of full employment and a constant capital stock, $\rho$ is constant. (Appendix 7-2 considers an economy with less than full employment and a cyclical relationship between output and expected profits per unit of physical capital.)

Equations (7-1) and (7-2) describe arbitrage among stocks and bonds. Money is assumed to be an inverse function of the common nominal return on nonmoney assets, $i = r^* + \dot{p}^*/p$. A balanced portfolio results when the demand for real cash balances equals the real money stock. Under a managed exchange rate money becomes endogenous, and equilibrium in the money market does not need to be considered explicitly, as it is in appendix 7-2.

Assume that the central bank avoids overvaluation by following a crawling peg and devaluing the exchange rate in response to increases in domestic prices in excess of increases in foreign prices. The central bank also looks at the current account and devalues faster if the exchange rate is overvalued. The central bank adopts the following devaluation rule:

(7-3) $$\dot{e}/e = \dot{p}/p - \alpha\,(x - \bar{x})$$

where $x$ is the real exchange rate and - is steady state values.

The system is now formed by equations (7-1), (7-2), and (7-3). In steady state, the real price of capital and the real exchange rate are constant:

(7-4) $$\dot{q}/q = 0 = \bar{r} - \alpha(x - \bar{x}) - \rho/q$$

(7-5) $$\dot{x}/x = 0 = -\alpha\,(x - \bar{x}), \text{ i.e., } x = \bar{x}$$

where $r$ is the real interest rate on foreign bonds and $\rho$ is profits per unit of physical capital.

**Figure 7.7 Phase diagram: Dynamics of the real price of capita and the real exchange rate**

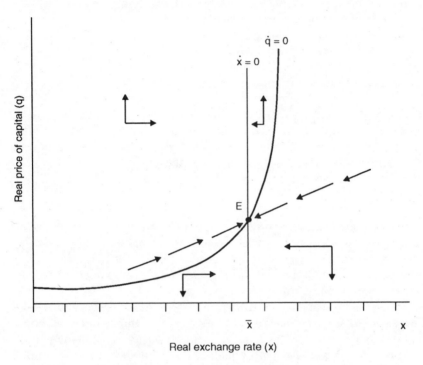

Real exchange rate (x)

*Note:* In the model the real exchange rate is defined as foreign prices divided by domestic prices. An increase in the real exchange rate indicates a real depreciation.

*Source:* Author's elaboration.

This system is represented in figure 7-7. The upward-sloping schedule, $\dot{q}/q = 0$, represents the combinations between the real exchange rate, $x$, and the real price of capital, $q$, for which the real price of capital is constant. To the left of the schedule $\dot{q}/q = 0$, the real price of capital is increasing; it is declining to its right. The vertical schedule $\dot{x}/x = 0$ cuts the x axis at the equilibrium real exchange rate, $\bar{x}$. If $x > \bar{x}$, the real exchange rate is falling; if $x < \bar{x}$, it is rising. Figure 7-7 also shows the unique path to equilibrium. The real price of capital can jump at any time, but the real exchange rate slowly follows the central bank rule.

*An adverse terms of trade shock*

A permanent decline in the terms of trade requires a higher real exchange rate in the new equilibrium and shifts both schedules to the right, as shown in figure 7-8. In response to the shock the real price of capital immediately falls because the expected real depreciation increases the domestic real

**Figure 7.8  A deterioration in the terms of trade**

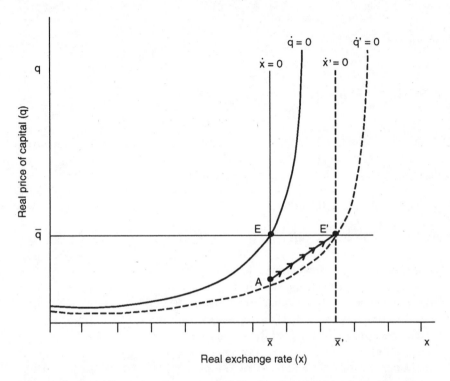

*Note:* In the model the real exchange rate is defined as foreign prices divided by domestic prices. An increase in the real exchange rate indicates a real depreciation.

*Source:* Author's elaboration.

interest rate above the foreign interest rate. From then on, as the real exchange rate depreciates, the real price of capital slowly recovers. During the adjustment the real price of capital and investment are below their equilibrium levels.

It might be expected that a permanent deterioration of the terms of trade would also reduce the real profit rate, $\rho$. In that case the schedule $\dot{q}/q = 0$ would shift further to the right, and the new equilibrium would move to a point below the one represented in figure 7-8. In this case the real price of capital would instantaneously fall more than before. Although it would increase during the adjustment, it would be permanently lower than under the hypothesis represented in figure 7-8.

## Terms of trade and investment

This section considers the effects of fluctuations in the terms of trade on investment. The focus is on two mechanisms. First is the effect of a change in the terms of trade on real income, as well as its impact on the profitability of the export sector and the extent to which this impact is multiplied if profits are positively correlated across sectors. This effect is called here the "Manaus Opera House effect." Second is the way a deterioration in the terms of trade affects the current account and induces contractionary measures. This second channel is here called the "IMF effect."

## The Manaus Opera House effect

A deterioration in the terms of trade reduces real income and has at least a transitory negative effect on investment. Because a deterioration in the terms of trade directly affects the profitability of investment in the export sector, it also reduces investment in that sector. If profits are positively correlated across sectors, bad news for the export sector is bad news for the economy as a whole, and an adverse terms of trade shock means poorer business prospects.

Conversely, a positive terms of trade shock will spread its benefits throughout the economy. The case of Brazilian natural rubber offers a good example. Between 1840 and 1911 the price of rubber increased from £45 to £512 per ton, as the industrial applications of rubber multiplied rapidly in the last quarter of the nineteenth century. Brazil exported 6,600 tons of natural rubber in 1870. By 1911 shipments amounted to 38,500 tons. Rubber gatherers spread throughout the Amazon valley, a phenomenon that gave new stimulus to the economic life of the region and led to the first effective settlement in the jungle, the city of Manaus. Built 1,000 miles up the river, it was the first city in South America to have streetcars; its residents sent their laundry to Lisbon to be washed. The Opera House, where the Ballet Russe once danced and Beniamino Gigli once sang, was completed in 1910, just before the collapse of the rubber boom. After 1911, a catastrophic decline in the price of rubber set in. Gatherers retired, and 10 years later Manaus scarcely retained a shadow of its former splendor. Investment vanished. Numerous similar examples abound. Buenos Aires before World War I was a monument to the impact of the rising terms of trade. The adverse terms of trade shock of the 1930s provoked a fantastic deflation to which the response was the implementation of import-substitution policies.

A deterioration in the terms of trade also affects the budget adversely— either directly if the government owns the export sector or indirectly by reducing the tax base. A deterioration in the budget will require corrective measures, and its deflationary effect will reduce investment. Even in the absence of corrective action, when the government spends what it earns, a reduction in taxes will automatically reduce spending, profits, and investment.

A movement in the terms of trade directly affects government revenues in countries where the main export sector is in the hands of public enterprises, such as in Chile (copper) and Mexico (oil). It is no accident that Chile's major recessions (in 1975 and 1982) coincided with a collapse in copper prices or that the Mexican investment boom in the second half of the 1970s accompanied an oil boom.

## The IMF effect

A deterioration in the terms of trade will worsen the current account balance. If people perceive the deterioration as permanent, the government will have to take corrective measures. Even if the deterioration is transitory but cannot be financed, it will have to take corrective measures. These measures may include fiscal and monetary policies that reduce expenditures, a step that will affect investment adversely. They may also include a devaluation of the exchange rate, which can only be translated into a real devaluation in the context of tight money.

Tight money works through different channels depending on a nation's financial structure and the details of financial intermediation. One possibility (with a deep capital market) is that it will raise the cost of capital and thus reduce the desired stock of capital and the optimal rate of investment. A second possibility, which may be parallel, associates tight money with tight credit. Credit rationing in turn reduces the rate of investment that can be financed. A third possibility is that tight money causes reduced profit flows and thus a reduced ability to self-finance. It may also lower the value of collateral. In one way or another these mechanisms convert tight money into reduced investment. Brazil in 1981-82 and Peru in 1983-84 provide good examples of the IMF effect.

## The empirical evidence

This section discusses the empirical evidence from regressions of the share of private investment in GDP on a group of variables, including the log of the terms of trade. The regressions use quadrennial panel data for the period 1970-85 in Argentina, Brazil, Chile, Colombia, Mexico, and Venezuela. These countries accounted for 86 percent of total GDP in Latin America. (The sources of the data are provided in appendix 7-3.) The equations do not use the real interest rate or any other variable as a proxy for the cost of capital. There are no continuous data for all countries in the sample. Moreover, the extreme variability of inflation and taxation suggests that no single variable will correctly capture the average opportunity cost of investment for all firms in the medium term. In different countries and at different times the long-term instruments in the credit market have vanished, and retained earnings have become the primary source of finance for significant periods.

## Real exchange rates and investment

The positive correlation between the decline in the shares of investment in GDP in the 1980s and the real depreciation observed after the debt shock (table 7-1) can lead to a mistaken belief that the real depreciation caused the decline in investment. Servén and Solimano (1990) survey mechanisms that link devaluation with investment, as well as empirical studies that find a negative impact of devaluations on investment (see, for instance, Faini and de Melo 1990). The rationale for these findings include the following. First, the adverse real income effect of a real depreciation (following the line of the "contractionary devaluation" literature) could reduce firms' desired capacity. Second, without monetary accommodation exchange rate depreciation may result in higher interest rates and depress investment. If these are the channels of transmission, a significant negative coefficient of real depreciation would not be expected in an investment regression that includes both income and interest rates. A third argument is that because a devaluation might raise the cost of imported capital, it could lead to a decline in investment. This argument would apply in the nontraded goods sector but not for investment in the traded goods sector. Thus, the effect of real devaluations on aggregate investment is uncertain. It should also be observed that the higher cost of imported capital could encourage investment with a high domestic content rather than investment with a high foreign exchange content without affecting the level of investment.

Servén (1990) assumes an exogenous real exchange rate. He shows that the long-run effect of a real devaluation is ambiguous, although an anticipated depreciation in the real exchange rate provides the incentive for a speculative reallocation of investment over time. When a real depreciation is expected, an investment boom is likely to develop if the import content of capital goods is high relative to the degree of capital mobility. The reason is that the expected depreciation promotes flight into foreign goods. A slump will follow the boom when the depreciation takes place because such devaluation amounts to a removal of a subsidy for investment. With high capital mobility the anticipated depreciation promotes flight into foreign assets and an investment pattern opposite to that described above.

The previous section presented a model with a crawling peg where the real exchange rate is determined jointly with the real price of capital. In that model an expected rate of real depreciation (in response to an adverse terms of trade shock) temporarily raises the domestic real rate of interest and reduces the real price of capital below its equilibrium level. The deterioration in the terms of trade causes both the real depreciation and the reduction in the real price of capital and investment. The results presented here, obtained using a model with perfect capital mobility, are consistent with Servén's results for his case of high capital mobility.

The first regression in table 7-4 shows the strong positive effect of an improvement in the terms of trade on investment. Table 7-4 also reports the reaction of the share of private investment in GDP in response to growth, to movements in the share of public investment in GDP, to the index of the real exchange rate, and to the rate of real appreciation. The hypothesis that the coefficients of the real exchange rate and of real appreciation are zero cannot be rejected. Growth, the share of public investment in GDP, and the terms

**Table 7.4  Regression analysis**
(dependent variable: share of private investment in GDP)

| | Independent variables | | | | |
|---|---|---|---|---|---|
| *Growth rate of GDP* | *Share of public investment in GDP* | *Log of terms of trade* | *Index of the real exchange rate* | *Rate of appreciation of the real exchange rate* | $R^2$ |
| 0.81 | 0.89 | -6.77 | | | |
| (6.72) | (4.39) | (-2.62) | | | 0.74 |
| 0.81 | 0.75 | | 0.003 | | |
| (5.04) | (3.24) | | (0.07) | | 0.65 |
| 0.81 | 0.75 | | | 0.002 | |
| (5.67) | (3.20) | | | (0.02) | 0.65 |

Note: Quadrennial panel data, periods 1970-73, 1974-77, 1978-81, and 1982-85.
The countries are Argentina, Brazil, Chile, Colombia, Mexico, and Venezuela.
The number of observations is 24.
Constant term is not reported. The t-statistics are in parentheses.
*Source:* Author's calculations.

of trade explain 74 percent of the variation in the share of private investment in output.[7]

*Private and public investment*

In Latin America the public sector accounts for a high proportion of investment. Between 1985 and 1988 public investment accounted for more than half of total investment in Bolivia, for approximately half of total investment in Argentina, Chile, and Colombia, and for more than one-third of investment in Brazil, Uruguay, and Venezuela. Public enterprises dominate a wide range of economic activities, including the banking, transport, and mining industries. In many countries the explanation for the large participation of government in production lies in considerations such as the absence of a private sector able to undertake major projects. Even though the performance of the public sector has been strongly criticized, the empirical evidence shows an important complementarity between public and private investment. Government investment in fixed capital crowds in private investment, possibly because it increases productivity by providing infrastructure and services. In the regressions presented here a 1 percentage point increase in the share of public investment in GDP raises the share of private investment in GDP by more than half a percentage point.

Complementarity between private and public investment does not rule out the possibility that an increase in total government spending, rather

## Table 7.5 Regression analysis
(dependent variable: share of private investment in GDP)

|  | | | Independent variables | | |
|---|---|---|---|---|---|
| Growth rate of GDP | Share of public investment in GDP | Log of terms of trade | Stock share of claims on government in total domestic credit | Flow share of claims on government in total domestic credit | $R^2$ |
| 0.74 (5.26) | 0.62 (2.64) | | -1.06 (-1.48) | | 0.68 |
| 0.76 (5.98) | 0.78 (3.52) | -6.21 (-2.39) | 0.78 (-1.18) | | 0.76 |
| 0.74 (5.17) | 0.75 (3.47) | | | -1.38 (-1.42) | 0.68 |
| 0.76 (5.89) | 0.88 (4.35) | -6.25 (-2.39) | | -1.00 (-1.13) | 0.76 |

Note: Quadrennial panel data, periods 1970-73, 1974-77, 1978-81, and 1982-85.
The countries are Argentina, Brazil, Chile, Colombia, Mexico, and Venezuela.
The number of observations is 24.
Constant term is not reported. The t-statistics are in parentheses.
*Source:* Author's calculations.

than just an investment outlay, could crowd out private investment. An increase in total spending that is not financed by an increase in taxes provokes a deficit that is in part financed by borrowing from the local credit market. This form of financing can have a detrimental effect on private investment. High fiscal deficits push up interest rates and reduce the availability of credit to the private sector.

Departing from the hypothesis of perfect capital markets, crowding out is tested for here by introducing the share of claims on government in total domestic credit as a variable in the regressions (table 7-5). One equation uses the share of the stock of claims on government in the stock of domestic credit; and the other uses the share of the flow of claims on government in the total domestic credit flow. In all equations the coefficients are negative as expected, but the t-statistics are small.

Bernanke (1983) shows that irreversible investment invites delay, as entrepreneurs wait for the resolution of uncertainty. Firms are cautious in their decisions to expand capacity under uncertainty because investment

**Table 7.6 Regression analysis**
(dependent variable: share of private investment in GDP)

| | Independent variables | | | | |
| --- | --- | --- | --- | --- | --- |
| Growth rate of GDP | Share of public investment in GDP | Log of terms of trade | Index of economic instability | Log of the ratio of external debts to exports | $R^2$ |
| 0.81 (6.72) | 0.89 (4.39) | -6.77 (-2.62) | | | 0.74 |
| 0.66 (4.23) | 0.69 (3.25) | | -1.55 (-1.79) | | 0.70 |
| 0.71 (4.90) | 0.83 (4.06) | -5.86 (-2.22) | -1.07 (-1.29) | | 0.76 |
| 0.70 (4.98) | 0.63 (2.93) | | | -3.55 (-2.01) | 0.71 |
| 0.74 (5.59) | 0.79 (3.65) | -5.49 (-2.00) | | -2.23 (-1.26) | 0.76 |

Note: Quadrennial panel data, periods 1970-73, 1974-77, 1978-81, and 1982-85.
The countries are Argentina, Brazil, Chile, Colombia, Mexico, and Venezuela.
The number of observations is 24.
Constant term is not reported. The t-statistics are in parentheses.
*Source:* Author's calculations.

today can lead to excessive capacity tomorrow if circumstances change. Substantial budget deficits have created financial instability in many Latin American countries such as Argentina and Peru. In these countries, volatility of output, interest rates, relative prices, and inflation increase uncertainty and thus reduce investment. Another source of uncertainty in the investment climate is the need in the future to carry out an external transfer to creditors, since that transfer might require increases in taxes and changes in relative prices.

The regressions in table 7-6 test the hypothesis that uncertainty affects the share of private investment in Latin America by bringing two additional variables into the picture, one at a time. One of the new variables is the log of the ratio of the total external debt to exports. The coefficient of the variable standing for the debt overhang has the expected negative sign. Its t-statistic is larger than 2 in the equation that does not include the terms of trade, but in the equation that includes the terms of trade the coefficient for the debt overhang is not significant.

The other variable is an index of instability built by adding the log of the debt ratio, the log of one plus the rate of inflation, and the log of the coefficient of the variation in the real exchange rate (calculated from monthly data during each of the four-year periods). Once again the coefficient has the expected negative sign but is not significant in the equation that includes the log of the terms of trade. Regressions with the three different uncertainty proxies entered separately were run; they did not obtain better results.

## Concluding remarks

The regressions in tables 7-4, 7-5, and 7-6 show that growth, the share of public investment in GDP, and the log of the terms of trade explain 74 percent of the variation in the share of private investment in output. The coefficients of these variables are significant and stable across specifications. A 1 percentage point increase in the growth rate increases the share of private investment in output by less than 1 percentage point. This result is consistent with other empirical studies that find a strong response of investment to changes in output.[8] The regressions presented here dampen the scope for any "excessive"[9] output-related variability of investment in the cycle by using four-year averages for the variables.

In the present regressions a 1 percentage point increase in the share of public investment in GDP raises the share of private investment in GDP by more than half a percentage point, a result that confirms the hypothesis of complementarity between private and public investment. This complementarity does not rule out the possibility that an increase in the budget deficit crowds out private investment. When testing the hypothesis that government borrowing from the local credit market crowds out private investment, as expected the coefficients in all equations were negative, but the t-statistics were small.

The coefficients of the variables standing for the debt overhang and macroeconomic volatility had the expected negative signs, but the t-statistics in the regressions that included the terms of trade were small. In all equations, the effect of an improvement in the terms of trade on investment was large and significant. Both the real exchange rate and the real rate of depreciation had no effect on investment behavior.

## Appendix 7A. Empirical studies of investment in Latin America

Investment regressions for Latin America use models that combine elements of different theories. Behrman (1972) explores the validity of putty-putty versus putty-clay assumptions across a number of different economic sectors in Chile. He finds that investment functions differed across sectors. Bilsborrow (1977) shows that the availability of foreign exchange to implement planned capital formation and the internal flow of funds were the most important determinants of investment in Colombia. Dailami (1987) finds a negative relation between the cyclical behavior of private investment in Brazil and the volatility of the stock market. Musalem (1989) shows that investment in Mexico was responsive to the real interest rate, the relative price of investment, and the rate of capital utilization and that there were complementary links between public and private investment. Ocampo (1990) surveys the literature on determinants of investment in Colombia. The evidence suggests that domestic demand was the major determinant of investment in Colombia. Simple accelerator models explain a large proportion of the variance in manufacturing investment. Investment was also sensitive to the relative price of capital goods, to direct import controls, to the internal funds of the manufacturing firms, and to the long-term availability of credit. Pinheiro and Matesco (1988, 1989) calculate historical series for the incremental capital/output ratio (ICOR) in Brazil since 1948. Solimano (1989) studies the impact of cycles of economic activity, relative prices, and policy inconsistencies on investment in Chile.

## Appendix 7B. The price of capital and the real exchange rate

This appendix develops a model of the real exchange rate and the real price of capital. The special features of the model are the presence of a stock market, full long-run flexibility of prices, and stickiness of the price of goods in the short run. The prices of stocks and exchange rates can jump at any time.

Initially it is assumed that the model incorporates full employment and a price level that rises when demand for domestic output exceeds its full employment level. The closed form solution of the dynamic system is discussed next. An extension of the model covers the case of an economy with less than full employment. Finally the model is discussed with a crawling peg regime.

*The model*

Consider a small open economy with flexible exchange rates and four assets: money, stocks, short-term domestic bonds, and foreign bonds.

Nonmoney assets are assumed to be perfect substitutes, and arbitrage ensures they have the same expected short-run rate of return. Therefore the expected real interest rate on domestic bonds, $r^*$, must equal the given real interest rate on foreign bonds, $\bar{r}$, plus the expected real rate of depreciation, $\dot{e}^*/e - \dot{p}^*/p$:

$$(7B\text{-}1) \qquad\qquad r^* = \bar{r} + \dot{e}^*/e - \dot{p}^*/p.$$

It is assumed in equation (7B-1) that the rate of foreign inflation is zero, and thus the real interest rate on foreign bonds is equal to its nominal interest rate.

Arbitrage also ensures that the expected real interest rate on domestic bonds, $r^*$, equals the real profit rate, $\rho/q$, plus expected capital gains, $\dot{q}^*/q$:

$$(7B\text{-}2) \qquad\qquad r^* = \rho/q + \dot{q}^*/q.$$

Under the assumption of full employment and a constant capital stock, $\rho$ is constant. (Analysis of an economy with less than full employment and a cyclical relationship between output and expected profits for a unit of physical capital is considered later.)

The expected real rate of interest on domestic bonds is defined as the difference between the nominal interest rate, $i$, and the expected inflation rate:

$$(7B\text{-}3) \qquad\qquad r^* = i - \dot{p}^*/p$$

where $i$ is the nominal interest rate.

Equations (7B-1), (7B-2), and (7B-3) describe arbitrage among stocks and bonds. Since money is held for transactions, money is assumed to be an increasing function of income, $y$, and an inverse function of the common nominal return on nonmoney assets, that is, the nominal interest rate. A portfolio is balanced when the demand for real cash balances equals the real money stock, $m \equiv M/p$:

$$(7B\text{-}4) \qquad\qquad m = y/vi.$$

where $m$ is the real money stock, $y$ is income, and $v$ is a constant.

It is assumed in equation (7B-4), in keeping with Mundell (1965), that velocity is a linear function of the opportunity cost of holding money. The nominal interest rate is assumed to be positive.

Equations (7B-1)—(7B-4) determine the price of capital, the nominal exchange rate, and domestic nominal and real interest rates ($q$, $e$, $i$, and $r^*$) as functions of: the foreign interest rate, $\bar{r}$; the policy variable, $M$; the price level, $p$; and expectations, $\dot{p}^*$, $\dot{q}^*$, and $\dot{e}^*$.

The behavior of the price level is specified next. It is assumed that prices increase whenever aggregate demand for domestic goods exceeds the full employment level of output. The aggregate demand for domestic goods is composed of investment spending, consumer and government expenditures, and net exports. Following Tobin, investment is an increasing function of the real price of stocks. Consumption is assumed to depend on permanent and transitory income and is constant under the assumption of full employment and a constant tax structure. Net exports depend on the real exchange rate, defined as $x \equiv e/p$. A real depreciation raises the competitiveness of domestic goods relative to foreign goods while increasing the demand for domestic goods and reducing domestic demand for foreign goods. It is further assumed that an increase in the real exchange rate expands net exports. From this argument it follows that the demand for domestic goods exceeds its full employment level whenever the real exchange rate or the real price of stocks exceeds its steady state level. The equation for the rate of change in the level of prices can be written as:

(7B-5) $$\dot{p}/p = \Theta(x - \bar{x}) + \phi(q - \bar{q})$$

where $\Theta$ is the product of the elasticity of aggregate demand relative to the real exchange rate times the speed of adjustment of prices and $\phi$ is the product of the elasticity of aggregate demand relative to the real price of stocks times the speed of adjustment of prices.

The model is closed by assuming rational expectations. It reduces to three differential equations describing the behavior of the real price of stocks, the real exchange rate, and the real money stock:

(7B-6) $$\dot{q}/q = y/vm - \rho/q - \Theta(x - \bar{x}) - \phi(q - \bar{q})$$

(7B-7) $$\dot{x}/x = y/vm - \Theta(x - \bar{x}) - \phi(q - \bar{q}) - \bar{r}$$

(7B-8) $$\dot{m}/m = -\Theta(x - \bar{x}) - \phi(q - \bar{q}).$$

It is assumed in equation (7B-8) that the nominal money stock is constant. Thus the growth rate of the real money stock equals the rate of deflation.

In a steady state, $\dot{q} = \dot{x} = \dot{m} = \dot{p} = 0$, and the real price of stocks is equal to the ratio between the real profit rate and the real interest rate, or $\bar{q} = \rho/\bar{r}$.

## The dynamics

Linearization of the system formed by equations (7B-6)—(7B-8) around its steady state is presented in the last section of this appendix. The system has three characteristic roots:

$$\lambda_1 = \bar{r}$$
$$\lambda_{2,3} = -A \pm (A^2 + \bar{r}\bar{x}\bar{\Theta})^{1/2}$$

where $A = (\bar{x}\Theta + \bar{q}\phi)/2$. Two roots are positive, and one is negative. The absolute value of the negative root is defined as $\lambda$. The steady state is a saddle point equilibrium. Given the value of the real money stock, there is a unique combination of the price of stocks and the exchange rate such that the economy converges to the steady state. The equations of motion along the stable arm are:

(7B-9)                              $m(t) = [m(0) - \bar{m}]e^{\lambda t} + \bar{m}$

(7B-10)                             $q(t) = (\bar{q}/\bar{m})m(t)$

(7B-11)                         $x(t) = (\bar{x}/\bar{m})B[m(t) - \bar{m}] + \bar{x}$

where $B = 1 + \bar{r}/\lambda$. Observe that $B > 1$. Equations (7B-9), (7B-10), and (7B-11) are derived in the last section of this appendix.

    In response to a shock, granted that the price of stocks and the exchange rate jump and move the economy onto a stable path to equilibrium, adjustment is faster (a) the larger the elasticities of aggregate demand are in relation to the real price of stocks and the exchange rate, (b) the faster prices move in response to excess demand, and (c) the higher the foreign interest rate is.

## Comparative dynamics

Consider an unanticipated monetary expansion. The steady state real price of capital, interest rates, and real exchange rates are invariant to nominal money, which only affects prices proportionately in the long run. To understand the short-run effects of a monetary expansion, it is assumed that the economy is initially in steady state when the unanticipated expansion in nominal money occurs. When it does take place, real balances increase since the price level does not adjust instantaneously. The nominal interest rate fails to maintain portfolio equilibrium, and the expected rate of inflation further decreases the expected real interest rate on domestic bonds. Arbitrage causes an immediate depreciation of the exchange rate and an immediate jump in the price of stocks. As the price level increases, real balances fall. Consequently, interest rates start to rise, the exchange rate slowly appreciates, the real price of capital falls, and the economy returns to steady state equilibrium. The adjustment is illustrated in figure 7B.1.

    Observe that initially the movement of the exchange rate exceeds that of the price of capital. At $t = 0$, when the monetary expansion takes place, the exchange rate relative to the value of stocks is:

(7B-12)                          $e(0)/p(0)q(0) \equiv B\bar{x}/\bar{q}$

where $\bar{x}$ and $\bar{q}$ are the values of $x$ and $q$ in the initial steady state and $B > 1$. The reason the depreciation in the exchange rate has to exceed the initial increase in the price of stocks is that expected movements in the real price

**Figure 7B.1  Unanticipated monetary expansion: Dynamics of the real price of capital and the real exchange rate**

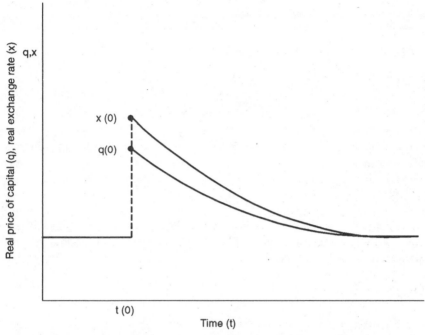

*Note:* In the model the real exchange rate is defined as foreign prices divided by domestic prices. An increase in the real exchange rate indicates a real depreciation.

*Source:* Author's elaboration.

of capital affect both the real profit rate and the expected capital gains, whereas movements in the exchange rate only affect expected capital gains, as can be seen in the following arbitrage equation:

(7B-13)          $i - \dot{p}^*/p = \rho/q + \dot{q}^*/q = \bar{r} + \dot{e}^*/e - \dot{p}^*/p.$

The initial jump in the price of stocks increases investment. The initial jump in the exchange rate makes domestic goods more competitive. Both effects contribute to an increase in aggregate demand and create inflation. As the price level rises, the economy returns to the steady state.

*An extension for economies with less than full employment*

The analysis is now extended to the case of the economies described by IS/LM-type models, where it is assumed that output is determined by aggregate demand, *yd*:

(7B-14) $$y = yd.$$

Equation (7B-15) is rewritten for the slow adjustment of prices as follows:

(7B-15) $$\dot{p}/p = h(1 - yd/\bar{y}) = \Theta(x - \bar{x}) + \phi(q - \bar{q})$$

where $h$ is the speed of adjustment of prices. It follows that:

(7B-16) $$yd/\bar{y} - 1 = (z/h)(x - \bar{x}) + (\phi/h)(q - \bar{q}).$$

The cyclical behavior of profits is considered next. IS/LM models assume mark-up pricing and a constant capital stock. These assumptions imply that the profits for a unit of physical capital are an increasing function of output:

(7B-17) $$\rho = ay.$$

Equations (7B-14) and (7B-17) are substituted into the system of differential equations formed by (7B-6)—(7B-8). Linearization of this system around its steady state gives:

(7B-18) $$\begin{bmatrix} \dot{q} \\ \dot{x} \\ \dot{m} \end{bmatrix} + \begin{bmatrix} \bar{q}\phi - \bar{r} & \bar{q}\Theta & \bar{r}\bar{q}/\bar{m} \\ \bar{x}\phi\gamma & \bar{x}\Theta\gamma & \bar{r}\bar{x}/\bar{m} \\ \bar{m}\phi & \bar{m}\Theta & 0 \end{bmatrix} \begin{bmatrix} q - \bar{q} \\ x - \bar{x} \\ m - \bar{m} \end{bmatrix} = 0$$

where $\gamma \equiv 1 - \bar{r}/h$.

This system has three characteristic roots: $z_1 = \bar{r}$ and $z_{2,3} = -F \pm (F^2 + \bar{r}\bar{x}\Theta)^{1/2}$, where $F \equiv (\bar{q}\phi + \bar{x}\Theta\gamma)/2$. As before, two roots are positive, and one is negative. The steady state is a saddle point equilibrium.

Two cases can be distinguished. If prices move fast, $h > \bar{r}$ and $1 > \gamma > 0$. In this case the absolute value of the negative root is called $\bar{z}$.

If prices move very slowly, $h < \bar{r}$, $\gamma < 0$ and $\bar{q}\phi < \bar{x}\Theta |\gamma|$. Under those last assumptions the absolute value of the negative root is called $\bar{\bar{z}}$. It is possible to verify immediately that $\bar{\bar{z}} < \bar{z} < \gamma$, where $\gamma$ is the absolute value of the negative root in the model with full employment. It can be concluded that the speed of adjustment to monetary shocks in an economy with less than full employment is slower than in the case of a full employment economy. During the adjustment to the steady state, in addition to inflation (or deflation), levels of activity above (or below) the activity level in steady state are observed.

For economies with less than full employment where prices move relatively quickly, the equations of motion along the stable arm are:

(7B-19) $$m(t) = [m(0) - \bar{m}]e^{\bar{z}t} + \bar{m}$$

(7B-20) $$q(t) = (\bar{q}/\bar{m})m(t)$$

(7B-21) $$x(t) = (\bar{x}/\bar{m})H[m(t) - \bar{m}] + \bar{x}$$

where $H \equiv 1 + \bar{r}[(1/\bar{z}) - (1/h)]$.

If prices move rapidly, $h$ is large, and $H > 0$. In this case the effects of a monetary expansion are qualitatively the same as in the case of the full employment economy. It leads to an overshooting of the exchange rate, a jump in the price of stocks, and an increase in aggregate demand. To the inflationary effects obtained in the full employment economy must now be added an expansion in output. The rise in output boosts the demand for real balances, a shift that leads to an initial reduction in the interest rate that is smaller than in the case of the full employment economy. It follows that the overshooting of the exchange rate in the present case is smaller than in the case of the full employment economy.[10]

Note that in equations (7B-10) and (7B-20), $q(0)$ is the same. This result can be readily understood. The expected cyclical profits that did not exist in the full employment case are now discounted at higher interest rates, which arise from the cyclical increase in the demand for real cash balances.

The model developed here is also useful in analyzing external shocks. Consider, for instance, an increase in the steady state foreign interest rate. It raises expected domestic interest rates by the same amount, so that the demand for real cash balances is reduced; the exchange rate immediately depreciates; and the price of stocks immediately falls. As a consequence the composition of aggregate demand changes, as investment spending is substituted by net exports.

*Calculating the characteristic roots*

Linearization of the system formed by equations (7B-6)-(7B-8) gives:

(7B-22) $$\begin{bmatrix} \dot{q} \\ \dot{x} \\ \dot{m} \end{bmatrix} + \begin{bmatrix} \bar{q}\phi - \bar{r} & \bar{q}\Theta & \bar{r}q/\bar{m} \\ \bar{x}\phi & \bar{x}\Theta & \bar{r}x/\bar{m} \\ \bar{m}\phi & \bar{m}\Theta & 0 \end{bmatrix} \begin{bmatrix} q - \bar{q} \\ x - \bar{x} \\ m - \bar{m} \end{bmatrix} = 0$$

The system has three roots: $\lambda_1$ and $\lambda_2$ are positive; and $\lambda_3$ is negative.

To obtain equations (7B-9), (7B-10), and (7B-11), the system is solved:

(7B-23) (i)
(ii)
(iii)
$$\begin{bmatrix} \dot{q} \\ \dot{x} \\ \dot{m} \end{bmatrix} + \begin{bmatrix} \bar{q}\phi - \bar{r} + \lambda_3 & \bar{q}\Theta & \bar{r}q/\bar{m} \\ \bar{x}\phi & \bar{x}\Theta + \lambda_3 & \bar{r}x/\bar{m} \\ \bar{m}\phi & \bar{m}\Theta & \lambda_3 \end{bmatrix} \begin{bmatrix} N_1 \\ N_2 \\ N_3 \end{bmatrix} = 0$$

Substitution of (iii) into (ii) gives

(iv) $$N_2 = B(\bar{x}/\bar{m})N_3$$

where $B \equiv 1 + \bar{r}/\lambda$ and $\lambda \equiv |\lambda_3|$.

Substitution of (iv) into (i) gives

$$N_1 = - (\,\overline{q}/\overline{m})[(\overline{Bx}z + \overline{r})/(\,\overline{q}\phi + \lambda_3 - \overline{r})]N_3$$

Observe that $[(Bxz + r)/q\phi + \lambda_3 - r)] = -1$, since

(7B-24)                    $\lambda^2_3 + (\,\overline{q}\phi + \overline{x}\Theta)\,\lambda_3 - \overline{x}\,\overline{r}\Theta = 0.$

The choice of the initial money stock establishes the value of $N_3$, and equations (7B-9), (7B-10), and (7B-11) immediately follow.

## Appendix 7C: Data used in the regressions

*Share of private investment in GDP and share of public investment in GDP*: average of the annual shares during each of the four-year periods. Source: World Bank, except for Brazil because of the discontinuity in the World Bank data, as discussed in appendix 7D. The shares of private and public total fixed capital formation, as reported in Contas Nacionais (National Accounts), were used for Brazil.

*Growth rate of real GDP*: average of the annual rates during the four-year period. Source: Economic Commission for Latin America and the Caribbean.

*Log of the terms of trade*: log of the average of the yearly indices relative to the country average for the whole period. The log of the average of the yearly indices was used with almost the same results. Source: World Bank, *World Tables*, 1989-90 edition.

*Index of the real effective exchange rate*: average of the monthly indices during the four-year period. Deviations from the country average for the whole period were also used with basically the same results. Source: Morgan Guaranty.

*Average real appreciation rate during the period*: average of the yearly real appreciation during the four-year period, calculated from the index above.

*Log of the coefficient of variation of the real exchange rate*: the coefficient of variation was calculated from Morgan Guaranty monthly data during each of the four-year periods.

*Log of one plus the inflation rate*: the inflation rate is the four-year period average inflation rate per year of consumer prices. Source: International Monetary Fund, *International Financial Statistics*.

*Log of the debt/exports ratio*: total external debt outstanding at the end of the year/exports of goods and services: both the total external debt and exports are from World Bank, *World Tables*, 1989-90 edition.

*Log of the ratio of the stock of claims on government to the stock of domestic credit*: the ratio is [1 - (line 32d/line32)], where line 32d in the *International Financial Statistics* represents claims on the private sector. The data for Chile are reported only until 1984. The 1985 numbers were obtained by telephone. Source: International Monetary Fund, *International Financial Statistics*.

## Appendix 7D: Looking at investment shares in GDP

The data on the share of investment in GDP in Latin America from different sources present many discrepancies. This section compares the statistics from a number of sources and discusses the reasons for the differences. Table 7D.1 shows the data for 19 Latin American countries[11] from Summers and Heston (1988), and table 7D.2 shows the data for 13 Latin American countries from the World Bank. Both represent the share of total gross investment, including variations in stocks in GDP. Summers and Heston's data show real gross investment divided by real GDP, whereas the World Bank data show nominal gross investment divided by nominal GDP. Much of the difference between the two series derives from the investment and GDP deflators Summers and Heston use.

These differences are explored a bit further here by looking at the data for Chile and Brazil. Table 7D.3 shows that the World Bank data for total nominal investment shares in the case of Chile are exactly the same as the data published by the Banco Central de Chile. Figure 7D.1 plots the shares of total gross investment in GDP as well as the share of gross fixed capital formation in GDP. The shares of total investment (which include variation in stocks) move more widely than do the shares of fixed capital formation. Strangely, the variation in stocks in a given year can appear positive when expressed in nominal terms and negative when expressed in real terms. The explanation is that variations in stocks in Chile are calculated as a residual.

The Banco Central de Chile also provides information on real investment shares (table 7D.3). Figure 7D.2 shows the shares of total nominal investment in nominal GDP and the shares of total real investment in real GDP. After 1974, when the principal episodes of Chilean inflation came to an end, the two series are very similar. Because the relative price of capital can move, there is no reason to expect that the real and nominal shares should coincide. In general, however, very high inflation seems to introduce uncertainty about the accuracy of deflators in many Latin American countries.

Figure 7D.3 shows Summers and Heston's data for real gross investment divided by real GDP and the same data from the Banco Central. They broadly follow the same pattern, but the shares reported by Summers and Heston are almost twice as large as the data reported by the Banco Central. This large discrepancy is attributable to the very different deflators used in the two sources. Data from Summers and Heston also show much larger shares than are likely for Argentina but not for the other Latin American countries.

Table 7D.4 shows the investment shares in Brazil between 1970 and 1988. The national accounts methodology changed recently, and the data for the years prior to 1970 have not been revised. The Instituto Brasileiro de

**Table 7D.1   Share of investment in GDP, 1950-85**
              (percent)

| Year | Argentina | Bolivia | Brazil | Chile | Colombia | Costa Rica |
|------|-----------|---------|--------|-------|----------|------------|
| 1950 | n.a.   | 8.20  | n.a.  | n.a.  | 21.11 | 11.06 |
| 1951 | n.a.   | 11.79 | n.a.  | n.a.  | 19.70 | 11.92 |
| 1952 | n.a.   | 11.16 | n.a.  | n.a.  | 19.63 | 13.88 |
| 1953 | n.a.   | 7.41  | n.a.  | n.a.  | 21.01 | 13.07 |
| 1954 | n.a.   | 9.90  | n.a.  | n.a.  | 23.75 | 11.94 |
| 1955 | n.a.   | 15.30 | 29.10 | n.a.  | 24.14 | 12.21 |
| 1956 | n.a.   | 14.29 | 26.91 | n.a.  | 23.65 | 13.63 |
| 1957 | n.a.   | 12.91 | 32.17 | 30.67 | 21.53 | 14.30 |
| 1958 | n.a.   | 11.87 | 29.87 | 29.85 | 18.54 | 11.14 |
| 1959 | 20.13  | 9.14  | 34.02 | 27.87 | 18.44 | 13.77 |
| 1960 | 26.80  | 12.11 | 30.53 | 33.33 | 20.36 | 12.17 |
| 1961 | 27.26  | 9.41  | 23.19 | 35.69 | 21.24 | 12.33 |
| 1962 | 25.77  | 14.38 | 23.04 | 34.18 | 18.49 | 13.81 |
| 1963 | 22.08  | 13.73 | 20.52 | 36.05 | 17.50 | 15.12 |
| 1964 | 24.96  | 13.88 | 21.62 | 33.70 | 18.47 | 11.21 |
| 1965 | 24.59  | 15.21 | 22.94 | 34.83 | 17.72 | 17.15 |
| 1966 | 22.90  | 14.56 | 23.82 | 33.94 | 19.67 | 13.26 |
| 1967 | 23.23  | 13.11 | 20.84 | 31.98 | 16.85 | 13.48 |
| 1968 | 24.50  | 16.87 | 22.92 | 32.99 | 19.09 | 12.46 |
| 1969 | 27.22  | 15.10 | 25.95 | 34.03 | 18.15 | 13.67 |
| 1970 | 27.80  | 15.28 | 24.35 | 33.93 | 19.25 | 14.34 |
| 1971 | 29.43  | 15.86 | 24.89 | 31.55 | 18.59 | 16.76 |
| 1972 | 28.93  | 17.97 | 24.67 | 26.88 | 17.22 | 14.58 |
| 1973 | 26.93  | 15.54 | 26.62 | 26.99 | 17.56 | 16.20 |
| 1974 | 26.06  | 14.39 | 28.88 | 32.01 | 19.74 | 16.62 |
| 1975 | 26.60  | 19.77 | 30.30 | 18.55 | 16.02 | 14.76 |
| 1976 | 28.08  | 16.70 | 27.69 | 21.27 | 16.32 | 17.64 |
| 1977 | 31.19  | 16.35 | 25.50 | 25.14 | 17.81 | 19.63 |
| 1978 | 29.02  | 16.07 | 24.29 | 28.86 | 17.29 | 18.42 |
| 1979 | 28.33  | 14.83 | 22.65 | 30.55 | 16.19 | 19.20 |
| 1980 | 29.68  | 11.45 | 23.31 | 35.52 | 16.79 | 20.43 |
| 1981 | 24.84  | 9.73  | 19.71 | 35.24 | 18.29 | 13.46 |
| 1982 | 22.72  | 5.46  | 18.79 | 20.44 | 18.82 | 7.67  |
| 1983 | 19.99  | 5.82  | 16.51 | 21.53 | 18.63 | 8.01  |
| 1984 | 16.16  | 5.36  | 15.55 | 22.28 | 16.79 | 15.04 |
| 1985 | 13.76  | 8.22  | 16.07 | 21.68 | 16.09 | 15.17 |

(continued)

| Year | Dominican Republic | Ecuador | El Salvador | Guatemala | Haiti | Honduras |
|------|--------------------|---------|-------------|-----------|-------|----------|
| 1950 | 10.12 | 17.80 | 5.39 | 7.94 | n.a. | 11.43 |
| 1951 | 10.10 | 20.89 | 6.15 | 7.66 | n.a. | 13.79 |
| 1952 | 17.20 | 17.18 | 6.07 | 5.84 | n.a. | 16.18 |
| 1953 | 14.83 | 21.73 | 5.88 | 6.26 | n.a. | 15.04 |
| 1954 | 13.07 | 24.70 | 5.58 | 5.96 | n.a. | 12.07 |
| 1955 | 15.86 | 25.81 | 5.49 | 9.20 | n.a. | 13.12 |
| 1956 | 15.70 | 25.14 | 7.23 | 12.22 | n.a. | 12.55 |
| 1957 | 15.54 | 24.28 | 7.60 | 12.23 | n.a. | 12.94 |
| 1958 | 15.56 | 23.25 | 6.28 | 9.90 | n.a. | 10.66 |
| 1959 | 11.68 | 23.89 | 4.61 | 8.56 | n.a. | 10.12 |
| 1960 | 9.16 | 24.43 | 8.65 | 7.72 | 3.73 | 11.05 |
| 1961 | 6.95 | 24.38 | 7.43 | 6.54 | 3.50 | 9.70 |
| 1962 | 9.92 | 22.47 | 6.82 | 6.45 | 3.58 | 12.20 |
| 1963 | 13.00 | 22.90 | 7.18 | 8.06 | 3.61 | 13.53 |
| 1964 | 14.97 | 22.33 | 9.58 | 9.27 | 3.29 | 12.85 |
| 1965 | 8.12 | 21.03 | 8.52 | 9.15 | 3.20 | 12.69 |
| 1966 | 12.44 | 18.99 | 9.31 | 7.67 | 2.79 | 13.50 |
| 1967 | 12.86 | 21.14 | 7.69 | 8.90 | 2.97 | 16.79 |
| 1968 | 12.75 | 22.78 | 5.75 | 10.67 | 3.19 | 15.65 |
| 1969 | 15.35 | 25.09 | 6.22 | 7.75 | 3.68 | 15.75 |
| 1970 | 16.70 | 25.62 | 6.69 | 8.83 | 5.48 | 14.97 |
| 1971 | 17.77 | 29.80 | 7.86 | 9.69 | 5.15 | 11.84 |
| 1972 | 18.42 | 23.75 | 6.89 | 7.59 | 6.03 | 11.75 |
| 1973 | 20.81 | 21.71 | 8.45 | 8.48 | 7.07 | 14.02 |
| 1974 | 22.75 | 26.67 | 10.23 | 10.89 | 7.44 | 18.07 |
| 1975 | 23.43 | 28.86 | 8.67 | 8.90 | 9.35 | 12.89 |
| 1976 | 20.82 | 25.58 | 9.04 | 11.64 | 10.16 | 12.05 |
| 1977 | 21.46 | 28.43 | 12.22 | 12.02 | 10.54 | 18.47 |
| 1978 | 21.66 | 29.87 | 11.85 | 12.59 | 11.20 | 16.91 |
| 1979 | 22.45 | 27.88 | 9.29 | 10.41 | 12.44 | 17.40 |
| 1980 | 21.01 | 28.59 | 6.85 | 8.52 | 11.79 | 17.60 |
| 1981 | 22.96 | 26.62 | 7.08 | 9.66 | 11.34 | 13.56 |
| 1982 | 16.47 | 24.05 | 6.35 | 8.05 | 9.23 | 9.85 |
| 1983 | 17.56 | 18.60 | 6.68 | 6.94 | 10.47 | 9.76 |
| 1984 | 22.62 | 21.62 | 7.23 | 6.79 | 12.18 | 14.52 |
| 1985 | 24.21 | 21.76 | 6.59 | 5.93 | 11.25 | 12.80 |

(continued)

## Table 7D.1 (continued)

| Year | Mexico | Nicaragua | Paraguay | Panama | Peru | Venezuela | Uruguay |
|------|--------|-----------|----------|--------|------|-----------|---------|
| 1950 | 13.18 | 8.60 | 2.92 | 18.42 | 13.34 | 11.75 | 15.60 |
| 1951 | 14.50 | 10.88 | 4.03 | 15.29 | 17.19 | 11.19 | 16.66 |
| 1952 | 15.44 | 12.58 | 5.61 | 13.99 | 19.03 | 13.95 | 15.41 |
| 1953 | 15.47 | 13.39 | 7.10 | 19.73 | 18.41 | 13.67 | 12.22 |
| 1954 | 15.77 | 14.52 | 5.72 | 15.85 | 13.42 | 14.51 | 15.07 |
| 1955 | 16.15 | 13.95 | 4.32 | 17.57 | 15.25 | 12.60 | 12.86 |
| 1956 | 18.76 | 12.87 | 4.14 | 20.23 | 17.55 | 12.06 | 11.63 |
| 1957 | 18.54 | 11.91 | 6.89 | 19.21 | 18.87 | 11.50 | 12.46 |
| 1958 | 16.61 | 11.52 | 6.39 | 21.16 | 15.76 | 11.62 | 9.08 |
| 1959 | 16.16 | 12.88 | 5.64 | 22.94 | 11.48 | 11.00 | 10.63 |
| 1960 | 16.87 | 11.27 | 6.78 | 19.32 | 13.65 | 7.39 | 11.49 |
| 1961 | 16.72 | 11.42 | 7.11 | 22.09 | 14.19 | 6.73 | 12.40 |
| 1962 | 15.86 | 13.06 | 6.60 | 22.82 | 14.39 | 6.53 | 11.06 |
| 1963 | 17.27 | 13.31 | 6.12 | 23.62 | 13.03 | 6.05 | 9,.96 |
| 1964 | 18.50 | 15.97 | 6.58 | 20.79 | 13.07 | 7.38 | 8.29 |
| 1965 | 19.61 | 16.76 | 8.17 | 21.70 | 13.84 | 7.03 | 7.92 |
| 1966 | 18.93 | 17.83 | 9.22 | 26.34 | 16.16 | 6.67 | 7.91 |
| 1967 | 19.42 | 16.60 | 9.61 | 25.61 | 15.24 | 6.60 | 8.88 |
| 1968 | 18.82 | 14.46 | 8.87 | 26.98 | 10.39 | 7.81 | 7.80 |
| 1969 | 19.30 | 16.03 | 8.90 | 28.67 | 10.30 | 7.10 | 9.35 |
| 1970 | 20.48 | 15.97 | 7.87 | 30.93 | 10.40 | 7.70 | 9.52 |
| 1971 | 18.73 | 15.84 | 8.21 | 34.14 | 11.43 | 8.81 | 9.51 |
| 1972 | 19.09 | 10.86 | 8.98 | 36.66 | 7.70 | 9.15 | 8.36 |
| 1973 | 20.27 | 18.63 | 11.70 | 36.32 | 13.59 | 10.21 | 5.93 |
| 1974 | 22.35 | 22.70 | 12.12 | 33.82 | 17.79 | 11.42 | 6.86 |
| 1975 | 22.24 | 14.01 | 12.19 | 31.97 | 16.19 | 14.32 | 9.95 |
| 1976 | 20.86 | 13.57 | 13.88 | 31.11 | 13.82 | 15.63 | 12.51 |
| 1977 | 20.22 | 20.06 | 15.28 | 21.90 | 10.21 | 19.16 | 15.14 |
| 1978 | 20.84 | 9.46 | 16.87 | 24.83 | 8.96 | 19.60 | 17.27 |
| 1979 | 22.33 | n.a. | 18.60 | 25.51 | 8.79 | 18.60 | 21.20 |
| 1980 | 24.96 | 11.81 | 19.40 | 26.62 | 12.11 | 17.88 | 20.07 |
| 1981 | 26.60 | 17.96 | 19.81 | 28.14 | 13.70 | 19.00 | 20.08 |
| 1982 | 19.40 | 14.23 | 17.87 | 25.79 | 11.14 | 19.23 | 17.64 |
| 1983 | 15.05 | 12.23 | 18.09 | 22.41 | 8.97 | 12.24 | 13.38 |
| 1984 | 16.64 | 14.39 | 12.45 | 17.44 | 8.07 | 12.79 | 13.31 |
| 1985 | 18.05 | 11.80 | 12.95 | 15.44 | 6.39 | 12.55 | 10.39 |

n.a. Not available.
*Source:* Summers and Heston (1988).

**Table 7D.2    Total gross investment as a share of GDP, 1970-88 (percent)**

| Countries | 1970 | 1971 | 1972 | 1973 | 1974 | 1975 | 1976 |
|-----------|------|------|------|------|------|------|------|
| Argentina | 21.6 | 20.8 | 20.7 | 18.1 | 19.3 | 25.9 | 26.8 |
| Bolivia | 14.3 | 14.5 | 15.1 | 17.4 | 15.1 | 18.4 | 19.0 |
| Brazil | 23.8 | 24.7 | 25.2 | 25.8 | 27.9 | 29.6 | 26.7 |
| Chile | 16.4 | 14.5 | 12.2 | 7.9 | 21.2 | 14.0 | 12.8 |
| Colombia | 20.2 | 19.4 | 18.1 | 18.3 | 21.5 | 17.0 | 17.6 |
| Costa Rica | 19.4 | 22.1 | 21.9 | n.a. | n.a. | n.a | 23.5 |
| Ecuador | 16.6 | 21.8 | 18.0 | 17.6 | 18.2 | 23.2 | 22.2 |
| Guatemala | 12.5 | 13.3 | 13.0 | 13.9 | 14.8 | 15.7 | 20.6 |
| Mexico | 19.8 | 17.8 | 18.9 | 19.2 | 19.9 | 21.4 | 21.0 |
| Paraguay | 14.8 | 14.0 | 15.5 | 15.6 | 17.9 | 19.9 | 21.7 |
| Peru | 13.3 | 13.9 | 13.7 | 15.7 | 18.3 | 18.6 | 17.4 |
| Uruguay | 11.8 | 11.5 | 9.8 | 9.0 | 10.3 | 13.3 | 15.5 |
| Venezuela | 22.2 | 23.3 | 25.8 | 25.4 | 18.6 | 24.3 | 31.6 |

| Countries | 1977 | 1978 | 1979 | 1980 | 1981 | 1982 |
|-----------|------|------|------|------|------|------|
| Argentina | 27.3 | 24.4 | 22.7 | 22.2 | 18.8 | 17.0 |
| Bolivia | 19.1 | 20.2 | 16.6 | 14.3 | 16.6 | 13.8 |
| Brazil | 25.2 | 24.4 | 22.3 | 22.9 | 22.8 | 21.4 |
| Chile | 14.4 | 17.8 | 17.8 | 21.0 | 22.7 | 11.3 |
| Colombia | 18.8 | 18.3 | 18.2 | 19.1 | 20.6 | 20.5 |
| Costa Rica | 22.4 | 23.0 | 26.2 | 23.9 | 24.1 | 20.3 |
| Ecuador | 23.6 | 26.2 | 23.7 | 23.6 | 22.3 | 22.6 |
| Guatemala | 19.0 | 20.1 | 18.6 | 16.4 | 16.8 | 15.0 |
| Mexico | 19.7 | 21.2 | 23.7 | 24.8 | 26.4 | 23.0 |
| Paraguay | 23.4 | 25.2 | 27.3 | 31.0 | 30.9 | 27.2 |
| Peru | 15.7 | 14.2 | 14.1 | 17.1 | 19.0 | 20.4 |
| Uruguay | 15.2 | 16.0 | 16.2 | 16.7 | 15.8 | 15.1 |
| Venezuela | 38.8 | 42.5 | 31.5 | 25.3 | 24.4 | 24.1 |

| Countries | 1983 | 1984 | 1985 | 1986 | 1987 | 1988 |
|-----------|------|------|------|------|------|------|
| Argentina | 17.4 | 14.5 | 12.3 | 13.0 | 13.0 | 14.0 |
| Bolivia | 16.4 | 8.7 | 7.4 | 9.5 | 10.2 | 13.5 |
| Brazil | 17.9 | 16.5 | 17.0 | 19.2 | 22.3 | 23.2 |
| Chile | 9.8 | 13.6 | 13.7 | 14.6 | 16.9 | 17.0 |
| Colombia | 19.9 | 19.0 | 19.0 | 18.0 | 19.3 | 19.6 |
| Costa Rica | 18.0 | 20.1 | 19.3 | 18.6 | 19.9 | 18.3 |
| Ecuador | 16.5 | 15.4 | 16.1 | 18.8 | 22.8 | 21.1 |
| Guatemala | 10.5 | 9.6 | 11.0 | 10.1 | 12.2 | 13.6 |
| Mexico | 17.6 | 17.9 | 19.2 | 19.4 | 18.9 | 18.5 |
| Paraguay | 25.6 | 21.6 | 20.7 | 23.6 | 23.7 | 23.1 |
| Peru | 23.7 | 22.6 | 22.4 | 23.3 | 23.6 | 28.5 |
| Uruguay | 11.0 | 9.3 | 7.5 | 7.9 | 9.0 | 9.6 |
| Venezuela | 16.7 | 16.4 | 16.8 | 19.0 | 19.1 | 21.5 |

n.a.  Not available
*Source:* World Bank

**Table 7D.3    Share of gross investment in GDP, Chile, 1957-88**
              (percent)

| | Banco Central de Chile | | | | | |
| Year | Nominal fixed capital formation/ nominal GDP | Nominal gross investment/ nominal GDP | Real fixed capital formation /real GDP | Real gross investment /real GDP | Summers and Heston | World Bank |
|---|---|---|---|---|---|---|
| 1957 | n.a. | n.a. | n.a. | n.a | 30.67 | n.a. |
| 1958 | n.a. | n.a. | n.a. | n.a. | 29.85 | n.a. |
| 1959 | n.a. | n.a. | n.a. | n.a. | 27.87 | n.a. |
| 1960 | 14.7 | 14.0 | 20.7 | 14.6 | 33.33 | n.a. |
| 1961 | 15.1 | 15.3 | 20.0 | n.a. | 35.69 | n.a. |
| 1962 | 15.2 | 12.5 | 21.4 | 13.9 | 34.18 | n.a. |
| 1963 | 16.1 | 14.9 | 23.1 | 15.6 | 36.05 | n.a. |
| 1964 | 15.3 | 14.2 | 21.4 | 18.6 | 33.70 | n.a. |
| 1965 | 14.7 | 14.9 | 19.9 | 17.9 | 34.83 | n.a. |
| 1966 | 14.2 | 16.3 | 18.5 | 23.1 | 33.94 | n.a. |
| 1967 | 14.2 | 16.1 | 18.3 | 20.3 | 31.98 | n.a. |
| 1968 | 14.7 | 16.3 | 19.3 | 21.3 | 32.99 | n.a. |
| 1969 | 14.3 | 15.1 | 19.6 | 22.0 | 34.03 | n.a. |
| 1970 | 15.0 | 16.4 | 20.4 | 23.3 | 33.93 | 16.4 |
| 1971 | 14.6 | 14.5 | 18.3 | 20.8 | 31.55 | 14.5 |
| 1972 | 13.1 | 12.2 | 14.8 | 15.2 | 26.88 | 12.2 |
| 1973 | 12.8 | 7.9 | 14.7 | 14.3 | 26.99 | 7.9 |
| 1974 | 16.9 | 21.1 | 17.4 | 25.8 | 32.01 | 21.2 |
| 1975 | 17.7 | 13.1 | 15.4 | 14.0 | 18.55 | 14.0 |
| 1976 | 13.3 | 12.8 | 12.7 | 13.6 | 21.27 | 12.8 |
| 1977 | 13.3 | 14.4 | 13.3 | 14.4 | 25.14 | 14.4 |
| 1978 | 14.7 | 17.8 | 14.5 | 16.5 | 28.86 | 17.8 |
| 1979 | 14.9 | 17.8 | 15.6 | 19.6 | 30.55 | 17.8 |
| 1980 | 16.6 | 20.9 | 17.6 | 23.8 | 35.52 | 21.0 |
| 1981 | 18.6 | 22.7 | 19.5 | 27.6 | 35.24 | 22.7 |
| 1982 | 14.6 | 11.3 | 15.0 | 11.1 | 20.44 | 11.3 |
| 1983 | 12.0 | 9.8 | 12.9 | 9.3 | 21.53 | 9.8 |
| 1984 | 12.3 | 13.6 | 13.2 | 15.3 | 22.28 | 13.6 |
| 1985 | 14.2 | 13.7 | 14.8 | 14.0 | 21.68 | 13.7 |
| 1986 | 14.6 | 14.6 | 15.0 | 15.1 | n.a. | 14.6 |
| 1987 | 16.0 | 16.9 | 16.5 | 17.9 | n.a. | 16.9 |
| 1988 | 16.3 | 17.0 | 17.0 | 18.1 | n.a. | 17.0 |

n.a. Not available.
*Source:* Banco Central de Chile (1990), Summers and Heston (1988), and World Bank.

## Table 7D.4 Share of gross investment in GDP, Brazil, 1970-88

| Year | | Contas Nacionais | | | Summers and Heston, real gross investment /real GDP | World Bank[a] |
|---|---|---|---|---|---|---|
| | Nominal capital formation/ nominal GDP | Real capital formation /real GDP | Real variation of stocks /real GDP | Real gross investment /real GDP | | |
| 1970 | 20.6 | 18.8 | 0.9 | 19.7 | 24.35 | 23.8 |
| 1971 | 21.3 | 19.9 | 0.7 | 20.6 | 24.89 | 24.7 |
| 1972 | 22.2 | 20.3 | 0.7 | 21.0 | 24.67 | 25.2 |
| 1973 | 23.6 | 20.4 | 1.4 | 21.8 | 26.62 | 25.8 |
| 1974 | 24.7 | 21.8 | 2.2 | 24.0 | 28.88 | 27.9 |
| 1975 | 25.8 | 23.3 | 2.4 | 25.7 | 30.30 | 29.6 |
| 1976 | 25.0 | 22.4 | 0.7 | 23.1 | 27.69 | 26.7 |
| 1977 | 23.6 | 21.3 | 1.0 | 22.3 | 25.50 | 25.2 |
| 1978 | 23.5 | 22.3 | 0.6 | 22.9 | 24.29 | 24.4 |
| 1979 | 22.9 | 23.4 | -0.2 | 23.2 | 22.65 | 22.3 |
| 1980 | 22.9 | 22.9 | 0.4 | 23.3 | 23.31 | 22.9 |
| 1981 | 22.8 | 21.0 | 0.2 | 21.2 | 19.71 | 22.8 |
| 1982 | 21.4 | 19.5 | -0.3 | 19.2 | 18.79 | 21.4 |
| 1983 | 17.9 | 16.9 | -1.5 | 15.4 | 16.51 | 17.9 |
| 1984 | 16.5 | 16.1 | -1.1 | 15.0 | 15.55 | 16.5 |
| 1985 | 17.0 | 16.7 | n.a. | n.a. | 16.07 | 17.0 |
| 1986 | 19.2 | 19.0 | n.a. | n.a. | n.a. | 19.2 |
| 1987 | 22.1 | 18.1 | n.a. | n.a. | n.a. | 22.3 |
| 1988 | 21.8 | 17.3 | n.a. | n.a. | n.a. | 23.2 |

n.a. Not available.
a. Until 1980 World Bank nominal shares include increases in stocks. From 1980 on they are approximately the same as column 1.
*Source:* Brazil, Fundacão Getúlio Vargas (June 1990), Summers and Heston (1988), and World Bank.

**Table 7D.5**   Public investment as a percent of GDP in Latin America, 1970-88

| Countries | 1970 | 1971 | 1972 | 1973 | 1974 | 1975 | 1976 |
|---|---|---|---|---|---|---|---|
| Argentina | 8.2 | 7.8 | 8.4 | 7.3 | 8.3 | 8.8 | 12.9 |
| Bolivia | 8.0 | 8.7 | 8.9 | 6.5 | 5.1 | 7.5 | 10.6 |
| Brazil | 7.2 | 6.5 | 7.6 | 6.1 | 8.2 | 8.7 | 10.6 |
| Chile | 6.9 | 8.0 | 7.7 | 7.4 | 12.0 | 10.7 | 8.0 |
| Colombia | 5.7 | 6.4 | 5.8 | 7.0 | 5.2 | 5.2 | 5.5 |
| Costa Rica | 4.4 | 5.7 | 6.8 | n.a. | n.a. | n.a. | 8.4 |
| Ecuador | 6.7 | 7.1 | 6.6 | 6.8 | 8.0 | 8.7 | 9.2 |
| Guatemala | 2.4 | 2.9 | 3.2 | 3.4 | 2.9 | 3.5 | 6.6 |
| Mexico | 6.6 | 4.6 | 6.1 | 7.5 | 7.6 | 9.0 | 8.2 |
| Paraguay | 4.0 | 3.7 | 4.5 | 3.3 | 2.7 | 4.2 | 8.1 |
| Peru | 3.6 | 3.4 | 4.1 | 4.6 | 7.8 | 6.6 | 5.8 |
| Uruguay | 3.0 | 3.2 | 2.3 | 1.9 | 2.6 | 4.6 | 6.5 |
| Venezuela | 5.2 | 5.4 | 9.8 | 9.0 | 6.0 | 8.5 | 13.0 |

| Countries | 1977 | 1978 | 1979 | 1980 | 1981 | 1982 | 1983 |
|---|---|---|---|---|---|---|---|
| Argentina | 12.9 | 11.9 | 10.2 | 9.2 | 9.4 | 8.1 | 9.5 |
| Bolivia | 12.2 | 13.4 | 9.7 | 7.0 | 11.1 | 7.8 | 11.4 |
| Brazil | 9.5 | 10.8 | 7.7 | 8.1 | 9.0 | 8.3 | 6.5 |
| Chile | 6.9 | 6.4 | 5.2 | 5.4 | 5.4 | 5.4 | 5.4 |
| Colombia | 9.1 | 6.8 | 5.8 | 7.6 | 8.6 | 9.4 | 8.9 |
| Costa Rica | 8.2 | 7.4 | 8.9 | 9.2 | 8.9 | 7.2 | 6.4 |
| Ecuador | 10.2 | 9.4 | 9.2 | 9.5 | 10.6 | 9.6 | 7.9 |
| Guatemala | 5.9 | 5.6 | 6.3 | 6.7 | 8.4 | 6.3 | 4.6 |
| Mexico | 7.8 | 8.4 | 10.2 | 10.9 | 11.7 | 10.3 | 7.6 |
| Paraguay | 7.2 | 6.8 | 6.0 | 5.3 | 5.2 | 4.8 | 8.3 |
| Peru | 4.9 | 3.7 | 4.6 | 5.6 | 6.4 | 7.9 | 6.8 |
| Uruguay | 7.0 | 8.0 | 6.5 | 5.3 | 5.1 | 7.2 | 4.1 |
| Venezuela | 15.2 | 18.0 | 13.4 | 12.3 | 14.6 | 16.4 | 11.7 |

| Countries | 1984 | 1985 | 1986 | 1987 | 1988 |
|---|---|---|---|---|---|
| Argentina | 7.6 | 6.8 | 7.0 | 6.2 | 6.0 |
| Bolivia | 3.7 | 3.7 | 4.9 | 6.3 | 8.2 |
| Brazil | 6.0 | 6.3 | 6.4 | 6.9 | 7.2 |
| Chile | 6.4 | 7.0 | 7.5 | 6.9 | 7.0 |
| Colombia | 9.0 | 9.6 | 8.6 | 8.4 | 8.1 |
| Costa Rica | 6.4 | 7.0 | 5.8 | 4.8 | 3.2 |
| Ecuador | 6.4 | 6.6 | 9.0 | 9.0 | 7.9 |
| Guatemala | 3.8 | 2.7 | 2.0 | 2.8 | 2.8 |
| Mexico | 7.1 | 7.0 | 6.1 | 5.4 | 2.6 |
| Paraguay | 8.0 | 5.7 | 4.8 | 4.3 | 4.8 |
| Peru | 7.5 | 6.6 | 5.5 | 6.0 | 6.0 |
| Uruguay | 4.1 | 3.0 | 3.2 | 3.2 | 3.4 |
| Venezuela | 7.4 | 6.4 | 7.2 | 7.5 | 7.4 |

n.a. Not available.
*Source:* World Bank.

## Figure 7D.1  Gross investment and fixed capital formation, Chile, 1965-88

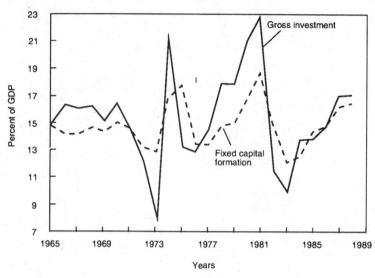

*Source:* Table 7D.3

## Figure 7D.2  Nominal and real investment shares, Chile, 1965-85

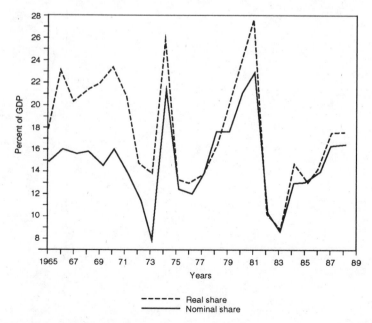

*Source:* Table 7D.3

**Figure 7D.3  Share of real investment in real GDP, Chile, 1965-85**

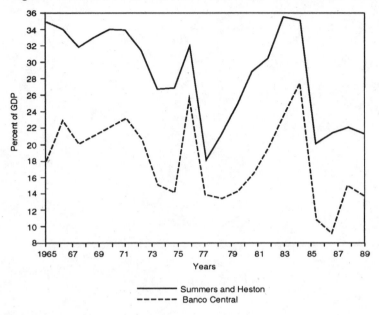

*Source:* Table 7D.3

**Figure 7D.4  Understanding the different measures, Brazil, 1970-1984**

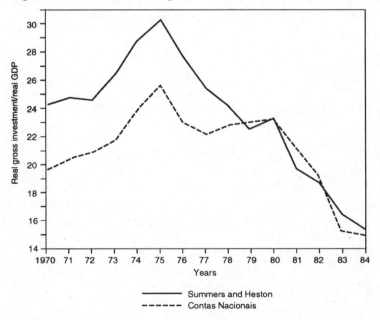

*Source:* Table 7D.4

**Figure 7D.5 Share of Fixed Capital Formation in GDP, Brazil, 1970-1988**

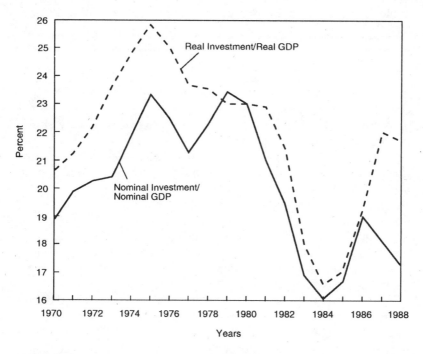

*Source:* Table 7D.3

Geografia e Estatistica, which is responsible for the Contas Nacionais published in *Conjuntura Economica*, recommends that the new data not be linked with those of different series. Also observe that there is no information on the variation in stocks after 1985. The only data after 1985 are for fixed capital formation, not total investment. Comparison of the first and last columns in table 7D.4 shows that the World Bank links data for total investment between 1970 and 1979 with data for fixed capital formation between 1980 and 1986.

Figure 7D.4 compares the shares of real total investment in real GDP reported by Summers and Heston with the information reported by Contas Nacionais, *Conjuntura Economica*. After 1978 the two sources report almost the same numbers. Summers' shares are larger in the 1970s and thus show a much bigger decline in the real share of investment in the 1980s relative to the 1970s than is true for the data recorded by *Conjuntura Economica*.

Figure 7D.5 shows real and nominal shares as reported by *Conjuntura Economica*. They broadly follow the same pattern until 1986. Inflation accelerated after 1986, and relative prices moved significantly. The price of investment goods increased less than the price of other components of GDP in 1987.

Table 7D.5 shows public investment as a percent of GDP in 13 Latin American countries.

## Notes

1. I thank Rudi Dornbusch, Luis Servén, and Andrés Solimano for their comments and suggestions.
2. See Williamson (1990) for a discussion of the extent to which adjustment has occurred in Latin America.
3. Appendix 7-2 uses a model of a small open economy with flexible exchange rates and four assets to discuss the dynamics of both the real price of capital and the real exchange rate in response to different shocks, including a change in monetary policy and an increase in external interest rates.
4. Since 1989, however, the Brazilian government has let the real exchange rate appreciate in an attempt to control inflation (figure 7-3). For the time being it has been able to live with the overvaluation by sticking to the external debt moratorium.
5. They expected this policy to lower inflation in three ways: by reducing the rate of inflation of import prices; by imposing discipline on price setters, who would have to compete with cheaper imports; and by providing a benchmark to which expectations about inflation could converge.
6. Murphy (1989) differs from Cardoso (1983) and Gavin (1989) by leaving aside the monetary question and allowing for capital accumulation in the context of an explicitly optimizing model.
7. Regressions that include both the terms of trade and the real exchange rate lead to similar results. Neither the significance of the terms of trade nor the lack of significance of the real exchange rate is affected when both variables are included in the same equation.
8. See regressions for 24 developing countries in Blejer and Khan (1984). They find that the degree of capacity utilization and availability of credit have an important positive effect on private investment. They also find evidence that public investment in infrastructure crowds in private investment.
9. High coefficients of the variable standing for change in output in investment regressions are considered excessive because part of the fluctuations in output is transitory.
10. Observe that $H < B$. In economies where prices move very slowly, the possibility of undershooting arises. For this perverse case to obtain, the elasticity of aggregate demand relative to the real price of capital has to be large enough to generate an expansion in income and thus an increase in the demand for money that exceeds the initial expansion in real balances.
11. Latin America includes 20 countries. Table 7D.1 excludes Cuba.

# References

Behrman, J. 1972. "Sectoral Investment Determination in Developing Economies." *American Economic Review* 62 (5)(December):825-41.

Bernanke, B. 1983. "Irreversibility, Uncertainty and Cyclical Investment." *Quarterly Journal of Economics* 98 (1)(February):85-106.

Bilsborrow, R. 1977. "The Determinants of Fixed Investment by Manufacturing Firms in a Developing Country." *International Economic Review* 18 (3) (October):697-717.

Blejer, M., and M. Khan. 1984. "Government Policy and Private Investment in Developing Countries." *IMF Staff Papers* 31(2):379-403.

Brazil. Fundaçao Geatúlio Vargas. Various years. Contas Nacionais. *Conjuntura Economais.*

Cardoso, E. 1983. "Exchange Rate Dynamics and the Stock Market." Discussion Paper Series. Center for Latin American Development Studies, Boston University, Boston, Mass. May.

———. 1990. "Debt Cycles in Brazil and Argentina," in D. Felix, ed., *Debt and Transfiguration.* Armonk, N.Y.: Sharpe.

Cardoso, E., and A. Fishlow. 1992. "Latin American Economic Development: 1950-1980." *Journal of Latin American Studies* 24:197-218.

Chile. Banco Central de Chile. 1990. *Indicadores Economicos y Sociales 1960-1988.* Santiago: Banco Central de Chile.

Dailami, Mansoor. 1987. "Expectation, Stock Market Volatility and Private Investment Behavior: Theory and Empirical Evidence for Brazil." World Bank, Country Economics Department, Washington D.C.

Dornbusch, R. 1976. "Expectations and Exchange Rate Dynamics." *Journal of Political Economy* 84 (6)(December):1161-76.

Economic Commission for Latin American and the Caribbean (ECLAC). 1989. *Preliminary Overview of the Latin American Economy, 1989.* Santiago, Chile: United Nations.

Faini, R., and J. de Melo. 1990. "Adjustment, Investment and the Real Exchange Rate in Developing Countries." World Bank, Country Economics Department, Washington D.C.

Gavin, M. 1989. "The Stock Market and Exchange Rate Dynamics." *Journal of International Money and Finance* 8 (2)(June):181-200.

Inter-American Development Bank. 1989. *Economic and Social Progress in Latin America.* Washington, D.C.: Inter-American Development Bank.

Montiel, P. 1989. "Empirical Analysis of High-Inflation Episodes in Argentina, Brazil and Israel." *IMF Staff Papers* 36 (3)(September):527-49.

Mundell, R. 1965. "Growth, Stability and Inflationary Finance." *Journal of Political Economy* 73 (2)(April):97-109.

Murphy, R. 1989. "Stock Prices, Real Exchange Rates, and Optimal Capital Accumulation." *IMF Staff Papers* 36 (1)(March):102-29.

Musalem, A. 1989. "Private Investment in Mexico: An Empirical Analysis." Working Paper no. 183. World Bank, Washington D.C.

Ocampo, J. A. 1990. "Investment Determinants and Financing in Colombia." Paper prepared for the World Bank Conference on Latin America: Facing the Challenges of Adjustment and Growth, Caracas, Venezuela, July 19-22, 1990.

Pinheiro, A. Castelar, and V. Matesco. 1988. "Investimento em Capital Fixo na Economia Brasileira: Estimativas Trimestrais para o Periodo 1975-87" [Fixed Capital Investment in Brazil: Quarterly Estimates, 1975-87]. Texto Para Discussao [Discussion Paper] no. 135. Instituto de Pesquisa Econômica Applicada (IPEA), Rio de Janeiro, Brazil.

———. 1989. "Relacao Capital/Produto Incremental: Estimativas Para o Periodo 1948-87" [Incremental Capital/Output Ratio, Estimates, 1948-87]. Instituto Pesquisa Econômica Applicada (IPEA), Rio de Janeiro, Brazil.

Servén, L. 1990. "Anticipated Real Exchange Rate Changes and the Dynamics of Investment." World Bank, Country Economics Department, Washington, D.C.

Servén, L., and A. Solimano. 1990. "Private Investment and Macroeconomic Adjustment in LDCs: Theory, Country Experiences and Policy Implications." World Bank, Country Economics Department, Washington D.C. August.

Solimano, A. (1989) "How Private Investment Reacts to Changing Macroeconomic Conditions. The Chilean Experience of the 1980s" World Bank, Policy, Research and External Affairs (PRE) Working Paper Series #212. Washington, D.C. Also in A. Chhibber, M. Dailami and N. Shafik, eds., *Reviving Private Investment in Developing Countries: Empirical Studies and Policy Lessons*. Amsterdam: North-Holland Publishing, 1992.

Summers, R., and A. Heston. 1984. "Improved International Comparisons of Real Product and Its Composition: 1950-1980." *Review of Income and Wealth*, series 30 (2)(June):207-19.

———. 1988. "A New Set of International Comparisons of Real Product and Prices." *The Review of Income and Wealth*, series 34 (1)(March):1-26.

Williamson, J. 1990. *Latin American Adjustment: How Much Has Happened?* Washington D.C.: Institute for International Economics.

World Bank. Various issues. *World Tables*. Washington, D.C.: World Bank.

# 8

# Investment and Macroeconomic Adjustment: The Case of East Asia

*Felipe Larrain*
*and*
*Rodrigo Vergara*

Every success in East Asia has unique features that have led some analysts to see each one as a special case.[1] Others have attempted to generalize and find *the* common East Asian pattern. It would be nice to be able to claim that all the countries had pursued a single strategy and that strategy was the key to economic development. That claim would, however, be mistaken. Further, it would not be accurate to describe all the successes as the victory of free enterprise, as Milton Friedman has argued:

> ...every successful country (Taiwan, South Korea, Singapore, Hong Kong, Japan) has relied primarily on private enterprise and free markets to achieve economic development. Every country in trouble has relied primarily on government to guide and direct its economic development. (Friedman 1983, 96, and as quoted in Sachs 1985)

In fact, only Hong Kong is a pure case of a free market with minimal government intervention.

Most analysts of East Asia tend to agree that the picture is more complex than that free market scenario. Governments there have used industrial and trade policies widely, and state intervention has been important (see, for example, Sachs 1985; Dornbusch and Park 1987; Sachs and Sundberg 1988; Collins 1988a; Collins and Park 1989), although with significant variations across countries. Even Lee Kuan Yew, the former prime minister of Singapore, described his country—although he was surely exaggerating—as a case of "socialism that works" (as quoted in Sachs and Sundberg 1988, 6). In reality, for the most part the policies pursued can be broadly described as "inspired intervention." The economic authorities have directly affected the allocation of resources through credit guidelines and trade restrictions. Nonetheless, they have generally respected basic economic principles such as fiscal and monetary restraint and have let the private sector take the leading role in the economy. Their intervention has tended to be pro-export, as opposed to the import-substituting bias in Latin America.

In spite of their differences, there are still factors common to almost all the successful East Asian economies. They share such elements as competitive real exchange rates, a stable macroeconomic environment, high saving/ investment ratios, relatively low degrees of income inequality, and rapid response to external shocks, all of which have been identified as keys to their success (see Kuznets 1988; Sachs 1985; Sachs and Sundberg 1988; Collins and Park 1989; Lin 1988; and Servén and Solimano 1990a, 1990b for a more detailed analysis of these and other points, also chapter 2 and 6, this volume).

One of the most impressive features of the East Asian economies has been their ability to maintain very high rates of investment. Beyond any doubt this factor has been crucial in determining their growth performance over the past three decades. This chapter presents an explanation of the evolution of investment in East Asian economies for the period from the early 1960s to the late 1980s. In particular, it identifies the determinants of private investment and measures its response to different variables.

The next section discusses the macroeconomic background of four East Asian economies—Korea, Singapore, Thailand, and Malaysia—over the last few decades. The following section describes the evolution of investment, distinguishing among several categories (public and private, machinery and equipment, infrastructure, and tradable and nontradable) and the sources of financing for investment. The fourth section presents an analysis at a conceptual level of the effect of different variables on investment; it draws a distinction between macroeconomic policies and structural variables. An econometric analysis of private investment is the subject of the subsequent section. Some conclusions and policy recommendations close the paper.

## Macroeconomic background

This section briefly describes the macroeconomic background of the four countries covered in this chapter.[2] The choice of countries was determined largely by the availability of data: since the main purpose was to study investment in East Asia, only countries with reliable and sufficiently long series of private and public investment were included. This prerequisite disqualified other interesting experiences such as those of Hong Kong, Indonesia, and Taiwan. Occasionally, however, reference is made to other countries.

Tables 8-1 to 8-4 present a summary of the major macroeconomic indicators for each of the four countries, averaged over relevant subperiods. The latter were chosen to coincide either with a change in policies or with internal or external events in each country that had an important impact on the economy.

## Korea

After the devastation of the Korean War, in which about one million people died, the country pursued an inward-oriented economic strategy supported by massive flows of American aid. The results, however, were disappointing. Political turmoil at the beginning of the 1960s gave way in 1961 to a military coup led by General Park Chung Hee.

General Park held power for the next 18 years, presiding over a massive transformation of the economy. In 1962 Korea started to organize its long-term economic policy according to five-year plans. The primary objective of the first plan was to switch from an import—substitution model to an active export—promotion strategy. To achieve this objective, the plan identified key variables that would have to be emphasized. First among these was a strong emphasis on investment. Other key parts of the plan were heavy intervention by the government in the credit market and an industrial policy to promote the tradable sectors. These policies were combined with moderate liberalization of trade. The authorities also recognized early on that overall macroeconomic stability and a high and stable real exchange rate to maintain external competitiveness were essential.

The results of this first phase were so good that they must have surprised even the strongest advocates of the new policy. Gross domestic product (GDP) grew at an average yearly rate of 9.8 percent between 1964 and 1969, which amounted to growth in per capita GDP of 6.9 percent a year (table 8-1). Exports increased from US$87 million in 1963 to US$658 million in 1969, a 40.2 percent yearly increase.[3] Inflation was relatively high,

**Table 8.1  Korea's major economic indicators**

| Indicators[a] | 1964-69 | 1970-72 | 1973-78 | 1979-82 | 1983-88 |
|---|---|---|---|---|---|
| GDP growth rate (%) | 9.8 | 8.0 | 10.6 | 4.4 | 9.9 |
| Per capita GDP growth rate (%) | 6.9 | 5.8 | 8.8 | 2.7 | 8.7 |
| Export growth rate (%)[b] | 40.2 | 36.8 | 42.6 | 13.5 | 19.8 |
| Inflation (CPI) (%) | 16.6 | 13.7 | 15.5 | 18.9 | 3.5 |
| Current account deficit (% of GDP) | 3.7 | 6.4 | 4.2 | 6.3 | -2.7 |
| Fixed investment (% of GDP)[c] | 20.0 | 22.5 | 25.9 | 29.6 | 28.5 |
| Domestic saving (% of GDP)[d] | 17.8 | 17.8 | 23.8 | 24.5 | 32.4 |
| External debt (% of GDP) | 15.0 | 31.3 | 33.4 | 43.3 | 42.8 |
| Real exchange rate (1980=100) | 90.5 | 89.4 | 108.1 | 95.6 | 110.4 |

a. Every figure corresponds to the average of the period.

b. Export growth rate refers to growth in dollar terms.

c. Fixed investment (% of GDP) in current prices.

d. Domestic saving (% of GDP) in current prices. Defined as total investment (fixed plus change in stocks) minus the current account deficit.

*Source*: International Monetary Fund (various issues, *International Financial Statistics*), World Bank data base, and Collins and Park (1989).

however, reaching an average of 16.6 percent a year during the same period. The current account was almost balanced for two years but then started showing a deficit that reached 7.5 percent of GDP on average during 1968-69. Fixed investment surged from 11.4 percent of GDP in 1964 to 26.1 percent in 1969. Given that saving did not grow as fast, the government financed the current account deficit with foreign credits. As a result, external debt went from 6.2 percent of GDP in 1964 to 27.5 percent in 1969. After two years in which growth slowed (to 7.6 percent a year on average during 1971-72) and saving dropped, the government decided to amend the economic strategy. It sensed that Korea's competitive position in the world markets would be eroded if the heavy focus on light manufacturing was maintained. In 1973 the authorities initiated a new phase known as the "Big Push," an industrialization program directed toward the creation of heavy and chemical industries (for a detailed description see Collins and Park 1989). To this end the government increased its involvement in the economy, especially through selective credit practices and import restrictions. When the first oil shock hit, Korea relaxed its monetary and fiscal policies. At the same time, and unlike many developing countries, it passed the increase in the world price of oil on to domestic prices. Inflation climbed to 24.8 percent in 1974-75, while the budget deficit reached over 4 percent of GDP. Saving fell. Since investment did not decline, the gap was again financed through external borrowing. The current account deficit reached 10.8 percent of GDP in 1974 and 8.9 percent in 1975.

Thus Korea, by pursuing a combination of expansive internal policies and external borrowing, made it through the first oil shock relatively unscathed. In 1976 GDP started to grow again at rates of over 10 percent. By 1978 fixed investment had surpassed 30 percent of GDP, while an amazing surge in domestic saving resulted in a drop in the current account deficit, which fell to 2.2 percent of GDP in 1978. The pace at which external debt was accumulating was reduced that year. The real exchange rate appreciated, and real wages increased beyond the rise in productivity toward the end of the 1970s.

The government instituted a change in strategy in 1979. Concerned about the distortions introduced during the "Big Push" era and about a stubborn rate of inflation, it decided to implement a program of gradual reduction of regulations and of fiscal and monetary restraint. However, internal problems and the second oil shock led to bad times. In 1980 GDP fell 3 percent, the first drop in output since the 1950s, and Korea faced a debt crisis. Fears that a big recession would bring an end to the "miracle" began to arise.

Once more Korea decided to apply expansionary internal policies and to use external borrowing to overcome the situation. In the period 1979-82 the current account deficit was, on average, 6.3 percent of GDP. The budget deficit surpassed 4 percent of gross domestic product (GDP) in 1981 and 1982 (4.7 percent and 4.4 percent respectively), and inflation averaged 18.9 percent. By 1982 external debt had climbed to more than 50 percent of GDP.

In 1983 Korea resumed its path of high growth. Between 1983 and 1988 GDP grew 9.9 percent annually. After two decades of deficits in 1986 the current account ran its first surplus, which reached 8.1 percent of GDP in 1987 and 1988. Some problems surfaced after 1988, particularly labor unrest and sharp increases in wages at the end of the authoritarian period and during the first years of the new democratic government. Nonetheless, GDP growth has continued at rates that Latin America would envy, although they were lower than what Korea was used to. External debt fell so dramatically that it would be incorrect to call Korea one of the highly indebted countries, a league to which it once belonged.

In summary, Korea's economic performance over the last three decades has been extraordinary. High rates of investment, saving, and growth, combined with external borrowing when necessary, have been some of the elements of Korea's success.[4] The promotion of exports has always been a top priority (in 1988 exports of goods and services were almost $60 billion, about 700 times their dollar value in 1963). The government has played a fundamental role in this strategy. Industrial and trade policies that promote the tradable sector have been the norm. In addition, the importance of a stable macroeconomic environment cannot be minimized. An excellent example of this stability has been the small variance in the real exchange rate (see table 8-1).

Korea's experience has not been without problems. The most serious came in 1979-80. What is most impressive about the country, however, has been its ability to overcome these problems rapidly and to resume growth.

*Singapore*

Singapore, as is true of Hong Kong, is a city–state. A young nation with a small population (2.7 million people in 1988) and an excellent geographic location between the Indian Ocean and the South China Sea, Singapore started its own government under British tutelage in 1959. In 1965 it became fully independent following its expulsion from the Malaysian Federation (which included Malaya and the British-controlled parts of Borneo). One prime minister, Lee Kuan Yew of the Peoples Action Party, led the country from 1959 to November 1990. During this period Singapore experienced breathtaking economic growth. Whereas in 1965 per capita GDP was US$1,753, by 1988 it was US$11,680 (Summers and Heston 1988).[5]

As in the case of Korea, Singapore has pursued an outward-oriented development strategy. In both cases, foreign capital has been crucial to financing investment. In Singapore, however, foreign investment was the most important form of foreign financing, whereas in Korea it was external credits. As a result of Singapore's policy of encouraging foreign investment, foreign firms accounted for 63 percent of manufacturing value added, 83 percent of manufacturing exports, and 70 percent of investment commitments to manufacturing in 1983 (Islam and Kirkpatrick 1986).

Singapore shifted to an export-led growth economy well before Korea did. By 1965 exports of goods were already 95 percent of GDP, and in 1988 the ratio of exports to GDP reached 155 percent, a level that made this city–state the most open economy in the world.

In 1967, two years after the Malaysian Federation expelled Singapore, Britain announced the end of its military presence. This decision posed a problem because the British employed about 20 percent of the labor force (Krause 1988). A concerned government decided to take a much more active role in the economy and to push for industrialization. Low wages, a large supply of relatively skilled labor, and open access to foreign investors made Singapore an ideal environment for foreign firms. Multinationals established themselves there and exported their production to the rest of the world.

The first stage was an astounding success. Between 1965 and 1973 per capita GDP grew at an average rate of 10 percent per year, manufacturing production at 20 percent (table 8-2). Gross fixed investment went from 21.1 percent of GDP in 1965 to an average 36.5 percent for the three years 1971-73. Given that saving was relatively low in this first phase, the government financed the resulting gap on the current account mostly through foreign investment. External credits were relatively unimportant, and the accumulation of foreign debt was low. In sharp contrast to Korea, Singapore was able to keep inflation at very low levels: the average rate for 1965-73 was 3.3 percent, and only in 1973 did it climb to 10 percent.

In the early 1970s the rapid economic expansion produced a tightening of the labor market. The government, fearing an uncontrolled increase in

**Table 8.2  Singapore's major economic indicators**

| Indicators[a] | 1965-73 | 1974-75 | 1976-84 | 1985-88 |
|---|---|---|---|---|
| GDP growth rate (%) | 12.1 | 5.2 | 8.4 | 5.0 |
| Per capita GDP growth rate (%) | 10.0 | 3.6 | 7.1 | 3.7 |
| Export growth rate[b] (%) | 18.1 | 27.0 | 18.7 | 15.3 |
| Inflation (CPI) % | 3.3 | 12.5 | 3.8 | 0.3 |
| Current account deficit (% of GDP) | 13.9 | 15.1 | 7.3 | -3.2 |
| Fixed investment (% of GDP)[c] | 28.0 | 37.1 | 41.0 | 37.5 |
| Domestic saving (% of GDP)[d] | 17.1 | 26.0 | 36.7 | 42.4 |
| External debt (% of GDP)[e] | n.a. | 10.0 | 11.9 | 11.6 |
| Real exchange rate (1980=100) | n.a. | n.a. | 94.6 | 105.8 |

n.a. Not available

a.  Every figure corresponds to the average of the period.

b.  Export growth rate refers to growth in dollar terms.

c.  Fixed investment (% of GDP) in current prices.

d.  Domestic saving (% of GDP) in current prices. Defined as total investment (fixed plus change in stocks) minus the current account deficit.

e.  External debt includes public and publicly guaranteed debt only.

*Source*: International Monetary Fund (various issues, *International Financial Statistics*), World Bank data base, and Collins and Park (1989).

wages, created the National Wages Council in 1972. Formed by representatives of workers, entrepreneurs, and the government, its main mission was to recommend wage increases that would maintain the country's external competitiveness. After the introduction of the New Economic Policies in 1979, the Wage Council started to suggest much larger wage increases. The objective was to move production out of low-skill, labor-intensive processes so as to reduce the economy's dependence on foreign workers.

The world recession caused by the first oil shock slowed Singapore's economy. In 1974-75 output grew at 5.2 percent a year, inflation reached 22.4 percent in 1974, and the current account deficit increased. After two years, however, in 1976, high growth resumed, and inflation fell to its previous level of 3-4 percent.

Singapore did not suffer the debt crisis of the 1980s, and its economy performed impressively until 1984. In that year saving climbed to more than 46 percent of GDP, a world record. Then in 1985 the country suffered its first recession since 1964, with output falling 1.6 percent. Although high growth resumed only in 1987, in 1986 Singapore did achieve its first current account surplus since 1966.

One effect of the 1985-86 crisis was to make many people wonder whether the government should lessen its involvement in the economy (Krause 1988). One of the often cited reasons for the 1985 recession was the government's policy of promoting large wage increases, a policy it had pursued since the end of the 1970s. It reduced Singapore's competitiveness in the very industries in which the country had been successful. The government reversed the policy soon after the recession.

Since its independence Singapore has had high rates of growth, high and increasing rates of saving and investment, and very low inflation. The economy has flourished in a regime of unrestricted capital mobility and virtually total openness to trade under a fixed exchange rate. Despite government involvement in other areas, it basically left trade to the marketplace. In 1988 total exports of goods were about $38 billion, with more than 70 percent of them comprised of manufactured goods (compared with a less than 30 percent share in 1963). In addition, Singapore is recognized for its macroeconomic stability, an achievement that has yielded a high level of confidence on the part of business. At the same time the country has shown great ability to adapt to external shocks.

## Thailand

In contrast to Singapore (and to a lesser extent Korea), Thailand is a resource-abundant country, with important reserves of tin, coal, iron, manganese, natural gas, and precious stones (especially sapphires and rubies). Agricultural land covers about 40 percent of its territory, forests almost another 30 percent. Despite its abundance of natural resources, Thailand has successfully managed a transition from a mostly agrarian to a modern economy based mainly on industry and services.

Thailand's growth performance over the last two decades is impressive by almost any standard, although it is not as high as Korea's and Singapore's.[6] Its 7.2 percent average rate of growth from 1965 to 1988 was still more than 1.5 percent lower than that of the other two countries. In per capita terms the difference is larger because of Thailand's higher rate of population growth. The country has also been successful in keeping inflation under control. Except for the years immediately following the two oil crises, inflation has been one-digit. Starting in 1959 and up to the early 1970s, Thailand implemented an import-substitution strategy. Low wages, tax exemptions for imported machinery, and guarantees against nationalization and competition from state enterprises encouraged domestic and foreign investment. In contrast to other countries that pursued import substitution, however, the government kept tariff rates relatively low— they ranged from 15 percent to 30 percent in this period. The Thai mix of import substitution and strict fiscal policies produced much better results than elsewhere, especially in Latin America. GDP grew at an average rate of 7.7 percent a year from 1960 to 1970, with the manufacturing sector leading the way. The government began to shift toward an industrial policy of export promotion in the early 1970s. Since 1972, for example, investment incentives started to discriminate in favor of exports. Exports grew an average of 14.5 percent a year between 1965 and 1976, although most of this growth occurred in the period 1971-76. The first oil shock, combined with the decline in American military spending in Vietnam, produced a slowdown in Thailand's economy. Growth dropped to 4.6 percent in 1974-75, and inflation peaked at 24.3 percent in 1974 (table 8-3). In 1976, during the fourth economic plan, Thailand moved further along the export promotion path.

The second oil shock did significant damage to the Thai economy.[7] In the beginning Thailand resorted to external borrowing to solve the problem, and the current account deficit climbed to 7.1 percent of GDP on average during 1979-81. Although growth declined a bit, external borrowing kept it at reasonable levels. Inflation went up—to 14.1 percent on average—but never reached worrisome proportions. Implementation of a sound set of macro policies—a willingness to adjust—and the low initial ratio of external debt to GDP allowed Thailand to obtain support from official lenders and thus to finance its current account deficit at a relatively low cost.

In 1984 the government devalued the baht to restore competitiveness, after a period of mild appreciation. Helped by the fall in oil prices during 1986, Thailand had its first current account surplus in 20 years. By the end of the 1980s the problems of the first part of the decade seemed mostly overcome. Between 1985 and 1988 exports more than doubled. Private investment was booming, and saving was on the rise. Growth was strong and inflation low.

A dominant characteristic of Thailand's economic performance has been the stability of its macroeconomic variables. Growth, for instance, has

## Table 8.3  Thailand's major economic indicators

| Indicators[a] | 1965-73 | 1974-75 | 1976-78 | 1979-81 | 1982-88 |
|---|---|---|---|---|---|
| GDP growth rate (%) | 8.2 | 4.6 | 9.9 | 5.5 | 6.4 |
| Per capita GDP growth rate (%) | 4.9 | 1.9 | 7.2 | 3.1 | 4.4 |
| Export growth rate[b] (%) | 12.1 | 24.6 | 23.3 | 19.9 | 13.8 |
| Inflation (CPI) (%) | 3.7 | 14.8 | 6.5 | 14.1 | 2.9 |
| Current account (% GDP) | 1.5 | 2.4 | 4.3 | 7.1 | 3.2 |
| Fixed investment (% GDP)[c] | 22.4 | 23.1 | 24.7 | 25.2 | 23.8 |
| Domestic saving (% GDP)[d] | 22.7 | 24.3 | 22.1 | 19.5 | 21.3 |
| External debt (% of GDP) | 10.0[e] | 8.8 | 15.9 | 27.0 | 39.4 |
| Real exchange rate (1980=100) | 96.3[e] | 99.9 | 103.5 | 101.8 | 108.1 |

a. Every figure corresponds to the average of the period.
b. Export growth rate refers to growth in dollar terms.
c. Fixed investment (% of GDP) in current prices.
d. Domestic saving (% of GDP) in current prices. Defined as total investment (fixed plus change in stocks) minus the current account deficit.
e. Average 1970-73.
*Source*: International Monetary Fund (various issues, *International Financial Statistics*), World Bank data base, and Collins and Park (1989).

never been under 3.5 percent since 1965. Investment and saving have been very steady, the former at around 24-26 percent of GDP and the latter 2 or 3 percentage points below (with the exception of 1966 and 1986). The economy's almost permanent current account deficit has resulted in an external debt that grew from 10 percent of GDP in 1970 to 41 percent in 1986-88.

Thailand's story is similar to that of Korea and Singapore. High rates of growth and investment, increased saving, and low levels of inflation have characterized this economy. Although the government financed the gap between investment and saving with external borrowing and external debt has reached significant proportions, the growth of exports has prevented it from becoming an issue to the extent it is in, for instance, Latin America.

### Malaysia

Malaysia is a multiracial society in which the Malays constitute slightly over half the population and the Chinese and Indians are very significant minorities. The racial situation has, as discussed below, been a central concern of Malaysian society.[8] The country is also endowed with a wealth of natural resources that still form the vast majority of its exports (rubber, tin, petroleum, timber, and palm oil).

Malaysia's growth has been the lowest of the four East Asian countries reviewed here. Since 1970 the average rate of GDP growth has been 6.7 percent, for a rate of per capita growth of 3.9 percent a year.[9] Although this rate of growth seems poor compared with that of Korea, Singapore, and even Thailand, it would be enviable in almost any other region of the world.

Since independence in 1957 the Government of Malaysia has been pursuing a strategy of structural change, attempting to move from a rural- to an industry-based economy. In the early years the approach was to provide fiscal and financial incentives for industrial investment, as well as tariff protection. Since the 1970s the government has decided to speed the process by investing directly in some industries. It has also lowered the level of tariff protection.

The New Economic Policies introduced in 1970 not only set a goal of transforming the traditional rural economy into a modern one by the 1990s, it also intended to reduce poverty and the inequality of income, variables that in the case of Malaysia were correlated with race.[10] Indeed, the majority race, the Malays, has the highest incidence of poverty compared with other racial groups (especially the Chinese).

Malaysia's sound economic policies, such as the open trade regime, commitment to growth, and low levels of inflation, have, despite govern- ment intervention, kept government-induced distortions at a relatively low level. As in Thailand, the early years (until the mid- to late 1960s) were characterized by an import-substitution strategy. Since then exports have played the leading role in the economy. Among them, manufactured exports have become increasingly important, going from 4 percent of merchandise exports in 1960-64 to more than 20 percent in the early 1980s. Primary products (such as rubber, palm oil products, timber, and petro- leum) are still, however, the main source of foreign earnings, accounting for about 70 percent of the total.

One distinguishing feature of Malaysia's economy has been its current account. Since 1965 the current account in Malaysia has run a surplus in more years than not. It did, however, run deficits for six years in a row (1980- 85), and by 1986 they had raised external debt to about 80 percent of GDP. Surpluses in the years since have reduced this ratio to less than 60 percent. In contrast, Korea, Singapore, and Thailand experienced current account deficits for about two decades and only reversed that pattern in the late 1980s.

The first decade and a half of the National Economic Policies was a big success. A high rate of growth (7.6 percent on average between 1971 and 1984), a low level of inflation (it reached two digits only in 1974-75), climbing exports (more than a tenfold increase between 1970 and 1984), and gross fixed investment that averaged 28 percent of GDP (financed almost entirely by domestic saving) are evidence of this golden period. In the early 1980s, however, some imbalances began to develop. Large current account deficits (11.6 percent of GDP on average during 1981-86), big budget deficits (22 percent of GDP in 1981), a corresponding increase in domestic and external debt, and an increasing set of policy-induced distortions were signs that something was wrong.

The recession of 1985-86, during which per capita GDP fell 4.1 percent and 1.5 percent respectively, convinced the government that deep changes were necessary. A first step was to implement policies to recover macroeconomic stability, such as a reduction in the budget deficit (which

## Table 8.4 Malaysia's major economic indicators

| Indicators[a] | 1971-80 | 1981-84 | 1985-86 | 1987-88 |
|---|---|---|---|---|
| GDP growth rate (%) | 8.0 | 6.7 | 0.1 | 7.0 |
| Per capita GDP growth rate (%) | 5.0 | 4.1 | -2.8 | 4.4 |
| Export growth rate[b] (%) | 25.3 | 6.9 | -8.6 | 23.8 |
| Inflation (CPI) (%) | 6.0 | 5.8 | 0.5 | 1.5 |
| Current account deficit (% of GDP) | 0.5 | 10.0 | 0.9 | -6.8 |
| Fixed investment (% of GDP)[c] | 26.1 | 35.1 | 28.1 | 23.5 |
| Domestic saving (% of GDP) | 25.7 | 25.1 | 27.2 | 30.3 |
| External debt (% of GDP) | 19.8 | 50.5 | 72.3 | 65.5 |
| Real exchange rate (1980=100) | 101.8 | 108.8 | 101.5 | 83.7 |

a. Every figure corresponds to the average of the periods.
b. Export growth rate refers to growth in dollar terms.
c. Fixed investment (% of GDP) in current prices.
d. Domestic saving (% of GDP) in current prices. Defined as fixed investment minus the current account deficit. Hence, it excludes the change in stocks.
*Source*: International Monetary Fund (various issues, *International Financial Statistics*), World Bank data base, and Collins and Park (1989).

had fallen to about 5 percent of GDP by 1987) and a prudent monetary policy. These austerity measures resulted in a current account surplus (6.8 percent of GDP on average during 1987-88), very low rates of inflation (1.5 percent on average during the same period), and a rate of saving that climbed to 30.3 percent of GDP (table 8-4). The second—and most profound—step was the implementation of a program of structural reforms. Among the steps the government has been taking are liberalization of the foreign investment code; reform of major public enterprises, with the development of a privatization program underway; reform of the banking system to eliminate the subsidies and discretion in the allocation of credit; freeing up of the labor market; and simplification of the tax and tariff systems. In summary, this resource-abundant country is moving toward a more free market-oriented strategy. In 1989 fixed investment—at 29 percent of GDP—returned to its usual level, with a strong performance by private investment and a drop in public investment to about 10 percent of GDP in 1988-89 from almost 20 percent in 1980-81.

## Trends in investment

Over the past two decades East Asian countries have attained unprecedented levels of investment, as shown in table 8-5. Among them, Singapore is in a league of its own, with an average ratio of investment to GDP of over 40 percent in the 1970-88 period. This rate grew substantially during the late 1970s and early 1980s, reaching a high of almost 50 percent of GDP in 1983-84. Since then it has declined to about 35 percent. Korea's rate of investment increased by almost 10 percentage points of GDP, from just under 25 percent

**Table 8.5 Public and private fixed investment as a percentage of GDP**
(in constant 1980 prices)

| | Korea | | | Singapore | | | Thailand | | | Malaysia | | |
|---|---|---|---|---|---|---|---|---|---|---|---|---|
| | Private | Public | Total | Private | Public | Total | Private | Public | Total | Private | Public | Total |
| 1970 | 19.2 | 6.4 | 25.6 | 29.6 | 7.2 | 36.8 | 18.8 | 7.9 | 26.7 | 13.0 | 6.2 | 19.2 |
| 1971 | 16.5 | 5.8 | 22.3 | 34.2 | 6.9 | 41.1 | 18.3 | 7.4 | 25.7 | 15.0 | 6.4 | 21.4 |
| 1972 | 16.1 | 5.7 | 21.8 | 30.8 | 9.2 | 40.0 | 17.6 | 7.4 | 25.0 | 14.1 | 8.0 | 22.1 |
| 1973 | 19.0 | 4.1 | 23.1 | 30.2 | 7.5 | 37.7 | 19.1 | 5.6 | 24.7 | 16.0 | 6.9 | 22.9 |
| 1974 | 19.8 | 4.0 | 23.8 | 31.1 | 9.1 | 40.2 | 20.1 | 3.8 | 23.9 | 18.7 | 7.4 | 26.1 |
| 1975 | 19.9 | 4.6 | 24.5 | 27.5 | 10.5 | 38.0 | 17.7 | 5.2 | 22.9 | 15.2 | 9.2 | 24.4 |
| 1976 | 20.5 | 5.1 | 25.6 | 25.2 | 11.9 | 37.1 | 16.5 | 6.9 | 23.4 | 13.7 | 9.3 | 23.0 |
| 1977 | 24.3 | 5.9 | 30.2 | 23.3 | 12.0 | 35.3 | 19.3 | 7.7 | 27.0 | 14.5 | 10.5 | 25.0 |
| 1978 | 29.2 | 6.1 | 35.3 | 25.3 | 11.4 | 36.7 | 18.7 | 8.2 | 26.9 | 15.7 | 9.0 | 24.7 |
| 1979 | 29.1 | 6.5 | 35.6 | 28.0 | 8.8 | 36.8 | 18.0 | 7.6 | 25.6 | 16.7 | 8.5 | 25.2 |
| 1980 | 24.3 | 5.5 | 29.8 | 30.7 | 9.9 | 40.6 | 16.3 | 8.9 | 25.2 | 19.6 | 11.7 | 31.3 |
| 1981 | 21.0 | 5.4 | 26.4 | 32.3 | 10.4 | 42.7 | 16.4 | 9.3 | 25.7 | 19.1 | 15.4 | 34.5 |
| 1982 | 25.2 | 6.8 | 32.0 | 34.3 | 13.9 | 48.2 | 15.6 | 8.2 | 23.8 | 17.6 | 17.6 | 35.2 |
| 1983 | 25.2 | 6.1 | 31.3 | 33.2 | 16.5 | 49.7 | 16.5 | 8.4 | 24.9 | 17.1 | 17.8 | 34.9 |
| 1984 | 25.0 | 6.3 | 31.3 | 33.4 | 16.5 | 49.9 | 17.3 | 9.1 | 26.4 | 17.9 | 16.2 | 34.1 |
| 1985 | 24.2 | 6.1 | 30.3 | 28.5 | 16.1 | 44.6 | 15.0 | 9.3 | 24.3 | 14.8 | 16.7 | 31.5 |
| 1986 | 24.1 | 5.8 | 29.9 | 23.0 | 16.6 | 39.6 | 14.2 | 7.7 | 21.9 | 10.2 | 15.0 | 25.2 |
| 1987 | 25.6 | 5.6 | 31.2 | 23.7 | 12.9 | 36.6 | 16.4 | 6.0 | 22.4 | 11.2 | 11.7 | 22.9 |
| 1988 | 26.2 | 5.3 | 31.5 | 26.6 | 8.3 | 34.9 | 18.8 | 5.4 | 24.2 | 15.1 | 9.2 | 24.3 |
| Average | 22.9 | 5.6 | 28.5 | 29.0 | 11.3 | 40.3 | 17.4 | 7.4 | 24.8 | 15.5 | 11.2 | 26.7 |

*Note:* These figures do not match exactly with the figures in tables 8.1-8.4, as those are in current prices.
*Source:* World Bank data base.

to just over 35 percent, between 1975 and 1979 (the time of the Big Push). It stabilized in the 1980s at slightly over 30 percent. The rates of investment in Malaysia and Thailand were the most stable (and lowest) of the four countries, at around 27 percent and 25 percent of GDP, respectively, during the 1970-88 period. Although this level of investment is not spectacular by East Asian standards, it would be a record in Latin America.

## Public and private investment

Traditionally the economic literature has seen an increase in public investment as crowding out private investment because it raises the interest rate. Recent contributions, however, challenge this view, stating that public investment may actually crowd in the formation of private capital (Aschauer 1989a, 1989b). According to this theory, public investment may increase the rate of return on private investment. Public capital—especially infrastructure such as roads, ports, and airports—appears to be complementary to private capital in production. Thus a mix of public and private investment may be very important to the overall production capacity of an economy.

Several studies have tried to verify this point empirically. Blejer and Khan (1984) use pooled data for 24 developing countries over the period 1971-79. They find that private investment is complementary with public investment in infrastructure, although that pattern is not necessarily true for other types of public investment. Greene and Villanueva (1990), using a sample of 23 developing countries for the period 1975-87, find evidence that the rate of private investment is positively related to the rate of public investment. This matter is investigated econometrically in a later section of this chapter for the four countries that are highlighted here besides chapter 6 and chapter 7 in this volume. At this point the emphasis is on the main trends in public and private investment.

Table 8-5 shows data on public, private, and total investment over the period 1970-88 for the four countries. Public investment accounted, on average, for slightly less than 30 percent of total investment in Singapore, about 19 percent in Korea, 30 percent in Thailand, and 42 percent in Malaysia. Interestingly, the simple average for the 12 Latin American countries included in Greene and Villanueva (1990) yields a 42.8 percent share for public investment.[11] Only Malaysia seems more in line with the Latin American countries than with the East Asian ones.[12] Since the rate of total investment was much higher in East Asia than in Latin America, the ratio of public investment to GDP was higher on average in the four East Asian countries (8.9 percent) than in the sample of 12 Latin American countries (7.9 percent).

The figures alone do not show a clear correlation between public and private investment across countries. Singapore, the country with the highest private investment ratio, also has the highest public investment ratio. Korea, however, has a lower public investment ratio than Thailand and Malaysia do, and a higher private investment one. Given that the correlation being discussed is just a simple one—the effect of other variables has not been controlled for—this conclusion is not robust. The fifth section pursues a more definitive answer through econometric analysis.

*Investment in the traded and nontraded sectors*

Specific data on investment by sector are not available. Nonetheless, the figures in table 8-6 make clear that a big proportion of investment has gone to the traded sector. An indirect way to estimate the share of investment going to tradables is to analyze the evolution of the share of exports in GDP. As the table shows, the share of exports of goods and nonfactor services rose substantially after 1965. In Korea exports increased from 8.6 percent of GDP in 1965 to 39.9 percent in 1988, while in Thailand they went from 18.3 percent to 34.5 percent. In Singapore the share of exports of goods alone went from 95 percent of GDP in 1965 to 155 percent in 1988. Malaysia's exports were 47.6 percent of GDP in 1965 and 67.8 percent in 1988.

*Construction and infrastructure versus machinery and equipment*

In an interesting recent article, De Long and Summers (1990) find evidence that investment in equipment has a larger influence on economic growth than investment in infrastructure. Using a cross-section of 25 countries over the period 1960-85, they find that on average for the group of countries each percentage point of GDP invested in equipment is associated with an increase in the rate of growth of GDP of a third of a percentage point a year.[13] When they use a 61-country sample, the explanatory power of the equation worsens, but investment in equipment remains significant.

Three of the countries highlighted here—Korea, Malaysia, and Thailand—are included in the 61 country sample. None has an impressive rate of investment in equipment. While Korea's is 5.57 percent of GDP, Malaysia's is 4.46 percent and Thailand's 3.95 percent.[14] De Long and Summers conclude from their regression analysis that investment in equipment was quite significant in explaining the growth in these three countries.

**Table 8.6 Exports of goods and nonfactor services**
(% GDP)

| Countries | 1965 | 1988 |
|-----------|------|------|
| Korea | 8.6 | 39.9 |
| Malaysia | 47.6 | 67.8 |
| Singapore[a] | 93.0 | 155.0 |
| Thailand | 18.3 | 34.5 |

a. Goods only.
*Source*: International Monetary Fund (various issues, *International Financial Statistics*), World Bank data base, and Collins and Park (1989).

## The financing of investment

Table 8-7 presents a decomposition of total saving for each of the countries in question. By definition total saving equals total investment (which includes fixed capital formation and inventory accumulation). Because there are no data on the accumulation of inventory, table 8-7 does not include it. The table breaks total saving into a national component and foreign saving (equal to the current account deficit). In turn, national saving is divided between public and private (except for Malaysia where the data were not available). This decomposition gives an accurate idea of the financing of investment.

Did these countries rely primarily on domestic or foreign saving? What were the relative contributions of private and public saving to the financing of investment? The figures clearly show that all the countries counted on a substantial savings base at home. Public saving was important in all three countries for which there were data, especially in Singapore. Fiscal auster-ity was the norm, although in difficult moments their governments resorted widely to fiscal expansion. Based on Malaysia's large budget deficits, it is likely that public saving were less important there. In Korea and Thailand private saving on average financed about 70 percent of investment. In Singapore the figure was substantially lower, about 45 percent. Foreign saving was also an important part of the overall picture.

For a long time Korea, Singapore, and Thailand used foreign saving extensively to finance their high levels of investment. As investment was directed toward the tradable sector, these countries did not have a foreign debt problem afterwards. In addition, when domestic saving dropped, these countries preferred to increase external borrowing rather than curb investment. Foreign saving supported the financing of investment tremen-dously, especially in Singapore (and in Korea) during the 1970s and early 1980s. Singapore ran current account deficits on the order of 20 percent to 30 percent of GDP in the early 1970s; Korea and Thailand experienced deficits of between 5 percent and 10 percent of GDP for sustained periods over the last two decades.

Why have foreigners been willing to finance these large deficits for so long? Two explanations are likely: first, as noted, each country had a strong domestic savings base; and second, and most important, the current ac-count deficit was attributable mainly to booming investment in the tradable sector. In the end the strategy of a high level of investment in tradables paid off. Since 1986 Korea, Singapore, and Thailand have started to run current account surpluses, which have reduced their net external liabilities in nominal terms.[15] The case of Malaysia is somewhat different. It did not run current account deficits for long periods, but when it did run them in the early 1980s, they were so huge that external debt problems resulted. Except in that period Malaysia has relied almost entirely on domestic saving to finance its investment. In the last three years it has ran large current account surpluses that have eased its external debt problems.

## Table 8.7 Components of Savings
(current prices, % of GDP)

| | Korea | | | | | Singapore | | | | |
|---|---|---|---|---|---|---|---|---|---|---|
| | Domestic saving | | | Foreign | Total | Domestic saving | | | Foreign | Total |
| | Private | Public | Total | Saving | Saving | Private | Public | Total | Saving | Saving |
| 1970 | 11.6 | 6.2 | 17.8 | 7.1 | 24.9 | -4.3 | 6.3 | 2.0 | 30.5 | 32.5 |
| 1971 | 8.2 | 5.5 | 13.7 | 8.7 | 22.4 | -1.6 | 6.1 | 4.5 | 32.2 | 36.7 |
| 1972 | 15.4 | 1.5 | 16.9 | 3.4 | 20.3 | 10.6 | 10.0 | 20.6 | 17.1 | 37.7 |
| 1973 | 17.2 | 3.6 | 20.8 | 2.2 | 23.0 | 15.8 | 6.9 | 22.7 | 12.5 | 35.2 |
| 1974 | 12.6 | 2.0 | 14.6 | 10.8 | 25.4 | 8.2 | 10.2 | 18.4 | 19.8 | 38.2 |
| 1975 | 13.3 | 2.7 | 16.0 | 8.9 | 24.9 | 14.7 | 10.8 | 25.5 | 10.4 | 35.9 |
| 1976 | 19.5 | 3.4 | 22.9 | 1.1 | 24.0 | 14.7 | 11.8 | 26.5 | 9.6 | 36.1 |
| 1977 | 23.5 | 3.4 | 26.9 | 0.0 | 26.9 | 16.9 | 12.6 | 29.5 | 4.5 | 34.0 |
| 1978 | 24.6 | 4.1 | 28.7 | 2.2 | 30.9 | 18.0 | 11.9 | 29.9 | 5.8 | 35.7 |
| 1979 | 21.9 | 4.3 | 26.2 | 6.4 | 32.6 | 17.7 | 11.1 | 28.8 | 7.8 | 36.6 |
| 1980 | 18.0 | 3.3 | 21.3 | 8.5 | 29.8 | 15.4 | 12.0 | 27.4 | 13.3 | 40.7 |
| 1981 | 17.1 | 1.9 | 19.0 | 6.7 | 25.7 | 21.7 | 11.3 | 33.0 | 10.6 | 43.6 |
| 1982 | 23.0 | 3.4 | 26.4 | 3.7 | 30.1 | 22.0 | 17.0 | 39.0 | 8.5 | 47.5 |
| 1983 | 22.5 | 4.7 | 27.2 | 2.0 | 29.2 | 26.4 | 17.6 | 44.0 | 3.5 | 47.5 |
| 1984 | 22.7 | 4.6 | 27.3 | 1.6 | 28.9 | 25.7 | 19.9 | 45.6 | 2.1 | 47.7 |
| 1985 | 22.7 | 4.5 | 27.2 | 1.0 | 28.2 | 24.8 | 17.4 | 42.2 | 0.0 | 42.2 |
| 1986 | 27.0 | 5.3 | 32.3 | -4.7 | 27.6 | 23.4 | 17.1 | 40.5 | -3.1 | 37.4 |
| 1987 | 31.0 | 5.5 | 36.5 | -8.1 | 28.4 | 28.5 | 9.8 | 38.3 | -2.8 | 35.5 |
| 1988 | 30.4 | 6.5 | 36.9 | -8.1 | 28.8 | 33.4 | 8.3 | 41.7 | -6.8 | 34.9 |
| Average | 20.1 | 4.0 | 24.1 | 2.8 | 26.9 | 17.5 | 12.0 | 29.5 | 9.2 | 38.7 |

| | Thailand | | | | | Malaysia | | | | |
|---|---|---|---|---|---|---|---|---|---|---|
| | Domestic saving | | | Foreign | Total | Domestic saving | | | Foreign | Total |
| | Private | Public | Total | Saving | Saving | Private | Public | Total | Saving | Saving |
| 1970 | 13.1 | 7.1 | 20.2 | 3.5 | 23.7 | n.a. | n.a. | 20.2 | -0.2 | 20.0 |
| 1971 | 14.2 | 6.7 | 20.9 | 2.4 | 23.3 | n.a. | n.a. | 20.6 | 2.5 | 23.1 |
| 1972 | 19.6 | 2.5 | 22.1 | 0.6 | 22.7 | n.a. | n.a. | 20.1 | 4.9 | 25.0 |
| 1973 | 20.2 | 1.9 | 22.1 | 0.4 | 22.5 | n.a. | n.a. | 26.3 | -1.4 | 24.9 |
| 1974 | 18.1 | 4.6 | 22.7 | 0.6 | 23.3 | n.a. | n.a. | 22.4 | 5.7 | 28.1 |
| 1975 | 15.6 | 3.1 | 18.7 | 4.2 | 22.9 | n.a. | n.a. | 22.5 | 5.3 | 27.8 |
| 1976 | 17.5 | 2.8 | 20.3 | 2.6 | 22.9 | n.a. | n.a. | 29.7 | -5.2 | 24.5 |
| 1977 | 16.3 | 4.1 | 20.4 | 5.5 | 25.9 | n.a. | n.a. | 28.8 | -3.3 | 25.5 |
| 1978 | 16.4 | 4.1 | 20.5 | 4.8 | 25.3 | n.a. | n.a. | 25.5 | -0.7 | 24.8 |
| 1979 | 14.1 | 3.9 | 18.0 | 7.6 | 25.6 | n.a. | n.a. | 30.8 | -4.4 | 26.4 |
| 1980 | 14.8 | 4.0 | 18.8 | 6.4 | 25.2 | n.a. | n.a. | 29.9 | 1.2 | 31.1 |
| 1981 | 11.8 | 5.5 | 17.3 | 7.4 | 24.7 | n.a. | n.a. | 26.1 | 9.9 | 36.0 |

(continued)

**Table 8.7  Components of Savings (continued)**

| | Thailand | | | | | Malaysia | | | | |
|---|---|---|---|---|---|---|---|---|---|---|
| | Domestic saving | | | Foreign | Total | Domestic saving | | | Foreign | Total |
| | Private | Public | Total | Saving | Saving | Private | Public | Total | Saving | Saving |
| 1982 | 19.1 | 1.5 | 20.6 | 2.8 | 23.4 | n.a. | n.a. | 22.9 | 13.4 | 36.3 |
| 1983 | 12.6 | 4.1 | 16.7 | 7.3 | 24.0 | n.a. | n.a. | 24.4 | 11.6 | 36.0 |
| 1984 | 14.5 | 4.9 | 19.4 | 5.1 | 24.5 | n.a. | n.a. | 27.0 | 4.9 | 31.9 |
| 1985 | 16.0 | 3.6 | 19.6 | 4.1 | 23.7 | n.a. | n.a. | 27.8 | 2.02 | 9.8 |
| 1986 | 19.1 | 3.2 | 22.3 | -0.6 | 21.7 | n.a. | n.a. | 26.5 | -0.22 | 6.3 |
| 1987 | 18.7 | 4.0 | 22.7 | 0.8 | 23.5 | n.a. | n.a. | 31.0 | -8.12 | 2.9 |
| 1988 | 16.1 | 6.8 | 22.9 | 2.9 | 25.8 | n.a. | n.a. | 29.5 | -5.4 | 24.1 |
| Average | 16.2 | 4.1 | 20.3 | 3.6 | 23.9 | | | 25.9 | 1.7 | 27.6 |

*Note*: The figures exclude change in stocks. Thus, total saving in the table corresponds to fixed investment in current prices (figures 1 to 4). For the same reason, domestic saving in this table is slightly different from the figures shown in tables 8.1-8.3. The difference is the change in stocks, which is excluded because data that would enable the change in stocks to be divided between private and public was unavailable.
n.a. Not available.
*Source*: International Monetary Fund (various issues, *International Financial Statistics*), World Bank data base, and Collins and Park (1989).

## Macroeconomic policies and their effect on investment

This section looks at the economic policies and characteristics of the four economies that have had an important influence on the formation of capital. The analysis emphasizes the determinants of private investment, which are also the focus of the econometric analysis in the next section.

### Monetary and credit policies

The literature emphasizes monetary and credit policies as important determinants of private investment. Restrictive monetary and credit policies depress investment by inducing an increase in the cost of credit and a reduction in the availability of credit (if quantitative constraints exist).

Credit policy can directly affect investment in repressed or controlled credit markets. The availability of funds will determine whether firms with investment opportunities can pursue them. Those firms or sectors with preferential access to the credit market will have higher levels of investment. This point is particularly important in developing countries, where repressed financial markets are more generally the norm than the exception. Different studies find that credit has a positive direct effect on investment, among them Blejer and Khan (1984) and van Wijnbergen (1982). Greene and Villanueva (1990) and Solimano (1989) find that higher interest rates have a negative effect on investment.

The figures on credit for Korea, Singapore, Thailand, and Malaysia, presented in table 8-8, show the growing importance of credit in these economies from 1965 to 1988. In Korea credit from the financial sector and the monetary authorities to the private sector climbed from 10.7 percent of GDP in 1965 to 56.1 percent in 1987, in Singapore from 37.6 percent to 87.6 percent, in Thailand from 14.0 percent to 50.0 percent; and in Malaysia from 12.7 percent to 64.0 percent.[16]

Korea pursued a rule of selective allocation of credit. The main objective was to promote certain industries, and the government used credit to achieve that goal. Its approach to development strategy was a highly controlled banking system that directed its credit mainly to target sectors

**Table 8.8  Credit to the private sector**
(% of GDP)

| Year | Korea | Singapore | Thailand | Malaysia |
|------|-------|-----------|----------|----------|
| 1965 | 10.7 | 37.6 | 14.0 | 12.7 |
| 1966 | 11.6 | 37.8 | 14.0 | 13.2 |
| 1967 | 17.6 | 36.2 | 16.0 | 14.3 |
| 1968 | 26.5 | 38.6 | 16.0 | 16.5 |
| 1969 | 33.1 | 42.3 | 17.0 | 15.8 |
| 1970 | 33.7 | 45.9 | 20.0 | 18.5 |
| 1971 | 35.5 | 45.6 | 20.0 | 19.9 |
| 1972 | 35.1 | 51.2 | 20.0 | 21.2 |
| 1973 | 35.1 | 60.2 | 22.0 | 24.5 |
| 1974 | 37.8 | 54.5 | 23.0 | 23.1 |
| 1975 | 34.8 | 57.5 | 26.0 | 27.2 |
| 1976 | 31.8 | 58.7 | 27.0 | 26.6 |
| 1977 | 31.1 | 59.3 | 29.0 | 27.7 |
| 1978 | 34.1 | 61.9 | 31.0 | 30.7 |
| 1979 | 36.8 | 66.6 | 32.0 | 31.5 |
| 1980 | 42.3 | 71.0 | 29.0 | 38.2 |
| 1981 | 43.1 | 77.9 | 30.0 | 43.4 |
| 1982 | 47.9 | 83.3 | 33.0 | 46.7 |
| 1983 | 48.9 | 88.7 | 40.0 | 50.9 |
| 1984 | 49.5 | 88.9 | 44.0 | 52.8 |
| 1985 | 53.7 | 92.9 | 46.0 | 61.7 |
| 1986 | 53.9 | 91.3 | 46.0 | 71.5 |
| 1987 | 56.1 | 87.6 | 50.0 | 64.0 |
| 1988 | 55.5 | 82.6 | 54.0 | 61.5 |

*Source*: International Monetary Fund (various issues, *International Financial Statistics*), World Bank data base, and Collins and Park (1989).

and big conglomerates. A financial nonbanking system (the curb market), which was less controlled, provided credit to other sectors basically along free market lines.

Korea partially liberalized its financial markets in 1965, at the beginning of the period of an outward orientation. Since 1982, and after some scandals, the financial sector was further liberalized in part. Subsequently the less regulated nonbanking financial sector experienced spectacular growth. Korea's financial market is, however, still far from being driven by market forces alone.

In Singapore monetary policy has been constrained by the openness of the country to foreign trade and capital. Typically the government maintained a restrictive monetary policy, but the access of the banking system to foreign capital markets eased liquidity pressures. Although the monetary authority did not control the money supply completely, it managed to keep inflation low and to produce a very favorable environment for domestic and foreign financial institutions.

The Government of Singapore, as noted, has intervened widely in the credit market, alongside private financial institutions. The government owns the largest saving bank (Post Office Saving Bank). Despite its involvement the government has always been mindful of the need to let the market take the lead. Thus it has kept interest rates in government financial institutions more or less in line with market conditions (that is, at moderately positive real levels) and has allowed broad participation by foreign banks. In terms of the allocation of credit, the huge surpluses generated by a compulsory savings mechanism and by government financial institutions allowed the government to undertake big infrastructure projects and to direct credit to priority areas.

In Thailand private banks have had a dominant role in the financial sector, with strong links to business groups and trading houses. The banking system, however, has been highly concentrated, with the five largest banks accounting for over 65 percent of bank assets (Robinson and others 1991). Although government involvement in the granting of credits has been minimal, banks have not been adequately efficient in allocating credit because big business interests have used them widely for cheap loans. The World Bank, among others, has proposed encouraging more competition in the financial sector to avoid this practice.

Malaysia has used directed credit widely to promote industrialization. In addition, especially after the New Economic Policies, credit policy has also reflected the government's objective of income redistribution. In 1970 foreign interests owned some 63 percent of company equity, non-Malay nationals 34 percent, and Malays only 1 percent (Young, Bussink, and Hasan 1980). Thus the government has promoted Malay ownership of equity capital through easy access to preferential credit (and through purchases of shares by government agencies).

Malaysia has allowed strong participation by foreign banks to encourage competition. The structural reforms of the late 1980s included liberalization of the financial markets as an important objective. Since 1985 direct credit practices and subsidies have become less important.

*Financial deepening*

McKinnon (1973) stresses the importance of an efficient financial market as a cornerstone of economic development. According to this point of view, "financial deepening" (the growth of the share of financial assets in the economy), which reflects an increasing use of financial intermediation by savers and investors and the monetization of the economy, allows the efficient flow of resources among people and institutions over time. This deepening can only occur in an economy with liberalized financial markets. Dornbusch and Reinoso (1989), however, challenge this conclusion, arguing that financial liberalization may be quite dangerous in periods of financial instability. The fact that financial deepening has paralleled improved growth performance in several cases does not, they contend, imply causality, since the better performance might be the result of other factors (such as adaptability to a change in financial resources).

Table 8-9 presents measures of financial deepening for the East Asian countries for selective years in the period 1962-88. The ratio of M2 (money plus quasi-money) to GDP is used. This ratio rose in all four countries. In Korea it went from 11.7 percent in 1962-65 to 39.0 percent in 1985-88; in Singapore from 52.6 percent to 81.8 percent; in Thailand from 23.9 percent to 62.9 percent; and in Malaysia from 27.3 percent to 68.9 percent. The policy of keeping real interest rates on deposits positive, as discussed below, was one of the factors behind this increase in financial savings.

Singapore has joined Hong Kong as an international financial center, and its high level of monetization comes as no surprise.[17] At the same time the relatively low degree of financial deepening in Korea likely is associated with its controlled financial market. The Malaysian government pursued an interest rate policy that favored saving with relatively few controls. This

**Table 8.9 Financial deepening**
(M2/GDP, percent)[a]

| Years | Korea | Singapore | Thailand | Malaysia |
|---|---|---|---|---|
| 1962-65 | 11.7 | 52.6 | 23.9 | 27.3 |
| 1970 | 33.3 | 66.3 | 27.8 | 33.9 |
| 1975 | 30.7 | 61.0 | 33.9 | 44.8 |
| 1980 | 33.0 | 64.0 | 38.2 | 51.5 |
| 1985-88 | 39.0 | 81.8 | 62.9 | 68.9 |

a. Currency and demand savings and time deposits as a percentage of GDP.
*Source:* International Monetary Fund (various issues, *International Financial Statistics*), World Bank data base, and Collins and Park (1989).

policy, as well as Malaysia's commitment to an anti-inflationary policy, has resulted in a high level of financial savings.

## Interest rate policy

It can be argued that Korea used credit policy quite actively (as did Singapore and Malaysia, although to a lesser extent) to direct investment to certain sectors deemed to be of high potential. In addition, it used ceilings on interest rates.

All four countries, with the exception of Thailand in the 1970s, maintained real interest rates that were positive and moderately high.[18] Although the market did not allocate investment entirely, private companies using the funds had to pay positive real rates. The government did not subsidize credit flagrantly even though it directed it. To some extent price has limited the demand for credit.

Maintenance of moderately high real interest rates appears to be closely associated with economic performance and financial deepening at the international level. The empirical evidence indicates that countries that have maintained moderately high real interest rates have outperformed by a considerable margin those that have favored negative real interest rates.[19] In the former group of countries the rate of growth of financial assets has been much larger, as the rate of expansion of output has been. Table 8-10 presents evidence on these issues for a group of 21 countries for the period 1971-80. Over a medium- to long-term horizon, the allocation of moderately positive real interest rates with higher growth rates is consistent with positive interest rates encouraging more efficient investment. The 21 countries in the table are divided into three groups according to their interest rate policies in the 1970s. Symptomatically those economies that espoused moderately positive real interest rates experienced the fastest growth in financial assets[20] (9.6 percent a year on average) and the quickest expansion in output (6.4 percent on average). At the other extreme, countries with *severely negative* real interest rates had dismal performance: on average their rate of growth of GDP was only 1.6 percent, and real financial assets declined. The group of countries with *moderately negative* real interest rates performed in between the other two groups, although closer to the group with positive real interest rates. The evidence is suggestive.

The quantitative controls on credit in East Asia (especially in Korea) are likely to have resulted in interest rates below their free market equilibrium, although positive in real terms. What justifications might a government have made for this policy? One may have been industrial policy, that is, the decision to favor certain economic sectors thought to have higher potential (a "pick-the-winners" strategy). Another one may have been adverse selection. At some point firms that are in financial distress will want to borrow at *any* interest rate to remain alive and pay wages. They could continue to demand large, and ultimately inflationary, amounts of credit

**Table 8.10 Interest rate policy, growth of financial assets, and rate of GDP expansion—selected developing countries, 1971-80**
(percent)

| Country/categories | Growth of financial assets | Growth of GDP |
|---|---|---|
| *Countries with moderately positive real interest rates* | | |
| Malaysia | 13.8 | 8.0 |
| Korea | 11.1 | 8.6 |
| Sri Lanka | 10.1 | 4.7 |
| Nepal | 9.6 | 2.0 |
| Singapore | 7.6 | 9.1 |
| Philippines | 5.6 | 6.2 |
| Average | 9.6 | 6.4 |
| *Countries with moderately negative real interest rates* | | |
| Pakistan | 9.9 | 5.4 |
| Thailand | 8.5 | 6.9 |
| Morocco | 8.2 | 5.5 |
| Colombia | 5.5 | 5.8 |
| Greece | 5.4 | 4.7 |
| South Africa | 4.3 | 3.7 |
| Kenya | 3.6 | 5.7 |
| Myanmar | 3.5 | 4.3 |
| Portugal | 1.8 | 4.7 |
| Zambia | -1.1 | 0.8 |
| Average | 5.0 | 4.8 |
| *Countries with severely negative real interest rates* | | |
| Peru | 3.2 | 3.4 |
| Turkey | 2.2 | 5.1 |
| Jamaica | -1.9 | -0.7 |
| Zaire | -6.8 | 0.1 |
| Ghana | -7.6 | -0.1 |
| Average | -2.2 | 1.6 |

*Source*: McKinnon (1989, table 3).

even with very high interest rates. For this reason monetary policy may require managing the interest rate to make sure that credit does not rise rapidly to bail out firms (both in the state sector and in the private sector) that *should* be pushed out of operation.

*Fiscal policy*

Expansionary fiscal policies push interest rates up and reduce the availability of credit for the private sector. Hence, these policies crowd out private investment. As mentioned, however, a distinction must be made between current and capital public expenditures. An expansion in public investment (for example, in infrastructure) may actually encourage private investment and thereby offset the interest rate/credit effect.

Korea, Singapore, and Thailand in general have had very responsible fiscal policies. Public saving has been positive every year since 1970 (see table 8-7), and the budget deficit, which includes public investment as an outlay, has never reached worrisome proportions. They used a moderate fiscal expansion for only very short periods to stimulate the economy when growth was sluggish. Moreover, when their budget deficits increased, the governments showed a remarkable ability to bring them down quickly, so that they did not jeopardize macroeconomic stability.

Thailand, however, ran fiscal deficits of around 5 percent of GDP from 1980 to 1985. Nevertheless, the Bank of Thailand has been as careful as possible to avoid the path of monetary finance, honoring its conservative reputation.[21] In 1987 the government made significant progress in restraining public spending and brought the budget into balance by 1988. The improvement is attributable to three main factors: the effect of economic growth on tax revenues; more conservative estimates of tax revenues in the fiscal budget; and an austere policy on public wages.

Malaysia has experienced even higher public deficits that Thailand has, with an annual average of over 6 percent of GDP during the 1970s and over 10 percent of GDP in several years of the 1980s.[22] The government, nonetheless, has carefully avoided resort to monetary financing, and since 1987 it has reduced the deficits significantly.

Thus, both Thailand and Malaysia have had access to credit markets (domestic and foreign) to finance their deficits. In no other way can the fact be explained that neither country has had inflation in excess of 6 percent since 1982, with Thailand having an annual average of 3.1 percent for 1980-88 and Malaysia a mere 1.3 percent (figure 8-1).

In short, in the four countries the public sector has managed to leave enough space for the private sector, which has taken the leading role in the economy. Table 8-11 shows the size of the state as measured by total government outlays as a percentage of GDP. On this basis Korea and Thailand have rather small governments (less than 20 percent of GDP in both cases). Government outlays in Singapore, the country with the highest per capita income in the sample, have risen above 30 percent since 1985, a

**Figure 8.1 Rate of inflation**
(annual rate of change in the Consumer Price Index, percent)

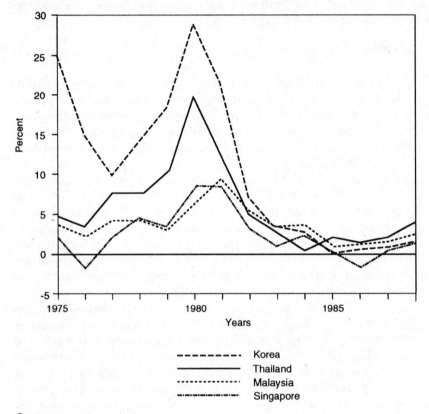

Source: World Bank data base.

level that is comparable with that of a developed country with a relatively small government (such as Japan, the United States, and Canada). Malaysia has had the largest ratio of government spending to GDP in the group, having been at times over 40 percent of GDP. By 1987, however, it had scaled expenditures down to 35 percent of GDP.

*Exchange rate policy*

The effect of the exchange rate on aggregate investment is theoretically ambiguous. If investment goods use both local and foreign inputs in their production, a devaluation encourages investment in the tradable sector and discourages investment in nontradables. In other terms, a high real exchange rate improves the profitability of investment in tradables. If imported inputs are a big share of the production of investment goods, and if tradables are relatively unimportant, a devaluation will tend to depress

**Table 8.11 Fiscal indicators—general government**
(% of GDP)

| Year | Korea a,b | | Singapore | | Thailand | | Malaysia | |
|---|---|---|---|---|---|---|---|---|
| | Tax revenue | Govt. expenditure | Tax revenue | Govt. expenditure | Tax revenue | Govt. expenditure | Total revenue b | Govt. expenditure |
| 1973 | 10.8 | 12.5 | 14.2 | 21.3 | 11.7 | 17.0 | 21.7 | 29.6 |
| 1974 | 12.2 | 13.6 | 15.2 | 19.9 | 14.4 | 14.4 | 24.1 | 31.2 |
| 1975 | 13.8 | 15.2 | 16.6 | 23.9 | 12.5 | 16.4 | 26.4 | 36.8 |
| 1976 | 15.1 | 16.4 | 16.1 | 23.2 | 12.2 | 18.2 | 26.1 | 33.3 |
| 1977 | 14.8 | 15.6 | 16.6 | 23.2 | 12.8 | 17.7 | 28.3 | 35.6 |
| 1978 | 15.3 | 15.6 | 15.8 | 22.2 | 13.3 | 18.8 | 27.2 | 33.1 |
| 1979 | 15.5 | 16.7 | 15.7 | 21.8 | 13.7 | 19.0 | 28.4 | 30.3 |
| 1980 | 15.6 | 17.3 | 16.8 | 23.3 | 14.0 | 20.5 | 31.1 | 37.7 |
| 1981 | 15.7 | 17.1 | 17.9 | 28.1 | 14.2 | 19.6 | 32.2 | 49.5 |
| 1982 | 16.1 | 19.1 | 19.1 | 26.7 | 13.6 | 21.8 | 31.9 | 49.3 |
| 1983 | 16.7 | 17.5 | 19.0 | 29.4 | 15.2 | 21.0 | 31.2 | 43.0 |
| 1984 | 16.1 | 17.2 | 18.5 | 25.3 | 15.1 | 20.6 | 30.3 | n.a. |
| 1985 | 16.0 | 17.7 | 16.5 | 36.0 | 14.9 | 22.4 | 31.2 | n.a. |
| 1986 | 16.0 | 17.3 | 13.3 | 36.8 | 15.0 | 21.8 | 32.9 | 44.2 |
| 1987 | 16.7 | 17.0 | 13.7 | 34.4 | 15.7 | 20.4 | 27.9 | 35.9 |
| 1988 | 15.9 | 15.2 | n.a. | n.a. | 17.8 | 18.8 | 28.4 | n.a. |
| Average | 15.1 | 16.3 | 16.3 | 26.4 | 14.2 | 19.3 | 28.7 | 37.7 |

n.a. Not available.
a. The figures for Korea correspond to the central government. Data for the general government until 1978 show that tax revenue as a percentage of GDP was between 1 and 2 points higher than the same figure for the central government. Government expenditure is between 2 and 5 points higher for the general government than for the central government.
b. Tax revenue figures are not available.
Source: International Monetary Fund (various issues, Government Finance Statistics).

**Figure 8.2 Real exchange rate**
(1980=100)

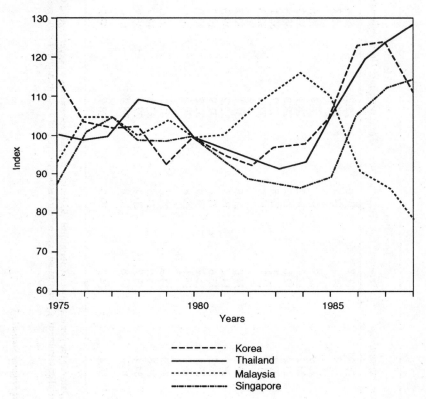

Source: World Bank data base.

total investment. Since the tradable sector is so dominant in the East Asian countries, however, the presumption is that a devaluation stimulates aggregate investment.[23]

The cornerstone of exchange rate policy in Korea, Singapore, Thailand, and Malaysia has been to maintain external competitiveness. With this purpose in mind they have kept the real exchange rate competitive and stable, supported by generally austere fiscal and wage policies. Figure 8-2 gives a clear picture of the stability of the real exchange rate in these four countries. Korea has experimented with different exchange rate systems. During 1975-80 it had a fixed exchange rate. Since 1980 it has followed a system of gradual adjustments to the nominal exchange rate, determined relative to a basket of currencies. After periods of real appreciation or external difficulties, the government has used one-shot devaluations to restore the competitiveness of exports. In Singapore, in contrast, the movement of the real exchange rate has been very mild, dominated by flows of foreign capital.

Thailand pegged its exchange rate to the dollar for most of the last three decades, with two devaluations—10 percent in 1981 and 14 percent in 1984.[24] In November 1984 it formally replaced the dollar peg with a basket of currencies. In reality, however, the *baht* follows the dollar closely. In general, low inflation has permitted a relatively high real exchange rate, and after periods of mild appreciation the government has used devaluations to restore competitiveness.

Malaysia has kept a stable and convertible currency, with the real exchange rate particularly stable over the last two decades. Only in recent years (1985-88) has the local currency, the *ringgit*, appreciated by a significant amount (almost 30 percent). Large inflows of foreign investment, which pushed up international reserves, were mostly responsible for the appreciation of the *ringgit*. This inflow of foreign investment is, however, a sign of a healthy economy and of confidence in the liberalization. At the same time, it is a cause of concern because of its effect on liquidity (and thus on potential inflation) and on competitiveness (through the exchange rate channel).

## Industrial and trade policies

All four countries have in some way used industrial and trade policies to promote target sectors, especially exportables. They have established many kinds of investment incentives to this end. Korea has used import restrictions widely, particularly during the industrialization stage of the 1970s. Although tariffs have not been high,[25] quantitative trade restrictions have implied a high degree of protection for some domestic industries. The idea has been to nurture some infant industries so that they can eventually grow up and become competitive in the world markets. This strategy, which worked so badly in Latin America, has produced some positive results in specific industries such as automobiles and steel (Collins and Park 1989). The government also made mistakes, however, which the authorities amended when they abandoned the Big Push strategy. Export subsidies have been used, mainly during periods of real appreciation such as in the late 1970s.

In terms of industrial policy, the five-year macroeconomic plans targeted certain industries that were to be helped with easy credit, tax incentives, subsidies, and other benefits. The government also, however, encouraged efficiency, and many of these industries have been exporting their production successfully. The experience of Hyundai in automobiles is a case in point, although lately it has run into some difficulties in the U.S. market.

After a brief period of import substitution (1965-67), Singapore has to a large extent left foreign trade to market forces. Its average nominal tariff rate in 1983 was only 6.4 percent, and it placed almost no other restrictions on imports. The government, however, has intervened in selected target sectors either by providing incentives (such as tax relief, subsidies, and easy credit) or by getting involved directly. As with Korea during the 1970s, Singapore has also promoted heavy industry.

Thailand followed an import-substitution strategy until the late 1960s, with high tariffs and other import restrictions, so as to promote domestic industries. The Investment Promotion Act of 1960, however, exempted taxes on imported capital machinery. This exemption encouraged investment and the use of modern technologies. In the early 1970s the strategy shifted toward export promotion, and a wide range of export incentives helped offset the effects of continued protection from imports (in the form of both tariff and nontariff barriers). Since the early 1980s the government has gradually phased out nontariff barriers. Tariffs have been more resilient.

Malaysia has maintained an open trade regime with very few nontariff restrictions and a low average tariff rate, although with a relatively high dispersion. According to some authors this low level of protectionism is related to the belief of the authorities that the beneficiaries of protectionism would be Chinese-run businesses (James, Naya, and Meier 1987). Industrial policies have also been influenced by racial factors. State involvement has pursued the development of Malay businesses vis-a-vis Chinese-run firms.

Malaysia has had active industrial policies since independence. All economic plans have included modernizing the country by developing a leading industrial sector. In 1958 the authorities provided fiscal incentives for industrial investment through the Pioneer Industrial Ordinance. A decade later they provided broader incentives under the Investment Incentives Act. With the New Economic Policies the government started to invest directly in some priority areas. In 1975 the new Industrial Coordination Act was introduced to accelerate achievement of the objectives of the New Economic Policies. As a result the manufacturing sector has led growth in Malaysia during the last two decades, going from 8.5 percent of GDP in 1961 to more than 20 percent in the 1980s.

### Role of the state

Given the information presented so far, it might be tempting to describe East Asian success stories as countries with very interventionist governments, in which market mechanisms have played a minor role. That conclusion would be wrong. Although the governments have been somewhat interventionist, they have relied mainly on the market. Further, there has been less government involvement in these four countries than in the less successful South Asian and Latin American countries. In East Asia intervention has always been directed toward promoting an outward orientation. In addition, as is stressed below, much of the government intervention in East Asia has been directed toward reducing economic uncertainty through stable and credible policies. For the most part state intervention has leaned in favor of, not against, market forces.

Among the successful East Asian economies Hong Kong has had the most laissez-faire government, while Korea is recognized as the most interventionist. In Korea the government has participated in the investment of the largest companies and helped organize export activities. Korean officials have been highly selective about foreign investment, allowing only that which brings a technology or marketing expertise unavailable at home. Economic decisions have been heavily centralized in the planning authority, which does the budgeting and coordinates fiscal and monetary policies, as well as industrial and trade policies. The Bank of Korea has depended on the Ministry of Finance, who is also the head of the monetary board. In short, monetary authorities have been subordinated to planners. Business conglomerates, on the other hand, have had close relationships with state-owned banks (Chu 1989).

Singapore's government has exercised less control over the economy than has Korea's,[26] and it has put more emphasis on state incentives to affect market outcomes. The financial markets, for example, have operated mostly outside the government's control. Of five local banks, only one is state-owned; foreign banks have provided two-thirds of domestic credit. In an effort to establish Singapore as a main international financial center, the government has progressively liberalized the capital markets. Foreign investment laws have been extremely liberal. A strong state enterprise sector has existed, however, in construction, health, petrochemicals, and shipbuilding; the state has provided for almost all basic needs. The financial requirements of public companies have nonetheless been subordinated to fiscal and monetary restraint. Singapore's central bank has been highly autonomous and by law has been precluded from lending money to the government.

In Thailand government involvement has been important during most of the 1960s, 1970s, and 1980s. The problems of the early 1980s, however, convinced the authorities that the market-based economic system needed to be strengthened. Liberalization of the financial system, lowering of trade barriers, elimination of most export taxes, a prudent wage policy, and so on have been part of the reorientation of the economic strategy.

The question remains, however, whether a freer economic system would have resulted in even better performance in these four countries. There is considerable debate and little agreement on this point. Some authors, while recognizing government mistakes, tend to give intervention significant credit for the success (for example, Collins and Park 1988). Others argue that these economies have been successful despite their governments. In the words of Vito Tanzi, a prominent exponent of the latter view,

> ...through its credit policies, incentive legislation and regulation of investments, the government [in Asia] has played too large a role in determining the area where investment should go, and for sure it has played too large a role in determining the composition of imports and even the users of these imports. (Tanzi 1988, p. 31)

*Stability and credibility of policy*

Authors such as Rodrik (1989), and Servén and Solimano (1990a and b,
chapter 6, this volume) have emphasized the role of uncertainty in investment. It is generally associated with the irreversibility of investment
(Pindyck 1989, chapter 3, this volume). The basic argument is as follows. If
macroeconomic conditions are uncertain, and given that once investment is
in place it is impossible to undo, it may pay to wait. The greater the
uncertainty and macroeconomic instability are, the lower the level of
investment is.

   Korea, Singapore, Thailand, and Malaysia are examples of economies
characterized by a high degree of stability. They have instituted no major
policy changes since the mid-1960s. Perhaps the most important was
Thailand's switch to an export-led growth strategy in the mid-1970s.
Korea's Big Push phase was an intensification of some policies started in the
1960s, and it did not last long; Malaysia's liberalization of the late 1980s was
a reorientation of a system that was becoming increasingly interventionist.
These changes are minor (and relatively few) compared with those in other
regions of the world. Latin American countries, for instance, have suffered
wide policy changes over the last 30 years. In addition to structural
adjustments, stabilization programs were the norm there throughout the
1980s, with resultant economic recession and relative price volatility. Many
countries have undertaken several stabilization efforts in the short period
of a few years, Argentina, Brazil, and Peru being the most prominent. There
have been few stabilization programs in the successful economies of East
Asia because they have rarely been necessary.

   In addition, and in contrast to Latin America, the East Asian countries
in general have maintained conservative fiscal policies that have helped
maintain the stable macroeconomic environment. As discussed, except for
Malaysia the public sector has made a significant contribution to the overall
saving effort.

   A measure of the stability in East Asia is the low variability of the real
exchange rate. Table 8-12 shows the average of the moving-average
coefficients of variation of the real exchange rate for the period 1975-88 in
the four East Asian countries, as well as in some Latin American economies.
The average of this measure for Korea, Singapore, Thailand, and Malaysia
is 0.041; the figure for a sample of seven Latin American countries is more
than twice this, 0.095. The figures for Singapore and Malaysia, the East
Asian countries with highest coefficients of variation (0.043), are lower than
the figure for any of the seven Latin American countries. The second
column in table 8-12 shows the coefficient of variation for GDP growth.
Again, the variability in East Asia is significantly lower than that in Latin
America. Here the difference is even more pronounced.

   Credibility in government policies, as stressed by Rodrik (1989, 1990),
can also affect private investment significantly. Again, it may pay to wait
until being sure that a government is going to hold to a given program.

**Table 8.12  Economic instability, 1975-88**

| | Average coefficient of variation[a] | |
| | Real exchange rate | GDP growth |
| --- | --- | --- |
| *East Asia* | | |
| Korea | 0.039 | 0.456 |
| Singapore | 0.043 | 0.422 |
| Thailand | 0.037 | 0.265 |
| Malaysia | 0.043 | 0.515 |
| Average | 0.041 | 0.414 |
| *Latin America* | | |
| Argentina | 0.170 | 11.362 |
| Brazil | 0.049 | 1.061 |
| Chile | 0.105 | 13.891 |
| Colombia | 0.065 | 0.340 |
| Mexico | 0.102 | 4.455 |
| Peru | 0.084 | 1.374 |
| Uruguay | 0.088 | 1.412 |
| Average | 0.095 | 4.842 |

a. Defined as the average of the moving-average coefficients of variation between periods t - 2 and t (from t = 1975 until t = 1988). The coefficients of variation are defined in absolute terms. *Source:* World Bank data base.

Although difficult to measure, it can be argued convincingly that government policies in the four East Asian countries have been credible and consistent. Their governments have emphasized the promotion of exports, saving and investment, and industrialization of the economy. Business people inside and outside the countries have perceived these goals as permanent, and government behavior has validated these expectations. This situation has produced an extraordinarily good environment for investment, as witnessed by the very high rates of private investment. The absence of major policy changes over the last three decades, as mentioned, has no doubt enhanced credibility.

*Income distribution*

One reason Latin American governments have been so erratic in their macroeconomic policies may be the significant inequality in income in these countries. It leads to social pressures that governments have attempted to relieve through populist policies. After one or two years of economic expansion inflation soars, real wages fall, unemployment starts to increase, and output declines. The policies prove unsustainable, and the government has to switch to another set of policies. Many countries in the region have suffered this populist cycle, some of them more than once.[27]

In East Asia the situation has been the opposite. A very equitable distribution of income has facilitated macroeconomic stability. Table 8-13 presents figures on income distribution for a group of East Asian and Latin American countries. The summary measure used is the share of national income of the top and the bottom quintiles of the income distribution. As the figures show, the ratio of top to bottom income is much lower for East Asian countries than for Latin American ones. In East Asia the richest 20 percent of the population on average has 8.7 times the income of the poorest 20 percent. In Latin America the ratio is 21.5 times. Moreover, with the exception of Malaysia the distribution of income in East Asia is within the range shown by developed economies. It is also worth mentioning that reduction of income inequality has been a major objective of the Malaysian government, as stressed in the New Economic Policies implemented since the early 1970s.

Recent work suggests that income inequality has a negative effect on economic growth (Alesina and Rodrik 1991). It may be conjectured that a key channel for this relationship is investment. More equitable distributions of income lead to less social conflict, a situation that reduces uncertainty and creates a more stable economic environment for investment. Unfortunately, no time series data on income distribution exist to test this point empirically for the four East Asian countries. For this reason an income distribution variable is not included in the empirical section.

*Debt overhang*

According to the debt overhang argument, emphasized by Krugman (1988) and Sachs (1989b), the larger the external debt burden is, the lower private investment is. The reason is two different yet complementary arguments. First, a high external debt can be seen as a source of macro instability because an external burden that is not known with certainty (as it depends on world interest rates and terms of trade, which are beyond the control of the country) will surely affect economic policies. From another point of view, an excessive level of debt acts as a potential tax on domestic investment.[28] Empirically, Greene and Villanueva (1990) find that private investment is negatively correlated with the debt service ratio and the debt to GDP ratio, see also chapter 6, this volume.

Korea and Malaysia are the clearest cases of successful East Asian countries that have experienced external debt problems; in the early 1980s Korea's debt to GDP ratio rose to over 50 percent. Since 1985, however, the ratio has fallen dramatically. The huge current account deficits of the early 1980s in Malaysia resulted in a debt to GDP ratio reaching almost 80 percent in 1986. Since then surpluses have brought this ratio to below 60 percent.

External debt increased rapidly in Thailand during the 1980s. Although

**Table 8.13 Income distribution: An international comparison**
(circa, 1988)

| | Percent of national income | | | Per capita income |
| | Bottom 20% | Top 20% | Ratio | (US$) |
| | (1) | (2) | (2/1) | (3) |
| --- | --- | --- | --- | --- |
| *Asia* | | | | |
| Hong Kong | 5.4 | 47.0 | 8.70 | 9,220 |
| Indonesia | 8.8 | 41.3 | 4.69 | 440 |
| Korea | 5.7 | 45.3 | 7.95 | 3,600 |
| Malaysia | 4.6 | 51.2 | 11.13 | 1,940 |
| Singapore | 5.1 | 48.9 | 9.59 | 9.070 |
| Taiwan | 8.8 | 37.2 | 4.23 | 2,530 |
| Thailand | 5.6 | 49.8 | 8.89 | 1,000 |
| Average | 6.3 | 45.8 | 7.27 | 3,971 |
| *Latin America* | | | | |
| Argentina | 4.4 | 50.3 | 11.43 | 2,520 |
| Brazil | 2.4 | 62.6 | 26.08 | 2,160 |
| Chile | 4.2 | 60.4 | 14.38 | 1,510 |
| Mexico | 2.9 | 57.7 | 19.90 | 1.760 |
| Peru | 1.9 | 61.0 | 32.11 | 1,285 |
| Venezuela | 3.0 | 54.0 | 18.00 | 3,250 |
| Average | 3.1 | 57.7 | 18.61 | 2,080 |
| *Industrialized countries* | | | | |
| France | 6.3 | 40.8 | 6.48 | 16,090 |
| England | 5.8 | 39.5 | 6.81 | 12,810 |
| Italy | 6.8 | 41.0 | 6.03 | 13,330 |
| Japan | 8.7 | 37.5 | 4.31 | 21,020 |
| United States | 4.7 | 41.9 | 8.91 | 19,840 |
| Fed. Rep. of Germany | 6.8 | 38.7 | 5.69 | 18,480 |
| Average | 6.5 | 39.9 | 6.14 | 16,928 |

*Source:* World Bank.

it remained moderate by international standards (only between 1985 and 1987 did Thailand's foreign debt surpass 40 percent of GDP), it became a source of concern for the authorities. Since 1987, however, the debt burden has been falling steadily.

In Singapore external debt has never reached worrisome proportions. At its peak in 1977, public and publicly guaranteed external debt was only 15 percent of GDP.

**Empirical analysis**

This section presents an empirical test of some of the hypotheses outlined above. How the different variables help explain private investment in Korea, Singapore, Thailand, and Malaysia is investigated with pooled cross-section—time series (panel) data. First, however, the efficiency of investment is reviewed briefly.

*The efficiency of investment*

East Asian countries have achieved both high rates of economic growth and high rates of investment. The question is whether their rates of growth are as high as they should be given the resources invested. The higher the level of investment, the less consumption there is today. Thus it is very important to invest efficiently so that the sacrifice is adequately compensated in the future.

Table 8-14 shows incremental capital/output ratios (ICORs) for the four East Asian countries. The same definition used by Faini and de Melo (1990) was used in computing them. That study distinguishes three groups of countries: manufacturing exporters; primary exporters; and developed countries. The ICORs for the period 1970-86 in the three groups are 2.72, 2.16, and 2.50, respectively.

A comparison of the four East Asian countries with those in the Faini and de Melo study reveals that investment in Korea, Thailand, and Malaysia was quite efficient. Their ICORs were within the range shown by the most efficient countries. The sharp and short-lived increase in Malaysia's figures during the mid-1980s was associated with the 1985-86 recession; in subsequent years its ICORs showed a marked improvement.

Only Singapore seems somewhat less efficient in terms of the growth associated with its rates of investment. Its ICORs seem relatively high when compared with those of other countries. Between 1971 and 1988, for example, Singapore's average rate of growth of GDP of 8 percent was lower than that of Korea (8.6 percent), while its rates of investment were substantially higher (tables 8-1 and 8-2). As with Malaysia, the economic recession in the mid-1980s greatly influenced Singapore's ICORs. In 1987 and 1988, however, the situation improved dramatically. Singapore's ICORs declined to levels below the average for the most efficient group in the Faini and de Melo sample, although not lower than those of the other three East Asian countries.

*Econometric estimation and results*

A private investment function for Korea, Singapore, Thailand, and Malaysia is estimated here. The period of estimation—1975 to 1988—was largely determined by the availability of data.

According to the earlier discussion, private investment is considered to be a function of:

**Table 8.14 The efficiency of investment, as measured by the incremental capital/output ratio** (ICOR)

| Year | Korea | Singapore | Thailand | Malaysia |
|---|---|---|---|---|
| 1971 | 1.47 | 2.37 | 2.25 | 1.78 |
| 1972 | 1.83 | 2.23 | 2.39 | 1.48 |
| 1973 | 1.23 | 2.30 | 1.61 | 1.37 |
| 1974 | 1.63 | 3.12 | 2.21 | 1.85 |
| 1975 | 1.80 | 3.61 | 2.04 | 3.14 |
| 1976 | 1.42 | 2.81 | 1.56 | 1.38 |
| 1977 | 1.86 | 2.57 | 1.78 | 1.82 |
| 1978 | 2.18 | 2.56 | 1.69 | 1.93 |
| 1979 | 2.65 | 2.48 | 2.23 | 1.69 |
| 1980 | 7.77 | 2.67 | 2.26 | 2.33 |
| 1981 | 2.03 | 2.82 | 2.06 | 2.65 |
| 1982 | 2.39 | 3.71 | 2.24 | 2.89 |
| 1983 | 1.84 | 3.55 | 1.88 | 2.80 |
| 1984 | 2.07 | 3.53 | 2.00 | 2.49 |
| 1985 | 2.33 | 8.07 | 2.39 | 5.21 |
| 1986 | 1.72 | 4.54 | 2.00 | 3.10 |
| 1987 | 1.85 | 2.44 | 1.61 | 1.96 |
| 1988 | 1.92 | 2.14 | 1.50 | 1.68 |
| Average 1971-88 | 2.22 | 3.20 | 1.98 | 2.31 |
| Average 1971-75 | 1.59 | 2.73 | 2.10 | 1.92 |
| Average 1976-80 | 3.18 | 2.62 | 1.90 | 1.83 |
| Average 1981-88 | 2.02 | 3.85 | 1.96 | 2.85 |

*Notes*: ICOR = Investment (t)/[GDP(t)-(1-d)GDP(t-1)]. d = depreciation = 0.07.
Investment and GDP in constant prices.
*Source*: World Bank data base.

(a) *Public investment.* Theoretically two factors relate public and private investment. On the one hand, as public investment increases, the productivity of private investment increases, with the resultant expectation of a positive correlation. On the other hand, there is the usual argument that crowding out results in reduced private investment. Thus, in this study there was no a priori expectation about the sign of public investment in the equation. It would depend on which effect dominated.

(b) *External debt as a percentage of GDP.* The debt overhang argument implies a negative correlation between the external debt burden (in this case measured by the debt to GDP ratio) and private investment.

(c) *Credit as a percentage of GDP.* The greater the amount of credit available to the private sector, the more projects will be carried out. As such, a positive correlation of credit and private investment is expected.

(d) *Interest rates.* Higher real interest rates make investment more costly. At the same time positive interest rates are often needed to promote saving and thus to have an efficient financial sector, an argument advanced by McKinnon (1973). This second factor would mean a positive correlation between interest rates and private investment. Therefore there is a range within which the correlation between both variables is unclear. Another source of ambiguity about the effect of the real interest rate is that the published interest rate in repressed credit markets probably does not mean much. In all four countries the free market forces operating in the financial sector have to some extent been repressed.

(e) *Uncertainty and stability.* The more predictable the future environment is, the larger private investment will be. The coefficient of variation of the real exchange rate will be used as a proxy for this variable.

(f) *Per capita growth.* Although not discussed in the previous sections, per capita growth is usually included in investment equations to capture the predictions of the flexible accelerator model. To avoid simultaneity problems the lagged value for this variable is used.

(g) *Country-specific factors,* captured by a dummy variable for each country. Thus the equation takes the following form:

$$(8\text{-}1) \quad IP/Y = f[PCGR(t-1), IPU, XD, CR, RIR, CVAR, W]$$

where $IP/Y$  =  real private investment as a percentage of real GDP (source as described in table 8-4).

$PCGR(t-1)$ =  lagged percentage change in per capita GDP (sources as described in tables 8-1—8-4).

$IPU$  =  real public investment as a percentage of real GDP (source as described in table 8-4).

$XD$  =  external debt as a percentage of GDP (sources as described in tables 8-1—8-4).

$CR$  =  credit to the private sector as a percentage of GDP (source as described in table 8-7).

$RIR$  =  real interest rate (from the World Bank data base).

$CVAR$ =  Coefficient of variation of the real exchange rate between year (t - 2) and year t (source as described in table 8-11).

$W$ =  A vector of dummy variables, one for each country in the sample, which takes the value of one for that country and zero for the others.

The econometric results are presented in column 1 of table 8-15. All signs confirm the previous hypotheses. Growth in per capita GDP enters with a positive sign and is highly significant. Public investment also enters with a positive sign and is significant at less than 1 percent. This finding supports the results obtained by Aschauer (1989a and b) for the United

**Table 8.15 Determinants of private investment—Korea, Singapore, Thailand, and Malaysia**
[Dependent variable: log (private investment as a percentage of GDP)]

| Variable | (1) | (2) |
|----------|-----|-----|
| PCGR (t - 1) | 0.019 | 0.018 |
|  | (4.764) | (4.466) |
| log(IPU) | 0.178 | 0.180 |
|  | (2.781) | (2.778) |
| log(XD) | -0.153 | -0.153 |
|  | (-3.391) | (-3.357) |
| log(CR) | 0.177 | 0.177 |
|  | (2.480) | (2.458) |
| RIR | -0.015 | -0.016 |
|  | (-2.204) | (-2.210) |
| CVAR | -1.402 | -1.467 |
|  | (-2.939) | (-2.873) |
| log(RER) |  | 0.052 |
|  |  | (0.386) |
| Adjusted $R^2$ | 0.919 | 0.918 |
| S.E. of regression | 0.082 | 0.083 |
| No. of observations | 54 | 54 |

*Note:* t-statistics are in parentheses.
*Source:* Authors' calculations.

States, by Greene and Villanueva (1990) for a group of developing countries, and by Blejer and Khan (1984) for a different group of developing economies, also chapter 6 and chapter 7, this volume. Thus it appears that the productivity effect dominates, so that public and private investment are complementary.[29]

As expected, external debt over GDP enters with a negative sign and is highly significant. The coefficient of credit as a percentage of GDP is positive and significant, as explained.

The real interest rate enters significantly in the equation with a negative sign. The implication is the interest rate's usual effects on the cost of credit are more important than those of the repressed financial market, the argument stressed by McKinnon (1973) and discussed above. This conclusion is in line with the findings of Greene and Villanueva (1990) in their study of private investment in 23 developing countries, where they find a negative relation between private investment and the real interest rate.

Finally, the measure of instability used here—the coefficient of variation of the real exchange rate—enters with a negative sign, significant at less than the 1 percent level. This result confirms the hypothesis that uncertainty and stability are important determinants of private investment. Furthermore, it is consistent with the findings of Solimano (1989) and Servén and Solimano (1990b).

Another variable that may be related to private investment is the real exchange rate, RER. As discussed, the sign of this variable is theoretically ambiguous. Column (2) of table 8-14 shows the results when the real exchange rate is included in the equation.[30] As observed, the real exchange rate does not have any important effect in the regression: its coefficient is not significant, and the rest of the variables have very similar coefficients and levels of significance.

The same regressions were run using lagged instead of contemporary values for the different explanatory variables (except for per capita GDP, which is already lagged). The signs remain the same, and the coefficients remain significant in almost all possible combinations. In sum, the results obtained here seem quite robust.

## Conclusions

East Asian countries have achieved unparalleled economic performance over the last two and a half decades. A distinctive characteristic of these economies has been their high rates of growth, which have been possible because of their major, sustained investment efforts. The ratios of investment to GDP in East Asia have reached world record levels. The high level of investment has been supported by a strong base of domestic saving and quite significant foreign saving. This performance has made important social improvements possible.

Table 8-16 provides some summary economic and social indicators for these countries. For purposes of comparison, the countries are divided into three groups—East Asia, Southeast Asia (in general, the term East Asia has been used in this chapter to refer to both regions), and Latin America. The primary distinguishing characteristics of the two groups of Asian countries are not only location, but—most important—natural resource endowments. The East Asian economies of Korea, Hong Kong, Taiwan[31], and Singapore are poor in natural resources, while the Southeast Asian countries (Malaysia, Thailand, and Indonesia) are rich. This division is important for international comparisons, because the major Latin American countries have abundant natural resources.

Although it may seem paradoxical, the poorly endowed economies have significantly outperformed their natural resource—rich neighbors. Malaysia, which had the highest fiscal deficits and the worst income distribution of the countries analyzed in this chapter, has also been the

**Table 8.16 East Asia, Southeast Asia, and Latin America — economic and social indicators**

| Regions/ countries | GNP per capita (% growth, 1965-88) | Inflation (annual average, 1980-88) | Life expectancy (years, 1988) | Adult illiteracy (%, 1985) | Infant mortality rate (per 1,000 live births) | | |
|---|---|---|---|---|---|---|---|
| | | | | | 1965 | 1988 | %change |
| *East Asia* | | | | | | | |
| Hong Kong | 6.3 | 6.7 | 77 | 15.5 | 27 | 7 | -74 |
| Korea | 6.8 | 5.0 | 70 | — | 62 | 24 | -61 |
| Singapore | 7.2 | 1.2 | 74 | 17.5 | 26 | 7 | -73 |
| Average | 6.8 | 4.3 | 73.7 | 16.5 | 38.3 | 12.7 | -69.3 |
| *Southeast Asia* | | | | | | | |
| Indonesia | 4.0 | 8.5 | 61 | 30.5 | 128 | 68 | -47 |
| Malaysia | 4.0 | 1.3 | 70 | 30.5 | 55 | 23 | -54 |
| Thailand | 4.3 | 3.1 | 65 | 10.5 | 88 | 30 | -66 |
| Average | 4.1 | 4.3 | 65.3 | 23.8 | 90.3 | 40.3 | -55 |
| *Latin America* | | | | | | | |
| Argentina | 0.0 | 290.5 | 71 | 5.0 | 58 | 31 | -47 |
| Brazil | 3.6 | 188.7 | 65 | 23.0 | 104 | 61 | -41 |
| Colombia | 2.4 | 24.1 | 68 | 12.5 | 86 | 39 | -55 |
| Chile | 0.1 | 20.8 | 72 | 6.0 | 101 | 20 | -80 |
| Mexico | 2.3 | 73.8 | 69 | 11.0 | 82 | 46 | -44 |
| Peru | 0.1 | 119.1 | 62 | 18.5 | 130 | 86 | -34 |
| Uruguay | 1.3 | 57.0 | 72 | 4.5 | 47 | 23 | -51 |
| Average | 1.4 | 110.6 | 68.4 | 11.5 | 86.9 | 43.7 | -50.3 |

*Source:* World Bank (various issues, 1990).

worst performer in everything but inflation. Consider growth in per capita GDP over the period 1965-88. The average annual increase in East Asia was 6.8 percent, whereas Southeast Asia achieved "only" 4.1 percent. Moreover, every East Asian country has a rate of GDP growth at least 50 percent higher than that of any Southeast Asian economy.

The rates of investment and saving in East Asia have been significantly higher than in Southeast Asia, especially in recent years, with the differences usually around 10 percentage points of GDP. A qualification about the efficiency of investment in Singapore is, however, necessary. Although its efficiency appears to have been lower than that in the other countries during the mid-1980s, it has since recovered significantly. Regarding inflation, the results have been remarkable and much better than those of industrialized economies. During the 1980s, for example, the average annual rate of inflation in both regions was 4.3 percent, with Singapore and Malaysia at slightly over than 1 percent. Here, there is no clear dominance of East Asia over Southeast Asia.

The differences between East and Southeast Asia appear to be minor when Latin America enters the picture. Average growth in per capita GDP amounted to only 1.4 percent during 1965-88 for the seven countries in the table. The rate of inflation was, at 110.6 percent on average, over 25 times higher than that of Asia. The gaps in these two indicators are indeed remarkable.

The progress in Asia has involved not just the economic scene. The social indicators have improved dramatically as well. The rate of infant mortality in East Asia declined by almost 70 percent on average between 1965 and 1988; in Southeast Asia the same indicator fell by 56 percent over the same period and in Latin America by 50 percent. Once more, the first region outperforms the second, which, in turn, outperforms the third. Furthermore, infant mortality rates in Singapore and Hong Kong (at 7 per 1,000 live births) are the lowest in the world after Japan, Finland, and Sweden. Life expectancy at birth in 1988 averaged 73.7 years in East Asia, 65.3 years in Southeast Asia, and 68.4 percent in Latin America. Adult illiteracy in 1985 was 16.5 percent, 23.8 percent, and 11.5 percent in the three regions, respectively.[32] Latin American performance as measured by these last two indicators improves. Moreover, in the case of the latter indicator, it shows the best performance.

Private investment has been a dominant factor in East Asia's growth. In Korea, the share of private investment in total investment has been over 80 percent, in both Singapore and Thailand over 70 percent, and in Malaysia about 58 percent. Thus the participation of private investment in total capital formation has been significantly higher in East Asia than in other developing regions, such as Latin America (with the exception of Malaysia, which has been comparable to Latin America). If the fact that total investment rates are much higher than in other regions is taken into account, it is clear that the rate of private investment to GDP is much higher in East Asia.

A handful of variables explains well econometrically the performance of private investment in East Asia. An increase in GDP growth, public investment, or credit availability exerts a strong and positive influence over private investment. Higher external debt, real interest rates, or variability in the real exchange rate are clear disincentives to private investment.

With these results it is tempting to make some international comparisons. Why has private investment been so much stronger in East Asia than in Latin America? Key differences appear to be the instability of macroeconomic variables (measured here by the coefficient of variation of the real exchange rate) and the ability (and willingness) to adjust to external shocks. By every possible measure macroeconomic stability has been much higher in East Asia, a result of more stable and consistent policies. As a result of these policies and the greater willingness to adjust, East Asia weathered the debt crisis much better than Latin America did. Of the four East Asian countries Singapore never had an external debt problem (it privileged foreign direct investment over external debt), and Thailand's problems with foreign debt were minor. By many indicators Korea had the greatest problem with foreign debt among the four countries. It quickly implemented an adjustment program, however, and also had the luck of suffering its debt crisis in 1979-80, before the generalized debt crisis erupted. According to Collins (1988a), in 1979-80 Korea was still able to borrow overseas to support high rates of investment, a strategy that would have been very difficult a few years later.

It is possible to conjecture that policy stability—and thus private investment and growth—has been facilitated in Asia by a much more equitable income distribution than Latin America's. Recent international evidence (Alesina and Rodrik 1991) backs this argument but, because data are not available, this issue could not be verified econometrically. The relations among income distribution, private investment, and economic growth remain a prominent issue on the research agenda.

## Notes

1.  We are very grateful to Susan Collins, Luis Servén, and Andrés Solimano for their insightful comments and suggestions. We have also benefitted from comments at seminars held at the Banco Central de Chile, Pontificia Universidad Católica de Chile, and the World Bank.
2.  These four countries are referred to here as East Asian, although the literature distinguishes between East Asian countries, or newly industrialized countries (NICs) (Korea, Singapore, Taiwan, and Hong Kong), and Southeast Asian ones (Indonesia, Thailand, Malaysia, and the Philippines).
3.  All dollars are current U.S. dollars unless otherwise specified.
4.  Collins (1988b) has argued that one of the differences in the development of Japan and Korea has been external borrowing. When personal savings fell in Korea, the government financed investment through increased external borrowing. In contrast, Japan curbed investment when savings fell.
5.  These figures are in real terms (1980 dollars) at purchasing power parity exchange rates. For the period 1986-88 growth rates from the national accounts were used. Based on the same source, Korea's per capita GDP went from US$797 in 1965 to US$4,112 in 1988, Thailand's from US$833 in 1965 to US$2,242 in 1988, and Malaysia's from US$1,309 to US$3,665.
6.  Interestingly, whereas foreign authors consider Thailand to be a success, Thai authors are much less enthusiastic (see Warr and Nijathaworn 1987).
7.  Corden (1990) estimates the cost at about 4 percent of GDP.

8.   A World Bank book on Malaysia, for example, is suggestively titled *Malaysia: Growth and Equity in a Multiracial Society* (Young, Bussink, and Hassan 1990).

9.   There is no good set of data before 1970.

10.  As will be discussed later, income inequality is one of the factors that most strongly differentiates Malaysia from other East Asian countries.

11.  The 12 countries are Argentina, Bolivia, Brazil, Chile, Colombia, Costa Rica, Ecuador, Guatemala, Mexico, Peru, Uruguay, and Venezuela. The period considered is 1975-87.

12.  The government undertook austerity measures after the 1985-86 recession that included an important decline in public investment—from 16.5 percent of GDP in 1981-86 to 10.5 percent in 1987-88.

13.  The criterion was to select countries with a 1960 per capita GDP at least 25 percent of the level in the United States. Data were taken from the Summers and Heston data set.

14.  For purposes of comparison the rate for Japan was 12.23 percent, the United States 7.62 percent, and the United Kingdom 6.94 percent.

15.  The pattern of going from current account deficits to surplus is embodied in the theory of "balance of payments stages" originally suggested by John Elliot Cairns in the nineteenth century. If the surpluses continue, in the next stage some of these countries will become net creditors vis-a-vis the rest of the world.

16.  Total credit to the private sector is not, however, a perfect measure of the importance of credit policies in these economies. A more complete picture must include the allocation of credit across sectors. A lack of data precluded more work on this issue.

17.  Hong Kong, however, pursued a more market-oriented strategy in the financial sector. This approach may be the reason the indicators of financial deepening show Hong Kong ahead of Singapore. The ratio of money plus quasi-money to GDP in Hong Kong was about 110 percent in 1988.

18.  The controls the government imposed on nominal interest rates in Thailand during the 1970s resulted in negative real interest rates. In the early 1980s the government relaxed these controls and raised the ceilings on interest rates. This move, coupled with declining inflation rates, resulted in positive real interest rates after 1982.

19.  Recall, however, the criticism of Dornbusch and Reinoso (1989) of this view.

20.  Defined as the sum of monetary and quasi-monetary deposits in the banking system, deflated by the consumer price index.

21.  Some trace the Bank of Thailand's conservatism to the rule of King Rama V (1868-1910), who had British financiers as economic advisors (Warr and Nijathaworn 1987).

22.  This figure, however, might not include revenues from public companies, especially the oil sector.

23.  Servén and Solimano (1990a and b and chapter 2 in this volume) present

    a detailed discussion of the effects of a devaluation on investment.
24. There was a brief period of floating rates between 1979 and 1981.
25. For example, the simple average tariff rate for 1982-83 was 23.5 percent (James, Naya, and Meier 1987, p. 37).
26. Control over the private lives of its citizens may, however, be much greater. The government, for example, concerned that highly educated women were not marrying, created a matchmaking agency for graduates. Military service is extended for those considered too fat, as obesity is almost considered a public offense.
27. Dornbusch and Edwards (1990) and Sachs (1989a) analyze the populist pattern in Latin America.
28. See Servén and Solimano (1990a and b and chapter 2 in this volume) for a discussion of the debt overhang argument.
29. The lagged value of the public investment to GDP ratio was also used, as it avoids a possible problem of spurious positive correlation that arises because both private and public investment are divided by GDP. The sign of the coefficient remained positive, but its significance fell.
30. The real exchange rate series were obtained from the World Bank data base and are the same as those in tables 8-1—8-4.
31. Taiwan is not included in the table because of a lack of data.
32. Unfortunately, there are no figures on adult illiteracy and life expectancy in these countries as of the late 1960s or early 1970s.

## References

Alesina, A., and D. Rodrik. 1991. "Distributive Politics and Economic Growth." Harvard University, Department of Economics, Cambridge, Mass. January.

Aschauer, D. 1989a. "Is Public Expenditure Productive?" *Journal of Monetary Economics* 23 (March):177-200.

———. 1989b. "Does Public Capital Crowd Out Private Capital?" *Journal of Monetary Economics* 24 (October):171-89.

Blejer, M., and M. Khan. 1984. "Government Policy and Private Investment in Developing Countries." *IMF Staff Papers* 331 (2):379-403.

Chu, Y. 1989. "State Structure and Economic Adjustment in the East Asian Newly Industrializing Countries." *International Organization* 43 (Autumn):647-72.

Collins, S. 1988a. "South Korea's Experience with External Debt." NBER Working Paper no. 2598. National Bureau of Economic Research, Cambridge, Mass. May.

———. 1988b. "Savings and Growth Experiences of Korea and Japan." *Journal of the Japanese and International Economy* 2 (3):328-50.

Collins, S., and W. A. Park. 1989. "External Debt and Macroeconomic Performance in South Korea," in J. Sachs, ed., *Developing Country Debt and the World Economy.* Chicago: University of Chicago Press.

Corden, M. 1990. "Macroeconomic Policy and Growth: Some Lessons of Experience." A paper presented at the World Bank Annual Conference on Development Economics, Washington, D.C., April 26-27, 1990.

De Long, B., and L. Summers. 1990. "Equipment Investment and Economic Growth." NBER Working Paper no. 3515. National Bureau of Economic Research, Cambridge, Mass. November.

Dornbusch, R., and Y. C. Park. 1987. "Korea's Growth Policy." *Brookings Papers on Economic Activity* (2):389-454.

Dornbusch, R., and A. Reinoso. 1989. "Financial Factors in Economic Development." *American Economic Review* 79 (May):204-09.

Dornbusch, R., and S. Edwards. 1990. "La Macroeconomía del Populismo en América Latina" [The Macroeconomics of Populism in Latin America]. *El Trimestre Económico* 57 (Enero-Marzo):121-62.

Faini, R., and J. de Melo. 1990. "Adjustment, Investment and the Real Exchange Rate in Developing Countries." *Economic Policy* 5 (October):491-519.

Friedman, M. 1983. "'No' to More Money for the IMF." *Newsweek*, November 14, p. 96.

Greene, J., and D. Villanueva. 1990. "Private Investment in Developing Countries: An Empirical Analysis." International Monetary Fund, Washington, D.C.

International Monetary Fund (IMF). Various issues. *Government Finance Statistics*. Washington, D.C.: IMF.

———. Various issues. *International Financial Statistics*. Washington, D.C.: IMF.

Islam, I., and C. Kirkpatrick. 1986. "Exports and the Distribution of Income in Singapore." *Cambridge Journal of Economics* 10 (June):113-27.

James, W. E., S. Naya, and G. M. Meier. 1987. *Asian Development: Economic Success and Policy Lessons*. San Francisco, Calif.: International Center for Economic Growth.

Krause, L. 1988. "Hong Kong and Singapore: Twins or Kissing Cousins?" *Economic Development and Cultural Change* 36 (April):S45-66.

Krugman, P. 1988. "Market-Based Debt-Reduction Schemes," in J. Frenkel, ed., *Analytical Issues in Debt*. Washington, D.C.: International Monetary Fund.

Kuznets, P. 1988. "An East Asian Model of Economic Development: Japan, Taiwan, and South Korea." *Economic Development and Cultural Change* 36 (April):S11-43.

Lin, C. 1988. "East Asia and Latin America as Contrasting Models." *Economic Development and Cultural Change* 36 (April):S153-97.

McKinnon, R. 1973. *Money and Capital in Economic Development*. Washington, D.C.: Brookings Institution.

———. 1989. "Financial Liberalization and Economic Development: A Reassessment of Interest Rate Policies in Asia and Latin America." International Center for Economic Growth, ICS Press, San Francisco.

Pindyck, R. 1989. "Irreversibility, Uncertainty and Investment." World

Bank, Policy, Planning, and Research (PPR) Working Paper no. 294. Washington, D.C. October. Also in *Journal of Economic Literature* 24, (September): 1110-1148, 1991.

Robinson, D., Y. Byeon, R. Teja, and W. Tseng. 1991. "Thailand: Adjusting to Success. Current Policy Issues." Occasional Paper no. 85. International Monetary Fund, Washington, D.C. August.

Rodrik, D. 1989. "Policy Uncertainty and Private Investment in Developing Countries." NBER Working Paper no. 2999. National Bureau of Economic Research, Cambridge, Mass.

———. 1990. "How Should Structural Adjustment Programs Be Designed." *World Development* 18 (July):933-47.

Sachs, J. 1985. "External Debt and Macroeconomic Performance in Latin America and East Asia." *Brookings Papers on Economic Activity* (2):523-73.

———. 1989a. "Social Conflict and Populist Policies in Latin America." NBER Working Paper no. 2897. National Bureau of Economic Research, Cambridge, Mass.

———. 1989b. "The Debt Overhang of Developing Countries," in R. Findlay, ed., *Debt, Stabilization and Development: Essays in Memory of Carlos Diaz Alejandro.* Oxford: Basil Blackwell.

Sachs, J., and M. Sundberg. 1988. "International Payment Imbalances of the East Asian Developing Economies." Harvard University, Department of Economics, Cambridge, Mass. December.

Servén, L., and A. Solimano. 1990a. "Private Investment and Macroeconomic Adjustment: A Survey." World Bank, Macroeconomic Adjustment and Growth Division, Washington, D.C.

———. 1990b. "Private Investment and Macroeconomic Adjustment in LDCs: Theory, Country Experiences and Policy Implications." World Bank, Macroeconomic Adjustment and Growth Division, Washington, D.C.

Solimano, A. 1989. "How Private Investment Reacts to Changing Macroeconomic Conditions: The Chilean Experience in the 1980s." World Bank, Policy, Planning, and Research (PPR) Working Paper no. 212. World Bank, Country Economics Department, Washington, D.C. Also in A. Chhibber, M. Dailami and N. Shafik, (eds). *Reviving Private Investment in Developing Countries: Empirical Studies and Policy Lessons.* Amsterdam: North Holland Publishing, 1992.

Summers, R., and A. Heston. 1988. "A New Set of International Comparisons of Real Product and Price Levels: Estimates for 130 Countries." The Review of *Income and Wealth* 34 (March).

Tanzi, V. 1988. "The Role of the Public Sector in the Market Economies of Developing Asia: General Lessons for the Current Debt Strategy." Working Paper. International Monetary Fund, Fiscal Affairs Department, Washington, D.C. January.

van Wijnbergen, S. 1982. "Stagflationary Effects of Monetary Stabilization Policies: A Quantitative Analysis." *Journal of Development Economics* 10 (April):133-69.

Warr, P., and B. Nijathaworn. 1987. "Thai Economic Performance: Some Thai Perspectives." *Asian Pacific Economic Literature* 1 (May):60-74.

World Bank. Various issues. *World Development Report*. Washington, D.C.: World Bank.

Young, K., W. Bussink, and P. Hasan. 1980. *Malaysia: Growth and Equity in a Multiracial Society*. Baltimore and London: Johns Hopkins University Press.

# 9

# Policies for the Recovery of Investment: Panel Presentations

This chapter presents edited versions of the panel presentations made at the conference on "Private Investment and Macroeconomic Adjustment in Developing Countries," held at the World Bank in March 1991.

**Rudiger Dornbusch**

The setting in which investment will flourish has several ingredients, among them: opportunities; prosperity; coordination; rules of the game; and finance.

*Opportunities*

Some regions are blessed; others can offer barely any opportunities, no matter how hard they try. Some regions of Africa fall into the latter category, and so do parts of Latin America, for example, Bolivia. They once offered opportunities, when their primary commodities benefitted from attractive world prices. Ruled by oligarchies or colonial administrations that single-mindedly fostered respect of property and the established order, they offered plausible outlets for foreign capital. Today the commodities are not worth much in the world markets, and political systems are unstable. It is hard to make up for the lack of a god-given opportunity. Scale economies favor production in industrial centers, transport costs are not extreme, and the result is that an economy may not be attractive for substantial investment. It will become depressed, and there is not much that can be done about it. Frankly, emigration may be the best answer. Note that this conclusion was voiced even for Ireland.

It might be argued that there is a wage in dollars low enough to make production for the domestic and world markets profitable. I doubt that argument is valid, because a wage that low becomes a political problem. That problem in turn creates new difficulties that get in the way of investment. I may be exaggerating this point about opportunity, but I believe we should be far more cautious in advancing the view that the right policies can make any place a place in the sun. A joint economic *and* political equilibrium may simply not exist in parts of the world that had good days but are now "economic deserts." Ghost towns in the Far West are examples. Dirt-poor countries may be undergoing the same phenomenon except that they cannot move away.

## Prosperity

The next ingredient for investment is prosperity—the feeling that things are getting better and that they will continue to do so. While prosperity is mostly in the minds of investors, for that very reason it is the chief driving force of a broad-based investment boom.

Prosperity can be created easily. Even populists can do so. Former President Alan Garcia of Peru is a good example. Two years of spending, and he received a standing ovation from the business community—and a healthy dose of investment. Three years later, however, the experiment crashed (Dornbusch and Edwards 1990). The danger with prosperity is that it may be built on sand and turn out to be very ephemeral, as was the case in Peru. Prosperity in Peru, as in many developing countries, was characterized by passion and unreason, by a fear of losing out on a good thing (for example, a good investment opportunity), rather than by the centuries of wise, moderate, and steady accumulation such as that underlying Swiss-style prosperity. Hyndman and Hobson (1967, 153-54) offers a good description of the former type of prosperity:

> Buenos Aires surpassed every other city in its luxury, extravagance and wholesale squandering of wealth. There was literally no limit to the excesses of the wealthier classes. While money, luxuries and material poured in on the one hand, crowds of immigrants from Italy and other countries flocked in to perpetuate the prosperity of the new Eldorado of the South. Railways, docks, tramways, waterworks, gas-works, public buildings, mansions, all were carried on at once in hot haste.

The commercial real estate experience of Massachusetts in the United States in the late 1980s presents another example of the same phenomenon. Prosperity is a powerful engine, but often for a risky trip.

## Coordination

The profitability of an individual investment is almost inevitably dependent on what happens elsewhere in the economy. This situation creates a serious problem for investment: as with two Germans at the door, everybody says, "After you, please." If nobody goes first, nothing happens in the economy (Dornbusch 1990). Even though everybody keeps saying the fundamentals are right, they all hold off on investments except of the most liquid kind.

Even though coordination is central to generating investment, often little can be done to bring it about. Occasionally there are extraordinary opportunities, as is the case in Mexico today. The large amount of flight capital abroad would, if returned, easily cement economic stability. The owners of the capital are waiting for the message to start the stampede. The creative use of a free trade agreement may well become the coordinating device that sends the message that all is well, that it is safe to come home. When that message spreads, coordination is a done deal, and prosperity will take off.

## Rules of the game

Luigi Einaudi, Italy's celebrated postwar finance minister and president, said that investors have the memories of elephants, the hearts of lambs, and the legs of hares. Institutions are there to assure investors of stability in property rights and economic management. Without an institutional setting, principal-agent problems cannot find a satisfactory resolution. When they go unresolved, opportunities dry up.

**Institutions.** Decentralization of responsibilities and decisions, specifically between lenders and producers, call for property rights that secure the interest of lenders without unduly interfering with the ability of managers to carry out long-term decisions. When property rights become insecure, capital markets dry up, and the horizon of firms shrinks to a year, a month, or a day.

In many places in Latin America, property rights are in question. There is no way of securing equitable judgments in court, and majority owners routinely deprive stockholders of their returns. Extremely low price/ earnings ratios on stocks often are a signal not of a country without opportunity but of a country without an effective legal system. Venezuela or Brazil are striking examples. Rules of the game also apply to macroeconomic management. If real interest rates and exchange rates and inflation rates are violently unstable, the horizon inevitably shrinks. With the shrinking horizon comes a decline in profitability and reduced incentive to invest. Of course, real interest rates and exchange rates are not the only variables that count. Even so, a comparison of Argentina and Chile is revealing. It is hardly surprising that in Argentina, which has three times the variability of Korea, investment is not only low—negative in net terms— but it also has too short a horizon (Table 9-1).

Interventionist policies, particularly the recurrent use of price controls and discretionary interference in firms' production and pricing plans add to the instability of real exchange rates.

**Continuity.** Investors abhor transitions. Unresolved issues, in the way discussed by Bernanke (1983), stand in the way of investment, whereas continuity supports commitment.

The sound rule in banking is "never lend in a transition." This rule applies with equal relevance to investment decisions. Governments there-

**Table 9.1  Variability of the real exchange rate**
(coefficient of variation)

|           | *Argentina* | *Korea* |
|-----------|-------------|---------|
| 1970-79   | 18.1        | 9.9     |
| 1980-90   | 29.2        | 10.8    |

*Source:* Author's calculations.

fore must make every effort to move quickly to a sustainable regime and to put in place mechanisms that ensure asset-holders against abrupt moves. Governments must have a *policy* and not engage in day-to-day discretionary reaction to events.  This idea is fundamental to what is called *Ordnungspolitik* in Germany—stability with rules (Stutzel and others 1982).

The critical missing link in many Latin American countries today is governance. Mexico exemplifies the critical role of purposeful government in fostering confidence, growth, and the return of flight capital.  Argentina (until recently) or Brazil show how the melting, or outright wrecking, of economic institutions ultimately undermines the willingness of citizens to invest.  In the end, the ensuing decapitalization undermines a country's ability to pay yesterday's wages.  Standards of living decline and make politics increasingly difficult because distribution rather than growth are at the center of public policy concern. Workers call for economic reactivation as the answer to their plight, but in fact the country's ability to sustain past standards of living has been dissipated.

*Finance*

Last but not the least determinant of investment is finance.  Here the focus is on three issues: the initial debt overhang; the government budget as a source of national saving; and, finally, the structure of financial intermediation.

**The Debt Overhang.**  Unresolved debt problems, not debt per se, are an obstacle to investment.  It is hard for a man to establish a relationship with a lender if the estranged wife keeps barging in claiming alimony.  Mexico has demonstrated that getting debt out of the headlines and off the front page, however good or disappointing the deal is, is a critical first step in focusing discussion on the far more important task of restructuring and growth.  The Brady Plan may not solve the debt problem, but it certainly is a first-rate way to push the problem to the sidelines where it belongs. Ultimately, after reconstruction, many countries can easily service their debt.  The chief issue is to take away its nuisance value today.

**Stability and the Budget.**  Anyone who invested in nominal assets in Argentina in the mid-1980s would in real terms have less than five cents on the dollar today.  Even if people save, nobody can expect them to invest that saving in a financial system that systematically robs them. In this environment of protracted financial instability, it is no surprise that capital flight is endemic. The first priority in the area of finance must be to establish financial normalcy. The essential elements of normalcy are a balanced fiscal budget and a stable exchange rate policy.

When rules are stable and prosperity abounds, so does saving. Feldstein and Horioka show that saving tends to be invested in the country. Thus, unless instability drives saving out, a shortage of resources should not be an issue. Moreover, if opportunities abound and the stability of the rules is not in question, external saving will be available for the asking.

In their investigations of the linkage between international saving and investment, Feldstein and Horioka find that saving tends to be predominantly invested in the country where it occurs. If it is true that what is saved is available for investment, it must follow that if the government saves more, more is available for private investment. Taxation is the most effective means of increasing public sector saving. More attention should be focused on creating broad-based, efficient tax systems that will reduce the budget deficits. This measure would promote stability and make more resources available for private investment.

**The Structure of Financial Intermediation.** There are important questions regarding financial intermediation. Financial institutions are in the business of intermediating between ultimate lenders and final borrowers. How well do they do their job? Recurrent crises in the markets for sovereign debt, the savings and loan scandal, and the fragility of commercial banks in the United States, and the same problem in many countries that have "opened up," suggest that the structure of intermediation must be viewed with extreme suspicion and subjected to the most thoughtful regulation.

A key consideration is to achieve an intermediation system that focuses on lending to small and medium-size firms for which the agency costs of the capital market are prohibitive. Unfortunately, banks do not find these businesses the most attractive and instead favor large projects such as the debt of developing countries or vast real estate developments. History is not on their side.

In the area of finance, equity markets are essential to avoiding an economy that is overindebted. While there are problems with equity, they fall short of the risks of an overly leveraged economy (Tirole 1991).

**Robert S. Pindyck**

Let me say a few things about investment at the risk of repeating some of what I said at the conference. The kinds of models and issues that I discussed yesterday essentially emphasize two parts of investment. The first is the generation of valuable options to invest, that is, the ability of firms in countries to invest productively. The second is the exercising of these options. When and how do firms actually make their investment decisions?

Most of the discussions at the conference (including my presentation and those of Ricardo Caballero and others) focused on the second of these issues. In other words, the concern was what encourages or discourages firms from exercising their investment options? In this context, we gave considerable attention to risk and the role of various kinds of uncertainty. In some sense, these discussions elaborated on the obvious. Clearly, if the economic environment is unstable and the rate of inflation is jumping from 1 percent a month to 20 percent a month, or if the country is politically unstable, it is unlikely a lot of investment will take place. Do complicated models really need to be developed to elaborate on this point? I say yes, for two reasons. Models help flesh out the story and identify how important the various kinds of uncertainty are. They also help in comparing the role of uncertainty and instability with other factors that can influence investment.

Nevertheless, the exercising of investment options is only one aspect of investment, and in some sense it is being overemphasized. The actual generation of these options is the other aspect. Where do they come from? How can we help countries create the conditions that generate options to invest? In the case of the World Bank, it may have to support more analyses at the micro level of industrial structure. It would be useful to look, for example, at strategic complementarities: does promoting investment in some sectors lead to greater investment in others, or does promoting infrastructure create spillovers that increase the value of investment options throughout the economy?

The conference somewhat neglected the topic of investments in human capital. I agree with Rudiger Dornbusch that education is a critical factor. If we look at Southeast Asia and compare economic development in Singapore and Hong Kong with that in Malaysia, clearly education has been very important. It seems almost obvious that education at various levels is going to play a key role in generating options to invest. While the exercising of those options and the role of stability and uncertainty are important, they may be secondary to the generation of these options in the first place. I would like to see more research aimed at getting a better understanding of the conditions needed to create options for investment.

## Dani Rodrik

I will discuss three sets of issues. The first has to do with the policy implications of the investment irreversibility paradigm. The second relates to a somewhat alternative perspective on private investment having to do with bandwagon expectations and self-fulfilling prophecies. Third are some "deeper" determinants of investment.

### Policy implications of investment irreversibility

The main message of the irreversibility paradigm is that uncertainty matters a lot. Indeed, it may matter so much as to render insignificant some of the traditional determinants of investment, such as the cost of capital, level of profitability, or tax incentives. Uncertainty is important both to the level of investment and its responsiveness to changes in the economic environment: policy and macro uncertainty not only hurt investment, they also make it less responsive to policy reforms.

We have heard surprisingly little on the policy implications of this approach. At one level, these implications are obvious: policymakers should avoid exacerbating uncertainty by establishing policies that are (or are perceived as being) credible and sustainable. That said, although that statement is valid and important, in practice it has little operational significance. We need to go further and state what the specific implications of that statement are for the design of World Bank lending programs and policy reforms.

Let me suggest a few implications. For *macroeconomic policy*, the irreversibility paradigm strengthens the orthodox message: ensure fiscal rectitude and avoid overvalued exchange rates. Large fiscal deficits and overvalued exchange rates are doubly bad—they wreak havoc with macroeconomic balances, and they increase uncertainty. Much of the uncertainty in developing countries can be traced to unsustainable macro policies. Unsustainability implies a future policy change. Even though the public can understand the need for policy change, neither the timing of the change nor what comes after it can be predicted with any degree of certainty. Hence, fiscal reform and currency devaluation (when used sparingly) are *good* for private investment because they *resolve* uncertainty.

At the *microeconomic level of project appraisal*, the irreversibility paradigm also has clearcut implications. When world prices and domestic policies are uncertain—in other words, most of the time—the traditional methods of project appraisal have to be augmented by irreversibility considerations. Waiting may often be a wiser course than building a plant that looks profitable under current and expected future conditions. The developing world is full of white elephants built before their time. Options pricing and dynamic programming methods can be usefully brought to bear on such decisions.

Next are the so-called *structural policies*, such as trade and financial sector reform. Here the implications of the irreversibility paradigm are not clear. In fact, they may contradict the orthodox prescription. Too often, structural reforms aim at replacing perfectly sustainable—if highly distorting—policies with more liberal ones. Viewed from the perspective of the irreversibility paradigm, such reforms have a hidden cost, as they often *increase* uncertainty. Many factors contribute to this outcome. First, structural reforms replace the rules of the game to which entrepreneurs were accustomed with a new set of rules whose workings take time to get used to. Second, the government's commitment to the reforms is often suspect, as the reforms are undertaken under pressure from creditor institutions. Third, in highly distorted settings the introduction of structural reforms can have highly unpredictable consequences. For all these reasons, waiting may be the investors' natural reaction to structural reform.

These considerations need not make structural reform undesirable. The point is that if the irreversibility paradigm is to taken seriously, such tradeoffs have to be considered explicitly and the appropriate implications drawn for the design of structural adjustment programs.

*Bandwagon expectations and self-fulfilling prophecies*

There is an alternative way of viewing the disappointing investment performance to date—through the self-fulfilling expectations paradigm. Private investment is susceptible to an externality of a particular type: the profitability of my investment depends on the investment of others. As such, aggregate investment is highly sensitive to psychological factors and bandwagon expectations. It is easy to get locked into a "bad" equilibrium, with no one investing simply because no one expects others to do so.

Susan Collins and I recently surveyed large companies about their investment plans in Eastern Europe and the former Soviet Union. One question concerned the main reason they were attracted to the region. We provided a list of some fundamental economic reasons as possible answers: proximity to the European Community's market; low labor costs; and the skill level of the region's labor force. Respondents ranked the "potential to beat out competitors by being first" higher than any of these others. This response brought home how interdependent investment decisions really are.

From this perspective, the investment shortfall in developing countries, whatever may have caused it initially, can be viewed as reflecting a massive failure in coordination. How do we get out of this low investment trap? Economic models are not of much help. One broad conclusion, however, is that large shocks, rather than marginal policy tinkering, are called for. Investors need to be pushed from the bad equilibrium to the good one. This shift can only be accomplished with large enough shocks. In practice, the implications are several. The required shock may be large-scale capital inflows from abroad, or it may be that governments undertake large-scale structural reform.

Note the potential conflict with the policy conclusions drawn from the irreversibility paradigm. If the problem originates from a failure to coordinate, shaking things up is a good idea, even if that measure increases uncertainty. Thus, the paradigm with which the problem is approached may make a big difference.

*Deeper determinants of private investment*

Finally, it is time to think more about some of the "deeper," more fundamental determinants of private investment. As summarized in chapter 6, "Economic Adjustment and Investment Performance in Developing Countries: The Experience of the 1980s," one of the lessons to be drawn from the evidence to date is the *diversity* of country experiences: investment has been more resilient in Brazil than in Argentina, despite very similar macro problems; private investment appears to have responded to structural reforms in Chile, Mexico, and Turkey, but not in Bolivia; the differences between Asian and Latin American countries are well-known. "Diversity" is really another name for ignorance: we simply do not know why these outcomes have been so different.

Moreover, the irreversibility paradigm is rarely helpful in understanding some of these differences. Too often, it leads to tautologous explanations. It is tempting to argue, for example, that the poor performance of Bolivian investment is the result of the continuing uncertainty in the policy and macro environment. However, the only evidence is the poor performance of Bolivian investment.

What are some of the deeper determinants of private investment? They are mainly structural and political in nature. In joint work with Sule Ozler, we tried to extend the usual private investment equation to consider the roles of some such variables. We derived two main results. First, private investment tends to be higher, controlling for the other usual determinants, in economies where political rights are more complete. Possible explanations have to do with the better provision of property rights in more open political systems or the greater willingness of organized labor to be accommodative in such environments. Second, higher levels of urbanization, again with the appropriate controls, are associated with more drastic reductions in investment in response to negative external shocks. The implication is that high levels of urbanization are more conducive to pernicious types of populist politics and make adjustment to shocks more difficult. Neither of these results goes too far toward accounting for the diversity noted above. However, they are indicative of the mileage that might result from looking at a broader universe of determinants of investment.

Another important determinant may well be the distribution of income. There is a growing body of evidence that suggests that countries with a more equal distribution of income grow faster, especially if the political system is democratic. One explanation is that a large middle class and a sufficiently widespread ownership of capital are necessary to ensure that growth-inducing resources (capital of various sorts) are not taxed too heavily.

Uncovering some of these deeper determinants may serve more than an academic purpose. They will help in understanding what portion of the observed diversity in investment performance is truly structural (and therefore not manipulable by policy) and what portion can be affected by policies. Governments may not be able to push urbanization levels back, for example, but they can certainly influence the distribution of income and wealth.

### Andrés Solimano

My presentation focuses on two areas. I first draw some general lessons from the results of this research project (including issues raised during the conference). I then point out some issues in the area of private investment and macroeconomic adjustment that merit further research. My discussion is selective rather than exhaustive.

*Main lessons*

First, the slowdown in capital formation in developing countries in the 1980s, which went well beyond a cyclical downturn, was closely linked to the dramatic cut in foreign financing that took place after 1982 in developing countries. This trend started to be reversed in the early 1990s, as capital flowed back to Latin America in response to interest rate differentials, new opportunities opened by privatization, and the structural reforms. However, the new cycle of capital inflows is not problem-free: it may be unsustainable; it generates a tendency for real currency appreciation that squeezes export profitability; and the sterilization of capital inflows may generate losses to the Central Bank. All this may affect the sustainability of the macro environment in which investment decisions are made.

Second, a main finding from the country experiences reviewed in this project is the variety of the responses of investment to both economic instability before reform and to adjustment policies. A clear example of that diversity is the responses of private investment (and growth) in Chile, Mexico, and Bolivia to adjustment and liberalization. In Chile, private investors reacted quite forcefully to the new structure of incentives in the late 1970s and late 1980s. In Mexico, the response of investment and growth to the structural reforms launched in the mid-eighties has been more moderate. In contrast, in Bolivia private investment has remained stagnant, as has per capita growth, in the aftermath of stabilization and reform. The experiences of Brazil and Argentina in the 1980s also illustrate the existence of diversity in the response of private investment to acute economic instability.

Third, the importance of macro stability and policy credibility for promoting capital formation was discussed *ad abstinato* in the conference. Certainly, stability and credibility are prerequisites for an adequate investment response to economic incentives. However, it is also clear that the practical implications for policy design of the "credibility approach" are still elusive (see also Rodrik's panel presentation). In fact, ways to increase credibility may include either shock treatment at the macro level and rapid liberalization or, to the contrary, gradualism so as to avoid the social hardship that can invite policy reversals in a process of economic reform. As is apparent, the "credibility approach" could be consistent with very different policy implications.

Fourth, euphoria and booms of private investment in periods of abundant credit should be treated with caution. Chile in the late 1970s-early 1980s offers a good example of how overoptimistic expectations by the private sector may lead to an investment boom that, in the end, turns out to be neither sustainable nor directed to the right sectors. The implications are clear: beware of the soundness of private investment decisions made at times of widespread euphoria.

Fifth, econometric estimates of investment equations using panel data show some robust results across time and space:

• Public investment (particularly in infrastructure) tends to be complementary to private investment.

• The level of the real exchange rate has an ambiguous and statistically insignificant effect on (aggregate) private investment.

• The variability of the real exchange rate and of the rate of inflation have a significantly adverse effect on private investment. This finding provides empirical support for the contention that the level of private investment is inversely related to the degree of macroeconomic in stability.

• The (high) ratio of external debt to GDP has a negative effect on the private investment ratio. This finding confirms the argument that the debt overhang is a powerful deterrent to private investment.

## Issues for future research

Let me focus on three areas where more research is needed. First, the research under this project focused mainly on the effects (and interactions) of adjustment policies on the level (or quantity) of private investment. Another important dimension is the *productivity* and *quality* of investment: more analysis of the efficiency of investment is required to understand better the crucial link between investment and economic growth.

The second, and related, area involves the need to explore the existence of differences in productivity across different types of capital goods (both physical and human). Moreover, the issue of externalities and complementarities between investment in human capital and physical capital, between foreign direct investment and national investment, and between public and private investment are worth exploring in more detail.

Third, a largely neglected but still important area where research is clearly insufficient is the relationship between the distribution of income and private investment. The degree of (in)equality in income distribution may affect the level of private investment through different channels. First, large income inequalities in the population may lead to social and political instability and discourage private investment. Second, the propensity of governments is to adopt populist policies that are destabilizing. Populism has often been a (misconceived) response to claims for income redistribution. Then a more equitable distribution of income may be a necessary condition for avoiding populist policies that ultimately have an adverse effect on long-term investment. Third, income distribution may affect the profit share and the level of profitability of investment. This puts limits on the room for redistribution that can affect investment by reducing profitability. New theoretical and empirical analysis in this field would be very welcome.

Fourth, this project chiefly focused on investment. However, a better understanding of the determinant of savings and the interactions and causality between investment, growth and savings is certainly necessary.

## Luis Servén

I want to emphasize three lessons that follow from what was discussed at the conference. The lessons themselves are sources of additional questions that require new work. The first lesson is that public investment seems to matter—and to matter greatly. However, this conclusion raises more questions that it answers. First, it indicates that we need to look in much more detail at the specific composition of public investment. We need to separate those ingredients that are directly competing with private investment (for example, public investment in manufacturing, where the private sector could be as competent as the public sector) from investment in items such as infrastructure, as was mentioned. Then we have to go one step beyond and include, among these complementary public expenditures, those related to human capital, education, health, and the like. These questions have to be looked at in more detail in a country—specific context. Answering them is crucial to the design of reasonable, as opposed to "irrational," fiscal adjustment.

My second lesson relates to another result emphasized at the conference. It seems that external debt matters a lot. A higher debt burden, however measured, is associated with worsened investment performance. Again, this conclusion raises more questions than it answers. Why is there a negative association between high debt and investment? Is it because the debt service has an adverse effect on the financing available to the country? Is it because of the uncertainty associated with the need to meet the future external transfers? Again, more work is needed in this area, in part because of its importance to the evaluation of alternative financing arrangements, such as alternative debt relief measures.

The third lesson relates to the role of uncertainty and instability. We find consistently that instability matters—and matters a lot. We have made significant analytical progress through the work of Robert S. Pindyck and Ricardo Caballero in understanding why uncertainty matters for investment decisions. We have also made progress in designing methods for evaluating how much it matters. One suggestion that emerges from recent work in this area is that the specific effect uncertainty has on investment is likely to depend very much on history, that is, on initial conditions. Specifically, when the starting point in the business cycle is at a low point (for example, a recession) and uncertainty is great, it may be very, very hard to stimulate investment. Again, this dependence on history suggests the need to look at specific country experiences and particular sources of uncertainty.

This issue also relates to problems I would like to include under the broad heading of uncertainty and instability. The first one is political instability, a crucial source of uncertainty in many countries that needs careful analysis. Second is one specific form of political instability (already mentioned) related to income distribution. More analytical work and an in-depth look at country experiences are needed to acquire a better idea of the implications of these two factors. They are quite important from the viewpoint of policy because, as Rodrik and Solimano suggest, they determine what types of policy reforms may be adequate and feasible. Let me add that they may also determine what the speed of policy reform should be. Some drastic reforms may simply not be possible under certain political circumstances—for example, under certain income distribution conditions.

### References

Bernanke, B. 1983. "Irreversibility, Uncertainty and Cyclical Investment." *Quarterly Journal of Economics* 98 (February):85-106.

Dornbusch, R. 1990. "New Classical Macroeconomics and Stabilization Policy." *American Economic Review, Papers and Proceedings* (U.S.) 80 (2)(May):143-47.

Dornbusch, R., and S. Edwards. 1990. "The Macroeconomics of Populism in Latin America." *Journal of Development Economics* 32:247-77.

Hyndman, H. M., and J. A. Hobson, eds. 1967. *Commercial Crises of the Nineteenth Century.* 2d ed. Reprints of Economic Classics. New York: Augustus M. Kelley Publishers.

Stutzel, W., and others. 1982. *Standard Texts on the Social Market Economy.* Ludwig Erhard Stiftung. New York: Gustav Fischer.

Tirole, J. 1991. "Privatization in Eastern Europe: Incentives and the Economics of Transition," in O. J. Blanchard and S. Fischer, eds., *NBER Macroeconomics Annual.* Cambridge, Mass.: MIT Press.